ENGENDERING AFRICAN AMERICAN ARCHAEOLOGY

Engendering African American Archaeology

————— A SOUTHERN PERSPECTIVE —————

Edited by

Jillian E. Galle and Amy L. Young

THE UNIVERSITY OF TENNESSEE PRESS / KNOXVILLE

Copyright © 2004 by The University of Tennessee Press / Knoxville.
All Rights Reserved.
Cloth: First printing, 2004.
Paper: First printing, 2016.

Library of Congress Cataloging-in-Publication Data
Engendering African American archaeology : a southern perspective /
    edited by Jillian E. Galle and Amy L. Young.— 1st ed.
    p. cm.
Includes bibliographical references and index.

ISBN 978-1-62190-193-8

1. African Americans--Southern States—Antiquities.
2. Excavations (Archaeology)—Southern States.
3. Sex role--Southern States—History.
4. Ethnoarchaeology—Southern States.
5. Social archaeology—Southern States.
6. African Americans—Southern States—History.
7. African Americans—Southern States—Social conditions.
8. Slavery—Southern States—History.
9. Southern States—Antiquities.
 I. Galle, Jillian E.
II. Young, Amy L.
E185.E555 2004
975'.00496073—dc22   2003026431

Contents

Illustrations

Figures

Maps

Tables

Acknowledgments

This volume has its beginnings in a 1998 Society for Historical Archaeology symposium titled "Engendering African-American Archaeology." As this project took shape, a common thread emerged. This thread was not a shared definition of gender or an agreed-upon feminist approach. Rather, the link was regional, a commitment to understanding ethnicity and gender within the social, political, and ideological structures of the eighteenth- and nineteenth-century American South.

The articles in this volume present different ways of studying gender and ethnicity through the archaeological record. The effectiveness of each theoretical and methodological approach is promising. The authors show how African-American women and men shaped their own lives, as individuals and as members of families and communities. They add an important archaeological dimension to the growing historical literature on African-American gender roles by revealing the subtleties of identity and religion, the complexities of work regimens and economic opportunities, and the intricacies of personal and familial relationships through material remains.

Amy Young and Melanie Cabak deserve thanks for organizing the symposium from which this volume sprang. Amy Young had the initial vision for this book and undertook the task of getting the volume underway. The comments of Charles Orser and an anonymous reviewer helped clarify and refine many aspects of this volume. Special thanks goes to Scot Danforth, our patient and supportive editor at the University of Tennessee Press. This book is the result of much perseverance, alacrity, and good humor. All of the contributors demonstrated these essential characteristics throughout the editorial process.

Jillian E. Galle

ENGENDERING AFRICAN AMERICAN ARCHAEOLOGY

Gender Research in African American Archaeology

ELIZABETH M. SCOTT

When asked to provide an introduction to this collection, I immediately responded "Yes," but in the next breath I expressed several doubts about the appropriateness of doing so. My direct experience with African American sites is quite limited: an analysis of faunal remains from Nina Plantation, circa 1820–1890, situated on the Mississippi River in central Louisiana (Scott 1999). It is a wonderful site, containing African American slave and tenant households as well as main-house contexts; the antebellum deposits are associated with French Creole owners, and the postbellum deposits with Anglo-American owners (Markell et al. 1999). The analysis touched not only on differences (and similarities) in subsistence between three ethnic groups but also on changes in African American labor and diet related to the postbellum shift to tenancy. So, although the research I have undertaken is limited, it did involve a fairly complex mix of variables.

I also have had a longtime interest in African American history and archaeology, stemming partly from my own background. I grew up not far from Atlanta in what used to be the small town of Lithonia, in a middle-class white southern family with parents who were college educated, free-thinking United Methodists, and liberal Democrats (yes, they do exist in the South). Despite coming of age in the 1960s and 1970s in a household that supported the Civil Rights movement and despite attending integrated public schools, I was nonetheless in the midst of racist, and in many ways still segregated, southern society. As a way of dealing with these conflicting realities, I absorbed all of the popular culture I could about African Americans, the South, and race relations.

When I left the South and went North, I was shocked to find the racism in present-day northern Michigan to be as strong as any in the South. Through archaeological and historical research at Michilimackinac, where the eighteenth-century community included enslaved Native Americans and a small number of enslaved African Americans, it became clear that this racism had its roots far back in America's colonial past and that it went beyond black and white. French and British colonists differed in their attitudes toward Native Americans, Africans, and Jews, and these could be contrasted with the attitudes of other colonizing groups in the New World. What also became clear was the intense ethnic, perhaps even racist, animosity that existed between various European groups, with centuries-long histories of rivalry, war, and ethnocentrism (Scott 2001).

Also along the way, mostly in graduate school, I was exposed to feminist perspectives on a whole variety of subjects, those in history and anthropology being most important here. I came along at a time when feminists were beginning to examine how gender was related to one's class, ethnic group, or race (defined as the socially constructed category) and how these (and other aspects) combined to shape much of daily life.

What has been of interest to me for more than a decade now is how historical archaeology might reveal the roots of our inequalities, be they gender, racial, ethnic, economic, or other kinds of inequities. Engendering African American archaeology is certainly one way to reveal those roots. It is to this that I would like to turn now, sharing some thoughts and observations and, of course, bringing all of the aforementioned baggage with me.

Looking Back

It is only within the past dozen years or so that archaeologists working with African American sites have begun to address the role of gender in their interpretations of those sites (Singleton and Bograd 1995:29–30). This has involved making African American women visible, as had been done with men, by revealing their labor, through the production of colonoware and the foods that filled those wares (Ferguson 1991, 1992), their purchases in store accounts (Heath 1997, this volume), their importance as healers and ethnomedical practitioners (Cabak et al. 1995; Edwards-Ingram 2001; Wilkie 1996, this volume), and their ability to exist as free property holders in southern cities and to manumit enslaved family members (Singleton 2001). Some authors have taken explicitly feminist approaches and revealed African American women's roles in maintaining family property ownership within and between generations (Muller 1994); in developing distinctively African American foodways and influencing southern cuisine in general (Franklin 2001a); in social reform groups (Spencer-Wood 1994); and in urban working-class households and brothels (Seifert 1991). Only a few archaeologists have addressed gender among free blacks or free mulattoes (for example, Ryder 1991; Singleton 2001) or the gender roles of African Americans, mulattoes, and other mixed-race categories in Spanish colonies in the New World (Ruhl and Hoffman 1997).

It is interesting to note that, although the majority of African American archaeology has focused on plantations (be they colonial, antebellum, or postbellum), the literature on gender has included a much broader range of African American contexts. These are important beginnings, and as the contributors to this volume will show, feminist and gender research continues to expand our understanding of African American lives in the past.

Looking Around

Several different feminist theoretical approaches have been put forth in historical archaeology (Franklin 2001b; Little 1994; Scott 1991, 1994; Spector 1983, 1991, 1993; Spencer-Wood 1991, 1996; Yentsch 1991a, 1991b). In an important recent article, Maria Franklin (2001b) proposes a black feminist-inspired archaeology that would be concerned not only with African American pasts but also with the structural hierarchies that have maintained the marginalization of other groups as well. In addition, there are studies by cultural anthropologists and social historians that could provide historical archaeologists with useful theoretical insights as well as substantive data. While not an exhaustive survey, the following are several that I have found especially helpful.

In this age of multiculturalism, with what sometimes seem like rote examinations of race-class-gender, Nancy Hewitt's use of a chemical compound as a model is a refreshing way to think about the complexity of people's identities:

> A compound is a substance composed of elements that are chemically bonded to each other, the composition of each being transformed so that the original components can no longer be separated from each other. The concept of compound identities forces us to recognize the integral relations among all dimensions of experience and the impossibility of studying any element in isolation without distorting the whole. (1992:318)

This captures the closeness of the connection between variables such as race, class, and gender and also the transformative effect of that connection. In the complex societies that concern historical archaeologists, it is not possible to talk about the genders of a site's occupants without also talking about their economic, ethnic, religious, and racial identities, vis-à-vis others in society. That is, archaeologists must situate those individuals within their social, political, and economic contexts.

Looked at in this way, it is clear that all women do not have the same gender, nor do all men (Brown 1992). For example, in a particular time and place, it means one thing to be African American and male and something quite different to be Euro-American and male or Native American and male. Of course there are also class, ethnic, and other differences (sexual, religious, etc.) within such broad categories. But, as Elsa Barkley Brown (1992) has pointed out, it is not enough to simply talk about differences in the lives of black and white (or other) men and women; archaeologists must talk about the relational aspect of the differences—that is, relations *between* these people. Culturally defined race had (and has) tangible effects on people's lives, positive for some, negative for others, and that needs to be put into the equation.

One of the ways to engender any historical archaeology is to look at the documentary and oral history evidence of gender roles in the division of labor and analyze the material and spatial manifestations of that labor. Several historians have dealt with the great variety of African American women's work and gender roles in African American families in colonial, antebellum, and postbellum periods (Bolles and D'Amico-Samuels 1989; Gaspar and Hine 1996; Jones 1985; Sobel 1987; White 1991). In her ethnography of Indianola, Mississippi, remarkable for the 1930s or even today, anthropologist Hortense Powdermaker (1993) provides myriad oral histories by African Americans, some extending back to Reconstruction. Through these and other data, she describes, for example, the variety of labor schedules characteristic of sharecropping, cash tenancy, and renting; house architecture and furnishings; foods and subsistence; and the practice of moving from plantation to town during the winter, all of which have ramifications for African American archaeology (75–110). Being white and female hampered her plans to interview African American men, so she relied heavily on African American women informants. This situation allowed African American women's views on life to be heard, precisely the kind of information that is often missing from official records and other sources that were weighted toward the male head of household. Given this group of informants, she was able to distinguish generational and class differences among African American women (Williams and Woodson 1993:xxxi–xxxiii).

Much scholarship in African American archaeology, history, and anthropology has focused on the eastern seaboard and southern United States. A much smaller body of data exists on African Americans in French and Spanish colonies and in the western United States. Daniel Usner (1987, 1992) and Carl Ekberg (1985, 1998), both historians, provide detailed evidence of the complex economic and social interactions between French, British, Spanish, African American, and Native American men and women that characterized the Mississippi Valley in the eighteenth century. While neither study explicitly examines gender as a structuring element in society, both provide many examples of African American gender roles and status in a system of slavery very different from British and Anglo-American systems. Farther west, Lynda Dickson (1997) documents African American women's clubs in Denver between 1880 and 1925, and two studies of African American Seminoles in Texas and Mexico reveal how gender structured specific communities there (Mock and Davis 1997; Rodgers and Schott 1997).

Interaction and cultural exchange between African Americans and Native Americans is a topic that has not been explored in depth by many historical archaeologists. Those who have recovered colonoware in their excavations have variously dealt with the question of whether African Americans or Native Americans produced and/or marketed those ceramic vessels. Leland Ferguson (1992) provides many examples of the complex relations between the two groups and the resulting exchange of ideas and materials, especially in the realm of foods and food-related objects. However, it is historians who have proposed that some aspects of African American culture may have Native American rather than African origins (Wright 1981:248–278). Theda Perdue (1998:68) suggests, for example, that the prominent role of women in slave society might be due to the presence of so many enslaved women from matrilineal southeastern Indian groups. Perdue also provides detailed discussion of the complex relations between African Americans and Cherokees in the eighteenth and early nineteenth centuries, including the rise and fall of the Native American slave trade, the rise of slaveholding Cherokee elites, and the trading and selling of enslaved Africans by Cherokee warriors. Historical archaeologists are uniquely qualified to investigate the evidence for and nature of multiple origins of present-day African American, Native American, Anglo-American, and other cultures; the search for one kind of origin should not blind one to the evidence for others.

As a final leave-taking from this look around, I would like to mention several African American feminist historians, anthropologists, and literary and social critics whose writings are an immense help in trying to see the past and present from an African American perspective. Elsa Barkley Brown's discussion of a womanist approach (1990), Faye Harrison's Marxist-influenced approach to anthropology (1991a, 1991b), and Maria Franklin's black feminist-inspired archaeology (2001b) all challenge the distinction between theory and action and call for a scholarship of the past that is nonetheless politically and socially engaged in the present. These works stress the need to be aware of whom it is that research serves, and to think about the ramifications that that research might have for various groups in present-day society. A powerful new collection, *Black Feminist Anthropology* (McClaurin 2001a), takes this idea a step further, revealing the significant contributions being made through "native" anthropology and auto-ethnography while also bringing the work of previous black feminist scholars out of the margins and into the center of the anthropological canon (Bolles 2001; Ebron 2001; Gilliam 2001; McClaurin 2001b, 2001c; Mwaria 2001; Rodriguez 2001; Shaw 2001; Simmons 2001; Slocum 2001).

Looking Ahead

So, what does all of this looking around have to do with future work toward an engendered African American archaeology?

First, I would like to echo others (Conkey and Gero 1991:15; Singleton and Bograd 1995:29–30) in pointing out what is hopefully obvious by now: that by looking at gender, by asking how gender helped shape lives in the past, focus is brought onto *people*. It is asking about gender that puts faces on those people who lived on the sites (Tringham 1991:93–94). You can have all the minimum vessel lists and all the price indexing you want, but it is not until you ask who was preparing, who was serving, and who was consuming food and drink from those vessels that you bring people into the picture. The same is true for any category of artifacts recovered. Just as one would not dream of omitting the material and spatial evidence for economic position and ethnicity or race, so one must include archaeological and historical evidence for gender on sites. It is also important to go *beyond* this, to interpret how gender, as well as economic position and race or ethnicity, actually structured past societies.

Singleton and Bograd (1995:29–30) discuss several avenues for future research that engenders African American archaeology. They recommend a reevaluation of plantations by looking at gendered activities and spaces apart from slave cabins and the main house and how these activities and spaces might have changed with the shift from slavery to tenancy. They also emphasize how production of colonoware is clear evidence of the importance of African American women's work and wonder how changes in plantation social organization might have affected pottery production. It might be useful to consider both African American women's and men's overall artisan production in the plantation setting, their production for the household, and their possession of specialized knowledge (medicinal or religious, for example), and how these factors affected variations in status within the enslaved community.

There are many relatively unexplored topics in African American archaeology that should also include attention to gender, and I will mention just a few here, in the form of research questions. How did African American gender roles on French and Spanish plantations compare with those on British and Anglo-American plantations? How did gender shape the lives of slaves in the North and in nonplantation settings? What were gender roles in free black or maroon communities such as Fort Mose in Florida and Palmares in Brazil, and how do they compare with those in both New World plantation and African settings?

What seem to be the gendered behaviors that have the greatest perseverance through time? How did gender roles and gender ideology among postbellum African Americans compare with those among European Americans? How might one see evidence of the impact of African American women's reform organizations or men's Masonic lodges and similar groups on later nineteenth-century African American households and gender roles? What do military camps and battlefield sites of the Buffalo soldiers and Black Seminoles look like, archaeologically, and how do they compare with nineteenth-century European-American western military sites? How do urban African American working-class households differ from urban European-American working-class households in terms of evidence for gender roles? Do African American households in western U.S. mining towns look different archaeologically from households of other groups, particularly in the evidence for gender roles and ideology?

It is clear that, regardless of the directions African American archaeology takes in the future, an understanding is needed of how gender combined with other aspects to shape daily life. I would like to suggest three things that seem to warrant thoughtful consideration by archaeologists working on African American sites. First, I would like to encourage scholars to more explicitly examine African American men's roles for the sites they study. They need to be very clear about how they think one's identification as a man versus a woman affected one's social position, labor, activities, and differential access to wealth or privileges. There is still that tendency to think that gender research is only about women (Hewitt 1992:315–316), and there certainly is a need to make African American women more visible in the past than they have been. But this is not the whole picture; both kinds of analyses are needed. Although much of the research in this volume emphasizes African American women, as is common when gender research is new to a field, many of the contributors to this volume also address men's roles in the African American past.

Second, it is important to be aware and think carefully about the fine line there is to be walked in portraying African American men and women as active shapers of their lives without denying the constraints of the slavery and societal racism in which they lived. This point is related to the debate about whether race or class had primacy in determining social position and daily life; if it is proposed that class was more important, that in essence denies the very real difference race made among folks in the same class. For example, white sharecroppers often had advantages within southern society, just by virtue of the color of their skin, that black sharecroppers with the same income did not. It may be difficult to discern this difference archaeologically, but every effort should be made to do so. Looking at gender might be one way to help reveal the difference race made, or did not make, between people in the same class; that is, if archaeologists compare the evidence of gendered activities and gender ideology between Anglo-American and African American (and other) communities, they might begin to see how race mattered.

Finally, I would like to touch on a topic not often mentioned in African American archaeology, yet one in which gender was key: the sexual assault and violence carried out by white men on African American women and men. Rape and the threat of sexual violence by white men was one way in which African American women's lives differed from African American men's. However, African American fathers, brothers, husbands, and sons, besides being emotionally affected by these acts, also underwent great physical and psychological harm at the hands of white men, including castration and lynching.

These forms of sexual oppression might be borne in mind speaking, for example, about activities on and off the plantation. There seems to be a tendency among present-day scholars to associate greater mobility for individuals with greater personal freedom. Mobility and access to town markets might not be especially desirable if one had to fear being sexually or otherwise assaulted on the way to and from the market, or other plantations, or elsewhere, before and after emancipation. And although many African American women and men nonetheless were mobile (by choice or because they had to be), it should not be assumed that that mobility had only positive connotations for them. Conversely, it should not be assumed that a lack of mobility had only negative connotations. Not only were the actions and habits of white men on the plantation well known in the African American community (offering a means of avoidance or deterrence), but there was also a strength in numbers not found on lonely roads or paths. It may indeed have been the case that African American men and women could assert more control over their lives, within the confines of slavery and racist society, by staying closer to home.

Looking to This Volume

Many of the research questions and issues raised in the preceding discussion are addressed in the highly varied case studies in this edited volume.

Barbara Heath, in chapter 1, examines consumer choices that affected the material goods deposited in slave quarter contexts at Thomas Jefferson's Poplar Forest in Bedford County, Virginia. By examining records from rural stores and plantation account books, she determines that enslaved men and women participated differently in economic activities. For example, men were more likely to sell produce from kitchen gardens, chickens, ducks, fish, and crafted items such as baskets and brooms. Similarly, enslaved men were more likely to visit local stores than enslaved women. However, once at the store, there were few differences in the products purchased by enslaved men and women.

In chapter 2, Jillian Galle examines how clothing production structured social relationships among enslaved African Americans at Andrew Jackson's Hermitage near Nashville, Tennessee. Archaeological data from three slave dwellings suggests that the enslaved seamstress held an important social and economic position at the Hermitage. Her specialized sewing kit indicates that she was a skilled seamstress and likely sewed for the big house as well as for the enslaved community. In addition to many buttons, children's toys and health-care-related objects were recovered in relatively high frequencies, suggesting that her house may have served as an important center of distribution for goods other than clothing.

Laurie Wilkie, in chapter 3, explores how granny midwives were more than just baby catchers. African American midwives also trained women to be mothers, serving as generational mediators. Archaeological data from the house of Lucrecia Perryman, a midwife in Mobile, Alabama, reveal her production of traditional remedies and her use of them in combination with commercially produced medicines. The midwife's use of magic and ritual also served to reinforce gender ideology in southern African American communities.

Brian Thomas and Larissa Thomas, in chapter 4, focus on how gender and social identity is expressed through clothing and accessories. Drawing on data from extensive excavations of slave houses at Andrew Jackson's Hermitage, they demonstrate how layered dress is in one way social and how gendered identity was expressed. Clothing and accessories served to display the multiple, concurrent personae that constituted that identity.

In chapter 5, Amy Young examines the roles of enslaved women in the big house and in the slave quarter community. She sees gender roles as flexible and situational so that the persona displayed by African American domestic slaves at the big house was likely not the same as that displayed in the privacy of the family and the quarter community. However, in both roles, women took opportunities to protect themselves and their families from the dangers inherent in the system of slavery.

Patricia Samford, in chapter 6, examines continuities between traditional Igbo gender roles (gleaned from ethnohistoric and ethnographic data) and those exhibited in eighteenth- and nineteenth-century enslaved communities in Virginia. Archaeological and historical evidence suggests that enslaved African Americans in Virginia defined new gender roles for themselves based on those they had known traditionally in Igbo society. Especially prominent in both Igbo and Virginia societies were the centrality of the family and the active interest and responsibility on the part of men and women for the economic well-being of their families.

In chapter 7, Garrett Fesler explores the gendered nature of social interactions between enslaved men and women at Utopia, an early-eighteenth-century Tidewater Virginia quartering site. Fesler focuses several interesting questions around one main topic: whether gender relations at Utopia were reinforced by African gender ideologies or whether the owner of Utopia, James Bray II, imposed Anglo-centric notions of gender roles on those he enslaved. Fesler investigates the architectural and artifact patterning at Utopia and incorporates historical and ethnographic data regarding Utopia and West and Central African cultures. Although Fesler concludes that understanding specific gender roles is difficult using the archaeological record, he convincingly demonstrates that single-sex barracks and some form of indigenous African compound activities, which separated men from women, were being used at Utopia.

Marie Danforth, in chapter 8, uses data from the Natchez City Cemetery in Natchez, Mississippi, to address the interaction between biology and gender. Her data, which nicely supplement archaeological and historical data, show that Natchez men were more likely to suffer from violence and accidents than women and that deaths from childbirth among women occurred in young adulthood. Additionally, infant mortality dropped after emancipation. Overall, however, the data confirm that health patterns seen in other African American populations are seen also in Natchez.

In chapter 9, Melanie Cabak and Kristin Wilson use data from six cemeteries in the southeastern United States to explore gender roles within the African American community between 1850 and the late 1920s. Cabak and Wilson ask a variety of questions concerning gender-based differences in grave goods and physical health in their analysis of 336 African American burials from cemeteries in Texas, Alabama, Arkansas, and Georgia. Their work reveals that personal adornment objects such as beads and jewelry were most often found with women and children. Based on their data, Cabak and Wilson suggest that the distribution of artifacts possibly related to African medicinal or spiritual beliefs may indicate that women played a larger role than men in maintaining folk beliefs. Skeletal data indicates that men were more susceptible to trauma and infection, while women were more likely to die as young adults. Fewer gender differences in activity-related stress suggest that both African American men and women had similar workloads.

Larry McKee's commentary in chapter 10, "An End to the Eerie Silence," draws connections between the volume's articles, demonstrating that in each case the authors recognize the powerful social and cultural role gender played in shaping African American life. McKee notes that the contributors "are clearly in favor of having gender and identity up front" in analyses of slavery and that the diversity of these case studies indicates that there need not be one monolithic approach to studying gender and archaeology. He sees this volume as a large step toward ending the silence about gender and archaeological research on the African American past.

With this volume, the door is opened wide on a whole new field of archaeological inquiry into the African American past. The following essays reveal how scholars are not simply talking about this; they are actually getting on with the work of engendering African American archaeology. Their research is eagerly anticipated.

ACKNOWLEDGMENTS

I want to thank Amy Young and Melanie Cabak for organizing the session at the SHA conference in Atlanta, from which this collection began, and for asking me to participate. I thank Amy Young, Jillian Galle, the other contributors, Charles Orser, an anonymous reviewer, and my husband, Donald Heldman, for helpful comments and suggestions on this essay. Any errors that remain are solely my responsibility.

REFERENCES

Bolles, A. Lynn
    2001   Seeking the Ancestors: Forging a Black Feminist Tradition in
           Anthropology. In *Black Feminist Anthropology*, edited by
           Irma McClaurin, pp. 24–48. Rutgers Univ. Press, New
           Brunswick, N.J.
Bolles, A. Lynn, and Deborah D'Amico-Samuels
    1989   Anthropological Scholarship on Gender in the English-Speaking
           Caribbean. In *Gender and Anthropology: Critical Reviews for Research
           and Teaching*, edited by Sandra Morgen, pp. 171–188. American
           Anthropological Association, Washington, D.C.
Brown, Elsa Barkley
    1990   Womanist Consciousness: Maggie Lena Walker and the Independent
           Order of Saint Luke. In *Unequal Sisters: A Multicultural Reader in
           U.S. Women's History*, edited by Ellen Carol DuBois and Vicki L.
           Ruiz, pp. 208–223. Routledge, New York.

1992   "What Has Happened Here": The Politics of Difference in Women's
History and Feminist Politics. *Feminist Studies* 18(2):295–312.

Cabak, Melanie A., Mark D. Groover, and Scott J. Wegars

1995   Health Care and the Wayman A.M.E. Church. *Historical
Archaeology* 29(2):55–76.

Conkey, Margaret W., and Joan M. Gero

1991   *Engendering Archaeology: Women and Prehistory*. Basil Blackwell,
Oxford.

Dickson, Lynda F.

1997   Lifting As We Climb: African American Women's Clubs of Denver,
1880–1825. In *Writing the Range: Race, Class, and Culture in the
Women's West*, edited by Elizabeth Jameson and Susan Armitage,
pp. 372–392. Univ. of Oklahoma Press, Norman.

Ebron, Paulla A.

2001   Contingent Stories of Anthropology, Race, and Feminism. In
Black Feminist Anthropology: Theory, Politics, Praxis, and Poetics,
edited by Irma McClaurin, pp. 211–232. Rutgers Univ. Press,
New Brunswick, N.J.

Edwards-Ingram, Ywone D.

2001   African American Medicine and the Social Relations of Slavery. In
Race and the Archaeology of Identity, edited by Charles E. Orser Jr.,
pp. 34–53. Univ. of Utah Press, Salt Lake City.

Ekberg, Carl J.

1985   *Colonial Ste. Genevieve: An Adventure on the Mississippi Frontier*.
Patrice Press, Gerald, Mo.

1998   *French Roots in the Illinois Country: The Mississippi Frontier in
Colonial Times*. Univ. of Illinois Press, Urbana and Chicago.

Ferguson, Leland

1991   Struggling with Pots in Colonial South Carolina. In *The Archaeology
of Inequality*, edited by Randall H. McGuire and Robert Paynter,
pp. 28–39. Basil Blackwell, Oxford.

1992   *Uncommon Ground: Archaeology and Early African America,
1650–1800*. Smithsonian Institution Press, Washington, D.C.

Franklin, Maria

2001a The Archaeological Dimensions of Soul Food: Interpreting Race,
Culture, and Afro-Virginian Identity. In *Race and the Archaeology of
Identity*, edited by Charles E. Orser Jr., pp. 88–107. Univ. of Utah
Press, Salt Lake City.

2001b A Black Feminist-Inspired Archaeology? *Journal of Social Archaeology* 1(1):108–125.

Gaspar, David Barry, and Darlene Clark Hine (editors)

1996   *More Than Chattel: Black Women and Slavery in the Americas*. Indiana Univ. Press, Bloomington.

Gilliam, Angela M.

2001   A Black Feminist Perspective on the Sexual Commodification of Women in the New Global Culture. In *Black Feminist Anthropology: Theory, Politics, Praxis, and Poetics*, edited by Irma McClaurin, pp. 150–186. Rutgers Univ. Press, New Brunswick, N.J.

Harrison, Faye V.

1991a   Anthropology as an Agent of Transformation: Introductory Comments and Queries. In *Decolonizing Anthropology: Moving Further Toward an Anthropology for Liberation*, edited by Faye V. Harrison, pp. 1–14. American Anthropological Association, Washington, D.C.

1991b   Ethnography as Politics. In *Decolonizing Anthropology: Moving Further Toward an Anthropology for Liberation*, edited by Faye V. Harrison, pp. 88–109. American Anthropological Association, Washington, D.C.

Heath, Barbara J.

1997   Slavery and Consumerism: A Case Study from Central Virginia. *African American Archaeology* 19:1–8.

Hewitt, Nancy A.

1992   Compounding Differences. *Feminist Studies* 18(2):313–326.

Jones, Jacqueline

1985   *Labor of Love, Labor of Sorrow: Black Women, Work, and the Family from Slavery to the Present*. Basic Books, New York.

Little, Barbara J.

1994   "She Was . . . an Example to Her Sex": Possibilities for a Feminist Historical Archaeology. In *Historical Archaeology of the Chesapeake*, edited by Paul A. Shackel and Barbara J. Little, pp. 189–204. Smithsonian Institution Press, Washington, D.C.

Markell, Ann, R. Christopher Goodwin, Susan Barrett Smith, and Ralph Draughon

1999   *Patterns of Change in Plantation Life in Pointe Coupee Parish, Louisiana: The Americanization of Nina Plantation, 1820–1890*. Submitted by R. Christopher Goodwin & Associates to the U.S. Army Corps of Engineers, New Orleans District.

McClaurin, Irma (editor)

2001a *Black Feminist Anthropology: Theory, Politics, Praxis, and Poetics.*
Rutgers Univ. Press, New Brunswick, N.J.

2001b Introduction: Forging a Theory, Politics, Praxis, and Poetics of Black
Feminist Tradition in Anthropology. In *Black Feminist Anthropology:
Theory, Politics Praxis, and Poetics*, edited by Irma McClaurin,
pp. 1–23. Rutgers Univ. Press, New Brunswick, N.J.

2001c Theorizing a Black Feminist Self in Anthropology: Toward an
Autoethnographic Approach. In *Black Feminist Anthropology: Theory,
Politics, Praxis, and Poetics*, edited by Irma McClaurin, pp. 49–76.
Rutgers Univ. Press, New Brunswick, N.J.

Mock, Shirley Boteler, and Mike Davis

1997 Singing to the Ancestors: Revitalization Attempts among the
Seminole Blacks in Texas and Mexico. Paper presented at the
Annual Conference of the Society for Historical Archaeology,
Corpus Christi, Tex., Jan.

Muller, Nancy Ladd

1994 The House of the Black Burghardts: An Investigation of Race,
Gender, and Class at the W.E.B. DuBois Boyhood Homesite. In
Those of Little Note: Gender, Race, and Class in Historical Archaeology,
edited by Elizabeth M. Scott, pp. 81–94. Univ. of Arizona Press,
Tucson.

Mwaria, Cheryl

2001 Biomedical Ethics, Gender, and Ethnicity: Implications for Black
Feminist Anthropology. In *Black Feminist Anthropology: Theory,
Politics, Praxis, and Poetics*, edited by Irma McClaurin, pp. 187–210.
Rutgers Univ. Press, New Brunswick, N.J.

Perdue, Theda

1998 *Cherokee Women: Gender and Culture Change, 1700–1835.* Univ. of
Nebraska Press, Lincoln.

Powdermaker, Hortense

1993 *After Freedom: A Cultural Study in the Deep South.* Univ. of
Wisconsin Press, Madison. Originally published 1939 by Viking
Press, New York.

Rodgers, B. Ann, and Linda Schott

1997 "My Mother Was a Mover": African American Seminole Women in
Brackettville, Texas, 1914–1964. In *Writing the Range: Race, Class,
and Culture in the Women's West*, edited by Elizabeth Jameson and
Susan Armitage, pp. 585–599. Univ. of Oklahoma Press, Norman.

Rodriguez, Cheryl
    2001 A Homegirl Goes Home: Black Feminism and the Lure of Native
          Anthropology. In *Black Feminist Anthropology: Theory, Politics,
          Praxis, and Poetics*, edited by Irma McClaurin, pp. 233–257. Rutgers
          Univ. Press, New Brunswick, N.J.
Ruhl, Donna L., and Kathleen Hoffman (editors)
    1997 Diversity and Social Identity in Colonial Spanish America: Native
          American, African, and Hispanic Communities during the Middle
          Period. *Historical Archaeology* 31(1):1–103.
Ryder, Robin L.
    1991 "An Equal Portion": Archaeology of Susan Gilliam, a Free Mulatto
          in Virginia, 1838–1917. Paper presented at the Annual Conference
          of the Society for Historical Archaeology, Richmond, Va., Jan.
Scott, Elizabeth M.
    1991 A Feminist Approach to Historical Archaeology: Eighteenth-
          Century Fur Trade Society at Michilimackinac. *Historical
          Archaeology* 25(4):42–53.
    1994 Through the Lens of Gender: Archaeology, Inequality, and Those
          "of Little Note": In *Those of Little Note: Gender, Race, and Class in
          Historical Archaeology*, edited by Elizabeth M. Scott, pp. 3–24.
          Univ. of Arizona Press, Tucson.
    1999 Vertebrate Fauna from Nina Plantation (16-PC-62). In *Patterns
          of Change in Plantation Life in Pointe Coupee Parish, Louisiana:
          The Americanization of Nina Plantation, 1820–1890*, by Ann
          Markell, R. Christopher Goodwin, Susan Barrett Smith, and
          Ralph Draughon, vol. 2, appendix 7. Submitted by R. Christopher
          Goodwin & Associates, Inc., to the U.S. Army Corps of Engineers,
          New Orleans District.
    2001 "An Indolent Slothfull Set of Vagabonds": Ethnicity and Race in a
          Colonial Fur-Trading Community. In *Race and the Archaeology of
          Identity*, edited by Charles E. Orser Jr., pp. 14–33. Univ. of Utah
          Press, Salt Lake City.
Seifert, Donna J.
    1991 Within Sight of the White House: The Archaeology of Working
          Women. *Historical Archaeology* 25(4):82–108.
Shaw, Carolyn Martin
    2001 Disciplining the Black Female Body: Learning Feminism in Africa
          and the United States. In *Black Feminist Anthropology: Theory,
          Politics, Praxis, and Poetics*, edited by Irma McClaurin, pp. 102–125.
          Rutgers Univ. Press, New Brunswick, N.J.

Simmons, Kimberly Eison

2001 A Passion for Sameness: Encountering a Black Feminist Self in Fieldwork in the Dominican Republic. In *Black Feminist Anthropology: Theory, Politics, Praxis, and Poetics*, edited by Irma McClaurin, pp. 77–101. Rutgers Univ. Press, New Brunswick, N.J.

Singleton, Theresa A.

2001 Class, Race, and Identity among Free Blacks in the Antebellum South. In *Race and the Archaeology of Identity*, edited by Charles E. Orser Jr., pp. 196–207. Univ. of Utah Press, Salt Lake City.

Singleton, Theresa A., and Mark D. Bograd

1995 The Archaeology of the African Diaspora in the Americas. *Guides to the Archaeological Literature of the Immigrant Experience in America*, no. 2. Society for Historical Archaeology, Tucson.

Slocum, Karla

2001 Negotiating Identity and Black Feminist Politics in Caribbean Research. In *Black Feminist Anthropology: Theory, Politics, Praxis, and Poetics*, edited by Irma McClaurin, pp. 126–149. Rutgers Univ. Press, New Brunswick, N.J.

Sobel, Mechal

1987 *The World They Made Together: Black and White Values in Eighteenth-Century Virginia*. Princeton Univ. Press, Princeton, N.J.

Spector, Janet D.

1983 Male/Female Task Differentiation among the Hidatsa: Toward the Development of an Archeological Approach to the Study of Gender. In *The Hidden Half: Studies of Plains Indian Women*, edited by Patricia Albers and Beatrice Medicine, pp. 77–99. Univ. Press of America, Washington, D.C.

1991 What This Awl Means: Toward a Feminist Archaeology. In *Engendering Archaeology: Women and Prehistory*, edited by Joan M. Gero and Margaret W. Conkey, pp. 388–406. Basil Blackwell, Oxford.

1993 *What This Awl Means: Feminist Archaeology at a Wahpeton Dakota Village*. Minnesota Historical Society Press, St. Paul.

Spencer-Wood, Suzanne M.

1991 Toward a Feminist Historical Archaeology of the Construction of Gender. In *The Archaeology of Gender*, edited by Dale Walde and Noreen Willows, pp. 234–244. Dept. of Archaeology, Univ. of Calgary, Calgary, Alberta.

1994 Diversity and Nineteenth-Century Domestic Reform: Relationships among Classes and Ethnic Groups. In *Those of Little Note: Gender,*

Race, and Class in Historical Archaeology, edited by Elizabeth M.
Scott, pp. 175–208. Univ. of Arizona Press, Tucson.

1996   Toward the Further Development of Feminist Historical
Archaeology. *World Archaeology Bulletin* 7:118–136.

Tringham, Ruth E.

1991   Households with Faces: The Challenge of Gender in Prehistoric
Architectural Remains. In *Engendering Archaeology: Women and
Prehistory*, edited by Joan M. Gero and Margaret W. Conkey,
pp. 93–131. Basil Blackwell, Oxford.

Usner, Daniel H., Jr.

1987   The Frontier Exchange Economy of the Lower Mississippi Valley
in the Eighteenth Century. *William and Mary Quarterly*, 3d ser.,
44(2):165–192.

1992   *Indians, Settlers, and Slaves in a Frontier Exchange Economy: The
Lower Mississippi Valley before 1783*. Univ. of North Carolina Press,
Chapel Hill.

White, Deborah G.

1991   Female Slaves: Sex Roles and Status in the Antebellum Plantation
South. In *Unequal Sisters: A Multicultural Reader in U.S. Women's
History*, edited by Ellen Carol DuBois and Vicki L. Ruiz, pp. 22–33.
Routledge, New York.

Wilkie, Laurie A.

1996   Medicinal Teas and Patent Medicines: African American Women's
Consumer Choices and Ethnomedical Traditions at a Louisiana
Plantation. *Southeastern Archaeology* 15(2):119–131.

Williams, Brackette F., and Drexel G. Woodson

1993   Hortense Powdermaker in the Deep South. In *After Freedom: A
Cultural Study in the Deep South*, by Hortense Powdermaker,
pp. ix–xl. Univ. of Wisconsin Press, Madison.

Wright, J. Leitch, Jr.

1981   *The Only Land They Knew: The Tragic Story of the American Indians
in the Old South*. Free Press, New York.

Yentsch, Anne

1991a   Access and Space, Symbolic and Material, in Historical Archaeology.
In *The Archaeology of Gender*, edited by Dale Walde and Noreen
Willows, pp. 252–262. Dept. of Archaeology, Univ. of Calgary,
Calgary, Alberta.

1991b   Engendering Visible and Invisible Ceramic Artifacts, Especially
Dairy Vessels. *Historical Archaeology* 25(4):132–155.

CHAPTER I

Engendering Choice: Slavery and Consumerism in Central Virginia

BARBARA J. HEATH

Beginning in the mid-1980s, historical archaeologists have increasingly sought to understand gender systems and ideologies within the groups they study, recognizing that gender, like ethnicity and class, acts as a primary structuring principal in the creation of culture. Departing from traditional social-scientific views that equated biological sexual identity with gender, archaeologists have recognized instead that gender is a social construct and that gender roles vary across time and space, and even within the lifetimes of individuals (Conkey 1990; Wylie 1991:38–40). During the past decade, gender studies in historical archaeology have become more numerous and diverse. Researchers have described fluid gender boundaries within Native American societies; explored the lives of individual women living in colonial societies in North and Latin America; traced the emergence of the woman's sphere in nineteenth-century New York and its relationship to class; assessed the benefits of "social visiting" between female kin and neighbors in mining camps; and examined gender relationships within Jamaican coffee plantations (Delle 2000; Jamieson 2000; Little 1994; Purser 1991; Seifert 1991; Spector 1993; Wall 1994, 1999, 2000; Whelan 1991).

During this period, historical archaeologists have also devoted considerable attention to the study of African American life, focusing particularly on the lives of enslaved men and women in the antebellum South. These studies include examinations of foodways and subsistence, housing and yard spaces, belief systems, medicine, and ritual—all aspects of life that were surely shaped by gender (Edwards-Ingram 1997; Ferguson 2000; Heath and Bennett 2000; McKee 1999; Russell 1997; Samford 1996; Stine et al. 1996; Wilkie 1997; Young 1996). Yet relatively little attention has been devoted specifically to an understanding of the creation, maintenance, and negotiation of gender roles

and boundaries within the quarter and between the enslaved and their owners (Delle 2000; Edwards-Ingram 2001; Singleton and Bograd 1995:29–30).

In studying slaves living in the American South during the eighteenth and
nineteenth centuries, historians have outlined the growth and maturation of kin
networks based on monogamy and increased birth rates (Fogel 1994:123–126,
150; Morgan 1998:501–511; Sobel 1987:161–162). Many large planters encouraged bondspeople to marry within the plantation, a policy that resulted in a
more stable home life for enslaved families and promoted owners' financial
interests. However, in regions where many enslaved men and women lived on
smaller farms, single adults often could not find a spouse at home. Others living on larger holdings chose not to marry within their plantation community.
Households headed by a single parent, usually the mother, resulted from such
"abroad marriages." These domestic arrangements, common in the late-
eighteenth-century Chesapeake, survived through midweek and Sunday visits
by absent spouses (Morgan 1998:508–510; Sobel 1987:161–162; White 1991:115).

One productive line of inquiry for historical archaeologists interested in
studying how gender played out in the African American communities of the
Chesapeake region may be the examination of economic strategies employed
by enslaved families. Such a study draws on both the historical evidence of
changing household composition and the material evidence recovered from a
variety of quarter sites dating from the mid-eighteenth through the early
nineteenth centuries. The examination of gender roles may help clarify the
timing, organization, and ultimate success of economic production within
individual households.

Historians differ in their attention to and interpretation of men's and
women's work in their analyses of the economic roles played out within
enslaved families. In his comprehensive, comparative treatment of slavery in
the Chesapeake region and Carolina Lowcountry, Philip Morgan rarely dis-
tinguished between gender roles as they related to production and consumption. While combining individual historic sources to make a point, he avoided
broad characterizations of sexual divisions of responsibility in terms of hunting, gardening, handicraft production, or other activities that contributed to
slaves' participation in the market economy. He did, however, acknowledge
women's participation in poultry raising in the Chesapeake and their importance as hawkers in Lowcountry markets (Morgan 1998:136–143, 250–252).

Historian Jacqueline Jones dealt more explicitly with gender. She asserted
that women "assumed primary responsibility for childcare and for operations

involved in daily household maintenance—cooking, cleaning, tending fires, sewing and patching clothes." Fathers and husbands, though denied the patriarchal role of free men, filled the role of "provider and protector." Jones credited fathers with most of the economic activity of the household, ranging from hunting and gardening to making handicrafts and earning small sums of money for work done on other estates (Jones 1995:36).

Jones's model stands in sharp contrast with the gender system that developed among eighteenth-century Caribbean slave societies. There, women's economic autonomy has been seen as an important factor in the retention of polygamy and polygyny and in the desire among women for "freedom of movement and choice" over motherhood and domesticity (Mullin 1994:172).

This chapter explores the economic lives of enslaved men and women in central Virginia, taking issue with Jones's homemaker/provider dichotomy and suggesting that a more complex and more flexible system of relationships was at work in the past. To date, comparatively little research has been done on the internal economy of slavery in Virginia (Schlotterbeck 1995). While it is true that Virginia slaves never achieved the same level of economic success as their Lowcountry or West Indian counterparts, an examination of the ways that gender roles and household composition affected their economic lives merits closer inspection.

As part of my research on quarters excavated at Poplar Forest, Thomas Jefferson's Bedford County holding, I have examined evidence of Virginia slaves as consumers and producers of goods independent of the larger economies of their home plantations. One goal of this research is a clearer understanding of how objects came to the quarter—the social dimensions of collection or production, trade, and barter that resulted in purchasing power. Another goal is to determine which objects slaves selected for themselves among the growing variety of consumables available in local stores. Whether men and women passively received objects or actively acquired them may reflect the value placed on them within the household and, perhaps, the uses to which they were put.

Although much is currently known about the gender roles assigned to bondsmen and women by white southerners (Morgan 1998:196–197, 204–254), much less is understood about the ways in which the enslaved constructed their own systems of gender relationships and gender identity. Approaching these questions through the lens of consumerism enables us to explore the interplay between gender and economics, shedding light on such issues as the structuring of households and the allocation of labor within them, the construction of self, and the maintenance of social ties.

The following questions framed this study. First, how did enslaved men and women vary in their approaches to generating surplus that could be sold or bartered at a store? Were stores equally accessible to both? Did men and women make substantially different choices of goods at the store? Finally, what are the archaeological implications of these similarities or differences when trying to interpret assemblages of objects recovered at slave quarters?

I approached these questions through the examination of a number of documents. The economic activities of enslaved women and men as producers within the plantation—the first step in a process that ultimately led to some form of consumption—has been recorded in plantation account books. Evidence of economic strategies that included a partial reliance on goods and services procured outside of the plantation—in this case at rural stores—is primarily preserved in detailed mercantile records and secondarily in probate records, wills, and deeds of sale. This chapter reviews a small sample of documentary evidence from Virginia between 1770 and 1810.

As with all questions addressing people whose lives were constrained by institutionalized slavery as it developed in the American South, the study of gender roles and relations within the quarter must also be seen through the filter of rules and limitations imposed by the free white community. An understanding of slaves as producers and consumers presupposes an understanding of behavior sanctioned by owners and shopkeepers. For example, white (male) shopkeepers' notions of appropriate credit terms, reflecting the primacy of men in formalized economic relationships, set the boundaries within which gender roles, developed at the quarter, could be played out. Similarly, owners set parameters on what goods slaves were allowed to gather, raise, sell, and own, and on the time they had available to pursue such activities. These restrictions limited the degree to which enslaved men and women were able to freely participate in the economic life of the community and to improve their own material standards of living.

Slaves as Producers

To understand gender and household relationships involved in generating surplus for sale, I have relied primarily upon a plantation account from Monticello dating to the opening decade of the nineteenth century. This small ledger kept by Thomas Jefferson's granddaughter Ann Cary Randolph records her weekly purchases from slaves living at Monticello and at Jefferson's outlying Tufton and Lego quarters. The vast majority of transactions described in the ledger deal with plants and fowl raised in garden plots and house yards. While contemporary merchants in central Virginia recorded that slaves used hunted resources, such as animal skins, or their own labor to settle accounts, the Monticello system of exchange did not provide an outlet for these types of transactions, and they do not generally appear in the Randolph ledger (Heath 1997).

Randolph recorded purchases between 1805 and 1808. These records indicate no real difference in the goods that men and women carried to the mountaintop each Sunday for sale. Slaves most commonly sold eggs. They also sold chickens, ducks, and fish; "messes of salad," lettuce, sprouts, and cabbages; root crops such as potatoes, onions, and beets; cucumbers, squash, and beans; a variety of fruits, including apples, watermelons, musk melons, peaches, and strawberries; hops, walnuts, beeswax, baskets, and brooms. Enslaved men and women raised most fowl, vegetables, and fruits in house yards, kitchen gardens, and plantation provision grounds; they gleaned others from meadowlands and fencerows. For the most part, slaves exchanged goods for cash rather than credit, although in some cases Randolph failed to note her method of payment in the account book.

While the goods they brought to sell did not differ significantly, the extent to which men and women were able to participate in sales varied markedly. In 1810, the closest year to the account period for which census data are available, 110 slaves lived at Jefferson's Albemarle County holdings, of which 56 percent were male and 44 percent were female (Betts 1987:128). Figure 1.1 shows this age distribution.

Because some members of the enslaved community shared the same names, it is impossible to determine the absolute numbers of people participating in the weekly exchanges. Numbers per year range from a high of thirty-two potential men and eleven women in 1806 to a low of twenty-three men and nine women in 1805. Overall, men trading with Randolph outnumbered women by a ratio of close to three to one (Figure 1.2).[1]

I next assembled composite biographies of the men and women who traded during 1806, looking at factors such as age, marital status, occupation within the plantation, and number and age of children.[2] The average age of the women listed was forty-two years, with actual ages clustered around this

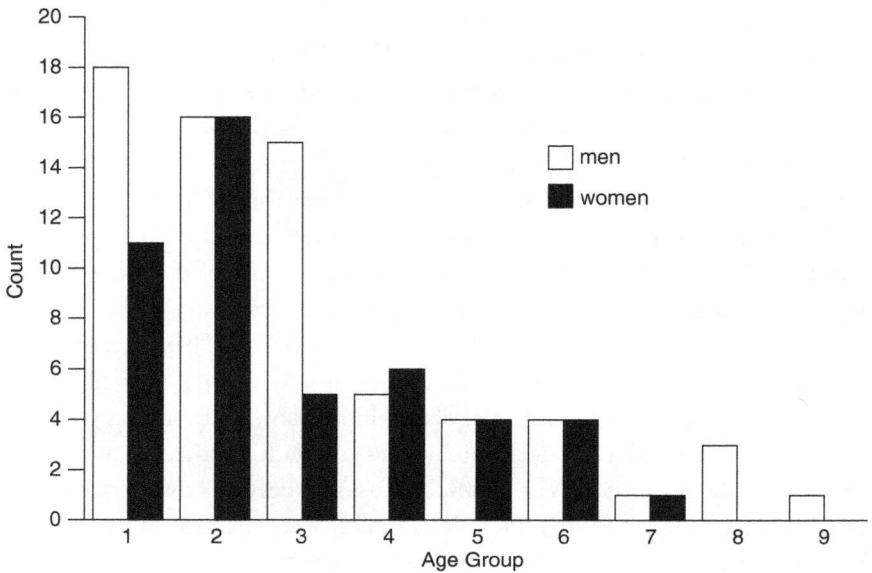

FIG. I.I.   Age distribution of Jefferson's Albemarle County slaves, 1810.

mean. While the average age of men in the account book was also forty-two, a closer examination of the data tells a different story. Nearly all were either young adults (in their late teens to early twenties), or they were more than forty years old (Figures 1.3 and 1.4).[3]

Half of the women involved in sales to the big house headed their own households, while most of the others were married and lived with their husbands. All but two were mothers; one was only eighteen and had not yet married, while another apparently never married. Among the men, a small majority lived with their wives within the Monticello slave community. Jefferson's census listed the remainder as living alone; in some cases as young men who had not yet found a wife; in others, as fathers supporting wives and children living on neighboring farms. Because men often lived separated from their families, it is impossible to know how many of the men in the account book had neither spouse nor offspring.

These Monticello families possessed a cross section of skills; husbands were both field hands and tradesmen; wives worked in the fields and as domestic servants. Occupation within the plantation seems to have had little to do with one's ability to earn extra cash through gardening, poultry raising, or the production of handicrafts.

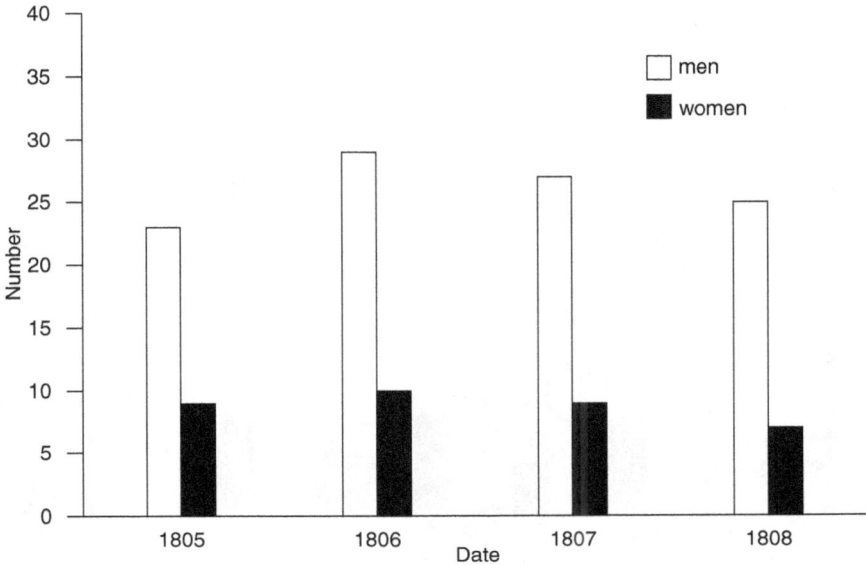

FIG. I.2. Monticello traders by gender, 1805–1808.

Much more important factors in the economic lives of these men and women appear to have been their ages, marital status, and the ages of their children. The two most productive gardeners (as measured by the number of different products they sold)[4] during the period that the account book covers were Squire, who was seventy-eight in 1805, and Goliah, his junior by four years. While the young couple Wormley and Ursula Hughes sold by far the greatest quantity of eggs—nearly four times as many as any other household—the other three largest egg producers were all men with no children under the age of ten living on the plantation. Indeed, of the fifteen to seventeen families represented in the account book, only three had children exclusively under the age of ten. The rest were both young men and women with a single infant less than a year old, or older couples with teenage or adult offspring.

It appears, then, that the ability to produce surplus goods for market hinged in part on need and in part on labor. For families with only young children, a dozen eggs, a "mess of sprouts," or a basket of apples served as necessary supplements to provisions. Tending, clothing, and feeding young children required time, energy, and, most likely, the contents of garden plots and poultry yards. Market activities likely took a backseat to child rearing. However, once children reached a productive age, defined by Jefferson as ten years

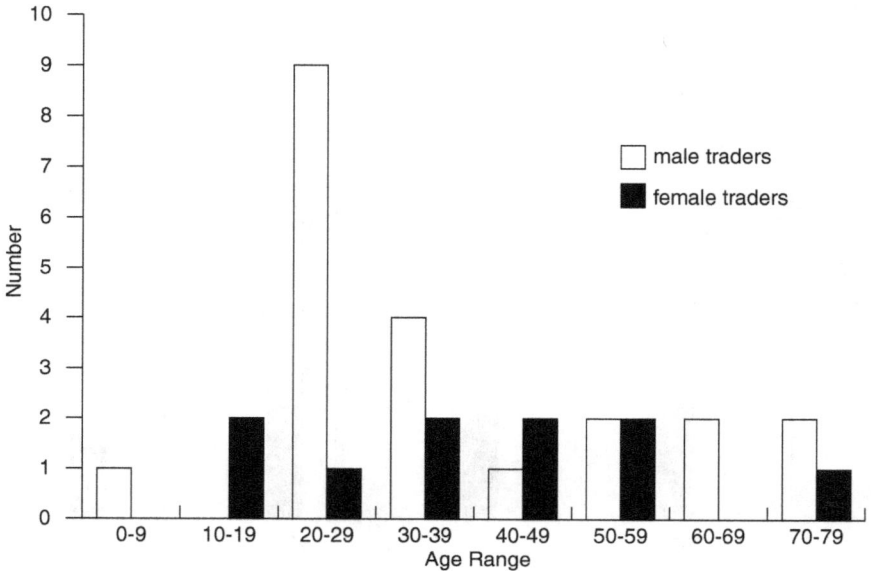

FIG. I.3.   Monticello trading by age and gender, 1806.

old, their labor in gardening and other moneymaking activities may have enabled families to produce a profitable surplus. How the exceptional families balanced parenting and marketing is unclear.

The Monticello data, of course, consist of a tiny sample of people, even within Jefferson's holdings, of nearly two hundred slaves. However, they provide the outlines of a model to be tested. Single young men living on their own and older adult men and women, with teenage or adult offspring, participated most fully in the marketplace as producers. Young women's activities seem to have been absorbed by the households in which they lived, and only one is represented in the account book. Families with small children, on the other hand, are poorly represented, perhaps due to a combination of limited time and an increased household consumption that precluded the production of surplus for market.

Slaves as Consumers

Virginian consumers in the late-eighteenth and early-nineteenth centuries could acquire goods through a variety of channels. The wealthiest among

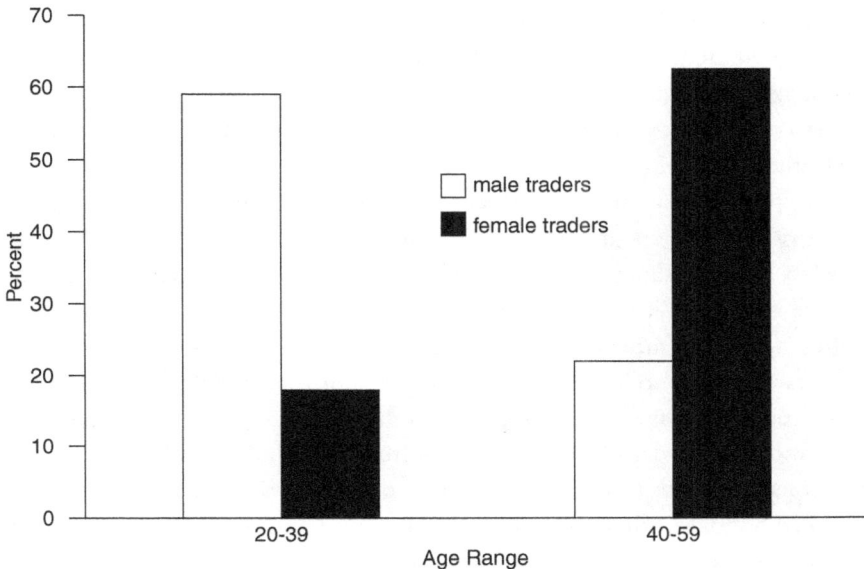

FIG. I.4.   Percentage of Monticello traders by age and gender.

them ordered supplies through agents in England or corresponded with urban merchants, who in turn selected goods and arranged for shipment to their customers. Middling and poorer people, including slaves, relied on local stores, weekly markets, vendors at court days and other public holidays, itinerant peddlers, and trade or barter between neighbors. The connection between slaves' production at Monticello and the conversion of this income into consumer goods is suggested by a nineteenth-century description of Charlottesville. There, stores were open on Sundays "to traffic and trade with the slaves, who came to town . . . to dispose of their garden truck" (Rawlings 1942:2). Other types of transactions are not well documented. Thus, although stores served slaves as just one point of access into the world of consumables, shop records remain the best sources for studying consumerism.

Shopkeepers kept a variety of records to track the purchases and payments of customers, both enslaved and free. Merchants used daybooks to record individual transactions made during each business day, including customers' names, what they bought, and how (or if) they paid. Daybooks also preserve patterns of consumption over time, including the months of the year when individual customers were most active, the days of the week most favored by shoppers, and even the order in which customers entered the store.

Merchants used daybooks to record not only long-term customers who had established credit accounts, but also walk-ins making occasional purchases, often against the account of a friend or relative. This category of shopper, the nonaccount holder, included a preponderance of both free women and slaves (Martin 1993:299, 307).

A preliminary analysis of these data from the daybook of eighteenth-century shopkeepers in Orange, Virginia, reveals that slaves were most often the last customers in a shop on Saturday and made most of their purchases on Sundays (University of Virginia 1785–1786). There does not seem to be any difference in the shopping schedules of enslaved men and women. Daybook entries often group slaves together, suggesting that people from the same plantation may have traveled together to the store, and, once there, may have met and socialized with other shoppers from neighboring farms. These data are consistent with other historic sources that suggest that slaves customarily claimed Sunday as their own, and they provide a glimpse into the network of social ties that slaves created and maintained through consumer behavior.

Merchants also compiled individual daybook entries to create ledgers arranged by customer. These documents preserve a longer-term record of economic activities. Ledger accounts often spanned a period of years, making it possible for merchants to assess an individual's credits and debits at a glance. These records preserve customers' long-term economic strategies in a format that is easily accessible, while obscuring some of the details preserved in the daybook.

I examined daybooks and ledgers of six businesses (in Bedford, Buckingham, Fauquier, King William, and Orange Counties), dating from the 1770s through 1810, to see if consumption patterns differed between enslaved men and women. Ann Smart Martin's work with records of a Bedford County store has demonstrated that among the general population, only one account holder in twenty was female (Martin 1993:299). Her research also suggests that women bought, on average, more fine cloth, ribbons, looking glasses, and other personal items than men, leaving her to posit that women were particularly influenced by changing fashions (307).

If only the enslaved population is considered, the daybooks show ratios of two men to one woman and six men to one woman as shoppers. The ledgers demonstrate an even greater inequality between the sexes, most probably reflecting the contemporary bias toward extending credit to men. Enslaved men holding long-term accounts outnumbered enslaved women by as little as five to one, and as much as thirteen to one. Though disparate, these gender differences are not as pronounced as among the free population. Though having less opportunity than men to visit the store, enslaved women appear to have had more direct access to stores than their free counterparts.

Evidence contained within individual accounts from one store demonstrates that enslaved men made purchases for others within the community. Jacob bought a hat for Celia, a young mulatto woman living on another plantation (Martin 1996:12–14). Isham bought sugar for his mother and paid his brother for corn and fodder. Daniel bought cloth for Phoebe, a hat for Plato, and paid his father for corn. It is likely that all shoppers, whether men or women, served as suppliers for a much larger population of family members and friends who did not, or could not, make the trip to the store for themselves.

Despite unequal access, once inside the shop, enslaved men and women made surprisingly similar purchases. Records from two central Virginia stores indicate that consumption patterns were remarkably similar at both (University of Virginia 1785–1786; Duke University 1788–1808, 1805–1809). Because many more men than women shopped, they selected a wider variety of goods, most as single purchases. From both stores, men alone bought tools such as awls, cuttoe knives and pruners, bar lead, shot and gunpowder for hunting, and iron for manufacturing.

Both men and women bought an assortment of foodstuffs and vessels for preparing and serving food. Alcoholic beverages, cloth, and adornment items were the most popular selections. Owners often rewarded their slaves at harvest time or holidays with gifts of rum or whiskey. That slaves frequently purchased liquor on their own may reflect their use of drink to escape the hardships of everyday life individually and as an accompaniment to social interactions. Dances, card games, and other informal gatherings may have been made merrier by the sharing of spirits. Although both men and women purchased quantities of rum, it appears that by the early nineteenth century, men drank whiskey and women brandy as their beverage of choice.

Like alcohol, cloth was in great demand by both men and women. If additional items relating to clothing are included to create a dress category for analysis, the pattern becomes even more distinct. Slaves chose from a variety of types of cloth, from coarse osnaburgs and rolls to broadcloth and silk. They bought cotton cards to process fibers; indigo, alum, and copperas to color plain fabrics; ribbons, buckles, and buttons to adorn them; thread, needles, pins, and scissors to create new fashions; and ready-made shoes, stockings, hose, hats, and handkerchiefs to cover themselves from head to foot in items of their own choosing (Heath 1997:1–8).

Runaway advertisements chart the increasing availability of clothing to slaves throughout the eighteenth and early nineteenth centuries. In the earliest period an owner could, with confidence, describe every detail of a runaway's attire. By the turn of the century, most slave owners penned some version of the following, "it is probably he may change his dress, as he has a number of other cloathing" (Meaders 1997:42; Heath 1999:52–57).

Within the context of slavery, clothing had both symbolic and actual value. In a system that demanded hard physical labor of both men and women and subjected both to harsh punishments, slaves used clothing and adornment items to establish gender identities and mediate relationships. Women's ribbons, men's fancy buttons, and colorful bandanna handkerchiefs all served to create a sense of self within a framework in which slaves defined appropriate appearances and behaviors for men and women (Heath 1999).

Archaeological Implications

This study suggests that an understanding of household structure within plantation communities is essential in interpreting the economic activities of late-eighteenth- and early-nineteenth-century enslaved men and women in Virginia. Both sexes engaged in economic activities and both served households as providers. While contemporary gender roles favored the participation of men over women in the marketplace, factors such as age, marital status, and family composition were crucial in determining production and consumption of goods.

What are the archaeological implications of an engendered study of consumerism? Differences in material culture between slave households have been explained by historians and archaeologists using a variety of models. During the 1980s, archaeologists examining households on Monticello's Mulberry Row interpreted these differences as evidence of a particular slave's or household's favoritism by Jefferson. This favoritism resulted in an increase in material wealth derived either from hand-me-downs, tips and gratuities, or preferential treatment (Crader 1990; Gruber 1990:79–80). Other arguments have stressed plantation size and slaves' proximity to or, conversely, distance from, the big house as key factors to understanding slaves' access to material goods

(McKee 1995:40; Morgan 1998:144; Samford 1996:92). All of these arguments place the relationship between slave and owner as a primary determinant of economic success.

The analysis of the Monticello account book suggests that other factors may have had a significant impact on the economic lives of slaves and, by extension, the variety and quantity of items they possessed. I suggest that archaeologists look more closely at the documented makeup of individual families living at the sites excavated. What may be seen reflected in artifact assemblages is information about household structure rather than master/slave relationships. Young families with small children may be represented by a relative lack of diversity or quantity of artifacts due to limited participation within the market economy, while a gradual increase in artifactual richness may occur as families age and establish market connections. The exception to this might be domestic deposits associated with young men who may be accumulating material goods prior to establishing families of their own, or single men who are part of abroad marriages.

Based on the evidence from store accounts alone, it is not possible to assign specific artifacts to activities that historically have defined gender roles. Women bought men's hats and shoes; men bought ribbons, knitting needles, and cotton cards, items usually associated with women's dress or activities. Thus an understanding of how objects are acquired may reflect their value on a household level, but it still falls short of revealing how they were used and valued by individuals. However, other sources of evidence, including runaway advertisements, plantation accounts, and archaeological findings indicate that certain types of objects, most notably those associated with dress, appear to have played an important role in the construction and maintenance of gender identity and gender roles within the slave community. Buttons, beads, buckles, thimbles, scissors, pins, and other tools associated with cloth production, sewing, and adornment are the physical residues of these complex social interactions.

Approaching consumerism through the lens of gender has raised important new questions about the connection between household size, structure, and the domestic economy and has added to archaeologists' understanding of the complexity of roles within Virginia slave communities. As this study continues, I hope to learn more about the domestic arrangements of the slaves who frequented central Virginia's shops, to trace their market participation over a longer period of time and to take a closer look at artifact assemblages at two Poplar Forest quarters. Together, these findings and the findings of others working with comparative data will help archaeologists approach an important aspect of gender relations within enslaved communities in eighteenth- and nineteenth-century Virginia.

ACKNOWLEDGMENTS

I would like to thank the Henry Luce Foundation for a two-year grant that supported excavation and analysis of a quarter site at Poplar Forest and Thomas Jefferson's Poplar Forest for continuing support of archaeological research. I am also grateful to Melanie Cabak and Amy Young for organizing the session "Engendering African American Archaeology" at the 1998 SHA Conference on Historical and Underwater Archaeology and to Amy and Jillian Galle for their hard work in bringing this volume to press. I appreciate comments made by Kristin Wilson, Brian Thomas, and other anonymous reviewers from the session, as well as Lucia Stanton of the Thomas Jefferson Foundation on earlier drafts of this chapter. Bree Detamore, Lori Lee, and Randy Lichtenberger provided useful editorial suggestions as the draft entered its final revisions, and Mark Freeman contributed his outside perspective and unfailing support. Each reviewer provided valuable input along the way. The interpretations presented here are not always in agreement with individual recommendations and remain, for better or worse, my own.

NOTES

1. Peter Hatch has recently published an analysis of the account book. While my counts of men versus women do not agree with his, our overall conclusions of age structure as it relates to gardening activities are in agreement (Hatch 2001:17–18). The counts for Figure 1.2 are based on minimum numbers of individuals. This and subsequent tables are labeled "Monticello traders" but involve slaves living at Monticello and Jefferson's outlying quarters of Lego and Tufton.

2. These biographies are based on an analysis of slave census data from Thomas Jefferson's *Farm Book* from the 1790s through 1810 (Betts 1987:30, 50–53, 57, 58a, 60, 128, 130, 134). Lucia Stanton's reconstruction of Monticello families has also been quite helpful in refining my understanding of family structure (Stanton 2000).

3. Figure 1.4 represents the percentage of traders in 1807, based on the account book entries for that year, and the total population counts for 1810.

No census was available for 1807. There may be some difference between the number of people living on the plantation in both years, but there is no reason to believe that this difference is significant.

4. Ideally, a more effective approach to measure success would be to compute overall earnings for each individual listed, but Randolph often does not record payments.

REFERENCES

Primary Sources

Thomas Jefferson Foundation
    1768–1769 Anne Cary Randolph Account Book in Record of Cases Tried in Virginia Courts.
Duke University, John Hook Papers
    1770–1776 Hook Petty Ledger.
    1788–1808 Account Book.
    1805–1809 Ledger.
University of Virginia
    1785–1786 Daybook, Barbour and Johnson Store.
    1803–1807 Ledgers of Blackwell and Pickett.
    1773 Merchants Ledger for Store in King William Courthouse.
    1797–1798 Merchandize Accounts, Buckingham County.

Secondary Sources

Betts, Edwin Morris (editor)
    1987 *Thomas Jefferson's Farm Book.* Univ. Press of Virginia, Charlottesville.
Campbell, Edward D. C., and Kym S. Rice (editors)
    1991 *Before Freedom Came: African American Life in the Antebellum South.* Univ. Press of Virginia, Charlottesville.
Conkey, Margaret W.
    1990 Does It Make a Difference? Feminist Thinking and Archaeologies of Gender. Paper presented at the 22d Annual Chacmool Conference, "The Archaeology of Gender," Calgary.
Conkey, Margaret W., and Joan Gero (editors)
    1991 *Engendering Archaeology: Women and Prehistory.* Basil Blackwell, Oxford.
Crader, Diana
    1990 Slave Diet at Monticello. *American Antiquity* 55(4):690–717.

Delle, James A.

2000 Gender, Power, and Space: Negotiating Social Relations under Slavery on Coffee Plantations in Jamaica, 1790–1834. In *Lines That Divide: Historical Archaeologies of Race, Class, and Gender*, edited by James A. Delle, Stephen A. Mrozowski, and Robert Paynter, pp. 168–201. Univ. of Tennessee Press, Knoxville.

Delle, James A., Stephen A. Mrozowski, and Robert Paynter (editors)

2000 *Lines That Divide: Historical Archaeologies of Race, Class, and Gender*. Univ. of Tennessee Press, Knoxville.

Edwards-Ingram, Ywone D.

1997 An Inter-Disciplinary Approach to African American Medicinal and Health Practices in Colonial America. *Watermark* 20(3):67–73.

2001 African American Medicine and the Social Relations of Slavery. In *Race and the Archaeology of Identity*, edited by Charles E. Orser Jr., pp. 34–53. Univ. of Utah Press, Salt Lake City.

Ferguson, Leland G.

2000 "The Cross Is a Magic Sign": Marks on Eighteenth-Century Bowls from South Carolina. In *I, Too, Am America: Archaeological Studies of African American Life*, edited by Theresa A. Singleton, pp. 116–131. Univ. Press of Virginia, Charlottesville.

Fogel, Robert William

1994 *Without Consent or Contract: The Rise and Fall of American Slavery*. W. W. Norton, New York.

Franklin, Maria, and Garrett Fesler (editors)

1999 *Historical Archaeology, Identity Formation, and the Interpretation of Ethnicity*. Colonial Williamsburg Research Publications, Colonial Williamsburg Foundation, Williamsburg.

Gruber, Anna

1990 The Archaeology of Mr. Jefferson's Slaves. Master's thesis, Winterthur Program in Early American Culture. Univ. of Delaware, Winterthur.

Hatch, Peter J.

2001 African American Gardens at Monticello. *Twin Leaf, Thomas Jefferson Center for Historic Plants Annual Journal and Catalogue* 13:14–20.

Heath, Barbara J.

1997 Slavery and Consumerism: A Case Study from Central Virginia. *African American Archaeology, Newsletter of the African American Archaeology Network* 19:1–8.

1999 Buttons, Beads, and Buckles: Contextualizing Adornment within the Bounds of Slavery. In *Historical Archaeology, Identity Formation, and the Interpretation of Ethnicity*, edited by Maria Franklin and Garrett Fesler, pp. 47–69. Colonial Williamsburg Research Publications, Colonial Williamsburg Foundation, Williamsburg.

Heath, Barbara J., and Amber Bennett

2000 "The Little Spots Allow'd Them": The Archaeological Study of African American Yards. *Historical Archaeology* 34(2):38–55.

Jamieson, Ross W.

2000 Doña Luisa and Her Two Houses. In *Lines That Divide, Historical Archaeologies of Race, Class, and Gender*, edited by James A. Delle, Stephen A. Mrozowski, and Robert Paynter, pp. 142–167. Univ. of Tennessee Press, Knoxville.

Jones, Jacqueline

1995 *Labor of Love, Labor of Sorrow: Black Women, Work and the Family, from Slavery to the Present*. Vintage Books, New York.

Little, Barbara

1994 "She Was . . . an Example to Her Sex": Possibilities for a Feminist Historical Archaeology. In *Historical Archaeology of the Chesapeake*, edited by Paul A. Shackel and Barbara J. Little, pp. 189–204. Smithsonian Institution Press, Washington, D.C.

McKee, Larry

1995 The Earth Is Their Witness. *Sciences* 35(2):36–41.

1999 Food Supply and Plantation Social Order: An Archaeological Perspective. In *I, Too, Am America: Archaeological Studies of African American Life*, edited by Theresa A. Singleton, pp. 218–239. Univ. Press of Virginia, Charlottesville.

Martin, Ann Smart

1993 Buying into the World of Goods: Eighteenth-Century Consumerism and the Retail Trade from London to the Virginia Frontier. Ph.D. diss., Dept. of History, College of William and Mary, Williamsburg.

1996 Sukey's Mirror: Consumption, Commodities and Cultural Identity in Eighteenth-Century Virginia. Paper presented at the Berkshire Conference on the History of Women, Chapel Hill, N.C.

Meaders, Daniel

1997 *Advertisements for Runaway Slaves in Virginia, 1801–1820*. Garland Publishing, New York.

Morgan, Philip D.

    1998   *Slave Counterpoint: Black Culture in the Eighteenth-Century Chesapeake and Lowcountry.* Univ. of North Carolina Press, Chapel Hill.

Mullin, Michael

    1994   *Africa in America: Slave Acculturation and Resistance in the American South and the British Caribbean, 1736–1831.* Univ. of Illinois Press, Urbana.

Purser, Margaret

    1991   "Several Paradise Ladies Are Visiting in Town": Gender Strategies in the Early Industrial West. *Historical Archaeology* 25(4):6–16.

Rawlings, Mary (editor)

    1942   *Early Charlottesville: Recollections of James Alexander, 1828–1874.* Albemarle County Historical Society, Charlottesville.

Russell, Aaron E.

    1997   Material Culture and African American Spirituality at the Hermitage. *Historical Archaeology* 31(2):63–80.

Samford, Patricia

    1996   The Archaeology of African American Slavery and Material Culture. *William and Mary Quarterly,* 3d ser., 53(1):87–114.

    2000   "Strong Is the Bond of Kinship": West African-Style Ancestor Shrines and Subfloor Pits on African American Quarters. In *Historical Archaeology, Identity Formation, and the Interpretation of Ethnicity,* edited by Maria Franklin and Garrett Fesler, pp. 71–91. Colonial Williamsburg Research Publications, Colonial Williamsburg Foundation, Williamsburg.

Schlotterbeck, John T.

    1995   The Internal Economy of Slavery in Rural Piedmont Virginia. In *The Slaves' Economy, Independent Production by Slaves in the Americas,* edited by Ira Berlin and Philip D. Morgan, pp. 170–81. Frank Cass, London.

Seifert, Donna

    1991   Within Sight of the White House: The Archaeology of Working Women. *Historical Archaeology* 25(4):82–108.

Shackel, Paul A., and Barbara Little (editors)

    1994   *Historical Archaeology of the Chesapeake.* Smithsonian Institution Press, Washington, D.C.

Singleton, Theresa A. (editor)

    1999   *I, Too, Am America: Archaeological Studies of African American Life.* Univ. Press of Virginia, Charlottesville.

Singleton, Theresa A., and Mark D. Bograd
   1995   The Archaeology of the African Diaspora in the Americas. Guides
           to the Archaeological Literature of the Immigrant Experience in
           America, No. 2. The Society for Historical Archaeology.

Sobel, Mechal
   1987   *The World They Made Together: Black and White Values in Eighteenth-
           Century Virginia*. Princeton Univ. Press, Princeton.

Spector, Janet
   1993   *What this Awl Means: Feminist Archaeology at a Wahpeton Dakota
           Village*. Minnesota Historical Society Press, St. Paul.

Stanton, Lucia
   2000   *Free Some Day, The African American Families of Monticello*.
           Monticello Monograph Series, Thomas Jefferson Foundation,
           Charlottesville.

Stine, Linda France, Melanie A. Cabak, and Mark D. Groover
   1996   Blue Beads as African American Cultural Symbols. *Historical
           Archaeology* 30(3):49–75.

Wall, Diana DiZerega
   1994   *The Archaeology of Gender: Separating the Spheres in Urban America*.
           Plenum Press, New York.
   1999   Examining Gender, Class, and Ethnicity in Nineteenth-Century
           New York. *Historical Archaeology* 33(1):102–117.
   2000   Family Meals and Evening Parties: Constructing Domesticity in
           Nineteenth-Century Middle-Class New York. In *Lines That Divide:
           Historical Archaeologies of Race, Class, and Gender*, edited by James A.
           Delle, Stephen A. Mrozowski, and Robert Paynter, pp. 109–141.
           Univ. of Tennessee Press, Knoxville.

Whelan, Mary K.
   1991   Gender and Historical Archaeology: Eastern Dakota Patterns in the
           Nineteenth Century. *Historical Archaeology* 25(4):17–32.

White, Deborah G.
   1991   Female Slaves in the Plantation South. In *Before Freedom Came:
           African American Life in the Antebellum South*, edited by Edward
           D. C. Campbell Jr. and Kym S. Rice, pp. 101–121. Univ. Press of
           Virginia, Charlottesville.

Wilkie, Laurie A.
   1997   Secret and Sacred: Contextualizing the Artifacts of African American
           Magic and Religion. *Historical Archaeology* 31(4):81–106.

Wylie, Alison

    1991   Gender Theory and the Archaeological Record: Why Is There No Archaeology of Gender? In *Engendering Archaeology: Women and Prehistory*, edited by Margaret W. Conkey and Joan Gero, pp. 31–54. Basil Blackwell, Oxford.

Young, Amy

    1996   Archaeological Evidence of African-Style Ritual and Healing Practices in the Upland South. *Tennessee Anthropologist* 21(2):139–155.

CHAPTER 2

Designing Women: Measuring Acquisition and Access at the Hermitage Plantation

JILLIAN E. GALLE

Gracy Bradley and Elizabeth Keckley led strangely parallel lives. Both were born in Virginia in the first quarter of the nineteenth century. Their skills as seamstresses took them to the White House—Gracy Bradley as the seamstress for Andrew Jackson and his family and Elizabeth Keckley as the dressmaker for Mary Todd Lincoln. Both were African American, and both used their talents to benefit themselves, their families, and their communities. There was, however, one significant difference between these two women: Gracy Bradley was a slave; Elizabeth Keckley was free.

Keckley's success story is an important starting point for this narrative about Gracy Bradley and her role as the seamstress at Andrew Jackson's plantation, the Hermitage, located outside of Nashville, Tennessee. Keckley, who spent thirty years as a slave, sewed her way to freedom. Born in Virginia, and moved by her owner to North Carolina and then Missouri, Keckley took in sewing in order to keep "bread in the mouths of seventeen persons" (Keckley 1868:45). Word of her expertise spread throughout St. Louis society, and her skills became so desirable that Keckley's female patrons purchased her freedom in 1855 for $1,200. When Keckley fully repaid this loan in 1860, she headed North, supporting herself and her son by teaching classes in dress cutting and fitting. Upon her arrival in Washington, she became the modiste for the wife of Jefferson Davis, then U.S. senator and soon-to-be president of the Confederacy. When she refused to return South with the Davises at the onset of the Civil War, Keckley was selected as the White House seamstress for Mary Todd Lincoln. She continued as Lincoln's supporter and confidant after her husband's assassination, and she went on to found the Black Contraband Relief Association in Washington, D.C. (Keckley 1868).

Keckley's story is an outlier on the historical landscape. Although few enslaved seamstresses earned their freedom with their needles, skilled seamstress work gave slaves opportunities in both the free and enslaved worlds. Enslaved seamstresses occupied a broader world than most slaves and their skills may have resulted in material and social benefits not afforded to the rest of the enslaved community. Their proximity and value to their owners most likely provided some seamstresses and their families with better quality food, clothing, housing, and other material objects. Their skills also gave them direct access to expensive fabrics and adornment items. Access to these objects, as well as knowledge of current fashions and textile and dressmaking techniques, may have helped seamstresses establish economic and social connections with slaves living in different quartering areas throughout the plantation community.

The archaeological record at the Hermitage is uniquely suited to test the hypothesis that an enslaved seamstress had access to material goods and knowledge not available to the majority of the slave community. Since the 1970s archaeologists have uncovered the extensive plantation landscape at the Hermitage (McKee 1992, 1995; McKee et. al. 1994; Russell 1997; Smith 1976; Thomas 1995, 1998). Archaeological data from three contemporaneous yet spatially separate quartering areas, the Mansion Backyard, the First Hermitage, and the Field Quarter, provide most of what is known about the more than 140 slaves living at the Hermitage by 1850 (Figure 2.1). To date, over thirteen dwelling units from these three slave quartering areas have been either archaeologically tested or fully excavated. These sites have generated hundreds of thousands of artifacts from a variety of contexts, providing archaeologists, historians, and the public with a rich and complex picture of plantation life at the Hermitage. As with most comparative archaeological work, however, sample size differences and a range of excavation strategies can impede useful comparisons between sites, especially when trying to understand differences in nonceramic assemblages. This has resulted in the assumption that various nonceramic artifact types, such as toys, buttons, beads, buckles, coins, and firearms, were evenly distributed across the plantation (Russell 1997; Thomas 1998).[1]

The proposed expectation for this study, however, is that quantitative measures of assemblage content should indicate that the enslaved seamstress had access to greater amounts of nonprovisioned objects than other enslaved individuals. The method of acquisition, such as purchase or special provisioning, in the form of gifts and hand-me-downs not accessible to every slave, cannot be determined. However, I propose that higher discard rates of non-provisioned items indicates a slave who received more gifts, and who had the means and opportunities to purchase or barter for items not usually provided by an owner.

Data from four slave-dwelling sites are used for this study. I first locate the seamstress' residence using a measure of artifact abundance known here as the Abundance Index (AI) (Galle and Neiman 2003; Neiman et. al. 2000; Ugan and Bright 2001). In order to measure variation in access and acquisition, discard rates of objects that would not necessarily have been provided by Jackson, such as adornment items, toys, musical instruments, and tobacco pipes, are then calculated using AI. These methods provide an accurate measure of assemblage variation for sites with different sample sizes and for difficult-to-quantify artifacts such as non-provisioned items.

The Hermitage

When Andrew Jackson first moved to the Hermitage property in 1804, he owned 9 taxable slaves. By 1820 that number had quadrupled to 44 slaves, and within five years that number had doubled to 85 taxable slaves. The enslaved population at the Hermitage continued to grow through natural increase and the occasional purchase until Jackson's death in 1845. Census records from 1850 indicate that 137 enslaved individuals lived at the Hermitage (Thomas 1995:34–39). These enslaved Africans maintained more than one thousand acres of cotton fields, raised Jackson's prizewinning thoroughbred horses, cultivated secondary crops of wheat and corn, labored in the peach and apples orchards, and tended the vegetable and flower gardens. At certain times of the year the cotton gin and cotton press required constant attention. An 1835 letter from one of Jackson's overseers indicates that the cotton cloth woven at the Hermitage was used to make clothing for slaves: "We have all of our winter cloth for the negroes done but two pieces to weave, we will soon be done with that Job. Our shoes I have not yet begun. I have been trying to get the leather for three weeks and have not yet got it" (Bassett 1937:361). Everything from cloth to leather was cut and assembled at the Hermitage to create the attire provisioned to the enslaved community.

Two inventories of the property offer some of the only evidence of the various occupations held by Hermitage slaves. In both the 1829 and 1846 inventories, four women, Gincy, Creasy, Big Sally, and Eliza, were listed as weavers.

One enslaved man, Ben, worked the cotton gin (Thomas 1995:145–155). Although the 1829 inventory does not list a seamstress, the 1846 inventory does identify Gracy Bradley in such a role. Check receipts from Jackson to a Mr. Hebbs of Virginia mark the purchase of Gracy Bradley, her mother, two sisters, and her brother in January and February 1833.[2] Gracy, who was around fifteen years old at the time, and her sister Louisa were slaves at the White House for several years while her mother, sister Rachel, and brother were sent to the Hermitage. Gracy and Louisa were probably moved to the Hermitage at the end of Jackson's presidential term in 1836. Within a year of her arrival at the Hermitage, she married one of the most prominent enslaved men on the plantation, Alfred Jackson, Andrew Jackson's wagoner. Gracy retained her surname and resided at the Hermitage until her death in 1882.

Gracy was certainly not the only enslaved person who sewed at the Hermitage. However, she was probably the only one trained in specialized clothing construction and design. Jackson's decision to purchase her in Washington as the seamstress for those in the White House suggests the importance she held for the Jackson family. Unfortunately, few primary documents or family papers survive regarding slavery at the Hermitage. Written sources do not indicate, for example, the extent of Gracy's duties or where she lived on the plantation. Only one garment possibly made by Gracy, a man's shirt, survives. Archaeology is therefore one of the main ways of understanding Gracy's role on the plantation.

The Sites

The data used in this study are taken from four slave-dwelling sites located in spatially separate quartering areas. Cabin 3 is one of four twenty-by-forty-foot double-pen brick dwellings located at the Field Quarter, an area one-third mile north of the Hermitage mansion (see Figure 2.1). As many as eighty enslaved individuals lived at the Field Quarter between the 1820s and the 1850s. Separated from the mansion and surrounding plantation dependencies, the Field Quarter likely housed field slaves rather than domestic or skilled slaves. This study uses data from excavations at Cabin 3 West, the western twenty-by-twenty-foot unit of Cabin 3.[3]

The South Cabin is located 540 feet northeast of the mansion in the area known as the First Hermitage. Like Cabin 3, the South Cabin was a twenty-by-forty-foot brick duplex occupied between the early 1820s and the late 1850s.

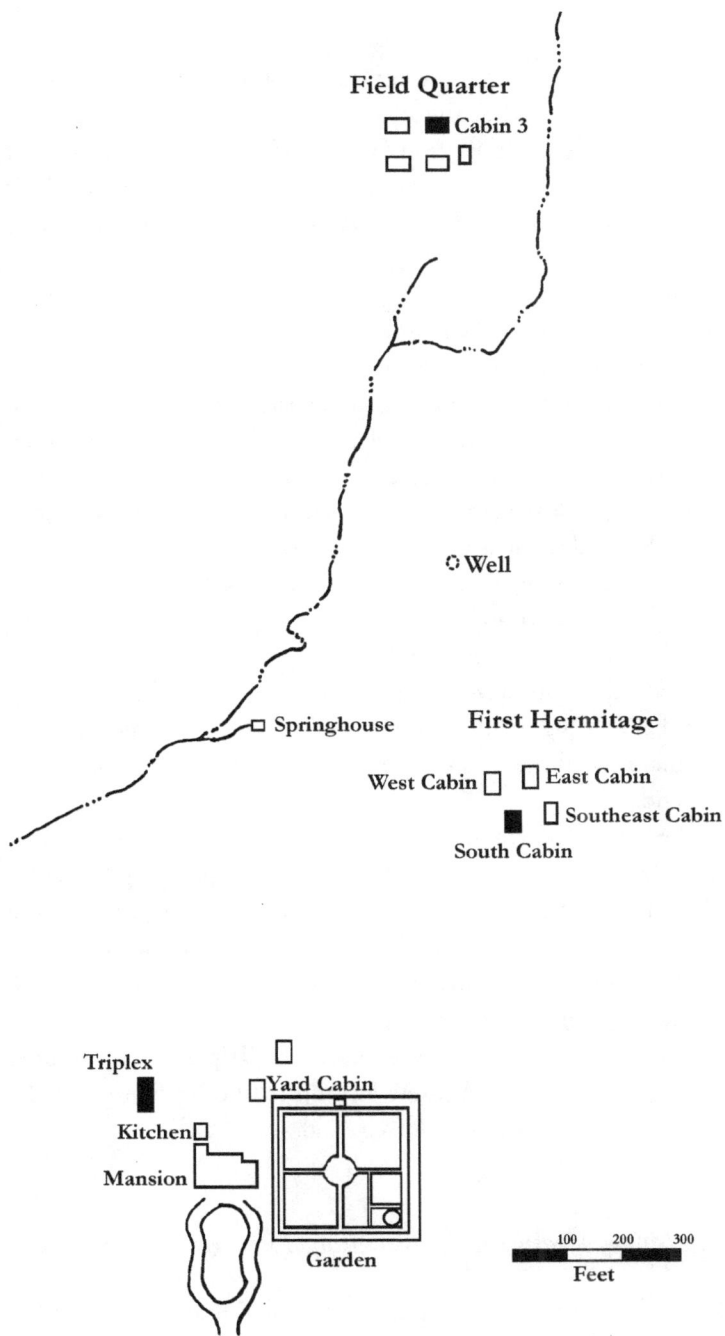

Field Quarter

☐ ◼ Cabin 3

☐ ☐ ☐

○ Well

☐ Springhouse   **First Hermitage**

West Cabin ☐   ☐ East Cabin

◼ ☐ Southeast Cabin

South Cabin

Triplex

☐ Yard Cabin

Kitchen ☐

Mansion

Garden

100   200   300
Feet

FIG. 2.1.   Hermitage Plantation (after Thomas 1995:41).

At least three other log structures, known as the East Cabin, the West Cabin, and the Southeast Cabin, stood at the First Hermitage. Built around 1804, these three structures housed the Jackson family and at least two families of slaves prior to the completion of the brick Hermitage mansion in 1821. These buildings were completely converted into slave houses shortly after the Jacksons moved into their new home (Smith 1976:114–119). Due to its proximity to the agricultural fields, gardens, and barns, a mixture of skilled and field slaves, and perhaps some domestic slaves whose responsibilities centered on the stables or the gardens, probably occupied the South Cabin (Thomas 1995:62–63).

The Triplex, located behind the Hermitage mansion just to the northwest of the detached kitchen, is a three-unit, twenty-by-sixty-foot brick dwelling. It is a variant of the brick two-unit slave dwellings that were constructed across the property in the early 1820s. Located behind the kitchen and smoke house, and across the yard from at least one other slave dwelling, the Triplex was part of a busy and dynamic mansion backyard that was home to as many as forty enslaved African Americans (see Figure 2.1). A person standing on the back porch of the Hermitage mansion could have observed the comings-and-goings of slaves and called any slave in the area by ringing call bells attached to the exterior of the building. In all likelihood, one or more members of each family living in these dwellings was required to work in the mansion or the surrounding dependencies.

Data from the Triplex North and Triplex Middle are used in this study. The Triplex North is the northern twenty-by-twenty-foot dwelling unit, and Triplex Middle is the central twenty-by-twenty-foot dwelling unit in the Triplex structure. A communicating interior door between the two units was unlikely, although there are no specific architectural data to confirm this. For this study, the Triplex North and Triplex Middle are analyzed as separate dwelling units containing different households. The Triplex was occupied until the mid-1850s, at which time Andrew Jackson Jr. and his family left the plantation amid financial difficulties (McKee et. al. 1994:19).

The Abundance Index: Measuring Consumption Through Discard Rates

One goal of this study is to measure variation in an individual's or household's ability to acquire goods through exchange, purchase or other mode of acquisition independent of slave owner provisioning. The ability to acquire goods over and above those items provided by the owner should be reflected in use rates and discard rates. For example, an individual or household that acquired more tobacco pipes should, theoretically, discard more pipes. A comparison of discard rates at Cabin 3 West, the South Cabin, the Triplex Middle, and the Triplex North is essential to testing the hypothesis that the enslaved seamstress had greater access to non-provisioned items than other Hermitage slaves.

How can we quantify non-provisioned items in the archaeological record in a manner that captures variation in discard rates and that pinpoints households that had more access to goods through their own agency and various modes of acquisition? Unfortunately, measuring and comparing discard rates using archaeological data is a difficult task. Currently many historical archaeologists use relative frequencies or percentages to measure assemblage variation among sites. Relative frequencies as measures of discard rates are problematic for inter-site comparisons. This is because relative frequencies are based on the assumption that the discard rate of the artifact class in the numerator is independent of the discard rates for all the other artifact classes that make up the denominator and that create the total sample size. A positive correlation between the discard rates of the numerator artifact class and any other artifact class that contributes to the total sample size in the denominator would attenuate variation in percentages between sites (Neiman et. al. 2000: 47).

In this study it would not be unexpected to find correlations between discard rates for non-provisioned classes of artifacts. Enslaved individuals or households with greater access to one class of non-provisioned items were likely to have greater access to other classes of non-provisioned goods. For example, a household that had access to decorative buckles and buttons might also have more access to beads. If relative frequencies are used to measure variation in buckles and buttons, variation among sites in the percentage of these artifact classes will be muted. It is important to remove beads from the denominator so that its correlation with buckles and buttons will not mask variation in the underlying discard rate values.

The Abundance Index works by choosing a single artifact class as the denominator value. By reducing the denominator to a single artifact class, one only has to be concerned with variation influenced by the correlation between two artifact classes, not variation within scores of artifact classes. It is important to select a denominator artifact class whose discard rate is either constant across assemblages or whose discard rate across assemblages varies in predictable ways.

TABLE 2.1
Total Ceramics

Artifact Description	South Cabin	Cabin 3 West	Triplex Middle	Triplex North	Total
Ceramic	3,758	2,936	1,220	2,424	10,388

Use of an artifact class with a relatively constant discard rate will result in a higher correlation between *AI* and discard rates than between percentages and discard rates.

Ceramics were chosen as the denominator artifact in this study for two reasons. First, most slave owners provided some ceramics, food, a small quantity of clothing, and bedding on a regular basis, although each owner distributed these goods at different intervals. Ceramics are one of the consistently and regularly provisioned items that remain in the archaeological record. Second, documents also tell us that owners provided slaves with the majority of their ceramics (Otto 1984; Rawick 1972). This was the case at the Hermitage (Thomas 1995: 66; Thomas 1998). Although some slaves most likely supplemented their ceramic rations with pieces acquired through purchase or exchange, ceramics were most likely provided by Jackson at a constant rate. Relatively constant provisioning of ceramics would result in a relatively constant discard rate, therefore making ceramics one of the more reliable artifact classes against which to measure access to goods independent of provisioning.

For this study the Abundance Index is estimated as:

$$AI = \frac{(Artifact\ Group\ 1)}{(Artifact\ Group\ 1) + (Artifact\ Group\ 2)}$$

where Group 1 is the artifact group whose variation we are interested in measuring and Group 2 is the artifact group against which abundance variation is measured. For this study, Artifact Group 1 is the sum of a chosen group of generally non-provisioned artifacts, such as adornment items. *Artifact Group 2* is the total sum of ceramics for each site. The ceramic total for each site provides a constant with which to compare these assemblages (Table 2.1).

This analysis begins with the calculation of a Sewing Equipment Index in order to gauge use frequencies and discard rates of sewing equipment at these four sites. The sewing equipment category consists of straight pins, scissors,

TABLE 2.2

Sewing Equipment Group Summary

Artifact Description	South Cabin	Cabin 3 West	Triplex Middle	Triplex North	Total
Awl/Drizzler			1		1
Crochet hook			1		1
Eye, clothing	7	4	2	10	23
Hook, clothing	14	12	19	7	52
Ivory needle case			1		1
Knitting needle guard			3		3
Lace needle			1		1
Needle		4	1		5
Scissors	1	3	1		5
Straight pin	45	12	323	60	440
Tambour hook			1		1
Thimble	5	1	2		8
Total	72	36	356	77	541

thimbles, needles, and miscellaneous bone needleworking implements (Table 2.2). Sewing equipment may have been provisioned to those slaves whose occupation depended on such tools. Sewing equipment would not have been provided to all slaves as part of an owner's standard allotment.

Table 2.2 reveals the variability in the numbers of types of sewing equipment recovered at each site. The most abundant sewing tools were straight pins, and all four sites contained them. Thimbles and scissors were the second and third most common pieces of sewing equipment, with fragments of both types found at Cabin 3 West, the South Cabin, and the Triplex Middle. The Triplex Middle contained a unique group of sewing tools, including a brass thimble stamped with the words "Tho Absent Ever dear," an ivory needle case, two mother-of-pearl knitting needle guards, and four specialized needlework implements: a tambour hook, a lace bobbin, an awl or drizzler, and a crochet hook. When these raw counts are put into the AI equation, the results indicate that residents at the Triplex Middle used and discarded ten times the number of sewing tools than those at Cabin 3 West, the South Cabin, and the Triplex North. The Sewing Equipment Index was calculated using 95 percent confidence limits (Figure 2.2).

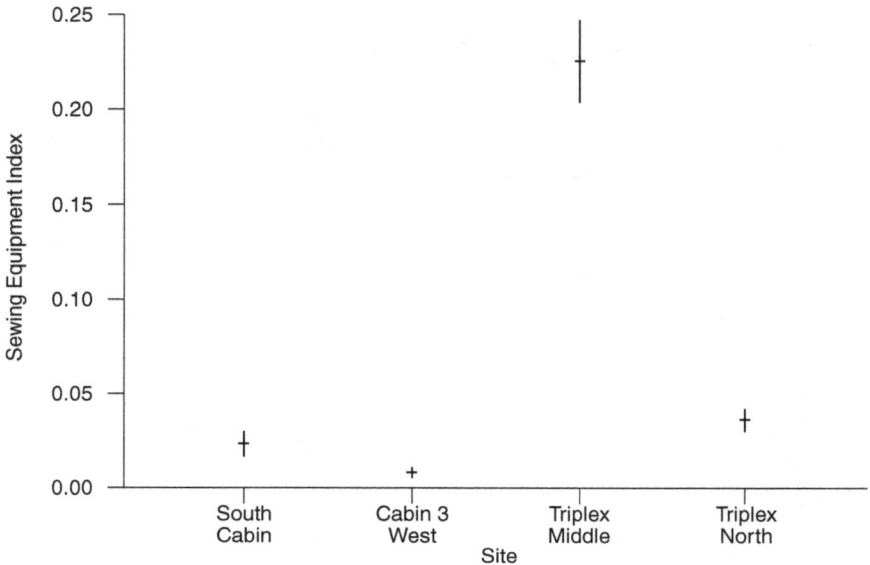

FIG. 2.2.   Sewing equipment index values with exact 95 percent confidence limits.

In contrast, residents at Cabin 3 West, the South Cabin, and the Triplex North discarded relatively few sewing items. The small number of straight pins, thimbles, and scissors most likely indicate that clothing repair and small-scale clothing production occurred at these sites. These artifacts not only demonstrate that slaves stretched their limited clothing supply as far as possible, but that they may have also had some degree of autonomy in respect to the creation and embellishment of garments to supplement their rations. The large quantity of basic sewing equipment, the unique presence of specialized needle-working tools, and the building's proximity to the mansion suggest that the Triplex Middle served as the center of highly skilled, and possibly large-scale, sewing activities at the Hermitage. It is likely that this dwelling unit was the residence of Gracy Bradley and her family or someone like her.

The Material Culture of Sewing and Needlework

The sewing toolkit found at the Triplex Middle represents a range of skills possessed by both enslaved and free seamstresses. As the use of lace and embroidered fabrics on garments and in home decor rose in popularity during the last quarter of the eighteenth century, greater value was placed on a woman's needlework skills (Baumgarten 2003). For elite and aspiring elite women, decorative needlework was an important mode of personal expression as well as social competition. Fine needlework was time consuming, however, and many women had difficulty producing the quantity of lace and embroidered fabric required to keep their family fashionable. Not surprisingly, the demand for skilled enslaved seamstresses rose throughout the early nineteenth century due partly to these changing fashions (Proctor 1990; Rogers 1983).

The mass production of sewing implements such as straight pins, thimbles, and bone needlework tools during the second quarter of the nineteenth century helped make it economically feasible to provide an enslaved seamstress with the tools she needed. Prior to the 1830s, for example, most sewing equipment was only sold in prohibitively expensive sewing tables or kits imported from China or Europe (Figure 2.3). The industrial revolution brought changes that directly affected the cost and availability of bone, ivory, and metal sewing equipment. In 1824 Lemuel Wright invented a straight pin machine that produced solid, machine-headed pins. These inexpensive and readily available straight pins replaced costly hand-headed pins. Similarly, the introduction of stamped brass thimbles in the 1820s provided a less costly alternative to imported silver, gold, and mother-of-pearl thimbles (Rogers 1983:95). By the mid-1830s, American manufacturers were also producing bone tools that copied expensive ivory needlework tools produced in east Asia and Europe (16–17).

The ivory needle case and two mother-of-pearl knitting needle guards found at the Triplex Middle are representative of imported needleworking tools. The mother-of-pearl knitting needle guards, usually purchased in pairs connected by either a ribbon or chain, became popular in the late 1840s (Figure 2.4). Placed on the end of knitting needles to keep the needle set together, they also prevented stitches from sliding off works in progress. Needle guards ranged in size from one-half inch to two inches in length and could easily accommodate thin, nineteenth-century knitting needles, which were often referred to as "pin[s], wire[s], or prick[s]" (Proctor 1990:112; Rogers 1983:201).

The four bone implements found at the Triplex Middle point to the production of detailed textiles such lace, tambour work, embroidery, and whitework. Bone and ivory tambour hook handles and lace bobbins were often intricately lathed. The recovered handle of a possible tambour hook would have been fitted with a metal hook. The neck of the lace bobbin was broken off, perhaps during use, and the broken edge was filed flat (Figure 2.5).

FIG. 2.3.   This sewing table was purchased for $50 in 1835 from the Philadelphia merchants, Barry and Kirkbaum. It was a gift from Andrew Jackson to his daughter-in-law, Sarah Yorke Jackson. Photograph courtesy Jean Fuller Guy and The Hermitage, Home of President Andrew Jackson.

The other two bone tools found at the Triplex were handcrafted rather than mass produced, and they may have been worked or modified at the Hermitage. In addition to crochet work, the flat bone crochet hook (Figure 2.5) may have also been used for pulling thread through eyelets or other openwork such as lace or white-work (Baumgarten, personal communication; Rogers 1983). A bone awl

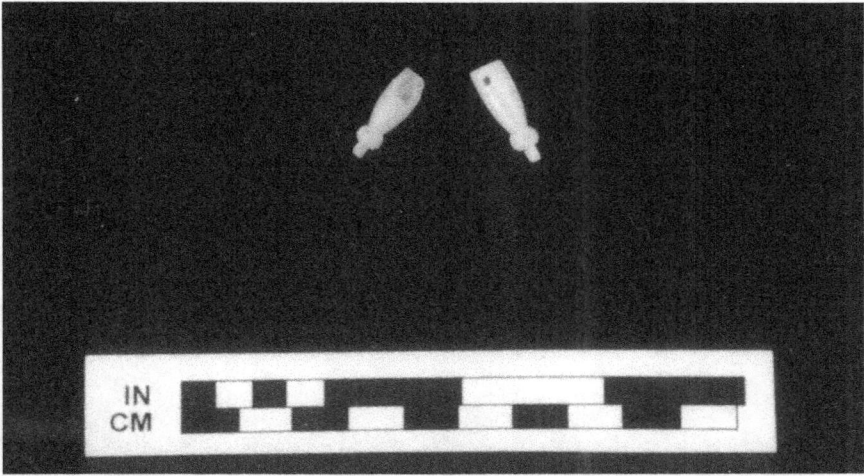

FIG. 2.4.   Mother-of-Pearl knitting needle guards from the Triplex Middle. Photograph by Larry McKee, by permission of the Archaeology Department, The Ladies Hermitage Association.

or stiletto was probably reshaped from a larger piece of bone (Figure 2.5). Its small, thin point may have been used in the creation of cutwork or for pushing thread through white work (Rogers 1983:207). It is also possible that the awl was used as a drizzler. Drizzlers were specialized tools used to draw precious silver and gold thread from worn cloth.

These tools excavated from the Triplex Middle suggest that a wide range of detailed needlework occurred within the cabin. The presence of the lace bobbin, tambour hook, and knitting needle guards indicate that a Hermitage seamstress, most likely Gracy, knew sewing techniques that few slaves at the Hermitage possessed. High-style nineteenth-century clothing included pleats, tucks, and seams that required several pins during the process of construction. The discovery of 347 straight pins suggests that the residents of the Triplex Middle were engaged in the production of the elaborate dress required by the Jacksons (Figure 2.6). The quantity of straight pins may also signal that this quarter, and perhaps the entire Triplex structure, served as a center for the production of all slave clothing at the Hermitage. The process of making clothing for 130 slaves would have required a large number of pins. The location of the Triplex Middle directly behind the mansion made it easily accessible to Rachel Jackson, Jackson's wife, and Sarah Yorke Jackson, Jackson's

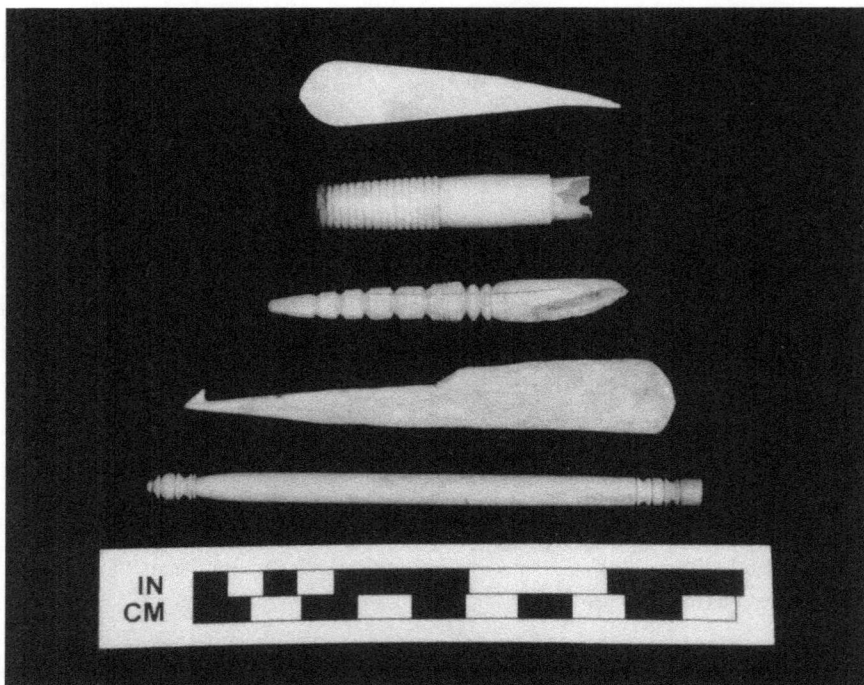

FIG. 2.5.   Bone and ivory needlework tools from the Triplex Middle. *From top to bottom*: Awl/Drizzler, Needle Case, Tambour Hook Handle, Crochet Hook, Lace Bobbin. Photograph by Larry McKee, by permission of the Archaeology Department, The Ladies Hermitage Association.

daughter-in-law, who likely supervised, and perhaps participated in, planta-tionwide sewing activities.[4]

A seamstress' specialized skills benefited the enslaved plantation commu-nity as well. The standard practice among planters was to distribute clothing twice a year, usually an allotment of two suits of a lightweight cloth such as osnaburg and two suits of heavy cloth such as wool (Breeden 1980; Joyner 1991:56). There were great discrepancies, however, in accounts of what a suit of clothing comprised and whether accessories, such as shoes and shawls, were included with the biannual distribution (Breeden 1980; Joyner 1991; Mellon 1988; Perdue et al. 1976; Rawick 1972). To save time and fabric, shapeless pat-terns that could be adapted to a multitude of body sizes were cut from coarse wool and osnaburg (Durand 1977:12–17; Fry 1990; Tandberg 1980:90–91).

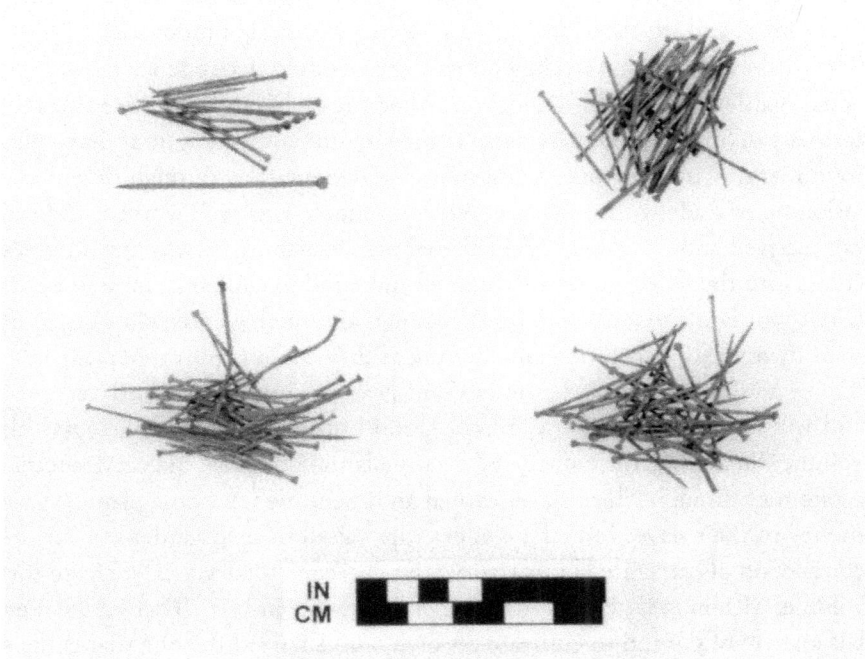

FIG. 2.6.   A sample of straight pins from the Triplex Middle. Photograph by
Larry McKee, by permission of the Archaeology Department, The Ladies
Hermitage Association.

As recipients of the coarse, misshapen clothing, enslaved individuals were
aware of the statements owners made by providing uncomfortable and unflattering apparel.

Masters' accounts and former-slave interviews demonstrate that clothing
was not only used to mark differences between free and enslaved groups, but
also to signal within an enslaved population differential access to goods and
possibly services. Many former slaves spoke of clothing items they had made,
while others described their ability to earn money to purchase "dress-up"
clothing (Baumgarten 1988, 1991; Fox-Genovese 1988; Mellon 1988; Perdue
et al. 1976:316; Rawick 1972). With a distinctive dress, headscarf, or waistcoat,
an enslaved individual could display his or her ability to supplement allot-
ments from owners. Several factors contributed to a slave's ability to procure
clothes beyond what was provided in the biannual allotment: an individual's

proximity to the plantation household; his or her use of informal plantation economies; and their personal skills at sewing and design innovation.

Slaves who labored in the house or surrounding dependencies as maids, cooks, gardeners, or stable hands were often dressed in uniforms or hand-me-downs provided by their owners. Hand-me-down clothing may have also found its way to fieldworkers and more isolated quarters through direct provisioning or trade within the enslaved community. Enslaved women who did not receive hand-me-downs often altered plain osnaburg by weaving different colors into the fabric, or by stitching on more fashionable buttons and beads (Fry 1990; Hunt 1996; White 1991). Women and men adapted clothing to fit their own needs, decorating and altering as they could (Hunt 1996:228).

In addition to hand-me-downs and personal innovation, enslaved men and women purchased fabric, ribbons, and buttons (Heath 1997, 1999, this volume; Smart-Martin 1991, 1996). Many plantations had organized internal economies through which slaves earned and spent money. Some planters gave money to their slaves in exchange for crops raised in their gardens or for the completion of specialized or unsavory tasks (Breeden 1980:257–275; Heath this volume; Mellon 1988:56). An Alabama planter wrote in 1852: "Each of the men has an acre of ground to cultivate his own, and I reward the one that gathers the largest and best crop. With the proceeds of their crop they purchase their Sunday clothing" (Breeden 1980:271–272). In addition, slaves made goods or traded labor for money or store credit (Heath, this volume). Groups of enslaved men and women may have participated together in the production of knitted crafts and quilts (Fry 1990; MacDonald 1988:23–25). Enslaved individuals also participated in informal exchanges with neighboring plantations.

Both the free and enslaved communities valued a seamstress' work (Durand 1977:12–17; Fry 1990; Tandberg 1980:90–91). For the free plantation community, ownership of a skilled seamstress meant that the household had access to a woman who could produce everyday clothes, linens, and fashionable dress for the family as well as manage the production of clothing for the rest of the enslaved community. Demand for these skills was so great during the nineteenth century that planters in seach of talented seamstresses placed want ads in the newspapers (Fry 1990:22). As a result of this demand, prices for enslaved seamstresses skyrocketed at the end of the eighteenth century, with their values rivaling the prices asked for healthy, young male slaves.

Although the plantation seamstress produced clothing unobtainable by other slaves, a skilled seamstress most likely had access to a wide range of fabrics and adornment items desired by the entire enslaved community. Experienced seamstresses were responsible for handling luxury fabrics needed for their owner's garments, and they might have exchanged fabric remnants and leftover buttons and beads for goods produced by other slaves. A skilled seamstress may have also made embroidered fabric, lace, or fashionable dresses for her own personal use. Her ability to produce or acquire ornate pieces of lace, needlework, or fabric may have been a powerful resource within a group that valued, but had little access to, high-quality, decorative clothing. If so, a seamstress may have used her work not only as a gift but also as a commodity that could be traded within an economy internal to the enslaved population at the Hermitage. For example, fine lace or a fancy vest may have been traded for goods, the services of another skilled craftsperson on the plantation, or for the ministrations of a traditional healer. Additionally, lace, embroidery, quilts, and a seamstress' design skills may have found a market outside of the plantation, thus providing cash money or a position from which to trade and barter (Benberry 1992; Fry 1990).

To test the hypothesis that an enslaved steamstress had greater access to non-provisioned items, discard rates were calculated using the abundance index for several artifact groups that were most likely acquired through purchase or special provisioning resulting from preferential access. The following artifacts groups are used for this analysis: adornment, appearance, amusement, medical, and tobacco pipes. The adornment group consists of artifacts that would have appeared on clothing (beads, buckles, buttons) or over clothing (beads, hand charms, watches, jewelry) or were worn and held in a way so as to enhance one's appearance (purses, parasols, hats, eyeglasses) (Table 2.3). The appearance group, although related to the adornment group, is made up of objects that enhanced one's physical appearance through hygiene or hairstyles (hair combs, brushes, hairpins, and toothbrushes) (Table 2.4). The amusement group contains toys such as marbles and dolls and musical instruments (Table 2.5). The medical group contains objects related to health care such as medicine vials and bottles and medical tools such as syringes (Table 2.6). The tobacco pipe group contains only tobacco pipes (Table 2.7).

Adornment Index

The widespread distribution of adornment artifacts at the Hermitage indicates the importance of decorative clothing items among the enslaved population.

TABLE 2.3
Adornment Group Summary

Artifact Description	South Cabin	Cabin 3 West	Triplex Middle	Triplex North	Total
Aiglet			1		1
Bead	28	19	14	18	79
Buckle	4	7	9		20
Button	197	200	287	139	823
Cane handle				1	1
Cane tip		2			2
Eyeglass parts		1	3		4
Eyelet	8	31	7		46
Fan blade				8	8
Hand charm		1			1
Jewelry				4	4
Purse		5	1		6
Rivet, shoe	1	2	6	6	15
Watch fob		2			2
Total	238	270	328	176	1,012

TABLE 2.4
Appearance Group Summary

Artifact Description	South Cabin	Cabin 3 West	Triplex Middle	Triplex North	Total
Hair Brush			2		2
Hair comb		5	3	1	9
Hair pin		1	1		2
Toothbrush	1		4	5	10
Total	1	6	10	6	23

TABLE 2.5

Amusement Group Summary

Artifact Description	South Cabin	Cabin 3 West	Triplex Middle	Triplex North	Total
Doll		21	4		25
Jaw harp	2				2
Marble	9	19	57	18	103
Music box		1			1
Probable gaming piece		2			2
Toy teapot fragment (porcelain)			2		2
Total	11	43	63	18	135

TABLE 2.6

Medical Group Summary

Artifact Description	South Cabin	Cabin 3 West	Triplex Middle	Triplex North	Total
Cu alloy syringe			1		1
Glass medicine vial	6	20	14	4	44
Surgical tool (possible)			1		1
Total	6	20	16	4	46

TABLE 2.7

Tobacco Pipe Group Summary

Artifact Description	South Cabin	Cabin 3 West	Triplex Middle	Triplex North	Total
Tobacco pipe fragment	32	43	18	27	120

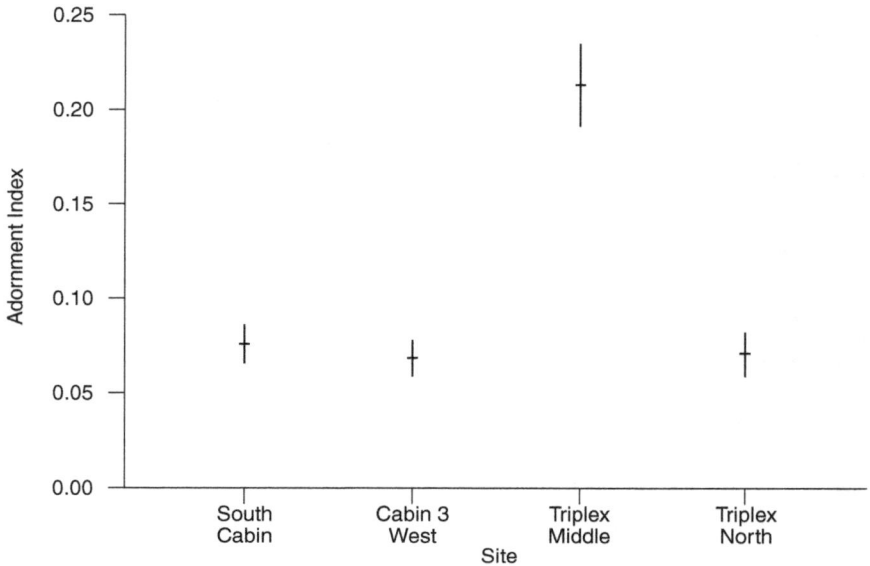

FIG. 2.7.   Adornment index values with exact 95 percent confidence limits.

All three sites investigated contain adornment artifacts such as buttons, beads, clothing buckles, cane tips, fan blades, and umbrella ribs. The raw counts for each site give the impression that slaves at the Hermitage had equal access to adornment artifacts. An adornment index suggests otherwise (Figure 2.7). The adornment index indicates that residents at the Triplex Middle were discarding adornment and appearance related objects at a greater rate relative to ceramics than residents at other quarters. If the Triplex Middle was the residence and workplace of Gracy, the enslaved seamstress, then an argument might be made that the adornment index values are influenced by the large number of buttons at the Triplex Middle, objects that might also be considered part of a seamstress' toolkit. An index for adornment items minus buttons was also calculated, and the resulting values were the same (Figure 2.8). Therefore, if one were to place buttons into the sewing equipment group, the adornment without buttons index values would still suggest that Triplex Middle residents had greater access to adornment items than even the household directly adjacent to them in the Triplex North.

Buttons found at Cabin 3 West and the South Cabin were roughly similar in terms of material and style.[5] Ranging in material from metal, bone, and

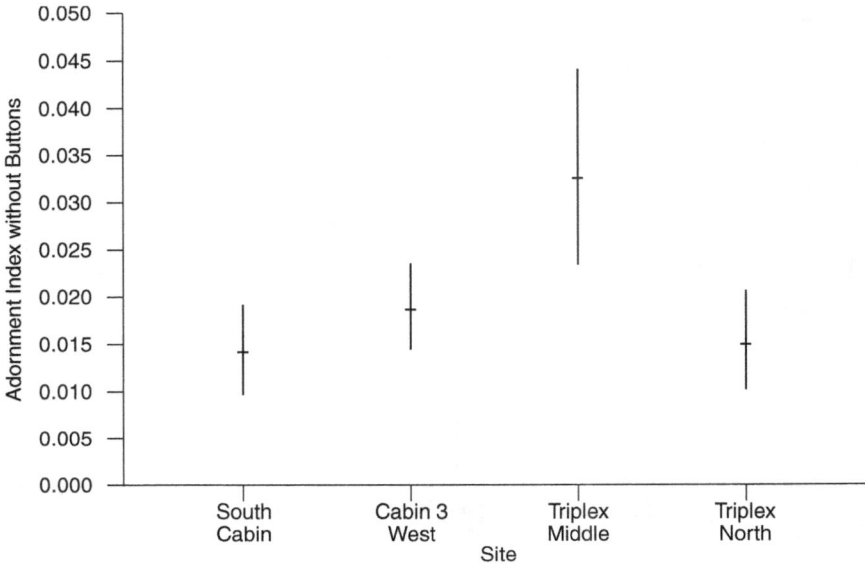

FIG. 2.8.   Index values with exact 95 percent confidence limits for the adornment group with buttons removed from the analysis.

shell to porcelain and rubber, these buttons represent a variety of men's clothing, including coats, breeches, trousers, shirts, waistcoats, and underwear (L. Rogers 1992:2; 1993:1–3). Shell buttons and bone disks with single holes would have been covered with cloth, crocheted threads, or beadwork, and they are suggestive of women's clothing (L. Rogers 1993:1–3). Small, ornate buttons reflect specialized garments such as fancy vests (popular from 1830 to 1860) that were probably not distributed as part of Jackson's clothing allowance (5). Their presence may be the result of hand-me-downs, purchases, or trades.

The button assemblage from the Triplex Middle stands out from the other two sites. Bone disks with single holes and high-quality shell buttons dominate the Triplex Middle's button assemblage. These buttons probably reflect the production of individualized, high-style clothing that required buttons covered with matching fabric or decorative stitching (L. Rogers 1995:3). The number of buttons and button blanks, along with the size of the sewing assemblage, reinforces the argument that the Triplex Middle was a locus of clothing production.

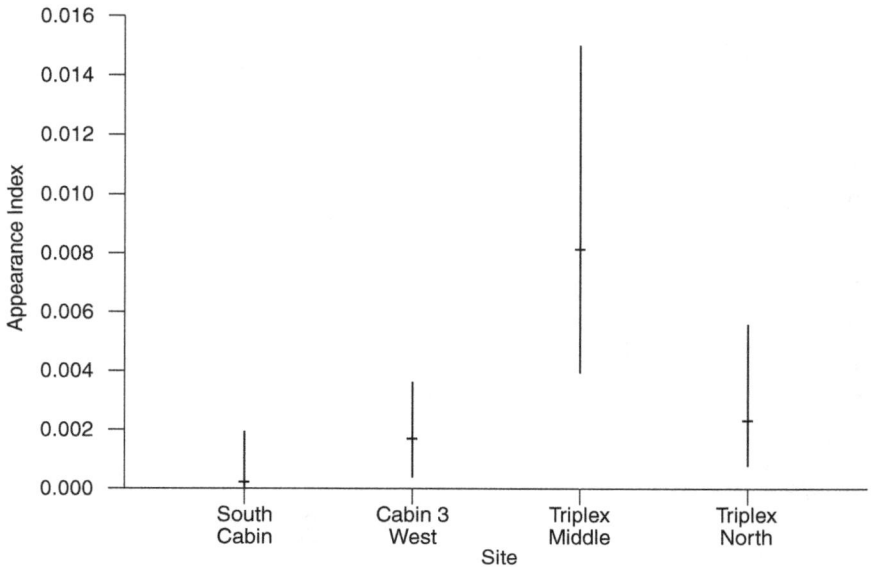

FIG. 2.9.   Appearance index values with exact 95 percent confidence limits.

Appearance Index

The appearance index is similar to the adornment index (Figure 2.9). Residents at the Triplex Middle had greater access to appearance-related artifacts as well, although residents at the Triplex North may have discarded nearly as many hair combs, hair brushes, and toothbrushes.

The adornment and appearance indexes indicate that objects such as beads, buckles, hair combs, and toothbrushes were not restricted to one localized group of enslaved individuals. Not unsurprisingly, Hermitage slaves were concerned with their appearance, and they acquired adornment items not necessarily provided by Jackson's clothing distributions. The ability to procure goods not channeled through Jackson meant that either slaves had some amount of purchasing power or that there was a well-established network of trade within the enslaved community.

A skilled seamstress with access to hand-me-down clothing and remnants of cloth, and with advanced clothing design and construction skills, might have been central in the trade and distribution of adornment items. She would have been able to create stylish dresses and vests for fellow slaves not as skilled in clothing construction. Additionally, the seamstress may have saved

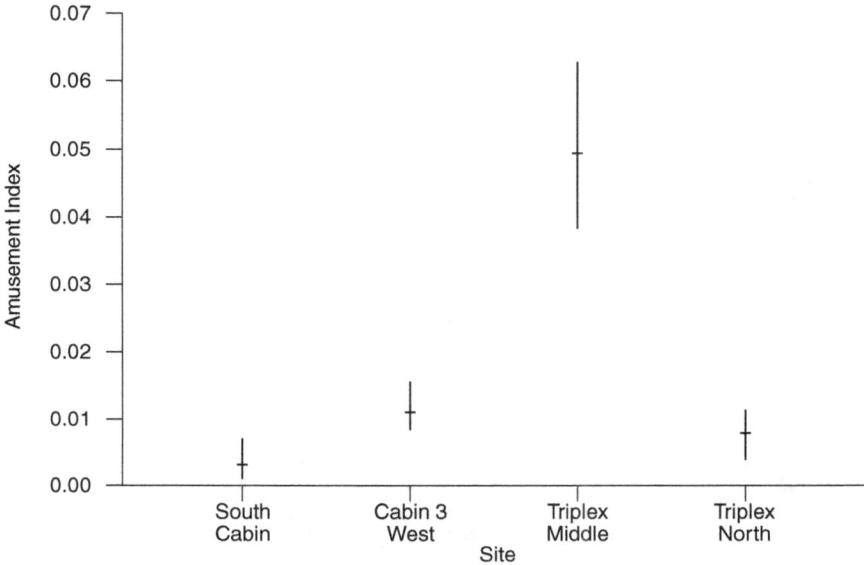

FIG. 2.10.   Amusement index values with exact 95 percent confidence limits.

fabric remnants and adornment items that she then traded or passed onto other enslaved persons. Her ability to provide these desired goods may have facilitated the expansion of a seamstress's social circle. It also would have given her more social "capital" with which to trade and barter for goods and services from other slaves. These indexes show that Triplex Middle residents also had more objects than those living in the Triplex North, which suggests that the variation in discard rates may have more to do with one's social and occupational identity than one's proximity to the mansion. In addition, although Gracy may have received more from her owners, it is also possible she had more to gain from other slaves since she had objects and skills desired by the rest of the enslaved community. The amusement, medical, and tobacco pipe indexes support this theory and add complexity to the story of the Triplex Middle.

Amusement Index

The number of amusement artifacts found at the Triplex Middle may also point to the seamstress's access to materials from the mansion as well as her ability to purchase or trade for such items. The Triplex Middle contains a strikingly large

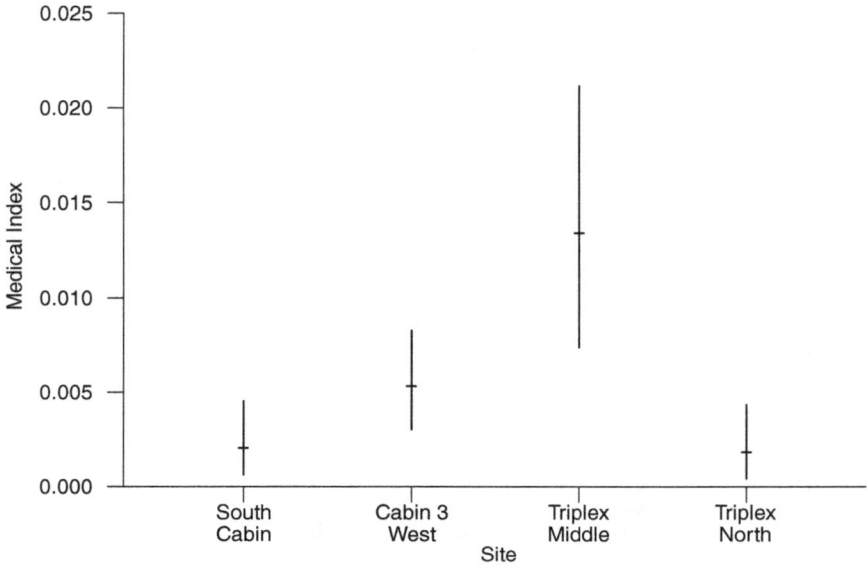

FIG. 2.II.   Medical index values with exact 95 percent confidence limits.

number of marbles (Table 2.5). Four porcelain doll parts and two fragments of a toy teapot found at the Triplex Middle further point to the leisure activities of children and adults. The amusement index (Figure 2.10) shows that Triplex Middle residents were clearly using and discarding many more recreational items relative to ceramics than those living in the other three dwellings.

Medical Index

Objects related to medical care might also be used to measure a household's access to goods (Table 2.6). Once again, the Triplex Middle has the highest index value, while the Triplex North has the lowest. All four dwellings have fragments of medicine vials and medicine bottles. The Triplex Middle also contains one possible surgical tool and one intact copper syringe that was found at the bottom of the dwelling's subfloor pit (Figure 2.11).

It is possible that residents at the Triplex Middle had more medical supplies available to them. Gracy's and Alfred's value to the Jackson family may have earned them preferential health care. It may also have been the case that the Hermitage had a place on the plantation set aside for the treatment of sick slaves. Accidents occurred often on plantations, and cramped, unsanitary living

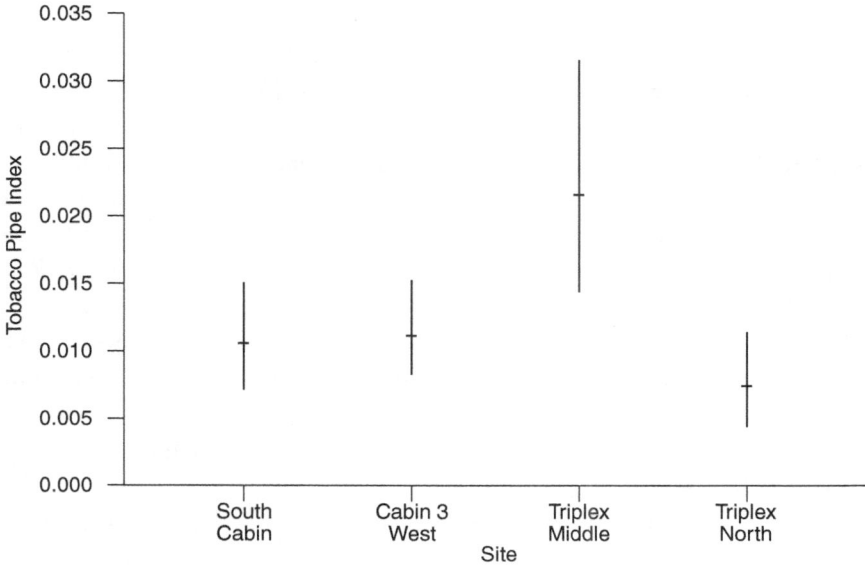

FIG. 2.12.   Tobacco pipe index values with exact 95 percent confidence limits.

conditions promoted diseases such as dysentery, worms, and typhoid fever (Savitt 1988:129). When such ailments were discovered by planters, slaves were quickly treated with harsh drugs, such as quinine, leeches, and lancets, all standard medical procedures for both the free and enslaved (142). The medicine vials and possible surgical tool indicate such treatments were available to slaves at the Hermitage.

Although planters and overseers rarely named the diseases that afflicted slaves, venereal disease was a persistent problem on plantations (139). In a surprising addendum to a letter to Andrew Jackson Jr. in 1835, Mr. Hobbs, a Hermitage overseer, wrote: "Aron the Blacksmith and Tom Franklin was both taken sick yesturday, verry hot fever all night. I gave them a large dose of Calomel and Jalap this morning, they are much better tonight. Littleton is laid up with the gonerea, he got it from his wife, he of course will do nothing for two or three weeks" (Bassett 1937).

Fearing that venereal disease would disable portions of their workforce for long periods of time, planters quickly treated the afflicted. Doctors used copper alloy syringes, similar to that found in the root cellar of the Triplex Middle, to treat venereal disease during the nineteenth century. Syringes allowed the directed application of disease-fighting lotions containing sulfates of zinc, alum, and tannin. A medical guide to prostitution first published in 1857 argued that a six-ounce syringe was the primary method by which diseases like gonorrhea were prevented and controlled (Acton 1972:85–87).

When the amusement and medical indexes are viewed in light of nineteenth-century documents, the argument that a seamstress could improve her social and economic access by way of occupational status becomes more complicated. Both planters' accounts and ex-slave interviews refer to the practice of having cooks and seamstresses watch over those unable to work in the fields, such as the young, the sick, or the elderly (Breeden 1980: 205–206, 281–288). The high amusement and medical indexes may indicate that the seamstress was looking after children while their parents were in the field or that she had the additional responsibility of caring for the sick.[6] The Triplex Middle's high tobacco pipe index also suggests that the dwelling might have been a gathering spot (Figure 2.12).

The placement of the Triplex Middle was ideal for overseeing the young and the indisposed. It is possible that the entire Triplex structure was used for these activities, although the indexes for the Triplex North are lower than the other dwellings. Currently, the child and health care roles of the seamstress at the Hermitage are speculative. However, if the Hermitage seamstress took care of the sick and the young, she may have employed them in activities related to clothing production. Masters' accounts indicate that sick women were often put to work sewing, spinning, or watching children.

Architecture and the Social Use of Space

The use of the Triplex Middle as the possible site of clothing production, childcare, and health care raises the larger question of architectural planning at the Hermitage. Archaeological research has shown that a double-pen dwelling was the standard for enslaved Hermitage families. Four brick duplexes were located at the Field Quarter: one brick and two log duplexes were at the First Hermitage area, and at least one duplex was located in the mansion yard area. Each duplex measured twenty by forty feet, suggesting that Jackson had a clear architectural type for Hermitage slave quarters.

The Triplex structure's variation from the standard duplex may result from specific ideas that Jackson had regarding use of that space. He may have wanted to consolidate multiple activities into one building close to the man-

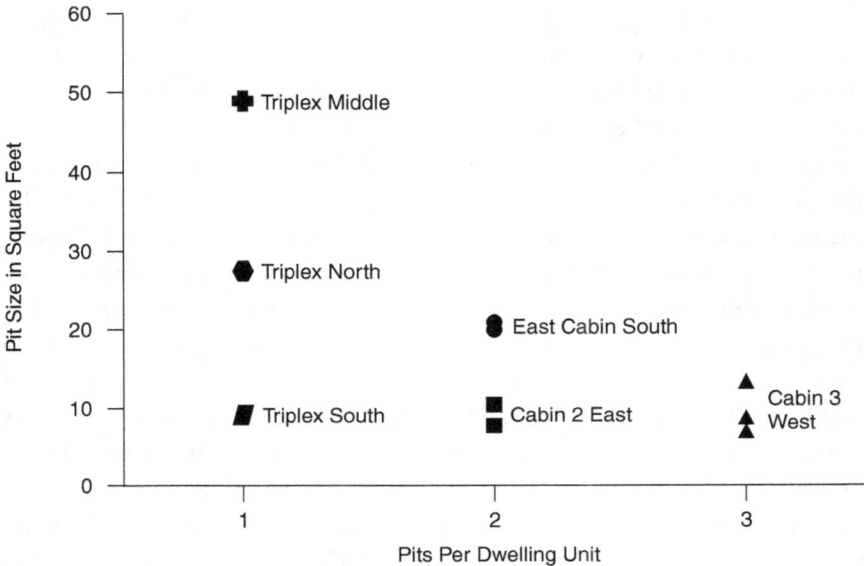

FIG. 2.13.   Subfloor pit quantity and size per dwelling unit at the Hermitage.

sion. In doing so, he would have created a locus of activity, purposefully designing the Triplex as an activity area, a site of domestic control where he could place a prominent enslaved person, or group of people, to preside over the activities of others. A fence line running between the mansion and the Triplex created a physical barrier between the yard spaces of the quarters behind the mansion and the mansion yard, yet the quarters were still close enough for easy supervision. For the enslaved population, however, a production space like the Triplex Middle may have become a place for trade, communication, and creative expression. If Jackson placed the seamstress as an overseer of the young, elderly, and sick, she would have been in frequent contact with much of the enslaved community.

One architectural feature of Hermitage slave dwellings, the subfloor pit or root cellar, may support this hypothesis. The subfloor pit at the Triplex Middle is by far the largest excavated at the Hermitage to date (Figure 2.13). At 6.5 x 7.5 feet, the pit's size may be directly correlated with the abundance indexes that suggest Triplex Middle residents had more personal items to store than other slaves at the Hermitage. The substantial, brick-lined cellar provided storage space for a variety of items ranging from food and dry goods to children's toys.

Recent work suggesting that subfloor pits functioned like safety deposit boxes in dwellings that contained non-kin-based residents applies nicely to the Triplex Middle (Neiman 1997). Neiman argues that slaves constructed pits to protect their belongings, particularly when individuals lived with non-kin or when dwellings were not easily secured. Dwellings with multiple, small pits point to households of unrelated, perhaps uncooperative individuals who maintained their own personal items in separate storage areas (ibid.). Following this argument, the Triplex Middle's single pit indicates that a cooperative, kin-based household occupied the unit. If their living space also functioned as an activity center through which many different people passed on a daily basis, those living in the Triplex Middle may have constructed a large and highly visible cellar for the storage and protection of their personal objects. A non-family member opening the large pit in the Triplex Middle would have drawn attention, therefore effectively discouraging pilfering.

The architecturally distinctive Triplex structure may have linked Jackson, Gracy, and the larger enslaved population. Although Jackson may have created the Triplex Middle space as the center of activity and daily control over a certain segment of the enslaved population, it is possible that slaves transformed a portion of the mansion backyard into a space receptive to their own economic and social needs. I suggest that the Triplex Middle served as a meeting place through which most of the enslaved at the Hermitage traveled at certain times. Goods such as fancy fabrics and clothing accoutrements may have been exchanged, as well as gossip and other forms of specialized knowledge. It is highly possible that the seamstress, with her knowledge of plantation activities and access to desired goods, transformed the Triplex Middle into a nexus of interslave social activity incongruous with its location within the socially controlled realm of the plantation backyard.

Conclusion

Enslaved individuals created and participated in economic and social systems based on their skills, interactions with the owners and overseers, and relationships with individuals outside the plantation. Gracy Bradley may not have earned her freedom as a seamstress but the Abundance Indexes suggest that she and her family had significantly more non-provisioned items than other enslaved households on the property. Abundance Index values from the

Triplex Middle are notably higher than at the Triplex North, suggesting that access to goods at the Hermitage was not simply a result of one's proximity to the mansion.

Gracy's work in the White House, Alfred's mobility as a wagoner, and their proximity to the mansion may have given them opportunities to earn money through tips. Their proximity to the Jackson family may have afforded them gifts not normally distributed to the other slaves. It is possible that Gracy's skills as a seamstress, and her direct access to adornment items, made her a desired trading partner within the enslaved community at the Hermitage.

If the Triplex Middle also served as a clothing production center and a quarter for the employment of the sick and young, it would have also linked enslaved individuals from all three areas of The Hermitage plantation— the Mansion Backyard, the First Hermitage, and the Field Quarter. Even if Jackson's intent was for the Triplex Middle to serve as a quarter for the supervision of sick or aged, it may have become an exchange center for trade and information. Gracy and her family possibly traded cloth remnants, lace, and other adornment items for the goods and services of slaves who passed through or near the building. Gracy's and Alfred's proximity to the Jackson family most likely gave them access to information and gossip that was useful to the rest of the enslaved community. The size of the Triplex Middle's subfloor pit and the tobacco pipe index value are other possible signs that slaves unrelated to Gracy and Alfred passed through the dwelling for work, trade, or socializing.

The use of Abundance Indexes from the remains of four enslaved households suggests that many complex relationships lie beneath the traditional models, posited by historians and archaeologists, that imply competitive and antagonistic relations between slaves assigned to field work and those who worked in and near the mansion. An enslaved individual's placement on the plantation landscape may have been a result of their occupation, but this study suggests that not all slaves living in proximity to the mansion received the same treatment and access to goods. Specialized occupations gave certain slaves access to money and goods and, when allied with similarly successful or valued individuals either through marriage or kinship, resulted in households with potentially more economic success than other households. This study explores the complexity of a single occupation at one plantation. It holds out the promise for future studies of enslaved women and men who, individually and together, used their skills and knowledge to create access to material and social capital within the bounds of slavery.

ACKNOWLEDGMENTS

This article has accrued many debts. I would like to thank the Ladies' Hermitage Association and Earthwatch for support of the Hermitage Archaeology Program, which made these excavations possible. Marsha Mullins, curator at the Hermitage, and Elizabeth Kellar, director of archaeology at the Hermitage, were exceptionally helpful and generous with their time and data. The comments of Charles Orser and one anonymous reviewer helped clarify my thinking on several points, and I am grateful to Barbara Clark Smith for our lively discussion about Elizabeth Keckly. This paper benefited greatly from the comments of James Deetz, Clifton Ellis, Garrett Fesler, Adria LaViolette, Larry McKee, Fraser Neiman, Drake Patten, Charles Perdue, Hal Sharp, Brian Thomas, Aaron Wunsch, and Amy Young. I am especially grateful to Larry McKee for supporting my work at the Hermitage. Special thanks are due to Clifton Ellis and Aaron Wunsch for enduring multiple drafts and to Fraser Neiman for helping to make the data come to life.

This material is based upon work supported under a National Science Foundation Graduate Fellowship. Any opinions, findings, conclusions, or recommendations expressed in this publication are those of the author and do not necessarily reflect the views of the National Science Foundation.

NOTES

1. Research conducted by Brian Thomas suggests that the enslaved community at the Hermitage created and participated in social relationships distinct from the disciplinary regime imposed by Jackson and his overseers (Thomas 1998). Although Thomas demonstrates complexity in ceramic assemblages among the Triplex Middle, the Yard Cabin, the South Cabin, and Cabin 3, he suggests that a relatively even distribution of artifacts such as beads, adornment items, children's toys, writing slates, and gun parts point to a complex set of cooperative social relations among the enslaved population (Thomas 1995, 1998).

2. The receipts indicate that checks for one hundred and four hundred dollars were written to Mr. Hebbs, owner of Gracy and her family (Dorris 1913; papers of Andrew Jackson). These receipts most likely represent a down payment or partial payment, since a family of five slaves would have commanded quite a bit more money.

3. Hermitage slave dwelling names were assigned by archaeologists in the 1970s and 1980s and have no historical connection to the nineteenth-century naming conventions at the Hermitage.

4. Rachel Jackson died in December 1827, prior to Jackson's departure for the White House. The Hermitage mansion was completed in 1821, and the Triplex was built shortly thereafter. Rachel Jackson would have only supervised work in the mansion backyard for about seven years before her death. Sarah Yorke Jackson married Jackson Jr. and took over house duties in the early 1830s.

5. Buttons from the Triplex North have yet to be analyzed to the same degree as buttons from other Hermitage residences. I have excluded discussion of Triplex North button types for this reason.

6. Gracy Bradley and Alfred Jackson only had two children. Although it is possible the high amusement index value points only to the activities of one family, I suggest that the large quantity of leisure items may indicate that the Triplex Middle was the location of broader community activities.

REFERENCES

Acton, William
    1972   *Prostitution Considered in Its Moral, Social, and Sanitary Aspects.*
            London: Frank Cass and Co. Originally published 1857.
Bassett, John S. (editor)
    1937   *Correspondence of Andrew Jackson, Volume 5.* Carnegie Institution of
            Washington, Washington, D.C.
Baumgarten, Linda
    1988   "Clothes for the People": Slave Clothing in Early Virginia. *Journal of
            Early Southern Decorative Arts* 14(2):26–70.
    1991   Plains, Plaid, and Cotton: Woolens for Slave Clothing. *Ars Textrina*
            15:203–221.
    2003   *What Clothes Reveal: The Language of Clothing in Colonial and
            Federal America.* The Colonial Williamsburg Foundation in
            Association with Yale University Press, New Haven.
Benberry, Cuesta
    1992   *Always There: The African-American Presence in American Quilts.*
            Kentucky Quilt Project, Louisville, Ky.
Breeden, James O.
    1980   *Advice among Masters: The Ideal in Slave Management in the Old
            South.* Greenwood Publishing Co., Westport, Conn.
Dorris, Mary C.
    1913   *The Hermitage: Home of General Andrew Jackson, near Nashville,
            Tennessee.* Brandon, Nashville, Tenn.

Durand, Sally Graham
　　1977　The Dress of the Antebellum Field Slave in Louisiana and Mississippi, 1830–1860. Master's thesis, Louisiana State Univ. and Agricultural and Mechanical College.
Fox-Genovese, Elizabeth
　　1988　*Within the Plantation Household: Black and White Women in the Old South*. Univ. of North Carolina Press, Chapel Hill.
Fry, Gladys-Marie
　　1990　*Stitched from the Soul*. Dutton Studio Books, New York.
Galle, Jillian, and Fraser Neiman
　　2003　Patterns of Tea and Tableware Consumption on Late-Eighteenth-Century Slave Quarter Sites. Paper presented at the Society for Historical Archaeology Annual Meeting, Providence, R.I.
Genovese, Eugene
　　1976　*Roll Jordan Roll: The World the Slaves Made*. Vintage Books, New York.
Heath, Barbara
　　1997　Slavery and Consumerism: A Case Study from Central Virginia. *African American Archaeology: Newsletter of the African American Archaeology Network* 19:1–8.
　　1999　Buttons, Beads, and Buckles: Contextualizing Adornment within the Bounds of Slavery. In *Historical Archaeology, Identity Formation, and the Interpretation of Ethnicity*, edited by Maria Franklin and Garrett Fesler, pp. 47–69. Colonial Williamsburg Foundation and Dietz Press, Richmond, Va.
Hunt, Patricia
　　1996　The Struggle to Achieve Individual Expression through Clothing and Adornment: African American Women under and after Slavery. In *Discovering the Women in Slavery*, edited by Patricia Morton, pp. 227–240. Univ. of Georgia Press, Athens.
Joyner, Charles
　　1991　The World of the Plantation Slaves. In *Before Freedom Came*, edited by Edward D.C. Campbell Jr. with Kym Rice, pp. 51–100. Univ. Press of Virginia, Charlottesville.
Keckley, Elizabeth
　　1868　*Behind the Scenes: Thirty Years a Slave and Four Years in the White House*. G. W. Carleton & Co., New York.
MacDonald, Anne
　　1988　*No Idle Hands: The Social History of American Knitting*. Ballantine Books, New York.

McKee, Larry
    1992   Summary Report on the 1991 Field Quarter Excavation. Ms. on file,
           Ladies Hermitage Association, Hermitage, Tenn.
    1995   The Earth Is Their Witness. *Sciences* (Mar./Apr.):36–41.
McKee, Larry, Brian Thomas, and Jennifer Bartlett
    1994   Summary Report on the 1993 Hermitage Mansion Yard Excavation.
           Ms. on file, Ladies Hermitage Association, Hermitage, Tenn.
Mellon, James (editor)
    1988   *Bullwhip Days: The Slaves Remember*. Avon Books, New York.
Morton, Patricia (editor)
    1996   *Discovering the Women in Slavery: Emancipating Perspectives in the
           American Past*. Univ. of Georgia Press, Athens.
Neiman, Fraser
    1997   Sub-Floor Pits and Slavery in Eighteenth- and Early-Nineteenth-
           Century Virginia. Paper presented at the Thirtieth Annual Meeting
           of the Society for Historical Archaeology, Corpus Christi, Tex.
Neiman, Fraser, Leslie McFaden, and Derek Wheeler
    2000   Archaeological Investigation of the Elizabeth Hemings Site
           (44AB438). Monticello Dept. of Archaeology Technical Report
           Series No. 2. at http://www.monticello.org/archaeology/
           publications/hemings.pdf.
Perdue, Charles, Thomas Barden, and Robert Phillips
    1976   *Weevils in the Wheat: Interviews with Virginia Ex-Slaves*. Indiana
           Univ. Press, Bloomington.
Proctor, Molly
    1990   *Needlework Tools and Accessories*. B. T. Batsford, London.
Rawick, George P. (editor)
    1972   *The American Slave: A Composite Autobiography*. Vol. 16. Greenwood
           Publishing Co., Westport, Conn.
Rogers, C. Lynn
    1992   Summary of South Cabin Site Button Analysis. Ms. on file. Ladies'
           Hermitage Association, Hermitage, Tenn.
    1993   Summary of Cabin Three Site Button Analysis. Ms. on file. Ladies'
           Hermitage Association, Hermitage, Tenn.
    1995   Summary of Triplex Middle Site Button Analysis. Ms. on file.
           Ladies' Hermitage Association, Hermitage, Tenn.
Rogers, Gay Ann
    1983   *An Illustrated History of Needlework Tools*. John Murray Publishers,
           London.

Russell, Aaron
 1997   Material Culture and African American Spirituality at the Hermitage. *Historical Archaeology* 31(2):63–80.

Savitt, Todd L.
 1988   Slave Health and Southern Distinctiveness. In *Disease and Distinctiveness in the American South*, edited by Todd L. Savitt and James Harvey Young, pp. 120–153. Univ. of Tennessee Press, Knoxville.

Smart-Martin, Anne
 1991   Buying Your Way to the Top: Acquisition Patterns of Consumer Goods in Colonial Virginia. Paper presented at the Society for Historical Archaeology Annual Conference, Richmond, Va.
 1996   Sukey's Mirror: Consumption, Commodities, and Cultural Identity in Eighteenth-Century Virginia. Paper Presented at the Berkshire Conference on the History of Women, Chapel Hill, N.C.

Smith, Samuel D.
 1976   *An Archaeological and Historical Assessment of the First Hermitage.* Division of Archaeology, Tennessee Dept. of Conservation, Nashville.

Tandberg, Gerilyn
 1980   Field Hand Clothing in Louisiana and Mississippi during the Antebellum Period. *Dress* 5:89–104.

Tandberg, Gerilyn, and Sally Graham Durand
 1981   Dress-Up Costumes for Field Slaves of Ante-Bellum Louisiana and Mississippi. *Costume* (15):41–48.

Thomas, Brian
 1995   *Community among Enslaved African Americans on the Hermitage Plantation, 1820s–1850s.* Ph. D. diss., Dept. of Anthropology, State Univ. of New York at Binghamton, New York. University Microfilms, Ann Arbor, Mich.
 1998   Power and Community: The Archaeology of Slavery at the Hermitage Plantation. *American Antiquity* 63(4):531–551.

Ugan, Andrew, and Jason Bright
 2001   Measuring Foraging Efficiency with Archaeological Faunas: The Relationship between Relative Abundance Indices and Foraging Returns. *Journal of Archaeological Science* 28:309–1321.

White, Deborah G.
 1991   Female Slaves in the Plantation South. In *Before Freedom Came*, edited by Edward D. C. Campbell Jr. with Kym Rice, pp. 101–122. Univ. Press of Virginia, Charlottesville.

CHAPTER 3

Granny Midwives: Gender and Generational Mediators of the African American Community

LAURIE A. WILKIE

"Ar'n't I a woman?" Sojourner Truth challenged an audience of white middle-class women after detailing the labors she performed and the oppressions she had endured (White 1985:13). Perhaps today the power of this question has been lost to us, for our understandings of what it is to be a woman have been so profoundly expanded—despite need for further progress. For Sojourner Truth and other African American women of her time, the reality was that their experiences and color clearly placed them outside of the box of "True Womanhood" carefully drawn in hegemonic discourse. Instead, black women were socially constructed in dominant debates as the foil of white woman-hood, its polar opposite. Whereas white women were pure (sexually unavail-able and uninterested), naturally doting mothers, and fragile, black women were constructed as sexually aggressive, miserable mothers, and destined for heavy manual labor (Davis 1983; Giddings 1984; Collins 2000).

The controlling images of black womanhood that became entrenched dur-ing enslavement—that of the loyal mammy, the sexually lascivious jezebel, and the dominating matriarch—continue to shape public perceptions and policies that affect the African American community (Collins 2000; Roberts 1997). While strictly documentary histories of the African American experience must draw upon materials that were constructed primarily from the dominant group's perspective, archaeology offers the opportunity to explore through materiality the ways that African Americans created and maintained their own expectations of gender roles, obligations, and ideologies. In such a way, we can de-center the views of the hegemonic discourse and explore practices of rele-vance to the African American community.

My vision of a realized engendered African American archaeology would be one that is politically engaged in feminist thought (after Franklin 2001) and one that focuses on a fine-grain level analysis of social relations and person-hood. An engendered African American archaeology should recognize not only the structures of economic, racial, and sexist oppressions that African Ameri-cans constantly confronted and their engagement with those discourses, but also, where appropriate, African American cultural innovation and autonomy.

Cautionary Tales

One of the great challenges facing scholars studying African American wom-anhood is to disentangle from their interpretations the influence that stereo-types of African American womanhood still have on present-day society. Whether it is the "matriarch" appearing in the guise of the "welfare mother" or "jezebel" parading as a "hoochy-momma" (Collins 2000), stereotypes of African American womanhood remain archetypal foils in public policy and social debate. Archaeologists studying the African American past must be aware of these controlling stereotypes as well as recognize the source of their origin: the white middle class and elite.

It is part of archaeologists' responsibility to acknowledge the violence done against African American women and their families during enslavement (Farnsworth 2000), but in doing so they must be careful not to venture into the briar patch of unintentionally reifying stereotypes or interpreting materi-als from the white middle-class perspective. So engrained are these stereotypes that looking at African American womanhood becomes a difficult terrain to navigate, even for those who are students of social inequality and use meth-ods of reflexivity. I would like to comment briefly on an example of these dangers. In a recent study on African American women in the Caribbean, James Delle (2000:177) discussed how birth records can be used to look at sexual relations on the plantation, referring to a woman who had children with more than one man. He elaborated no further on this circumstance. By drawing attention to this "historical fact" but not contextualizing it further, Delle has inadvertently reinforced the notion that African American women are sexually promiscuous and do not form stable monogamous relationships—a stance a majority of the white population is today comfortable to believe. Instead, Delle could have then discussed the planter practice of forcing par-ticular women to have children with particular men in hopes of breeding a stronger slave population (Bush 1990).

Delle made a similar misstep when he erroneously referred to a pessary as a contraceptive device. "The plantation account ledger indicates that at one point the plantation purchased a pessary, an intrauterine contraceptive device used in the nineteenth century, listing it under purchases. It would appear that at least one of the white males on the estate was engaged in a sexual relationship with an enslaved woman" (Delle 2000:177). Delle missed an opportunity to explore the nature of labor demands on women's bodies. Pessaries were a commonly used intrauterine device in the nineteenth century, but as a treatment for prolapsed uteruses, not contraception. A prolapse occurs when the uterus slumps into the vaginal track.

Among the elite, there is strong evidence to suggest that the practice of tight corseting, which ironically was supported by physicians, led to increased incidences of prolapsed uteruses for white women (Summers 2001). For African American women, however, who generally did not corset, a high incidence of prolapsed uteruses was related to the harsh physical demands placed on these women's bodies during pregnancy and the short recovery time allowed to them following delivery (Bankole 1998). The condition is extremely painful, the treatment, which basically used a pessary to prop the uterus back out of the vagina, rendered most white women suffering from the condition invalids (Leavitt and Walton 1984). It is impossible to imagine the excruciating pain experienced by women required to work in the fields with this condition. Delle's work indicates how even socially aware scholars can fumble in the arena of interpreting African American women's experiences.

While it is important to acknowledge clearly and forthrightly the violence done unto women's bodies and psyches as a result of enslavement and ongoing racial oppression they endured following emancipation, this is just one historical narrative with which archaeologists should engage. Women's responses to oppression should also be considered. One arena that work has begun to address this is childcare (for example, Wilkie 2000; Edwards-Ingram 2001). For instance, bioarchaeologists (Corrucini et al. 1985; c.f. Blakey et al. 1994) studying weaning ages of enslaved children found evidence of enslaved infants being breastfed longer than would be indicated by planter preferences. This trend can be seen as a reassertion of maternal authority by enslaved women. There is the potential for much productive scholarship focusing on engendered resistance to structures of inequality in slavery and freedom.

It is not enough to think of the archaeological record only as a source of information on resistance and protest against hegemonic discourses, for to do so only legitimates the planter's view of the past. Instead, scholars need to recognize that Africans and African Americans, during and beyond the periods of enslavement, constructed their own notions of gender relations and responsibilities that were independent (though of course articulated with and influenced by) European perspectives (Collins 2000; Davis 1998). To differing degrees throughout the Diaspora, a sense of African-ness, and shared heritage was an important unifying force among black peoples. The archaeological record must be interrogated for insights into how African sensibilities may have shaped gender ideologies and the ways that these ideologies served to shape gender and familial relations.

Gender in Archaeology

The archaeology of gender is often interpreted as the archaeology of women, rather than as the relationship between different gender ideologies and roles. Gender is culturally and historically situated, not only through the broader tapestry of time but also during the course of an individual's life, and articulates with other facets of social identity (for example, Moore and Scott 1997; Sofaer-Derevenski 1994, 2000; Wilkie 1998, 2000). I have found it useful to think of gendered interpretations not as an end in themselves, but as part of a broader project of studying "personhood" archaeologically. I see personhood as a socially situated and performed identity that is the sum of a person's achieved and ascribed statuses. This notion of personhood is influenced by the recent works of Ian Hodder (2000), Rosemary Joyce (2000), and Lynn Meskell (1999). As such, my intent is to go beyond gross categories such as "men" and "women" and instead look at socially situated personae like "lineal elder," "unmarried youth," etc. Such a model more explicitly recognizes stage of life as an important component of identity.

All aspects of individuals' identities, be they ethnic, religious, class, or gender, are constantly negotiated between individuals and their cultural context throughout their life. Different stages of life bring new responsibilities, obligations, and expectations. "Childhood," "adulthood," "old age," are examples of culturally defined stages of life that bring shifts in gender roles and ideologies. Within a household, not only multiple genders, but also multiple generations of genders, interact with one another. As the gender ideologies of the broader community or society shift and change, within the household the gender expectations of one generation may clash with another.

African American families reconstructed a culturally meaningful social and communal context in which to rebuild their families and way of life under enslavement and beyond. At the community level, a number of individuals served as gender and generational mediators who facilitated the maintenance of gender-age ideologies. This discussion will focus upon one of these groups of individuals: midwives. Before elaborating on the role of African American midwives, however, I would first like to briefly discuss insights into African American gender ideologies evidenced from the documentary and ethnohistoric records.

Gender and Generational Mediators

African American gender ideologies may have some root in West African norms. African American men and women are often perceived as having different but complementary spiritual natures. An excellent example of this is the early-twentieth-century Ashanti *ntoro* practices recorded by Rattray (1979:51). Ntoro was the recognized male essence, necessary for reproduction, and passed through the male line. To ensure a safe and healthy pregnancy, a woman would have to observe the ntoro food taboos of her husband. The mother's essence, which was associated with her blood, was the necessary female contribution to pregnancy. The distinct natures of men and women on the metaphysical plane could be seen etched in the spatiality and temporality of daily life. African house compounds could be highly gendered spaces, with men and women even occupying separate houses or rooms (Aniakor 1996; Cruickshank 1966; Denyer 1978; Gray 1825;), a practice seen in the New World among the Saramake peoples of the Suriname (Price and Price 1999). Throughout the Caribbean, it is still typical for spaces to be seen as gendered primarily "male" or "female" (Pulsipher 1993; Wilkie 1996). In West Africa and many parts of the Diaspora, women's reproductive cycles, be they menstrual, gestation, or breastfeeding, could often dictate variations in sexual access, food preparation, sleeping arrangements, and the performance of particular labors (Aniakor 1996; Rattray 1979).

Based upon a review of late-nineteenth- and early-twentieth-century oral historical and ethnographic literature, the notion of the distinct but complementary spiritual natures of men and women was established in the African American community (for example, Dollard 1988; Herskovits 1941; Hurston 1990; Hyatt 1973; Powdermaker 1993). A consideration of these texts demonstrates that a male/female spiritual dichotomy not only affected mundane daily routines but also shaped African American ethnomedical and magical practices. The spiritual dichotomy clearly fell along the lines of biological definitions of manhood and womanhood. As spiritually distinct beings, men and women could combine their strengths in productive ways or, on the other extreme, could be potentially dangerous to one another. Menstrual blood, semen, urine, hair, and other exuviae, which are tied to the differences in biological sex, could have been used inadvertently or intentionally to cause harm to another person. Ironically, the threat of opening oneself up to magical attack would be a strong deterrent to meaningless sexual encounters—exactly the type of encounters African Americans were portrayed in the popular media as regularly succumbing to. Family conflicts could take place simultaneously on both physical and metaphysical planes. Children were particularly vulnerable to magical attack, both from human and nonhuman sources.

A number of specialists within the plantation population served to mediate tensions between men and women and to serve the interests of families, be they conjurers, root doctors, or clergy. These practitioners reinforced gender ideologies and roles within the community. Conjurers and root doctors preserved, maintained, and made accessible to their clientele traditional magical and medicinal realms. Competition between practitioners, however, ensured that creativity, distinctiveness, and even a sense of "modernity" were incorporated into the magical repertoire. Conflicts between the sexes were often the focus of root doctors and conjurers. Love, jealousy, and other magically and naturally caused illness were treated and healed by these practitioners (Fraser 1998; Hyatt 1973; Matthews 1992a, 1992b; Puckett 1968; Wilkie 1997).

Midwives also served as gender mediators for the African American community. However, while the others acted as mediators in disputes between the sexes, midwives, as gender mediators, emphasized birth as a time when male and female power combined in a powerful and healing way. Whereas conjurers and root doctors acknowledged the potential harms related to procreation, midwives recognized the mingling of male and female essence not only as the source of conception but also as a source of power for women facing the ordeal of birth. For instance, it was believed that labor pains were lessened for a woman who was able to wear the hat of the baby's father during birth (Campbell 1946:114; Coe 1995; Fraser 1998).

During enslavement, African American midwives were often the sole source of care for women. Formerly enslaved women often spoke of midwives in warm and respectful ways, emphasizing their strength and competence. It was not uncommon for the calling to midwifery to have a lineal dimension, with the position being passed from women of one generation to another. Following enslavement, African American midwives continued to be the primary source of black women's healthcare. Midwives were also important sources of prenatal, perinatal, and postnatal care. Prior to the end of this century, without midwives most free black women (and many of those enslaved) in the rural South would not have had any access to medical care during their pregnancies, nor would they have had access to medical care during delivery. African American midwives learned their medical knowledge through apprenticeships with older active midwives. A woman was not recognized as a midwife until she had witnessed, assisted, and finally supervised the birth of numerous babies. In contrast, many medical students during the late nineteenth and early twentieth centuries were able to graduate as obstetricians without having witnessed, let alone supervised, a single birth (Susie 1988:1).

In addition to their medical expertise, midwives served as important generational mediators. Midwives, through their apprenticeships to older women, created a cross-generational chain of magical and medical continuity. Typically, a woman was called to midwifery after she had raised her own children and was beyond child-bearing years herself (Coe 1995; Susie 1988). It was not unusual for a woman to begin her career in midwifery after she was already in her forties or fifties. Women in their eighties were reputed to still be actively working as midwives. Unlike white society, whose commitment to the modern led to the favoring of younger practitioners, age and experience were valued by African American patients (Fontenot 1994; Logan 1989). Given their long careers, midwives linked multiple generations of families, often delivering the children of children they had delivered (Campbell 1946; Fraser 1998; Susie 1988), thereby providing cultural and structural continuities within the African American community. Midwives passed important cultural knowledge from one generation of women to another.

Midwives did not merely catch babies, but trained women to be mothers. In the postpartum period, midwives would spend extensive amounts of time, sometimes actually living with the new mother, teaching her how to feed, clean, and care for the baby (Susie 1988). The work of midwives was truly an example of what Patricia Hill Collins (1994) refers to as "mother work," or mothering done on the behalf of one's community. Midwives were chronically underpaid but justified continuing to give care out of commitment to their communities and due to their understanding that their abilities were directly a gift from God, and it was his intention they be shared (Logan 1989). Midwives supervised the introduction of infants to the broader world and used magical and medical rituals to protect the infant from disease and malevolent spirits (Campbell 1946; Dougherty 1978). In teaching the basics of motherhood, mid-wives actively modified the traditions of one generation to suit the new reali-ties of the next, combining cultural conservatism and innovation within their practices (Campbell 1946; Susie 1988).

Within the material culture of midwifery, it is possible to see this combi-nation of conservatism and innovation. The conservative aspect of their prac-tice allowed for an ongoing sense of shared heritage between women of differ-ent generations who attended at a friend or relative's birth. Innovation allowed African American women to participate in changing attitudes regarding moth-ering in American society. African American activists were well aware of how African American mothering was perceived by the dominant white popula-tion. Reforming this perception was the focus of many African American women's groups (Smith 1995) and was communicated through churches and public education outlets. The archaeological evidence suggests that midwives were engaged in the broader social uplift movements of their time by making dominant ideologies of childcare, such as "scientific mothering," available to young women. It was the ability of midwives to meet the changing needs of new generations that encouraged continuities in gender ideologies.

By the 1920s the American Medical Association (AMA), hoping to expand opportunities for the overabundance of doctors being trained in the United States, had targeted midwives as undesirable competition for patients in the new field of gynecology and obstetrics (Matthews 1992a; Susie 1988). The AMA successfully waged a smear campaign in the northern United States against European immigrant midwives, leading to the eradication of their practices. After their success in the North, they turned their efforts to the South, where the vast majority of practicing midwives were of African American descent. The AMA helped with the preparation of state reports that alleged that African American midwives were unsanitary, superstitious, and dangerous to their patients, citing unsubstantiated reports of high infant mortality. Elite African

American civil rights activists did not support the midwives against the assault, instead supporting the growth of black nursing schools (Smith 1995). Southern states began to require that midwives gain state training, supervision, and licenses, thus forever altering African American midwifery (Dougherty 1978, 1982; Kobrin 1984).

In the 1980s feminist scholars became interested in midwifery (for example, Fildes et al. 1992; Logan 1989; Matthews 1992a; Susie 1988; Ulrich 1991) and conducted a number of studies demonstrating that infant mortality increased after the abolition of African American midwifery. Interviews were conducted with former midwives and used to contradict reports of incompetence and superstition. Unfortunately, the vast majority of the midwives interviewed either had not practiced or did not speak about midwifery practices prior to regulation. The oral histories fail to represent the full role of midwives as magical mediators. Archaeology thus remains the best means for attempting to understand holistically the experiences of African American midwives and their patients.

The Material Culture of Lucrecia Perryman

In the late summer of 1994, during a grading project in Crawford Park, Mobile, Alabama, three archaeological features associated with a late-nineteenth- to early-twentieth-century house site were discovered. Among the features discovered was a sealed well, filled with domestic refuse (Wilkie and Shorter 2001). Documentary research into the site revealed that the parcel of land had been owned, farmed, and lived on by Lucrecia Perryman and her family. Perryman had been born into enslavement in North Carolina around 1836 (Federal Population Census 1870). Perryman and her husband, Marshall, were recorded as owning the land as early as 1869. Following Marshall's death in 1885, Lucrecia turned to midwifery to support her young children. According to city directories, she remained a practicing midwife through the first decade of the twentieth century (Wilkie and Shorter 2001).

The materials discussed in this chapter were recovered from the filled well located on the property. The vast majority of the materials date from the late 1890s to the early 1900s, corresponding to the period when Lucrecia is described as working as a midwife/nurse. The well was filled quickly, as demonstrated by cross-mends in glass and ceramic vessels found throughout the

TABLE 3.1

Commercially Produced Goods of African American Midwifery
Recovered from the Perryman Well

Product	Documented Uses	Number Recovered
Vaseline	Coat newborn, lubricant for delivery, treat after pains, rub on mother during fussing	10
Fletcher's Castoria	Cathartic to clean out mother for labor and delivery, speed contractions, clear afterbirth	1
Pitcher's Castoria	Cathartic to clean out mother for labor and delivery, speed contractions, clear afterbirth	3
Burnett's Cod Liver Oil	Cathartic to clean out mother for labor and delivery, speed contractions, clear afterbirth	1
Lazell's Perfumes, New York	Beautify the body during fussing	3
Ed Pinaud, Perfumers, Paris	Beautify the body during fussing	1
Colgate Perfumers, New York	Beautify the body during fussing	2
Ponds toilet water	Beautify the body during fussing	1
Unidentified toilet waters and perfumes	Beautify the body during fussing	3
French Gloss skin cream	Beautify the body during fussing	1
Mum Mfg. Co. deodorant	Beautify the body during fussing	3
Unid. skin creams	Beautify the body during fussing	4
Seven Sutherlands Sisters Hair Grower	Beautify the body during fussing	1
Pocketknives	Put under mattress to "cut" pains during labor	2
Metal vaginal douche pipe	Treatment of fallen ovaries (prolapsed uterus)	1

extent of the deposit. The *terminus post quem* for the well is 1909, roughly the same time that Perryman retired from midwifery (Federal Population Census 1910). The assemblage associated with her household presents a rare glimpse into preregulation midwifery. It is important to note from the outset that I recognize that the materials I discuss had many other possible uses than just those considered here (Table 3.1). My intent is to encourage the recognition that these materials had meanings specific to a midwifery context.

Conservatism: Seeing Labor and Birth as Ritual

Whether an African American woman was having her first or fifth child, birth for her remained a transformative event as the child left the womb, welcomed by a community of kin. A child was the physical manifestation of the powerful combined force of men's and women's essences. The laboring body was a body in transition, with a climax that required the intense focus and effort of the woman. Birth represented a change in status for the infant, moving the child from the realm of the unborn to the born. African American midwifery recognized birth as a ritualized event comprising a series of expected steps. By ritualizing the process of labor and delivery, midwives offered women the comfort of knowing how to act and what to expect. "Natural" childbirth was the norm for these women, not the socially and medically informed choice available to many women in Western societies today. In a very real way, black and white women of all classes confronted the possibility of their own deaths to bring life to their children in the late nineteenth and early twentieth centuries (Leavitt and Walton 1984). Midwives offered strength and support through a terrifying time.

Today, medical science recognizes labor, the first stage of childbirth, as having three phases, early, active and transition (Savage and Simpkin 1987). Early phase labor is characterized by short, irregular contractions, often spaced as far apart as twenty minutes and lasting no more than forty-five seconds at a time. During this phase, the initial dilation and effacement (thinning) of the cervix takes place. Active labor is characterized by shorter periods of time between longer contractions. By the end of this period contractions may be separated by only three to four minutes and last up to sixty seconds. At the end of this phase, the cervix is typically eight centimeters dilated and 80 percent effaced. The remaining dilation and effacement takes place during the transition phase. This is typically the most physically challenging portion of labor, with contractions of sixty to ninety seconds separated by periods of equal length. Women are often exhausted and experiencing intense and unrelenting pain. After the completion of effacement and dilation, the woman then experiences the desire to bear down and delivers the child, which is considered the second stage of childbirth. The third stage is the delivery of the afterbirth (Savage and Simpkin 1987).

African American midwifery practice seems to have acknowledged these stages as well, and particular techniques and treatments took place at specific times during childbirth. In other words, the natural rhythms of this process served as the ritual structure midwives followed during childbirth. The timing of these practices served to structure the birth experience in a familiar and comfortable way for women and to encourage them to rally their physical and spiritual strength when most necessary. Midwives were typically called during early labor, with experienced mothers waiting longer to call than first-time mothers.

At this point, a woman might be surrounded by family and friends. Early labor can be of long duration, particularly for a first pregnancy. If a midwife felt that contractions were not progressing quickly enough, she might tell the woman to drink a catnip or sassafras tea or to take a dose of castor oil (Campbell 1946; Coe 1995; Logan 1989). One bottle of "Burnett's Cod Liver Oil" and four Castoria bottles were found in the well. Some oral histories make mention of such cathartics being given to mothers immediately after birth to "clean the mother out and to heal her up inside" (Coe 1995:18), while others discuss the use of castor oil to clean the bowels and speed contractions during labor (Logan 1989:53).

During the early stages of labor, midwives engaged in what later public health officials would refer to as "fussing." Fussing involved beautifying a woman's body in preparation for the transformative event of birth. A woman's hair was braided and pomaded, her calves and legs greased, her arms and groin talcum powdered, and her person sprinkled with sweet water, or perfume. Mongeau (1985:84) describes "fussing items," such as Vaseline, cocoa butter, rose water, talcum, toilet waters, pomades, face creams, and sweet soaps as some of the items banned from midwives' bags following regulation.

Among the products recovered from the well was a minimum of eighteen toiletry/cologne bottles that could have been used in Perryman's midwifery practice as easily as by her family. Fussing has physiological as well as ritual functions. The rubbing, combing, and massaging would relax and comfort the mother as well as provide a distraction during first stage labor, which can go on for hours. Female family members and other friends may have been in attendance at this time, and fussing provided a time for female support and encouragement to be expressed. The woman was encouraged to experience pleasure in the beauty and strength of her body and to make the exterior as welcoming and comforting to the child as her womb had been. Ritually, the body was made beautiful in anticipation of greeting the new child. Strong, positive smells, provided by the perfumes and lotions, could counteract any ill will that might linger in an area, providing yet another layer of protection for the newborn child.

As contractions grew stronger and more difficult to endure, women were encouraged to move around the room, to find positions comfortable for them. Midwives continued to massage a woman's back and legs to ease labor pains and prevent cramps. Tea made from eggshells was believed to ease labor pains and might have been offered as labor intensified (Campbell 1946). As pain became more intense, a midwife might then employ magical means of providing pain relief.

There are recorded in the ethnographic and oral historical literature a number of magical practices associated with midwifery. Marie Campbell (1946:27) wrote of the period of regulation:

> Nurses also watch for contraband in the midwife bag, because the grannies used to carry very little or nothing in the way of supplies except patent medicines, pills, brew of roots, herbs, etc.; homemade salves, all sorts of "remedies" with which they dosed their patients. They are now forbidden to do this. Nurses have learned to look under the removable lining of the bag. There may be found such things as coins tied into the corners of a handkerchief, a piece of rope, a box of snuff, a bottle of homemade tonic or "bitters," a rabbit's foot, or some other good luck charm.

Magical cures took the form of charms, rituals, and potions. A small number of artifacts were recovered from the Perryman site that could be indicative of magical midwifery practices. It is important to remark briefly on the nature of these magical practices relative to their gendered magical implications. Two practices in general, the placing of knives or axes under the mattress and the wearing of the father's hat (Campbell 1946), were employed during the part of labor when pains were particularly intense and women were likely to be despairing (while the terminology is not used in the ethnohistoric literature, it is likely that midwives were describing the transition period of labor). Based on my reading of the ethnohistoric literature, I think that these two items are particularly drawn upon at this time in labor because they have strong male associations. As such, the use of these practices draws male spiritual power—in the case of the hat, specifically the power of the father—into the birth process at a critical juncture.

Among the artifacts recovered from the site were two pocketknives. While these are multiuse artifacts, given that each was discarded in working condition and the midwifery context, it is worth considering their potential magical value. Knives and axes are both described as being placed under mattresses to "cut" labor pains (Campbell 1946; Coe 1985; Fraser 1998). Knives and axes bear magical meanings in other Diaspora contexts as well. Within Santeria and Voodoo, they are strongly associated with the Yoruban male Orisha Eshu-Elegba and Ogun (Thompson 1983). The use of knives and axes in the context of labor and delivery may also have associations with male power. While the pocketknives recovered from the Perryman site were likely used in a variety of contexts and for a variety of functions, the possibility that they were also used within Perryman's midwifery practice should not be discounted.

Hats served a variety of roles in the magical quest for love and lust. For instance, a woman wishing to attract a particular man could do so by treating his hatband with perfume (Hyatt 1973:2,663), while a man wishing to make a woman love him could do so by wearing her hair in his hat band (1,895). Within midwifery, wearing the hat of the baby's father was thought to reduce labor pains. If looking at the importance of the hat just in the realm of love spells, one might think that the purpose of the perfume in the hat might be merely a sympathetic magical attempt by a woman to keep a man's mind on her or, in the case of the wearing a woman's hair in the hat, a way to let her know she was on his mind. This would be a simplification of the prevalence of hat-related magical practices. African American healers and conjurers often describe themselves as having "a second set of eyes" or being "two-headed" (Hyatt 1973; Puckett 1968), thus indicating that the head is an important center for the consolidation of spiritual power. Women's hats do not show up in the literature, suggesting that the symbolic conflation of the head and spiritual power is specifically a male association. In contrast, women often use their menstrual blood as a means of binding a man or drawing his attention (Hyatt 1973, 1974; Puckett 1968).

In using hats and knives, objects that have clear male associations, midwives were actively engaged in consolidating male and female spiritual power in the context of the birth room. Even though fathers were ultimately banned by most midwives from the birth room, the use of their hats made them important actors at a critical time in the labor.

Although midwives used magic during labor, this does not appear to have been the case for the actual delivery. Midwives prided themselves on their ability to deliver babies without vaginal tearing and without invasive techniques. The ability to avoid tearing may be directly related to the fussing period. Midwifes were oblique in discussing what the nature of massage was, and some informants did refer to midwives preparing their bodies with massage and such (Litt 2000). It is likely they were engaged in the massage of the perineum. Today, perineum massage, which serves to relax and expand the tissue at the mouth of the vagina, is a technique used by doulas and midwives to prevent tearing or the need for episiotomies. Vaseline is described as being used to aid in the passage of the baby through the vaginal track (Logan 1989), and it may be that Vaseline was a massage medium. Some midwives coated newborns with a greasy ointment or Vaseline to protect their skin and help them maintain body heat (Coe 1995). It is interesting to note that a similar practice was described by Francis Moore in the Senegambia region in 1738. "When a child is newborn, they dip him over head and ears in cold water three or four times in a day, and as soon as they are dry they rub them over with Palm Oyl [*sic*], particularly the back bone, small of the back, elbows, neck, knees and hips" (Moore 1738:131).

A range of protective amulets intended to protect the newborn from malevolent forces are described in the ethnohistoric literature, such as the commonly recovered birth coins (for example, Fontenot 1994; Puckett 1968), but I have not found evidence that these were provided by the midwife. It may be that other female attendants cared for these aspects of the newborn's needs while the midwife tended to the delivery of the afterbirth. This is not to say that midwives were not involved in the spiritual caretaking of the infant. There is an account of a Florida midwife who supervised the official introduction of a newborn to the world outside of its birth home on his ninth day of life. The ritual basically enacted in the physical space around the home the Bakongo cosmogram (Wilkie 2003). Likewise, midwives encouraged women to stay in bed with their child for at least seven to nine days and to keep the windows closed during that time to protect children from malevolent forces. There is much to suggest that African practices that postponed naming a child until its ninth day were continued in parts of the Diaspora (Fraser 1998), and this practice seems to arise from an understanding that the child is not fully rooted in this world until that time. The act of naming the child serves to legitimate its personhood.

The delivery of the afterbirth is an anticlimactic event but an important conclusion to delivery. With ruptured placentas a woman could bleed to death, and an impartially delivered placenta could lead to serious infections.

To ensure the safe delivery of the afterbirth, midwives relied upon medical and magical techniques. Castor oils were used to maintain the contractions necessary for delivery of the afterbirth. Some midwives required their patients to drink water or buttermilk to hasten the afterbirth (Dougherty 1978).

In the magical context, women's power was drawn upon. It was believed that blowing into a blue glass bottle could cause the release of a retained placenta (Campbell 1946:35). The color blue is often associated with the pursuit or destruction of love. In part, this relationship between the color and emotion may be related to the association between blue and Yemalia, the Yoruban *Orish* who is syncretized in the Diaspora with the Virgin Mary, and strongly associated with motherhood, love, and water (Thompson 1983). Blue candles, blue stone, and blue bottles are all commonly employed in spells intended to draw, repel, or rekindle love or destroy it (for example, Hyatt 1973). Sixty-one blue-colored bottles were recovered from the site and certainly could have been reused in this way. Particularly intriguing from this perspective are the six blue ten-sided Phoenix mineral water bottles. The shape of the bottles combines the paneled look of the gothic—associated with mothering and womanhood in ceramic assemblages (Claney 1996; Wall 1994)—with the blue color of Yemalia. It is tempting to wonder whether this particular mineral water bottle, with its shape and color conveying the importance of domesticity from two different cultural discourses, played a role within Lucrecia's midwifery practice, either for the use of the contents or as a breathing device.

The archaeology of Lucrecia Perryman's midwifery practice does suggest that the African American medical practice included elements that could have been presented as evidence of superstitions by outsiders. These practices were not arbitrary cultural holdovers, but instead key elements in socially structuring the experience of childbirth. Midwives had to lead this ritual for a variety of audiences. The laboring mother, if it was her first time, would be terrified by the prospect of the unknown. An experienced mother might have brought expectations regarding how the birth should take place based on previous experiences. Concerned friends and family may have included multiple generations of women, each with their own experiences and expectations. Midwives worked to create a birth experience that ensured the best outcome for mother and child while also comforting and drawing upon the collective strength of the woman's community.

It is impossible to overemphasize the importance of midwives' generational mediator role. Gertrude Fraser studied a Virginia African American community's perceptions of the demise of midwifery. The way that older women who had relied upon midwives rationalized their disappearance is most fascinating. These women asserted that old medicines would not work on new, modern bodies. Instead, African American women's bodies were conceptualized in their communities as having changed in fundamental ways through the generations since midwives were abolished (Fraser 1998:164). Grandmothers no longer found the bodies of their granddaughters intelligible. The sense of generational connection, fostered in part by lay midwives and their approach to multigenerational participation in birthing, had been fractured by medicalization. The communal body had been ruptured.

Scientific Mothering and Nutritive Foods

I do not intend to communicate the idea that African American midwives were so steeped in tradition that they were out of touch with the realities of the broader medical paradigms of their times. It is in the realm of mothering activities where there is evidence of innovation. One of the roles of midwives was to train young women how to be proper mothers. Stereotypes of African American women pervaded the American consciousness, and African American reformers saw it as their duty to elevate the perception of black mothers promoting adoption of scientific mothering practices.

Rapid advances in science and technology accompanied the last quarter of the nineteenth century. Science was increasingly viewed as a means of improving the quality of everyday life. "Germ theory," or the notion that contact with germs leads to illness, became quickly entrenched in much of American society after its introduction in 1870 (Tomes 1997:37). An increased emphasis on the importance of sanitation, clean water and food, and personal hygiene (and associated rituals of good hygiene) characterized this period of American society. These practices were part of a growing movement of preventative medicine, intended to stop disease before it developed rather than to merely treat symptoms and illnesses already suffered. As scientism became a larger part of daily practice, a new mothering ideology developed, that of "scientific mothering" (Apple 1997). Initially, scientific mothering was an empowering ideology that stressed the ways that knowledgeable mothers could use scientific findings to better care for and raise their children. Like any other professional, the woman who worked as a mother was responsible for being up-to-date, in the parlance of modernity, so that she could construct the most efficient and safe environment in which children could be raised (Apple 1997; Litt 2000).

Perhaps one of the best-known examples of this early manifestation of scientific mothering is found in Catharine Beecher and Harriet Beecher Stowe's "The American Woman's Home; or, Principles of Domestic Science." This volume was first published in 1869 but was reprinted regularly. Beecher and Stowe compiled it upon sensing the imbalance between the ways that men were trained for professions versus the lack of formal training for women running households. With thirty-eight chapters (five hundred pages) in length, there were few topics not discussed by the authors. In addition to the expected subjects of child care, cooking, manners, and the overseeing of servants, a good amount of space was allotted to the necessities of exercise and healthy diet; the importance of cleanliness and the proper lighting, ventilation, and modes of heating a house were just a few of the topics covered.

Scientific mothering was embedded in larger African American social movements striving to improve public health. By establishing women's clubs that focused on serving particular communities or causes, African American women embraced what was known in domestic science circles as "municipal housekeeping" (Stage 1997:30). The community existed as an extension of the household. Through club work and church work, African American women were able to participate and shape changes in public health policy (Cash 2001; Higgenbotham 1993; Neverdon-Morton 1989; Smith 1995).

Women's voluntary groups took the form of church groups, female auxiliaries, and women's clubs (Smith 1995:1). Through their volunteerism, African American women, from both the middle and working classes, built schools, hospitals, day cares, and provided support for working women. So instrumental were women's clubs to reform and political movements that the National Association for Colored Women was founded in 1896 to represent the network of women's clubs. For middle-class African American women, improvements in public health represented another avenue of social uplift for the poorer classes. Through the efforts of church groups, working-class African American women also participated in the Progressive movement. The "Politics of Respectability" became a means of contesting and resisting the dominant culture (Higgenbotham 1993).

I have discussed the impacts of scientific mothering ideologies on the Perryman family specifically, and on African America more broadly, in another venue (Wilkie 2003). However, in this chapter I would like to discuss one aspect of scientific mothering evidenced in the food medicines prepared within the household and purchased from commercial sources.

Food Medicines

Nine food medicines were recovered from the site, including Horlick's Malted Milk, Mellin's Infant Food, Johan Hoff's Extract Malt, and Liebig's Extract Malt. These products were sold as nutritive food medicines that would provide infants, children, women recovering from childbirth, or the elderly with additional energy and sustenance.

In addition to commercially produced food medicines, faunal materials from the site suggest that Perryman may have prepared these products as well. A total of 278 bone fragments were recovered from the well. Of these bones, 194 fragments were probably from large mammals but were too fragmentary to be identifiable as to species or element. The unidentified bones included 100 burned fragments. Only 85 of the bone fragments were identifiable. Cow (*Bos taurus*) comprised the largest number of identifiable bone (72, of which 24 were teeth), followed by pig (*Sus scrofa*) (7), an unidentified bony fish (4), and chicken (*Gallus gallus*) (1). The cuts of beef recovered from the site are, at first glance, suggestive of a poor diet. Almost exclusively, beef cuts at the site were drawn from either the head (45) or the lower limbs of the cow (22). Scapho-lunars (1), naviculo cuboids (2), astraguli (3), and calcanea (4) are found at the lowest extreme of the animals' legs and provide little in the way of meat. These bones were recovered complete, without evidence of butchering, from the site. The presence of these foot elements could be related to Perryman's midwifery activities. One dish that utilizes a cow's lower limbs is calf's foot jelly, which is made by boiling a calf's feet to make gelatin. Making the jelly was time consuming and arduous, requiring hours of slow boiling. Considered an invalid's food, the jelly was fed to the weak or young to restore strength (Beeton 1907:1,371).

Whether food medicines were purchased prebottled or made in the home, their origin is the same—the food science research of Justus von Liebig in the mid-nineteenth century. Liebig was an organic chemist from Giessen whose research suggested that valuable juices in flesh should be sealed by roasting meat at a high temperature before cooking it at low temperature, and he promoted stewing as the most nutritious way to cook. His research led him to develop beef tea (Bagnell 1999), which was essentially a very concentrated beef essence in a liquid form. The beef tea was supposed to be easily digestible and ideal for children, invalids, and nursing mothers. This product was marketed widely, and to promote the product's use the Liebig Company published a cookbook. The Liebig Extract Malt bottles recovered from the site were examples of another food medicine marketed by the company. Collectively, the idea that food could be used to treat illness was greatly influenced by the scientific writing of Liebig and domestic scientists who made his ideas available to homemakers—particularly mothers. The impact of Liebig's findings can be seen in the proscriptive housekeeping literature of the time, as well as in pediatrician's literature (for example, Cambell 1881; Grulee 1916:137–138; Parloa 1910).

Perryman's incorporation of these ideas into her midwifery practice, and presumably within her own family, demonstrates that she was engaged with current discourses on scientific mothering and sought where appropriate to introduce innovation into her practice. In this particular example, by choosing to engage in scientific mothering ideologies, Perryman was also engaged in mother's work to benefit her community and was part of the movement to redefine public perceptions of black womanhood.

Conclusion

Individuals do not engage with the gender ideologies of their communities and societies in any single manner. In her various roles as an African American woman, mother, and midwife, Lucrecia Perryman was situated within a number of competing gender ideologies. As a black woman and mother, she had to confront the realities of white racism and stereotypes; as a midwife, she was engaged both in working within her community's value system in overseeing the ritual of birth and in promoting social uplift. Perryman's experiences are not unique, but too often archaeologists forget that there is not one gender discourse at any particular point in history but multiple, competing, and often contradictory notions regarding gender.

In exploring the experience of birth as ritual, and the ways that African American notions of spiritual complementarity between the sexes, I am looking at a particular gendered embodiment of labor and delivery. African American midwives drew upon established norms of thinking about gender difference to coax women through the physically and emotionally draining experience of birth. Midwives did this in a way that drew upon the collective strength of laboring women and their support networks and upon the spiritual essence of the father. Birth was an event that allowed women of different generations to maintain a connection and shared identity through shared experience. It is clear that the loss of midwives did cause a rupture in ties between the generations.

It was the midwives' attention to ritual and tradition within the birthing room that led the American Medical Association to attack their professionalism. It is ironic that many of the medical practices advocated by midwives, such as walking and moving during labor, perineum massage, body massage, and choosing one's own birthing position, are now seen as enlightened approaches to a woman-centered birth. Archaeological analysis also demonstrates that midwives were knowledgeable about shifts in medical paradigms outside of their own practices. While not discussed here, there was evidence that in addition to incorporating nutritive foods into her practice, Perryman was also engaged in sanitation discourses (Wilkie 2003). Applying the principles of scientific mothering into her midwifery was not merely a means for Perryman to keep her practice modern; it was also politically motivated. As persons who educated African American mothers in proper childcare, midwives were at the forefront of the effort to rehabilitate the image of African American women in the postemancipation world.

ACKNOWLEDGMENTS

There are many people who have helped the development of this project. Foremost, I would like to thank George Shorter for involving me in this project and for directing most of the site's fieldwork and preliminary historical research. George has been a constant source of support and good humor. I would also like to thank colleagues at Berkeley, Meg Conkey and Rosemary Joyce, who have served as sounding boards for different aspects of this project. The Committee on Research at Berkeley funded different aspects of this research as part of their junior faculty mentor grant program and through a sabbatical-year fellowship. I would also like to thank Amy Young for initially involving me in this volume, and Jillian Galle for her efforts to ensure that the volume was completed. Finally, I would like to thank Alexandra Wilkie Farnsworth, who made possible my firsthand experiences with labor and delivery.

REFERENCES

Aniakor, Chike
    1996   Household Objects and the Philosophy of Igbo Social Space. In *African Material Culture,* edited by M. J. Arnoldi, C. M. Geary, and K. L. Hardin, pp. 214–242. Indiana Univ. Press, Bloomington.

Apple, Rima D.
    1997   Constructing Mothers: Scientific Motherhood in the Nineteenth and Twentieth Centuries. In *Mothers and Motherhood,* edited by R. D. Apple and J. Golden, pp. 90–110. Ohio State Univ., Columbus.

Bagnell, Ann
    1999   Introduction. In *Liebig Company's Practical Cookery Book.* Southover Press, London. Originally published 1894.

Bankole, Katherine
    1998   *Slavery and Medicine: Enslavement and Medical Practices in Antebellum Louisiana.* Garland Publishing, New York.

Beecher, C. E., and H. B. Stowe
    1870   *The American Woman's Home.* J. B. Ford and Co., New York.

Beeton, Isabelle
    1907   *Mrs. Beeton's Book of Household Management.* Lock, Ward and Co., London.

Blakey, M., T. E. Leslie, and J. P. Reidy
    1994   Frequency and Chronological Distribution of Dental Enamel Hypoplasia in Enslaved African Americans: A Test of the Weaning Hypothesis. *American Journal of Physical Anthropology* 95:371–383.

Bush, Barbara
    1990   *Slave Women in Caribbean Society, 1650–1838.* Univ. of Indiana Press, Bloomington.

Cambell, Helen
    1881   *The Easiest Way in Housekeeping and Cooking.* Fords, Howard and Hulbert, New York.

Campbell, Marie
    1946   *Folks Do Get Born.* Rinehart and Co., New York.

Cash, Floris B.
    2001   *African American Women and Social Action: The Club Women and Volunteerism from Jim Crow to the New Deal, 1896–1936.* Greenwood Publishing Co., Westport, Conn.

Claney, Jane

  1996   Form, Fabric, and Social Factors in Nineteenth-Century Ceramics
          Usage: A Case Study in Rockingham Ware. In *Historical Archaeology
          and the Study of American Culture*, edited by Lu Ann De Cunzo
          and Bernard Herman, pp. 103–149. Univ. of Tennessee Press,
          Knoxville.

Coe, Emily

  1995   Granny Midwives: Grandmother to Nurse Midwives. Paper pre-
          sented at the American Anthropological Association Meetings,
          Washington, D.C.

Collins, Patricia Hill

  1994   Shifting the Center: Race, Class, and Feminist Theorizing about
          Motherhood. In *Mothering: Ideology, Experience, and Agency*,
          edited by E. N. Glenn, G. Chang, R. Forcey, pp. 45–66. Routledge,
          New York.

  2000   *Black Feminist Thought: Knowledge, Consciousness, and the Politics of
          Empowerment*. 2d ed. Routledge, New York.

Corruccini, Robert S., Jerome S. Handler, and Keith Jacobi

  1985   Chronological Distribution of Enamel Hypoplasias and Weaning in
          a Caribbean Slave Population. In *Human Biology* 57:699–711.

Cruickshank, B.

  1966   *Eighteen Years on the Gold Coast of Africa. Volume Two*. Frank Cass
          and Co., London. Originally published 1853.

Davis, Angela

  1983   *Women, Race, and Class*. Vintage Books, New York.

  1998   *Blues Legacies and Black Feminism*. Vintage Books, New York.

Delle, James

  2000   Gender, Power, and Space: Negotiating Social Relations under
          Slavery on Coffee Plantations in Jamaica, 1790–1834. In *Lines
          That Divide: Historical Archaeologies of Race, Class, and Gender*,
          edited by James A. Delle, Stephen A. Mrozowski, and Robert
          Paynter, pp. 168–201. Univ. of Tennessee Press, Knoxville.

Denyer, Susan

  1978   *African Traditional Architecture: An Historical and Geographical
          Perspective*. Africana Publishing Co., New York.

Dollard, John

  1988   *Caste and Class in a Southern Town*. Univ. of Wisconsin Press,
          Madison.

Dougherty, Molly C.

    1978   Southern Lay Midwives as Ritual Specialists. In *Women in Ritual and Symbolic Roles*, edited by Judith Hoch-Smith and Anita Spring, pp. 151–164. Plenum Press, New York.

    1982   Southern Midwifery and Organized Health Care: Systems in Conflict. In *Medical Anthropology* 6:113–126.

Edwards-Ingram, Ywone D.

    2001   African American Medicine and the Social Relations of Slavery. In *Race and the Archaeology of Identity*, edited by Charles Orser, pp. 34–53. Univ. of Utah Press, Salt Lake City.

Farnsworth, Paul

    2000   Brutality or Benevolence in Plantation Archaeology. In *International Journal of Historical Archaeology* 4(2):145–158.

Federal Population Census

    1870   Population Schedule of the Ninth Census of the United States, Mobile County, Alabama.

    1910   Population Schedule of the Thirteenth Census of the United States, Mobile County, Alabama.

Fildes, Valerie, Lara Marks, and Hilary Marland (editors)

    1992   *Women and Children First: International Maternal and Infant Welfare, 1870–1945*. Routledge, London.

Fontenot, Wonda

    1994   *Secret Doctors: Ethnomedicine of African Americans*. Bergin and Garvey, Westport, Conn.

Franklin, Maria

    2001   A Black Feminist-Inspired Archaeology? *Journal of Social Archaeology* 1(1):108–125.

Fraser, Gertrude

    1998   *African American Midwifery in the South*. Harvard Univ. Press, Cambridge.

Giddings, Paula

    1984   *When and Where I Enter: The Impact of Black Women on Race and Sex in America*. William Morrow and Co., New York.

Gray, William

    1825   *Travels in West Africa*. John Murray, London.

Grulee, C. G.

    1916   *Infant Feeding*. W. B. Saunders Co., Philadelphia.

Herskovits, Melville

    1941   *Myth of the Negro Past*. Beacon Press, Boston.

Higgenbotham, M. E.
    1993   *Righteous Discontent: The Women's Movement in the Black Baptist Church, 1880–1920*. Harvard Univ. Press, Cambridge.

Hodder, Ian
    2000   Agency and Individuals in Long-Term Process. In *Agency in Archaeology*, edited by Marcia-Anne Dobres and John Robb, pp. 21–33. Routledge, London.

Hurston, Zora Neale
    1990   *Mules and Men*. Harper and Row, New York.

Hyatt, Harry Middleton
    1973   *Hoodoo-Conjuration-Witchcraft-Rootwork, Vol. 3*. Harry Middleton Hyatt, St. Louis, Mo.

Joyce, Rosemary
    2000   *Gender and Power in Prehispanic Mesoamerica*. Univ. of Texas Press, Austin.

Kobrin, Frances E.
    1984   American Midwife Controversy: A Crisis of Professionalization. In *Women and Health in America*, edited by Judith Walzer Leavitt, pp. 318–326. Univ. of Wisconsin Press, Madison.

Leavitt, J. W., and W. Walton
    1984   Down to Death's Door: Women's Perceptions of Childbirth in America. In *Women and Health in America*, edited by J. W. Leavitt, pp. 155–165. Univ. of Wisconsin Press, Madison.

Litt, Jacquelyn
    2000   *Medicalized Motherhood: Perspectives from the Lives of African American and Jewish Women*. Rutgers Univ. Press, New Brunswick, N.J.

Logan, Onnie (as told to Katherine Clark)
    1989   *Motherwit: An Alabama Midwife's Story*. E. P. Dutton, New York.

Matthews, Holly
    1992a Killing the Medical Self-Help Tradition among African Americans: The Case of Lay Midwifery in North Carolina, 1912–1983. In *African Americans in the South*, edited by Hans A. Baer and Yvonne Jones, pp. 60–78. Univ. of Georgia Press, Athens.
    1992b Doctors and Root Doctors: Patients Who Use Both. In *Herbal and Magical Medicine: Traditional Healing Today*, edited by James Kirkland, Holly F. Matthews, C. W. Sullivan III, and Karen Baldwin, pp. 68–98. Duke Univ. Press, Durham.

Meskell, Lynn
    1999   *Archaeologies of Social Life*. Blackwell, Oxford.

Mobile, Alabama, City Directory
  1871 George Matzenger, Mobile.
  1892 George Matzenger, Mobile, vol. 27.
  1901 George Matzenger, Mobile, vol. 26.
  1902 J. Wiggins Co., Mobile, Vol. 37.
  1904 R. L. Polk and Co., Mobile.
  1905 R. L. Polk and Co., Mobile.
  1906 R. L. Polk and Co., Mobile.
  1907 R. L. Polk and Co., Mobile.
Mobile, Alabama, County Death Certificate
  1917 Alabama Center for Health Statistics, Death Certificate for Lecretia
        [*sic*] Perryman, Feb. 4, 1917.
Mongeau, Beatrice
  1985 The "Granny" Midwives: A Study of a Folk Institution in the Process
        of Social Disintegration. University Microfilms, Ann Arbor, Mich.
Moore, Frances
  1738 *Travels into the Inland Parts of Africa Containing a Description of
        the Several Nations for the Space of Six Hundred Miles up the River
        Gambia.* Edward Cave, St. Johns Gate, London.
Moore, Jenny, and Eleanor Scott
  1997 *Invisible People and Processes: Writing Gender and Childhood into
        European Archaeology.* Leicester Univ. Press, London.
Neverdon-Morton, Cynthia
  1989 *Afro-American Women of the South and the Advancement of the Race,
        1895–1925.* Univ. of Tennessee Press, Knoxville.
Parloa, Maria
  1910 *Home Economics: A Practical Guide in Every Branch of Housekeeping.*
        Century Co., New York.
Powdermaker, Hortense
  1993 *After Freedom: A Cultural Study in the Deep South.* Univ. of
        Wisconsin Press, Madison.
Price, Sally, and Richard Price
  1999 *Maroon Arts: Cultural Vitality in the African Diaspora.* Beacon
        Press, Boston.
Puckett, Niles Newbell
  1968 *Folk Beliefs of the Southern Negro.* Greenwood Publishing,
        New York.
Pulsipher, Lydia
  1993 Changing Roles in the Life Cycles of Women in Traditional
        West Indian Houseyards. In *Women and Change in the Caribbean,*

edited by J. J. Momsen, pp. 50–64. Univ. of Indiana Press,
Bloomington.

Rattray, Robert S.

1979   *Religion and Art in Ashanti*. Clarendon Press, Oxford.

Roberts, Dorothy E.

1997   *Killing the Black Body: Race, Reproduction, and the Meaning of
Liberty*. Pantheon Books, New York.

Savage, Beverly, and Diane Simpkin

1987   *Preparation for Birth: The Complete Guide to the Lamaze Method*.
Ballantine Press, New York.

Smith, Susan L.

1995   *Sick and Tired of Being Sick and Tired: Black Women's Health Activism
in America, 1890–1950*. Univ. of Pennsylvania Press, Philadelphia.

Sofaer-Derevenski, Joanne

1994   Where Are the Children? Accessing Children in the Past. *Archaeological Review from Cambridge* 13(2):8–20.

2000   *Children and Material Culture*. Routledge, London.

Stage, Sarah

1997   Ellen Richards and the Social Significance of the Home Economics
Movement. In *Rethinking Home Economics: Women and the History
of a Profession*, edited by S. Stage and V. Vincenti. Cornell Univ.
Press, Ithaca, N.Y.

Summers, Leigh

2001   *Bound to Please: A History of the Victorian Corset*. Berg, London.

Susie, Debra Anne

1988   *In the Way of Our Grandmothers: A Cultural View of Twentieth-
Century Midwifery in Florida*. Univ. of Georgia Press, Athens.

Thompson, Robert Farris

1983   *Flash of the Spirit*. Random House, New York.

Tomes, Nancy

1997   Spreading the Germ Theory: Sanitary Science and Home Econom-
ics, 1880–1930. In *Home Economics: Women and the History of a
Profession*, edited by S. Stage and V. Vincenti. Cornell Univ. Press,
Ithaca, N.Y.

Ulrich, Laurel T.

1991   *A Midwife's Tale: The Life of Martha Ballard, Based on Her Diary,
1785–1812*. Vintage, New York.

Wall, Diane DiZerega

1994   *The Archaeology of Gender: Separating the Spheres in Urban America*.
Plenum Press, New York.

White, Deborah G.

    1985   *Ar'n't I a Woman? Female Slaves in the Plantation South.* W. W. Norton and Co., New York.

Wilkie, Laurie A.

    1996   House Gardens and Female Identity on Crooked Island. *Journal of the Bahamas Historical Society* 18:33–39.

    1997   Secret and Sacred: Contextualizing the Artifacts of African American Magic and Religion. *Historical Archaeology* 31(4):81–106.

    1998   The Other Gender: The Archaeology of an Early-Twentieth-Century Fraternity. In *Proceedings of the Society for California Archaeology* (Fresno) 11:7–11.

    2000   *Creating Freedom.* Louisiana State Univ. Press, Baton Rouge.

    2003   *The Archaeology of Mothering: An African American Midwife's Tale.* Routledge, New York.

Wilkie, Laurie A., and George Shorter

    2001   Lucrecia's Well: An Archaeological Glimpse of an African American Midwife's Household. *University of South Alabama Archaeological Monograph 11.* Univ. of South Alabama Center for Archaeological Studies, Mobile.

CHAPTER 4

Gender and the Presentation of Self: An Example from the Hermitage

BRIAN W. THOMAS AND LARISSA THOMAS

Identity—that intangible human quality whereby we create ourselves and are created by others—helps us structure our social environment at the same time that our social environment is structured by it. Social identity is a complex, multifaceted aspect of human interaction, one that is never fixed but rather shifts according to the social context in which this interaction takes place. The fluidity of identity was just as true for African American slaves in the antebellum South as it is for other people who have greater liberty to define themselves and the nature of their participation in all sorts of social relationships.

There are a number of characteristics that contribute to one's social identity. These factors may include gender, age, class, work role, religion, ethnicity, and kinship ties. Within the constraints imposed by the various components of one's identity, there also are numerous means by which identity may be expressed—through speech, mannerisms, behavioral patterns, physical traits, dress, and material symbols or markers. Sociologist Erving Goffman (1959) has proposed an approach called dramaturgical theory as a way to model the strategies pursued by individuals in presenting themselves to others in the context of social interactions in which the participants occupy roles based upon their social identities. While archaeologists do not have access to the actual interactions of individuals in the past, with all of their intricacies and nuances, important elements in those interactions often remain strewn among the debris of archaeological sites: the props used by individuals in their performances as they presented themselves and pursued their interests in myriad social encounters. People express themselves and participate in social discourse through the material culture they create or select and through the order they impose on the natural world. Material culture and the built environment in part reflect aspects of social identity that people expressed through the course of their daily lives. Even enslaved African Americans, who lived highly regimented lives within an order imposed by their owners, found ways of acquiring material culture used in the presentation and in the construction and reproduction of social identity.

It is important to keep in mind, however, that social identity is fluid. In any given social arena, some aspects of identity may take precedence over others with respect to how an individual defines him- or herself, as well as how that individual is defined by others. At one moment a woman may be a mother, giving love, guidance, and discipline to a child. At another moment, or perhaps at the same time, her identity may be as a neighbor or a friend. At yet another moment—or again, perhaps at the same time—this woman's identity may be heavily influenced by the fact that she is interacting with a woman who legally owns her and her children and who dictates much of what she will do throughout the day. The point being made is twofold: (1) that social identity is fluid, not fixed, and (2) that it is always contingent upon social interaction. The individuals or parties with whom we interact and the social context of our interaction plays as important a role in our social identity, as does our own view of ourselves. As a result, personal items of material culture cannot be read as simplistic reflections of a monolithic notion of social identity. Rather, personal objects must be understood in terms of their use in the construction and reproduction of various aspects of social identity, and in terms of the multiple meanings they conveyed for various participants in social interaction.

Gender enters into social identity in a fundamental way. By gender, we refer specifically to the socially constructed categories, roles, relationships, and expectations defined—whether tangentially or directly—on the basis of perceived sexual differences. Although socially constructed, gender categories take on objective reality in the lived experience of individuals. Social identity is experienced, reproduced, and sometimes transformed through practice. As a fundamental component of social identity, gender has the ability to affect nearly every aspect of a person's life. It structures how individuals relate to other people, it influences the nature of their economic role in society, and it influences how individuals understand themselves and their cosmology. However, for many people past and present, gender is not the only "master status," a term used by sociologists to denote a factor or characteristic that has primacy in influencing the multiple roles an individual fills (Martin and Greenstein 1983). For enslaved African Americans in the antebellum South, race—which was the key attribute defining their status as property—was also

TABLE 4.1

Slave Population Totals at the Hermitage

Year	Number	Source
1820	44	Fourth Census of the U.S.
1825	80	Davidson County Tax List
1829	95	Hermitage Farm Journal[1]
1830	94	Fifth Census of the U.S.
1840	105	Sixth Census of the U.S.
1845	110	Probate Inventory[2]
1850	137	Seventh Census of the U.S.

NOTES: [1]Western Reserve Historical Society (1817–1832).
[2]On file at The Hermitage.

a master status, perhaps more important than gender, influencing every aspect of their existence.

With these points in mind, our purpose is to explore the relationship of dress to social identity among African American men, women, and children during the antebellum period, including the role that gender had in the expression of identity.[1] We draw primarily on archaeological and historical research conducted at the Hermitage plantation, located just east of Nashville, Tennessee (for example, Galle 1997; McKee 1991, 1993; McKee et al. 1994; Russell 1997; Smith 1976; Smith et al. 1977; Thomas 1995, 1998; Thomas et al. 1995), although we borrow from other more general sources as well. The Hermitage was an antebellum cotton plantation that was home to former President Andrew Jackson, his family, and a large number of African American slaves. The plantation was in operation between 1804 and the late 1850s, but it was from 1830 onward that the slave population was at its highest (Tables 4.1 and 4.2). With a slave population numbering over 100 in the 1840s and 1850s, the Hermitage was in the top 1 percent of slaveholdings in Tennessee. Behind the numbers noted on inventories, of course, were people. This community of enslaved people consisted of girls and boys and men and women. These people had the legal status of slaves, but they also were cooks, carpenters, and fieldworkers. They were sisters, uncles, mothers, and grandfathers. They were friends,

TABLE 4.2
Slave Demographics at the Hermitage, 1829 and 1850

| 1829[1] (n=95) | | | 1850[2] (n=137) | |
Females	Males	Age	Females	Males
20	18	<1–9	29	23
6	15	10–19	22	15
4	3	20–29	8	4
8	6	30–39	3	3
1	6	40–49	8	2
4	4	50–59	1	5
0	0	60–69	6	4
0	0	70+	3	1
43 (45.3%)	52 (54.7%)		80 (58.4%)	57 (41.6%)

N O T E S : [1]Western Reserve Historical Society (1817–1832). [2]Seventh Census of the U.S.

acquaintances, and, at times, adversaries. Acknowledging these roles is important because they helped to define the relationships in which peoples' identities were both formed and experienced at the Hermitage and at places like it throughout the plantation South.

A Layered Approach to Personal Appearance and Social Identity

The visual effect of costume is important. "Social roles are partly implemented and learned from dress. . . . Appearance provides a means of social communication concerning relationships between individuals or groups and it gives a unique understanding of the construction and symbolic reflection of social categories" (Sorenson 1991:122). An individual's appearance communicates to others before, or in the absence of, verbal interaction (Barnes and Eicher 1992:1). Messages communicated through dress can relate to group affiliation (including race or ethnicity), prestige, wealth, social role, kinship, age, gender, and many other social variables alone or in combination (Eicher and Roach-Higgins 1992:23). Because appearance can simultaneously have many alternative or layered meanings, it is important to seek a contextual understanding of what messages people conveyed through their dress.

While certain social variables may be marked by dress, dress is not a passive reflection of social reality. Appearance—conveyed, in part, through material culture—is actively used to constitute that social reality (for example, Barnes and Eicher 1992; Cannon 1991; Renne 1995; Rugh 1986; Sorenson 1991; Weiner and Schneider 1989). At many levels of social interaction, dress affects behavior (Eicher and Roach-Higgins 1992:8). Dress provides visual cues about a person, allowing viewers to respond accordingly. Like any form of representation, appearance takes place in a social context, motivated by interests, limited and structured (but not determined) by historical and cultural conventions, and is directed at various audiences.

It is clear, then, that the material culture of personal appearance participates in social interaction and takes part in the presentation of self. But just as provenience is the most crucial piece of archaeological information, the context in which material culture was used is crucial to understanding its role in social interaction. In the case of items used to construct and embellish personal appearance, context of use and even provenience on the body can be important to the meaning conveyed. Martin Wobst (1977:329) was the first archaeologist to observe the fact that material culture, which is broadly visible (such as the exterior of structures or the outer layers of clothing), communicates messages (including messages about identity) to a large audience of viewers. Applying this insight specifically to dress, one could argue that ornaments and articles of dress concealed by outer layers of clothing are intended for a narrow audience, while items worn on the exterior are intended for broader viewing. The messages contained in different layers of dress vary accordingly.

Goffman's dramaturgical theory is relevant for understanding how material culture worn in different layers of dress takes part in the presentation of self in different social contexts. Goffman uses the concepts of "front region" and "backstage" to refer to different settings of social interaction in which people either enact a performance based upon expectations defined by their given roles or they step out of character in a more private setting to "be themselves," so to speak (Goffman 1959:22, 112). Backstage behavior is kept hidden from those who do not share critical aspects of identity (113)—whether that is gender, occupational role, or one's status as slave. For African American slaves in the antebellum South, the clearest distinction in front region and backstage behavior corresponded to social settings in which whites were present versus social settings in which they were not.

Dress participates in the performances people offer as they present themselves in various social settings. People choose different costumes to wear in different situations, and different elements of dress worn simultaneously are more or less visible to others. Those elements carry meanings that are comprehensible to different viewers to varying degrees. For example, enslaved African Americans usually wore different clothing for work (especially work in the fields) than they wore for special events such as social dances or church (Foster 1997:176; Tandberg 1980; Tandberg and Durand 1981). In addition to the ragged, uniform clothing slaves were given for daily work, most slaves also had a finer set of clothing and ornaments to be worn on special occasions—items they usually obtained or made for themselves through various means (Foster 1997:176). Moreover, on occasions when African American slaves dressed elegantly, their dress differed in settings in which whites were present as opposed to those in which they were free to socialize on their own (177–186). The backstage contexts of social interaction for African American slaves were the least documented historically, as they were largely inaccessible to whites. It is in these contexts that slaves exercised the greatest freedom of self-expression and probably made use of the diverse array of ornaments and other personal objects often found in archaeological sites. The archaeological record, then, bears witness to the drive toward self-expression—the "will to adorn," as Zora Neale Hurston (1934, cited in Foster 1997:71) described it—that existed among African American slaves struggling to assert their identity within a hegemonic social order.

Because relationships provide the social context in which identity exists, people define their identity and have their identity defined through interaction with others. Dress is one locus of the social negotiation in which individuals both define themselves and are defined by others. In any social context, there is a degree to which people can create or influence their own appearance and a degree to which their appearance is dictated by cultural norms, constraints related to economic or social position, and rules applied to specific groups. African American slaves on antebellum plantations experienced significant limitations on how they could present themselves. Most slave owners issued one or perhaps two outfits to last slaves for the entire year (Foster 1997:146). Thus, the daily work clothes that slaves wore reflected choices made by their owners—choices usually governed by an interest in cutting costs and in some cases dehumanizing slaves (Foster 1997:147, 157, 161–164, 170–171). However, it is clear that enslaved African Americans sought out ways to influence their appearance—from using the little money they came by for the purchase of clothing and ornaments, to requesting hand-me-downs from whites, to making their own clothing and ornaments out of materials available to them (see Heath, this volume; Heath 1999).

The dress of enslaved African Americans during daily work, and their dress for special occasions, included some combination of things chosen by themselves and things given to them by others—usually white owners. Some of these elements of dress were broadly visible, and others were seen or known only to intimate friends and relations. One way to view these elements of personal appearance is as a series of layers: the body, items worn next to the body, clothing, and accessories. These different layers of appearance can express different aspects of identity, and each layer may be more or less visible and comprehensible to different audiences. Furthermore, each of these layers functions somewhat differently in terms of the aspects of social identity that they communicate or reinforce.

The Body

The first layer of appearance that is relevant to social identity is corporeal; that is, the body itself. One aspect of the body that was particularly salient on antebellum plantations was skin color, for it was the primary trait used to categorize people in the antebellum South. Although Native Americans also were victims of the institution of slavery, most slaves in North America were of African descent and were identified as such by virtue of their skin color. Recent commentaries on race, while focusing on the social construction of the concept, recognize the importance of the physical in this aspect of identity. Kwame Appiah and Henry Louis Gates (1995:3), for example, note that "Racial identities, like those along the dimensions of gender and sexuality, are defined in a peculiarly corporeal way: one's identity as an African American is rooted in one's embodiment as a black body." As the first, most basic level of how individuals appear to others, the body is fundamental to how we categorize ourselves socially and how others categorize us as well.

The ideology that equated a socially constructed racial category (that is, black) with forced servitude has a history (Fields 1990; Smedley 1993). Despite early beliefs that blacks and whites were separate species, it became clear that interracial sexual unions actually produced fertile offspring.[2] These sexual relationships—mostly between white men and black women and mostly coercive—resulted in children with lighter skin color, referred to as "mulatto" and "yellow." In the testimony and narratives of former slaves, it is clear that color distinctions did, at times, cause tensions among enslaved African Americans.

Examples of the social tensions created by color differences, and the effect that it had on social identity, can be found in narratives and interviews of former slaves. One former slave, interviewed in the 1920s, recalled: "A white woman would have a maid sometimes who was nice looking and she would keep her and her son would have children by her. Of course, the mixed blood, you couldn't expect much from them" (Fisk University 1945:3). In an 1842 interview published in an abolitionist newspaper, a fugitive slave named Lewis Clarke discussed how slaves viewed other slaves of mixed blood. "The slaves used to debate together sometimes, what could be the reason that the yellow folks couldn't be trusted like the dark ones could. . . . and I'll tell you what we concluded was the reason—we concluded it was because they was sons of their masters, and took after their fathers" (Blassingame 1977:154). Clarke went on to describe how he "felt ashamed of the white blood that was in me." Some slaves considered it superior to be fully black, primarily because they were "honest got" (649).

Slave sources frequently refer to the ridicule of mulattoes. Dora Franks, a former house slave interviewed during the 1930s, recalled the treatment she received by other slave children because of her lighter color: "I knew dat dere was some difference 'tween me and de rest o' chillen, 'cause dey was all coal black, and I was even lighter dan I is now. Lord, it's been to my sorrow many a time, 'cause de chillen used to chase me round and holler at me, 'Old yallow nigger.' Dey didn't treat me good, neither" (Yetman 1970:127). Bruce, a former slave who published his autobiography in 1895, also talked about the attitudes of some slaves toward mulattoes. He wrote, "I remember when we lived in adjoining cabins [to another slave family] that they were very quarrelsome people, and did not want their son Isaac to play with me, because, they said, I was a 'yarler nigger'" (Bruce 1969).

Although anecdotal, it should be clear from statements such as these that tensions existed among African Americans concerning skin color. The tensions were not, however, about color per se. Rather, color was an emblem of social relationships. Criticism of mixed-race slaves may have derived from the ambiguous identity of these individuals and from general protest against the circum-stances in which mixed race children were conceived. Color was a physical reminder of the power relations that governed the institution of slavery and had direct consequences on outward appearance and on social identity.

Color was also an important factor of identity on antebellum plantations because it often helped to define planters' notions of appropriate work roles for slaves. Although a single drop of black blood legally made an individual black, planters recognized differences and often assigned mulatto slaves to work roles that put them in closer contacts with whites (for example, domes-tic and skilled positions). Since there does appear to have been a strong corre-lation between the work role of a slave's parents and the role they eventually filled on the plantation, the connection between lighter color and domestic work was reinforced through time (Johnson 1986).

Beyond visibly defining who was free and who was not, we know little about how skin color influenced social relations at the Hermitage, particularly within the slave community itself. Only about a half dozen Hermitage slaves are specifically identified as mulatto, yellow, or "of fair complexion" in corre-spondence or bills of sale. All of these were either domestic slaves or skilled slaves, which is consistent with what we know from many other slaveholdings. However, individuals who worked in skilled or domestic positions were more likely to be mentioned in correspondence by Jackson family members, making it difficult to draw certain conclusions about skin color at the Hermitage.

Other aspects of the body that were fundamental in defining social iden-tity were sex-specific features. Perceived sexual differences, the basis for assign-ing gender, were obviously very closely tied to biological differences between men and women. Being a biological female did influence the types of work roles assigned to enslaved individuals, as was true at the Hermitage. Table 4.3 illustrates the various roles assigned to men and women at the Hermitage, as gleaned from plantation records dating between the 1820s and 1850s. Although there is some overlap, certain gender conventions were followed. Consistent with what Elizabeth Fox-Genovese (1988:293) has observed, African American men at the Hermitage were rarely assigned to tasks that would have been con-sidered inappropriate for white men, such as weaving, spinning, and washing clothes. On the other hand, black women did tasks that would have been seen as inappropriate for white women—at least for those of means.

One role filled by black women that was not viewed as an appropriate role for white women was work as field laborers. Jacqueline Jones (1985) notes

TABLE 4.3
Slave Occupations at the Hermitage

Roles Assigned to Men	Roles Assigned to Women
Blacksmith	Cook
Carpenter	Domestic
Cattle feeder	Field
Cook	Milker
Domestic	Poultry overseer
Field	Seamstress
Foreman	Spinner
Gardener	Washer
Ginner	Weaver
Groom/horse trainer	
Hog feeder	
Wagoner	

NOTES: The occupations of many slaves at the Hermitage have been gleaned from published correspondence between Andrew Jackson and family members or colleagues (Bassett 1926–1935), visitors' accounts (e.g., Brinkerhoff 1900), and an 1841 Hermitage farm journal entry (Western Reserve Historical Society 1845–1877).

that black women, who had toiled in the fields as slaves, left the fields in large numbers after emancipation, something noted by primary and secondary sources on Reconstruction. This fact suggests that they, like most white southerners, viewed fieldwork as inappropriate for women. Some scholars have viewed this movement on the part of black women to leave the fields as an attempt to imitate white values, which held that women should stay indoors to care for children and run the household, while males had the primary responsibility to provide income for the family. But, as Jones notes:

> In fact, however, the situation was a good deal more complicated. First, the reorganization of female labor resulted from choices made by *both* men and women. Second, it is inaccurate to speak of "removal" of women from the agricultural work force. Many were no longer working

for a white overseer, but they continued to pick cotton, laboring according to the needs and priorities established by their own families. (59)

Furthermore, idealized gender roles were difficult to maintain with the economic realities faced by newly freed African Americans. After emancipation,
black families continued to depend heavily upon the fieldwork of women
as well as children—a situation uncommon among whites. In 1870, for
example, "more than four out of ten black married women listed jobs, almost
all as field laborers" compared to 98.4 percent of white women who were
"keeping house" (63).

Against the Body

The body was the first and most fundamental layer in personal appearance. It
helped to define key aspects of identity among African Americans in the antebellum and postbellum South. The second layer of personal appearance
includes those things that were worn close to the body. These items of material culture, such as jewelry and charms, factored into the expression of identity in a more subtle way than the body. Forming a layer that remained relatively hidden from public view, such items probably had more to do with
reinforcing group identity rather than gender identity.

The second layer of personal appearance, and those aspects of identity
that it represented, differs dramatically from the first. First, it is constructed
with objects, many of which are found on archaeological sites. Examples from
the Hermitage and elsewhere include beads, cowrie shells, pierced coins, crys-
tals, and small hand charms (Figure 4.1). Second, unlike the body, white-
defined gender roles and institutions played little part in how identity was
expressed and perceived through these objects. For example, the association
of black skin color and servitude was an ideological construction created by
whites. It was an open, visible characteristic used to define important aspects
of social identity. The second layer, however, was not visible to all. While
some of the objects worn close to the body, such as glass beads, may have been
visible to others, most probably remained out of view. Some such hidden
objects—waist beads, for example—may have been viewed only by partners
in an intimate relationship. Some objects worn close to the body may have
represented and reinforced community values, or at the very least aesthetics,
defined by African Americans rather than whites.

FIG. 4.1.   Hand charms recovered from Hermitage slave contexts. Reprinted by permission of the Ladies' Hermitage Association.

Several copper-alloy hand charms recovered from the Hermitage represent one such item. These small charms, two of which are less than a centimeter in diameter, all represent minor variations of the same image (see Figure 4.1). Unfortunately, precious little is known about their origin and meaning. Sam Smith (1976:210–211), who directed the project that recovered the first charm, suggests that they may be "associated with African oriented spiritualist cults" or may be related to the term *hand*, which appears in slave narratives and is often described as a charm used to "keep witches away." Although there is no indication that the term *hand* (also commonly called a jack) refers to a physical representation of a human hand, these charms may have operated in the same magico-religious belief system (for a discussion of the importance and fusion of magic and religion among African Americans, see Wilkie [1997]). Thus, these hand charms probably had very special meanings for those who wore them—meanings that were shared by other members of the community, whether or not they had knowledge of who wore one.

Other objects, such as beads, likely functioned in similar ways (Figure 4.2). Although beads are common on African American sites, we know little about how beads were worn during the antebellum period. It is clear from the Hermitage that glass beads were accessible to all slaves, regardless of where they lived on the plantation and what work role they occupied. While there may be a tendency to think of beads as gender-specific, little evidence exists outside of mortuary practices to support this view—not surprisingly, given the somewhat

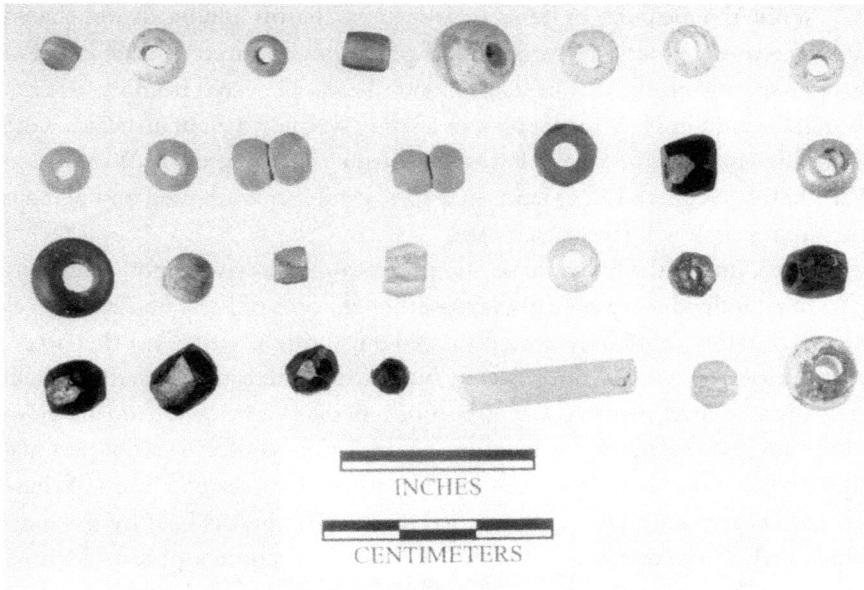

FIG. 4.2.   Glass beads from the South Cabin at the Hermitage. Photograph by Vince Macek, by permission of the Ladies' Hermitage Association.

hidden nature of this layer of appearance. Consider the blue beads that are prevalent on African American sites. Their association with good luck is equally applicable to males and females, based at least on what is known about them and the color blue from more recent accounts (for example, Stine et al. 1996). This short poem, entitled "Anniversary," by Rita Dove (1986:59), former U.S. poet laureate, illustrates this point. The poem is set in the late 1920s to early 1930s and is part of a collection that recalls the lives of two African Americans, Thomas and Beulah:

> *Twelve years to the day*
> he puts the blue worry bead into his mouth.
> The trick is to swallow your good luck, too.
> Last words to a daughter . . .
> and a wink to remember him by.[3]

Although we should not directly project the meaning and use of blue beads from the 1930s into the 1850s, it does seem clear that these artifacts fit into a set of beliefs shared by African Americans regardless of gender.

While the meaning in items such as hand charms and beads was shared among African Americans regardless of gender, there are some indications of gender-specific bead use. One collection of beads recovered from the African Burial Ground in New York represent a string worn on a woman's waist, a use of beads common in parts of western Africa (LaRoche 1994; Wilson and Cabak, this volume). Other items may have gender-specific uses, and perhaps further research will reveal such uses.

Thus, unlike the body, items worn next to the body were not necessarily part of an individual's *public* display—although some of these objects, such as beads, certainly could have been displayed outwardly as well, like other accessories. However, when worn privately by African American slaves, these small items represented personal and group beliefs that whites were not likely to understand. As such, they were important material manifestations of personal identity as well as corporate identity. The somewhat hidden nature of these objects meant that they were intended to reinforce beliefs held by the individuals who wore them, as well as to communicate certain aspects of identity to those with whom they were close. Although gender may have been a contributing factor in who more appropriately wore such items, it seems to have played a secondary role in how such items fit into a larger set of beliefs shared in slave communities.

Clothing

The third layer of personal appearance involves clothing. Clothing expresses various aspects of group and personal identity, and on a day-to-day basis on antebellum plantations it minimally conveyed information about work role, age, and gender. Because the exterior layers of clothing are broadly visible, they immediately communicate information about the wearer's identity to all within viewing range. For clothes made or chosen by African American slaves themselves, the information communicated to some degree reflected their own decisions about how to present themselves. But for clothes given to slaves by their owners, clothing reflected white ideals about slave identity and the social and economic agenda of planters. Therefore, the layer of appearance formed by clothing took on a very different character when enslaved African Americans were at work under the surveillance of their owners and when they were finely dressed for a social or sacred occasion in the company of other slaves.

The clothing that African American slaves wore to work typically was manufactured by slaves under the direction of overseers or members of the plantation household, or it was given to slaves directly (Foster 1997:146). At least some of the cloth used at the Hermitage was produced on the plantation. In an 1833 letter to Andrew Jackson, William B. Lewis reported that Jackson's overseer had the spinning wheel on the property and looms constantly going, along with "some of the old women spinning by hand" (Lewis 1833). It is likely that part of the seamstress' job at the Hermitage was making clothing for other slaves according to the specifications of her owners and overseers. Expressions of identity made by these clothes—produced in bulk almost as uniforms— were, therefore, expressions made by slave owners. Work clothes minimally expressed an individual's identity as slave, a fact recognized in eighteenth-century South Carolina, where the law explicitly required that slaves wear coarse clothing to mark their inferior status (Genovese 1976:559). Although the law was generally ignored, it reflected the dominant view that clothing was a useful tool for visually reinforcing the degradation of African American slaves. Dressing slaves in coarse, tattered garments served dual purposes for planters: reducing their expenditures, thus increasing their profits, and humiliating slaves. That shabby work clothes were felt to be humiliating is evident in the strong impulse African American slaves had to obtain nicer clothing and orna-ments for themselves (Foster 1997:77).

Some planters, however, may have used their slaves' clothing as a reflection of their own wealth and status. Some planters may have dressed their slaves bet-ter simply to display their ability to spend the money necessary to do so—this was especially true in the case of domestic slaves who would have been more visible to visitors than field slaves. Andrew Jackson may have dressed his slaves better than the average slaveholder, considering the fact that he was an impor-tant public figure with many visitors to his plantation. Indeed, the archaeolog-ical remains of one of the slave cabins closest to the Hermitage mansion may reflect a concern with public appearances. The Triplex cabin was a set of three connected brick structures built on a foundation of carefully dressed limestone blocks matching those used for the Hermitage mansion itself. This foundation differed from those of other brick cabins on the property, located away from the mansion, which were constructed of roughly hewn blocks. The yard area of the Triplex also appears to have been swept clean (unlike the yards of more remote cabins on the property) to create the appearance of a tidy, well-kept plantation.

Like the cabins, domestic slaves were part of Jackson's "front region," and it is likely that he insisted that they be appropriately attired.

Domestic slaves usually were dressed in respectable clothing, at least according to what whites deemed suitable for their role. Because field slaves were given cheaper, minimally functional clothes that quickly became worn through the rigors of agricultural labor, clothing served as an immediate visual cue to slaves' work roles on the plantation. Work clothing, as a readily visible exterior layer, was a clear marker of occupational identity and other aspects of identity as well. Whites in the antebellum South conceived of a hierarchy in which domestic slaves occupied a superior status than field slaves. However, there is evidence that the ideology of a slave hierarchy was not widely accepted by slaves themselves (Blassingame 1976; Thomas 1995). This ideology may have been subverted in part through choices African American slaves made about their own personal clothing.

Despite the differences that existed between the work clothes of domestic and field slaves, it is clear at the Hermitage that slaves in all work roles were able to obtain garments and ornaments of their own choosing to wear at secular and religious events. Nearly all cabins that have been excavated at the Hermitage have featured coins among the antebellum deposits. These coins, found at the former residences of domestic slaves as well as field slaves, suggest that all slaves, regardless of work role, had access to enough money that some of it was lost. Whatever the source of this money, slaves very likely used it to buy clothing and ornaments among other things. Widespread access to personal items of dress may have acted to minimize distinctions reflected in the occupational dress of domestic and field slaves and may have undermined planter-imposed notions of a slave hierarchy based on occupational roles.[4]

Although planters normally issued work clothes to their slaves, it appears that slaves at the Hermitage may have had a modicum of influence over the appearance of that clothing. Pieces of sewing equipment such as pins, thimbles, and scissors have been found in all cabins excavated at the plantation in varying numbers, including one cabin with a large and diverse assemblage of sewing equipment that probably belonged to the plantation seamstress (see Galle, this volume). In addition to the presence of sewing equipment in the cabins, all Hermitage slave cabins have many buttons—more than would be expected from normal breakage or loss. These buttons may have come from recycled clothing used for quilts, warm undergarments, winter wraps, or patches for worn-out clothes. Narratives of former slaves across the South indicate that many slaves made some clothes for themselves out of any materials they could find or make, to supplement the often inadequate wardrobe issued to them by their owners (Foster 1997:147–150). Because there was such wide access to sewing equipment at the Hermitage, it is likely that African Americans living there made some clothing or at least repaired or otherwise modified garments given to them. They were constrained, however, by the materials available to them, such that their work clothes probably did not depart dramatically from what was issued to them by the Jacksons. It is unlikely that African American slaves invested great amounts of time embellishing their work clothes. Given their demanding work schedules and their limited resources, it is more likely that they made do with work clothes that minimally met their needs and spent more time and resources to make or purchase fancy clothing for special occasions.

Just as work clothes marked that aspect of slaves' identity tied to occupational role, clothing also served as a marker of age. By numerous accounts, the clothing worn by slave children across the South consisted of a long shirt, worn by both girls and boys (Foster 1997:152–158). At the Hermitage, as elsewhere, children dressed alike, wearing what was described as "one coarse long garment to cover them" (Dorris 1915:122). In Figure 4.3, a stereograph taken of former Hermitage slaves in the late 1860s, one can see the rough, one-piece homespun that is the children's primary article of clothing. While clothing among adults was gender-specific, with children it acted to neutralize gender distinctions.

Unlike the children in Figure 4.3, the woman (their great grandmother, according to the inscription found on the back of an identical stereograph) wears gender-specific clothing, including a long dress; perhaps even two, one over the other. Partially covering her upper body is a cloak-type garment, which appears to be made from a piece of damask. While the cloak was likely a garment worn for special occasions, the remainder of the woman's clothing appears well worn. Overall, her attire is gender specific, as were the work clothes of African American field slaves: pants for men and long skirts for women (Foster 1997:159–172). Although these clothes were gender specific, women's dresses usually were unflattering and "unfeminine" by the standards of the day—made of coarse fabrics in drab colors, without ornamentation and tailoring to accentuate the female body. Given the efforts of planters to minimize their expenses, the provisioning of unattractive work clothes to African American slave women is not surprising. In some cases, however, these clothes may have been unflattering by design, as white women who often oversaw the

FIG. 4.3.   Stereoscopic image of former Hermitage slaves, circa 1867. Reprinted by permission of the Ladies' Hermitage Association.

production of clothing for slaves attempted to downplay the sexual appeal of African American girls and women (Foster 1997:157). In reaction to the ragged clothes worn on a daily basis, enslaved African American women must have relished the expression of personal style and femininity made possible with their "Sunday best."

A further extension of gender represented in the woman's clothing in Figure 4.3, but one that also reflects group identity, is found in her head wrap—an article worn by many African American women both prior to and well after emancipation. Foster (1997:272–315) argues that although the head wrap is probably West African in origin, it did not become popular in West Africa or the Americas until the eighteenth century. More important, the head wrap as worn in the Americas acquired "a complex of subtle functions not traditional" to its use in Africa (312). Although long viewed as a symbol of servitude by whites, Foster argues that "the headwrap acquired significance as a form of self- and communal identity" for African American women. The head wrap is certainly ubiquitous in images of African American women before and after emancipation, and it seems to have been worn at work, in domestic settings, and on special occasions (see, for example, paintings in McElroy [1990] and Seibels [1995]). Head wraps became a stigma in the eyes of whites, but they were not generally viewed negatively by African Americans. Foster argues that head wraps were a marker of ethnic identity and solidarity, and acted as "a badge of resistance against the servitude imposed by whites" (Foster 1997:312). The common use of head wraps for several hundred years by African and African American women reflects the strength of their adherence to an African-derived tradition as they forged a new ethnic identity in the American South.

Clothing, then, reflected several aspects of identity. Among adult slaves, clothing certainly reinforced gender-based notions of appropriate dress. Among women, it also expressed and helped to sustain an African-derived cultural identity. But clothing also acted to differentiate African Americans, particularly on larger plantations such as the Hermitage, where certain slaves were assigned principally to domestic tasks. Nonetheless, slaves had the ability to embellish their own personal appearance with clothing made or obtained by themselves for occasions separate from their work. In the "backstage" contexts of social interaction within slave communities such as the one at the Hermitage, African Americans found ways to present themselves in dress of their own choosing and creation, and people's attire on these occasions reflected personal and community ideals separate from and even antithetical to the agenda of white planters (see also Hunt 1996).

Accessories

A fourth layer to personal appearance and social identity includes accessories; that is, items on the person that appear outside of clothing. One example is the tobacco pipe, which is fairly common on archaeological sites from the antebellum period. Pipes have an obvious functional role, but they also can be part of an individual's public presentation. Representations of African American men and women often depict individuals with pipes, suggesting that such items were important to how they presented themselves to others. Tobacco pipes recovered from Hermitage slave contexts also testify to the role such items played in how the self was presented. Consider, for example, the differences in statements of social identity communicated by the pipes in Figures 4.4 and 4.5. A person who used the elaborate pipe depicted in Figure 4.4 was certainly "showing off" to some extent, differentiating him- or herself in a unique way. While it is true that this display may have been intended to demonstrate status or better access to material goods, it also helped to form and exhibit that individual's view of self. Using this pipe rather than a cheaper, more common pipe such as that depicted in Figure 4.5 was a statement about identity.

Thus, in this layer of appearance one is more likely to see greater individualized expression rather than expressions of corporate identity. Other examples that could be classified as accessories might include pieces of jewelry meant to be visible to the viewer (including beads), decorative buttons designed to accentuate clothing, and objects such as canes and umbrellas—all of which served as part of the overall image individuals created of themselves. These items were worn or used to make personal statements, to draw attention to oneself. Archaeologically, items such as these are rarely discussed in site reports because they occur in low numbers and thus defy quantification. However, as a reflection of idiosyncratic personal behavior, they can inform us of the ways that individuals sought to express their uniqueness. At the Hermitage, for example, a large number and diversity of buttons (with well over 1,000 buttons representing over 100 different styles), as well as tobacco pipe fragments, brooches, cane tips, parasol parts, and purse clips have been found, suggesting that African American slaves had considerable discretion in this aspect of how they presented themselves.

FIG. 4.4.   Ball clay pipe from the Triplex South dwelling unit at the Hermitage.
Photograph by Vince Macek, by permission of the Ladies' Hermitage Association.

FIG. 4.5.   Clay pipe from Cabin 2 at the Hermitage. Photograph by Vince Macek, by permission of the Ladies' Hermitage Association.

Appearance and Gender

Taken together, these four layers of personal appearance—the body, items worn next to the body, clothing, and accessories—helped to reflect and structure social identity among enslaved African Americans at the Hermitage and elsewhere in the South. As they did so, gender played a central role.

Although biological sex and gender, a cultural construct, are not equivalent, most societies assign appropriate gender roles based on biological sex. In

the case of African Americans in the antebellum South, the body was fundamental in this designation and, in large part, defined gender-based expectations. The extent to which African American–defined gender roles correlated
with those of whites is difficult to know with certainty, although there does
seem to have been a good deal of overlap.

Unlike the body, items worn next to the body were probably not as important in expressing gender as they were in reflecting acceptance of group beliefs
among African Americans. These beliefs were anchored in a shared cultural
heritage that underwent important transformations in the Americas as well as
a shared culture that emerged out of the common experience of slavery in the
U.S. Items such as charms and beads also reflected individual tastes that may
have been influenced by gender-based expectations, but which did not overtly
express them.

Gender certainly was an important component in how appearance was
expressed through clothing. Clothing concurrently signaled other aspects of
identity such as work role and age. Throughout the plantation South, travelers,
planters, and former slaves noted differences in the clothing worn by domestic
and field slaves. And, at least for adults, culturally constructed notions of gender were central in defining appropriate dress. While gender was not typically
expressed in children's clothing, boys and girls who worked and/or lived in the
big house often wore gender-specific clothing as well.

Contrary to the importance that clothing had in expressing gender, accessories less clearly reflected gender and were more closely tied to individual
choices that expressed personal identity. This is an area where personal aesthetics likely factored most prominently.

The information conveyed through these layers of identity was not equally
conveyed to all observers. Different material items related to layers were likely
viewed by different people/groups in different ways. For example, whites probably viewed items worn by African Americans differently than African Americans did. The head wrap is one good example; beads are a second example.
Each required a certain amount of cultural knowledge to correctly read the
messages embodied in them. Many scholars have pointed out that the presence of European or European-American material culture within slave households can have multiple meanings (for example, Brown 1993; Brown and
Cooper 1990; Ferguson 1991, 1992; Franklin 1995; Orser 1992:100–101; Vlach
1978, 1980), and the objects that helped to define and transmit social identity
among African American slaves functioned similarly.

The layers of dress worn by African American slaves embodied the fluid social relations that existed on plantations. As a group, slaves were people caught in the middle of dynamic and complicated relationships, and appearance was part of how they navigated through these relationships to minimize conflict, communicate acceptance of communitywide values, make personal statements, and even show off. African American slaves sometimes acted as members of a community first (acting on an identity in which in-group versus out-group distinctions are salient), while at other times they acted as individuals (where personal identity is salient). For example, slaves used symbols like hand charms and head wraps as additions to their work clothes, and these symbols were likely understood by slaves as signifiers of community values and solidarity in opposition to the planter-imposed ideology of subservience. On the other hand, the lively clothing, ornaments, and other personal effects embellishing the appearance of slaves attending a dance was intended for individual expression and differentiation (Heath 1999; Hunt 1996). African American slaves made choices about how to present themselves in the "front region" of interaction with whites, and in the "backstage" context among other slaves. The collective and individual expression of African Americans was constrained by the limitations inherent in the institution of slavery. And yet African American slaves were not powerless, and they manipulated the layers of dress to their advantage.

There are few who would argue that gender and social identity are not intimately intertwined. In fact, one might argue that there are no social situations in which gender is not a key aspect of an individual's identity. Although planters often ignored gender in making demands of enslaved men and women in the fields, it is clear that enslaved women asserted their understanding of gender nonetheless (see, for example, Foster 1997:81–84; Stevenson 1996). Gender was an important component of identity, but it was never experienced independently. African American dress in the antebellum South embodied the experience of gender alongside other aspects of identity and illustrates the complex manner in which it was expressed.

ACKNOWLEDGMENTS

We would like to thank Elizabeth Kellar, director of archaeology at the Hermitage, and the Ladies' Hermitage Association for their assistance and permission to photograph artifacts and reprint photographs. We also would like to express our gratitude to Dr. Rita Dove for allowing us to reprint her poem, "Anniversary." Thanks also to Vince Macek for his photographic talents. Funding for research at the Hermitage was provided by the Ladies' Hermitage Association, Earthwatch, the National Endowment for the Humanities, and the National Science Foundation. Finally, we would like to recognize Larry McKee for over a decade of leadership in the archaeological study of the former slave community at the Hermitage.

NOTES

1. By the term *dress* we refer to "an assemblage of body modifications and/or supplements displayed by a person in communicating with other human beings" (Eicher and Roach-Higgins 1992:15). This assemblage includes "the body, all direct modifications of the body itself, and all three-dimensional supplements added to it" (13), and thus is not limited to clothing.

2. Early racial theorists argued that blacks and whites were distinct species. As Kawash (1997:5) notes, "The word *mulatto* derives, after all, from a reference to the sterile hybridity of the mule. Just as the mule proved the horse and donkey were distinct species, so the mulatto proved that white and black were forever separate and distinct."

3. "Anniversary" from *Thomas and Beulah*, Carnegie-Melon Univ. Press, © 1986 by Rita Dove. Reprinted by permission of the author.

4. See Thomas (1998) for a more comprehensive discussion of the ideology and praxis of slave community.

REFERENCES

Appiah, Kwame Anthony, and Henry Louis Gates Jr.
  1995   Editor's Introduction: Multiplying Identities. In *Identities*, edited by Kwame Anthony Appiah and Henry Louis Gates Jr. Univ. of Chicago Press, Chicago.
Barnes, Ruth, and Joanne B. Eicher
  1992   Introduction. In *Dress and Gender: Making and Meaning in Cultural Contexts*, edited by Ruth Barnes and Joanne B. Eicher, pp. 1–7. Berg, Providence, R.I.
Bassett, John Spencer (editor)
  1926–1935   *Correspondence of Andrew Jackson*. 7 vols. Carnegie Institute of Washington, Washington, D.C.

Blassingame, James W.
    1976   Status and Social Structure in the Slave Community: Evidence from New Sources. In *Perspectives and Irony in American Slavery*, edited by Harry P. Owens, pp. 137–151. Univ. Press of Mississippi, Jackson.
Blassingame, James W. (editor)
    1977   *Slave Testimony: Two Centuries of Letters, Speeches, Interviews, and Autobiographies*. Louisiana State Univ. Press, Baton Rouge.
Brinkerhoff, Roeliff
    1900   *Recollections of a Lifetime*. Robert Clarke Co., Cincinnati.
Brown, Kenneth L.
    1993   Material Culture and Community Structure: The Slave and Tenant Community at Levi Jordan's Plantation, 1848–1892. In *Working Toward Freedom: Slave Society and Domestic Economy in the American South*, edited by Larry E. Hudson Jr., pp. 95–118. Univ. of Rochester Press, Rochester.
Brown, Kenneth L., and Doreen C. Cooper
    1990   Structural Continuity in an African American Slave and Tenant Community. *Historical Archaeology* 24(4):7–19.
Bruce, Henry C.
    1969   *The New Man. Twenty-nine Years a Slave. Twenty-nine Years a Free Man*. Negro Universities Press, New York. Originally published in 1895 by P. Abstadt & Sons, York, Pa.
Cannon, Aubrey
    1991   Gender, Status, and the Focus of Material Display. In *The Archaeology of Gender: Proceedings of the Twenty-second Annual Conference of the Archaeological Association of the University of Calgary*, edited by Dale Walde and Noreen D. Willows, pp. 144–149. Archaeological Association of the Univ. of Calgary, Calgary.
Dorris, Mary C.
    1915   *Preservation of the Hermitage*. Ladies' Hermitage Association, Hermitage, Tenn.
Dove, Rita
    1986   *Thomas and Beulah*. Carnegie-Mellon Univ. Press, Pittsburgh.
Eicher, Joanne B., and Mary Ellen Roach-Higgins
    1992   Definition and Classification of Dress: Implications for Analysis of Gender Roles. In *Dress and Gender: Making and Meaning in Cultural Contexts*, edited by Ruth Barnes and Joanne B. Eicher, pp. 8–28. Berg, Providence, R.I.

Ferguson, Leland

    1991   Struggling with Pots in Colonial South Carolina. In *The Archaeology of Inequality*, edited by Randall H. McGuire and Robert Paynter, pp. 28–39. Basil Blackwell, Cambridge.

    1992   *Uncommon Ground: Archaeology and Early African America, 1650–1800.* Smithsonian Institution Press, Washington, D.C.

Fields, Barbara Jeanne

    1990   Slavery, Race, and Ideology in the United States of America. *New Left Review* 181:95–118.

Fisk University

    1945   *Unwritten History of Slavery.* Social Science Institute, Fisk Univ., Nashville. Reprinted in *The American Slave: A Composite Autobiography*, Vol. 18, edited by George P. Rawick. Greenwood Publishing Co., Westport, Conn., 1972.

Foster, Helen Bradley

    1997   *"New Raiments of Self": African American Clothing in the Antebellum South.* Berg, Oxford.

Fox-Genovese, Elizabeth

    1988   *Within the Plantation Household: Black and White Women of the Old South.* Univ. of North Carolina Press, Chapel Hill.

Franklin, Maria

    1995   Rethinking the Carter's Grove Slave Quarter Reconstruction: A Proposal. *Kroeber Anthropological Papers* 79:147–164.

Galle, Jillian E.

    1997   Designing Women: Social Networks and the Occupation of Seamstress at the Hermitage Plantation, Hermitage, Tennessee. Master's thesis, Dept. of Anthropology, Univ. of Virginia, Charlottesville.

Genovese, Eugene D.

    1976   *Roll Jordan Roll: The World the Slaves Made.* Vintage Books, New York.

Goffman, Erving

    1959   *The Presentation of Self in Everyday Life.* Double Day, Garden City, N.Y.

Heath, Barbara J.

    1999   Buttons, Beads, and Buckles: Contextualizing Adornment within the Bonds of Slavery. In *Historical Archaeology and Current Perspectives on Ethnicity*, edited by Maria Franklin and Garrett Fesler, pp. 47–69. Colonial Williamsburg Research Publications, Dietz Press, Richmond.

Hunt, Patricia K.
    1996   The Struggle to Achieve Individual Expression through Clothing
            and Adornment: African American Women under and after Slavery.
            In *Discovering the Women in Slavery: Emancipating Perspectives on the
            American Past*, edited by Patricia Morton, pp. 227–240. Univ. of
            Georgia Press, Athens.
Hurston, Zora Neale
    1934   Characteristics of Negro Expression. In *Negro: An Anthology*, edited
            by Nancy Cunard. Wishart & Company, London. Reprinted in
            The Sanctified Church, Turtle Creek, Berkeley (1981).
Johnson, Michael P.
    1986   Work, Culture, and the Slave Community: Slave Occupations in the
            Cotton Belt in 1860. *Labor History* 27:325–55.
Jones, Jacqueline
    1985   *Labor of Love, Labor of Sorrow: Black Women, Work, and the Family
            from Slavery to Present*. Basic Books, New York.
Kawash, Samira
    1997   *Dislocating the Color Line: Identity, Hybridity, and Singularity in
            African American Narrative*. Stanford Univ. Press, Stanford.
LaRoche, Cheryl J.
    1994   Beads from the African Burial Ground, New York City: A Prelimi-
            nary Assessment. *Beads* 6:3–20.
Lewis, William B.
    1833   Letter to Andrew Jackson, Apr. 21, 1833. In *Correspondence of Andrew
            Jackson*, 7 vols. (1926–1935), edited by John Spencer Bassett, V:65.
            Carnegie Institution of Washington, Washington, D.C.
Martin, Harvey J., and Theodore N. Greenstein
    1983   Individual Differences in Status Generalization. *Journal of Personal-
            ity and Social Psychology* 44:641–662.
McElroy, Guy C.
    1990   *Facing History: The Black Image in American Art, 1710–1940*. Bedford
            Arts and the Corcoran Gallery of Art, Washington, D.C.
McKee, Larry
    1991   Summary Report of the 1990 Hermitage Field Quarter Excavation.
            Tennessee Anthropological Association Newsletter 16(1):1–17.
    1993   Summary Report on the 1991 Hermitage Field Quarter Excavation.
            Tennessee Anthropological Association Newsletter 18(1):1–16.
McKee, Larry, Brian W. Thomas, and Jennifer Bartlett
    1994   Summary Report on the Hermitage Mansion Yard Area. Ms. on file,
            Ladies' Hermitage Association, Hermitage, Tenn.

Orser, Charles E.
   1992   Beneath the Material Surface of Things: Commodities, Artifacts,
          and Slave Plantation. *Historical Archaeology* 26(3):95–104.
Renne, Elisha
   1995   *Cloth That Does Not Die: The Meaning of Cloth in Bunu Social Life.*
          Univ. of Washington Press, Seattle.
Rugh, Andrea B.
   1986   *Reveal and Conceal: Dress in Contemporary Egypt.* Syracuse Univ.
          Press, Syracuse.
Russell, Aaron E.
   1997   Material Culture and African American Spirituality at the Hermitage.
          Historical Archaeology 31(2):63–80.
Seibels, Cynthia
   1995   *The Sunny South: The Life and Art of William Aiken Walker.* Saraland
          Press, Spartanburg, S.C.
Smedley, Audrey
   1993   *Race in North America: Origin and Evolution of a Worldview.*
          Westview Press, Boulder.
Smith, Samuel D. (editor)
   1976   *An Archaeological and Historical Assessment of the First Hermitage.*
          Research Series No. 2, Division of Archaeology, Tennessee Dept.
          of Conservation, Nashville.
Smith, Samuel D., Fred W. Brigance, Emanuel Breitburg, Stephen D. Cox,
and Michael Martin
   1977   Results of the 1976 Season of the Hermitage Archaeology Project.
          Report prepared for the Ladies' Hermitage Association and the
          Tennessee American Revolution Bicentennial Commission,
          Nashville.
Sorenson, Marie Louise Stig
   1991   The Construction of Gender through Appearance. In *The Archaeol-
          ogy of Gender: Proceedings of the Twenty-second Annual Conference of
          the Archaeological Association of the University of Calgary*, edited by
          Dale Walde and Noreen D. Willows, pp. 121–129. Archaeological
          Association of the Univ. of Calgary, Calgary.
Stevenson, Brenda E.
   1996   Gender Convention, Ideals, and Identity among Antebellum
          Virginia Slave Women. In *More Than Chattel: Black Women
          and Slavery in the Americas*, edited by David Barry Gaspar and
          Darlene Clark Hine, pp. 169–190. Indiana Univ. Press,
          Bloomington.

Stine, Linda France, Melanie A. Cabak, and Mark D. Groover
  1996   Blue Beads as African American Cultural Symbols. *Historical
          Archaeology* 30(3):49–75.
Tandberg, Gerilyn
  1980   Field Hand Clothing in Louisiana and Mississippi during the
          Antebellum Period. *Dress* 5:89–104.
Tandberg, Gerilyn, and Sally Graham Durand
  1981   Dress-Up Costumes for Field Slaves of Antebellum Louisiana
          and Mississippi. *Costume* 15:41–48.
Thomas, Brian W.
  1995   *Community among Enslaved African Americans on the Hermitage
          Plantation, 1820s–1850s.* Ph.D. diss., Dept. of Anthropology,
          State Univ. of New York at Binghamton, Binghamton. University
          Microfilms, Ann Arbor, Mich.
  1998   Power and Community: The Archaeology of Slavery at the
          Hermitage Plantation. *American Antiquity* 63(4):531–551.
Thomas, Brian W., Larry McKee, and Jennifer Bartlett
  1995   Summary Report on the 1995 Hermitage Field Quarter
          Excavation. Ms. on file, the Ladies' Hermitage Association,
          Hermitage, Tenn.
Vlach, John M.
  1978   *The Afro-American Tradition in Decorative Arts.* Cleveland
          Museum of Art, Cleveland.
  1980   Arrival and Survival: The Maintenance of an Afro-American
          Tradition in Folk Art and Craft. In *Perspectives on American Folk
          Art*, edited by M. G. Quimby and Scott T. Swank, pp. 177–217.
          W. W. Norton, New York.
Weiner, Annette, and Jane Schneider (editors)
  1989   *Cloth and the Human Experience.* Smithsonian Institution Press,
          Washington, D.C.
Western Reserve Historical Society
  1817–1832   Hermitage Farm Journal. Otto Miller Collections. Western
          Reserve Historical Society, Cleveland, Ohio.
  1845–1877   Andrew Jackson II Account Books. Ms. 1880. Western
          Reserve Historical Society, Cleveland, Ohio.
Wilkie, Laurie A.
  1997   Secret and Sacred: Contextualizing the Artifacts of African American
          Magic and Religion. *Historical Archaeology* 31(4):81–106.

Wobst, H. Martin
    1977   Stylistic Behavior and Information Exchange. In *For the Director: Research Essays in Honor of James B. Griffin*, edited by Charles E. Cleland, pp. 317–342. Anthropological Papers No. 61. Museum of Anthropology, Univ. of Michigan, Ann Arbor.
Yetman, Norman R. (editor)
    1970   *Voices from Slavery*. Holt, Rinehart and Winston, New York.

CHAPTER 5

Risk and Women's Roles in the Slave Family: Data from Oxmoor and Locust Grove Plantations in Kentucky

AMY L. YOUNG

While gender roles and gender ideology are fundamental aspects of all human cultures, how they are manifested and operate in different societies is extraordinarily complex. Gender in African American slave culture is no exception. Any examination of gender ideology and the role of enslaved black women and men, because of the nature of slavery, must be addressed from two separate domains: (1) within the slave community, which might be considered private, and (2) within the white slaveholding society (the interaction of slaves with owners), which might be considered public.

This study focuses on the public and private roles of enslaved women in Kentucky and how these women used their gendered roles to minimize risk and improve life chances. The earliest attempts by scholars to investigate the roles of black women in slave society were primarily based on evidence from the sphere of interaction between slave and slave owners and assumed that this also represented the role of women within the slave community. The public domain is most visible to researchers and has led to some misinterpretations concerning the role of women within their households and within the slave community. Very few data sources reveal much about the interaction of slave women in their private world within the slave community and within the family (White 1985:23). In fact, tactics concerning survival in the slave community were probably hidden from outsiders, much as Zora Neale Hurston (1990:2) describes as "a feather-bed resistance" in early-twentieth-century black southern communities. In actuality, however, both domains need to be addressed in order to understand how gender structured the lives of slaves and how slaves structured their gender roles and ideologies.

Two separate data sets are employed to examine public and private gender roles. First, the documentary record from Oxmoor Plantation in Kentucky is used to investigate the public domain—specifically, the roles of slave women who served as domestics in the big house. The use of gendered kin terminology is interpreted as a strategy by which enslaved African American women coped with risk and capitalized on opportunities at Oxmoor when dealing with their owners. Second, the archaeological record from Locust Grove in Kentucky is used to discuss the private domain of women and gender ideology within the slave community. White (1985:22) has stated that "the jobs and services performed by slave women for the community were not peripheral but central to slave survival." Archaeological data from Locust Grove are used to interpret how slave women might have coped with risks to their family and community. Three seasons of archaeological fieldwork focused on three slave house sites, or slave households, gives material evidence concerning how gifting or sharing may have been used and controlled by women to strengthen kinship and other bonds between slaves and also to protect individuals in the slave community from harm. Both plantations are located near each other in the same county just outside Louisville, Kentucky (Map 5.1).

It is important to recognize that the same slave woman may have had different gender roles or personae in different domains (Duranti 1992; Ochs 1992). My approach is to view these multilayered gender roles as if they were situational use of language (code switching). Such an approach allows us to tease out the often convoluted but certainly complex meanings associated with the behaviors of the past. But, more importantly, I find that there is good evidence to suggest that slaves, especially slave women, were able to capitalize on the gender and kinship roles that were "assigned" to them in the public domain through occupation, such as mammy, and use the obligations that these gendered kinship terms implied to protect themselves and their families. In the slave quarters, another role or persona would have been assumed, and from this position women tightened kinship and reinforced solidarity as a means to cope with the dangers of slavery. Thus, the situational use or manipulation of gender roles was utilized by slave women to reduce or minimize risk.

Risks on Kentucky Plantations

Many have assumed that since there were few overseers on Kentucky and other Upland South plantations, slave populations there were relatively low

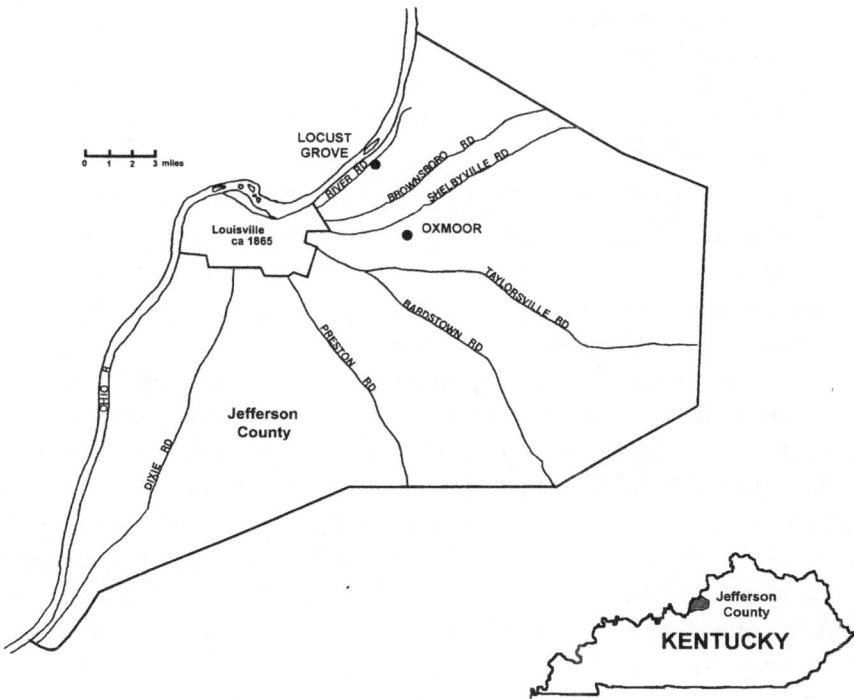

MAP 5.1.   Location of Oxmoor and Locust Grove in Jefferson County, Kentucky.

compared to the Deep South, and because slaves may have worked more closely with their masters, that slavery was easier in this region. Slaves in Kentucky may have had better housing (because winters were harsher) and may have had better diets (although this is still being debated) (Young 1997a). However, there were threats to existence that were common to all slaves as well as threats or risks peculiar to slaves in the Upland South (Young 1997a). Analysis of Kentucky former slave narratives recorded during the Great Depression by Works Progress Administration writers and fugitive slave accounts showed that there were a number of risks perceived by slaves. These risks, in order of frequency of references, are the following:

1. Being beaten
2. Being sold and separated from family and friends
3. Being sold "down the river"

4. Starvation, scarcity of food, malnutrition
5. Disease/Death
6. Injury/Death
7. Other (inadequate shelter or clothing, lack of education, harassment, rape)

The fear of being sold down the river was particularly terrifying for slaves in Kentucky, as was the fear of being beaten, which was common to all. Blassingame (1979:295–298) suggested that physical abuse from masters and being sold away from the family were the greatest fears of all slaves. The remainder of risks also posed serious threats to the slaves.

It is obvious that slaves in the Upland South perceived risks to their existence. How slave women may have functioned within their gender roles to manage or minimize these risks would lead to a much greater understanding of how African American culture operated in the antebellum period. Wiessner (1982) outlined a number of general strategies for reducing risk that are applicable to diverse groups in a variety of situations from hunter-gatherers to agriculturalists. One strategy involves pooling risk by sharing, or generalized reciprocity, often through gifting. Giving gifts, especially nonfood items, is a way of symbolically extending and strengthening family ties or kinship bonds. Such a strategy has been documented among the !Kung San (Wiessner 1982) and the Basarwa (Cashdan 1985), among others. This same strategy was described by Stack (1974) and Aschenbrenner (1973) in twentieth-century black ghetto communities.

For the antebellum period, Webber's (1978:158) study illustrates how "family" became synonymous with "slave community" in socializing children and meeting the basic needs of the members of that slave community. According to Webber (66–68), relationships with nonkin were established, or created, by reciprocal obligations. These quasi-familial relationships often extended off the plantation as well. Many of the helping characteristics described in various studies are viewed as African in origin (Foster 1983; McDaniel 1990; Sudarkasa 1980, 1981) and probably existed on many plantations and farms throughout the South. Further, the activities of raising children and providing goods and services usually involved women and resulted in feelings of solidarity within slave populations. Family and community solidarity were the slaves' best defense against racial, economic, and political oppression, because by standing together African Americans could successfully resist pressures from the dominant white society (Blassingame 1979:315–317).

Oxmoor Plantation and Enslaved Women in the Public Domain

Oxmoor is located in eastern Jefferson County, Kentucky, just outside Louisville. This part of the county contains the best agricultural land, and most of the largest slaveholdings were located there rather than in the western and southern districts of the county. Oxmoor was built in the late eighteenth century and operated as a hemp plantation by the Bullitt family. It continues to be owned and operated by the same family today. The mansion house is still occupied by the Bullitts. Several former slave houses built in the 1840s are also still standing and occupied by retired black employees of Oxmoor. Other surviving antebellum structures include a detached kitchen, a smokehouse, an icehouse, an overseer's house, a springhouse, and a slave kitchen. The slave kitchen (now a pool house and art studio) is a double-pen brick structure. The pen with the very large hearth probably served as the kitchen, while the other side probably served as the cook's residence (Young 1997b).

The Bullitt family recently moved their extensive collection of personal documents to the Filson Club in Louisville. These documents, uncataloged and disorganized, fill more than twenty, four-drawer file cabinets plus uncounted cardboard boxes. The documents span the time from the 1770s until the 1950s. During the summer of 1996, I spent time going through some of these documents looking for references to the slaves at Oxmoor (Young and Hudson 2000).

Oxmoor was established by Alexander Scott Bullitt and his wife, Priscilla Christian Bullitt, in 1784. The Bullitts and Christians came into the bluegrass of Kentucky from Virginia. Personal and public records, as well as a memoir written by a grandson, Thomas Walker Bullitt, reveal that hemp was the primary moneymaking crop (Bullitt 1995). According to Jefferson County tax lists, Alexander Scott Bullitt owned twenty-three slaves and about one hundred acres on Beargrass Creek at Oxmoor in 1789. The following year he was taxed on forty slaves and by 1795 he owned seventy. Tax records from 1795 until 1814 indicate that the slave population fluctuated between sixty-five and eighty. It is not known if the increase in the slave population was primarily due to purchases, inheritance, or births. Because it was quite substantial, I think the increase was due largely to purchases.

In 1810 Alexander Scott Bullitt was the second largest slave owner in Jefferson County. Thus, in the early era of statehood for Kentucky, he was master of a showplace plantation and a member of the economic and political elite in the commonwealth. In fact, he served as the first lieutenant governor of Kentucky from 1800 until 1804. The will of Alexander Scott Bullitt in 1816 mentions ninety-eight slaves by their first names. The slaves were divided among his heirs, including his second wife, Mary Churchill Bullitt, who inherited nine slaves. Children William Christian, Ann, Cuthbert, Thomas James, and Mary each inherited either seventeen or eighteen slaves.

The next master of Oxmoor was William Christian Bullitt. He and his wife, Matilda Ann Fry Bullitt, lived there from the time of his inheritance in 1816 until the Civil War, when he abandoned the plantation and moved into town. Like his father, William Christian Bullitt raised hemp, but he also grew corn and garden produce, kept cattle, and maintained horses for transportation. There is some question as to the number of slaves William Christian Bullitt owned. Thomas Walker Bullitt, his son and author of the memoir, stated that there were about one hundred slaves at Oxmoor. However, Jefferson County tax records and census data suggest that there were actually closer to fifty slaves.

The Bullitt family records, especially the personal letters written by plantation mistress Matilda Bullitt and her daughters, provide a glimpse of the roles of female domestic slaves at Oxmoor. Five slave women are prominently mentioned in letters. They are Aunt Betsy the cook, Charity, Lucinda, Beck, and Louisa, who was also called Mammy Teush.

Most of our knowledge about female slaves derives from memories of whites concerning women who served in the big house rather than as field slaves. Of all the different types of slave occupations (seamstress, cook, laundress, nurse, etc.), Mammy is the most well known. The role of Mammy has received much attention from historians and other social scientists (Fox-Genovese 1988:291–292; Genovese 1976:353–361; White 1985:46–61). Some have viewed Mammy as a myth of southern white creation. She was the ideal house slave that melded the best feminine attributes (submissive, maternal caregiver) with the best slave attributes (loyalty) (Fox-Genovese 1988:291–292). According to this view, Mammy was (from the white perspective) completely devoted to the white family, especially the children, and was given authority over domestic chores. In many ways, Mammy was a surrogate mother and plantation mistress (White 1985). Mammy's very title is "steeped in maternal sentiment" and because of the meaning that white southerners attached to her occupation, the woman filling that role became entitled to certain traditional rights and privileges. The ways that white slave owners treated Mammy were imbued with tradition associated with mothering, thus dictating the type of relations between her and her owners.

Another, less powerful kin term sometimes applied to female slaves, especially domestic slaves, was "Aunt." Both Mammy and Aunt imply a fictive kinship, presumably associated with rights and obligations. The traditional meanings associated with Mammy and Aunt, I argue, were used or accepted by slave women to protect themselves and their children from risks and fall at one end of a continuum of traditional gendered roles filled by enslaved women in the big house.

Through excerpts from Bullitt family letters, the duties of Mammy and other female domestic slaves at Oxmoor are illustrated, as are some of the special considerations they gained from their owner. The letters also indicate how female domestic slaves attempted to utilize the traditional meanings associated with their roles and titles to reduce risk. The letters here date primarily from 1840 until 1851, although I also examined documents dating from the eighteenth and early nineteenth centuries. References in letters to Oxmoor slaves varied from very brief mentions or greetings to paragraphs or even pages describing incidents or actions by slaves.

It appears that domestic slaves at Oxmoor were more commonly female than male. Male domestic slaves were elderly. For example Uncle Billy, who lived to the ripe age of one hundred, ran errands as an elderly man in his seventies and eighties. Most of the duties of domestic slaves mentioned in letters involved cooking, cleaning, laundry, sewing, and ironing. The duties of Mammy Louisa, her daughter, Beck, and Lucinda and Charity involved house cleaning and nursing the sick. For example, one letter stated, "Louisa, Lucinda, and Beck, were determined after Josh left to rid the house of dirt." Another letter dated May 15, 1842, said, "Lucinda has made the house shine from one end to the other since you left."

The plantation mistress, Matilda Bullitt, was in charge of overseeing the domestic slaves. In 1846 she wrote: "I asked Carity [Charity] to day if she cleaned all the litter from under Mas' John's window and ordered your carpet put down." Aunt Betsy, the cook, is almost always mentioned with reference to kitchen duties and never as having other chores. In a letter from Matilda Bullitt to her son in 1846, she explains: "Betsy has done her best on the ham which she wishes gone, as she is weary of hearing that this ham must be baked particularly well as it is for Mas' John." When Aunt Betsy was sick, the Bullitt family had other slaves in the kitchen. A letter from Susan Bullitt (Matilda

Bullitt's daughter) to her brother in 1849 described that "father is at home and with aunt Dinah's assistance nurses mother . . . We have Rose & Armstead to cook for us as aunt Betsy is sick, & they get along famously together—quarrel of course at a grand rate."

Duties of female domestic slaves were not confined to cleaning, cooking, and laundry. In 1851 Matilda Bullitt described that she "made Lucinda paint the porch floor yesterday, & it looks very nice." In 1842 Matilda Bullitt wrote that her two-year-old son "James is fairly weaned from Beck as a nurse."

Caring for the sick and injured seems to have occupied quite a bit of time, in addition to cleaning and cooking. Although enslaved women were most often nurses, male slaves were sometimes employed to nurse the sick if all female domestics were ill. Matilda Bullitt and Mammy Teush (Louisa) appear to have spent a great deal of time nursing Louisa's son Smith. A letter dated February 3, 1847, stated that "mother has continued her labors of attending to and nursing the sick—poor little Smith, Teush's youngest, seems to be at the point of death—he has been lingering thus for five or six weeks." A few weeks later, Matilda Bullitt wrote: "Poor Smith has left me busy in mind & body for the last month or more; indeed Louisa & I have done little else than nurse him for the last eight weeks. We now have strong hopes for his recovery, altho he is by no means out of danger; but for the most vigilant nursing he must have died a long time since. Louisa has frequently urged me to let him alone, that he might die in peace."

A little later that year, Matilda Bullitt wrote: "Nursing it seems, is to be my employment for the rest of my days. You know the servants have kept me busy . . . Mary commenced bleeding from her lungs . . . & lingered until yesterday morning . . . Smith will soon follow Mary. Louisa has had a hard time since you were here." Smith did not die immediately. He was ill again (or still an invalid) in 1850.

The work in and around the big house was sometimes difficult and stressful. The labor, however, seems to have been associated with special privileges or rights. For example, a letter dated 1841 illustrates not only the special place domestic slaves occupied in the Oxmoor big house but also the extent of the privileges that Mammy Louisa felt she deserved.

> I have been busy lately making a wedding dress; Becky is to be married on the 27th day of this month. I suspect she will have a very fine wedding; Teush wanted me to write invitations to all the company; but I rather thought it would be a burlesque on fashion to be writing

invitations to people that couldn't read, so we gave that up. Teush
wants you & brother Josh to be specially invited to the "wedding."
I suspect it will make almost as much fuss as Sally's [friend of the
Bullitt family daughters].

Following the wedding, a letter dated January 17, 1842, described "Beck was
married in the holidays & as *they* thought looked very beautiful, & had quite
a handsome entertainment, & a select company. Cynthia & Martha [Bullitt's
daughter] presided at the brides toilette, & arranged the table; every thing
went off to their satisfaction with the exception of a disappointment in the
brides cake." There were other slave weddings at Oxmoor at the same time as
Beck's. These did not seem to garner the same attention in the big house, reinforcing my interpretation that Mammy Teush, and perhaps her daughter Beck,
earned special consideration from the Bullitts. One of Matilda Bullitt's daughters wrote to her brother John on January 25, 1842, that "I suppose sister & the
papers have told you all the news: about Becky and Harry Howard, Aunt Betsy
and Uncle Jack, Caroline and Ben all being married. These are all the marriages among the blackies that I know of; and now for the white folks. . . . "

The descriptions about preparations for Beck's wedding and the party
afterward seem to illustrate that some negotiation of rights and obligation
between Louisa and the Bullitt family occurred. Relations seem to be rather
tightly balanced. It is interesting, too, that sometimes the kinship terms Aunt
or Mammy are used and at other times they are omitted. In the passage about
all the slave weddings, it may also be significant that Aunt Betsy's wedding to
Uncle Jack received so little attention from the Bullitts because Betsy was
their cook. Caroline was also a cook, but she probably worked in the slave
kitchen rather than the Bullitt kitchen.

Concerning Beck's wedding, the Bullitt family seemed obliged to provide
a dress, food, and possibly entertainment. However, they did not seem ready
to recognize this as a legitimate wedding since the term was placed within
quotation marks.

Louisa, or Mammy Teush, apparently earned a very special place within
the Bullitt family. An 1846 letter illustrates this: "Mammy, Cousin Annie
Blair, mother and I went inside the carriage; Daniel & black Harry were on
the box." John Christian Bullitt invited Mammy Louisa for a visit in Philadelphia. Louisa replied through a letter to John from his sister. "I have just rec'd
your letter, and must give you Teush's answer to your message. She says she
will certainly come to see you if the abolitionists don't steal her." Evidently

Louisa felt she had some choice as to whether she would make the journey to Pennsylvania. She could have refused and strengthened her refusal with fears concerning abolitionists. Nevertheless, Louisa's answer seems to fall into the category of a calculated move to demonstrate loyalty to the family.

In many ways, Mammy Teush seemed to have assumed the role of a mother when she communicated through others' letters. One of the Bullitt girls wrote in 1840 that "'Teush' (you know she is an oracle of wisdom) says I have the air of a very fashionable lady." In an 1846 letter, a Bullitt girl wrote, "Teush has just been in here, giving me a discourse on various subjects; she says 'tell Mas John to make haste & get married.'"

The most obvious attempt to influence future events is illustrated by Beck's actions. In 1846 Beck communicated via a letter from Matilda Bullitt to her son. "Beck asked me to let you know she has a fine little waiting maid for you. She insists on it her children must all belong to you." Probably knowing that the death of the master of Oxmoor might well result in splitting up families, Beck attempted to control where her children might go. If successful, it meant that all her children would remain together, and likely in predictable circumstances. If for some reason Beck's children went to John Christian Bullitt and she remained at Oxmoor, she knew she would not completely lose touch. When Beck's daughter Dolly, mentioned above as a possible waiting maid, became older, she was taken into the big house by Matilda Bullitt to begin her training as a domestic. A letter dated January 1847 from Matilda Bullitt to her son John Christian Bullitt states, "I have taken Dolly in the house she displays as many airs & graces as she did in the dance. Beck says after a while she can furnish you with an office boy."

The traditional meanings associated with female domestic slaves, especially those associated with Mammy, resulted in a limited but possibly significant source of power that enslaved women employed to protect themselves and their children. It is obvious that Mammy Teush was trying to attain more for her daughter Beck's wedding. Beck was obviously reminding her owner of those traditional rights and obligations when she informed John Christian Bullitt that he owned all her children. Slave women working in and around the big house used opportunities to ease their situations and must have been presented with opportunities to minimize risk or make material gains, only a small sample of which may have been recorded in family letters.

It appears that female domestic slaves, at least Lucinda, Charity, and Beck, had their own houses. A letter dated 1846 states, "The field back of

Lucinda's house is in preparation for hemp, part of which is sown." In 1850 a letter described that "Charity lifted a heavy something, & is in her quarters." And in 1851 a letter stated, "The hands are cutting wheat in the field back of Beck's house." Mammy Louisa may have lived in the big house. Aunt Betsy's house was not mentioned in letters I examined, but she and her husband and children may have lived in or above the kitchen. Interestingly, none of the letters that I examined referred to slave houses as belonging to a male slave. This point needs further exploration in other sources.

The tone of the Bullitt letters seems to indicate that Mammy Teush, Beck, and others used the traditional meanings associated with gendered kin/occupational terms they were assigned by the Bullitts to remind their owners of reciprocal obligations. Slave women used the power they gained from these roles to protect themselves and their family and to ensure the security or happiness of children. The terms *Mammy* and *Aunt* were imbued with tradition and history, and the slave women at Oxmoor used this when they could to control over where their children might reside and the kind of occupation their children assumed on the plantation. The same power may have been used to protect the entire slave community.

The roles of female domestic slaves do not necessarily reflect how these women acted within the slave community. Rather, the roles of Mammy Louisa, Aunt Betsy, and others must be viewed as personae displayed to the white slave owning family in the public domain. When they retired to the slave quarters for the night or in old age, their roles vis-à-vis the slave community was probably different. When Lucinda and Beck went home to their quarters, they may have switched roles from female domestics to some other persona, much as individuals switch dialect or vocabulary as the situation demands. How did enslaved women operate within their private domain in the quarters, and were they able to reduce risk at home? These questions are addressed with data from Locust Grove plantation in Kentucky.

Locust Grove and the Private Domain

Like Oxmoor, Locust Grove is located in eastern Jefferson County, Kentucky, just outside Louisville. It was established in the late 1780s by William Croghan and his wife, Lucy Clark Croghan. The Croghan and the Clark families moved to Jefferson County from Virginia. Locust Grove was a diversified plantation and was large relative to most other farms in the area. There were forty slaves living and working at Locust Grove when William Croghan died in 1822.

The eldest son of William Croghan, Dr. John Croghan was the master of Locust Grove from 1835 until 1849, when he died of consumption. Not only did John Croghan have a substantial slave population at Locust Grove during his tenure (usually around twenty slaves), he also owned extensive properties around Kentucky, including Mammoth Cave. One of the famous slave guides at Mammoth Cave was married to an enslaved woman at Locust Grove. This sort of "abroad marriage," where each spouse lived on different properties, was fairly common in Kentucky since most slaveholdings were too small to offer a chance of finding a mate. Because of this pattern of exogamy, as well as the traditional association of females with child rearing and other house-keeping activities in American and African cultures, maintenance and organization of the household may well have fallen to the women.

Three seasons of archaeological excavations at Locust Grove from 1987 through 1989 uncovered the remains of three single-pen slave houses (Map 5.2). The south and central houses were constructed between 1780 and 1800 and dismantled around the time of the Civil War (Young 1995; Young et al. 1998). The north house was probably constructed around 1820 and it was occupied until the 1920s. Each house excavation resulted in large ceramic assemblages and other domestic artifacts (Young 1997a).

The documentary record of Locust Grove is infuriatingly silent regarding the slaves who lived there. Other than tax lists and census data, there is virtually no record of their everyday lives. Slaves were mentioned only twelve times in more than two hundred letters among the surviving family documents (Young 1995). How slaves coped with the risks they faced is not readily apparent from the documentary record. The three field seasons, however, provide archaeological data that can be brought to bear on this issue.

Evidence from the archaeological record suggests that slaves at Locust Grove lived in at least three households; each of the three slave houses contained a family. Each family may have been extended or conjugal. I suggest that these families sought to create ties with each other and with other families on neighboring farms and plantations and with slave and free black families in the town of Louisville. Kinship ties, unfortunately, are difficult to detect archaeologically; however, items like decorated ceramics, glassware, and buttons obtained in matched sets might be used to track how artifacts were distributed across the plantation and may reflect gifting. Matched items in

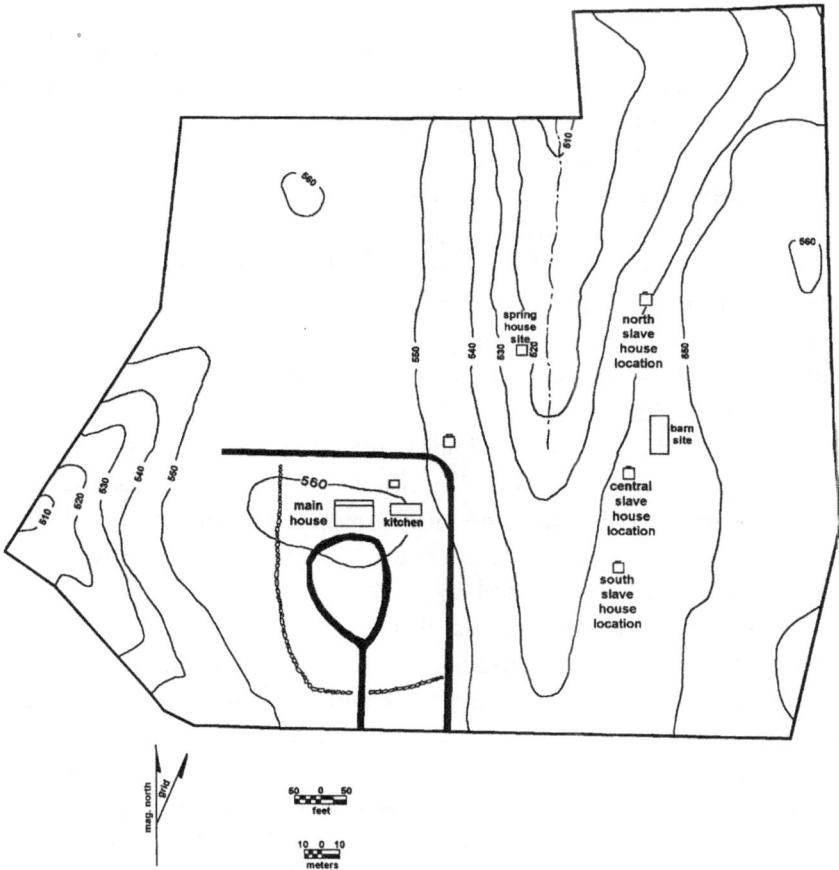

MAP 5.2.   Layout of antebellum Locust Grove Plantation.

ceramics and other artifacts not resulting from cross-mending or resulting from hand-me-downs from the main house may indicate that these objects were shared among slave families on the plantations.

The analysis of ceramics from the three slave houses was accomplished in a series of steps. First, a type collection of decorated ceramics and other items was constructed for each slave house. From the south house, a total of 199 different decorative patterns were identified. From the central house, 123 additional decorative types were identified. The analysis of ceramics from the north house identified only 40 additional decorative types. The planter's house assemblage consisted of 130 types, 14 of which were matched in the three slave house assemblages and removed from the sample. Each decorated ceramic sherd was compared carefully to the type collections from the other slave houses and from the main house. Only exact matches were recorded. Vessel form (plate, saucer, etc.) was also recorded for each ceramic sherd in the assemblages.

The result of the analysis of decorated ceramics was that thirty-two different ceramic types were shared among the slave families at Locust Grove. The south and central households shared twenty different ceramic types, the south and north households shared seven, and the central and north households shared five ceramic decorative types. When vessel forms were added into the analysis, it was not uncommon to find one decorative pattern on a whiteware or pearlware teacup from one house and matching decoration on a saucer from a different house.

Analysis of glass tableware did not result in any identifiable patterns that would indicate sharing or gifting. The glass tableware assemblages from each of the three slave houses were quite small. However, button analysis did reveal a match. A single blue transfer printed (calico) milk glass button was recovered from each of the three slave house sites.

The data presented here suggest that some amount of sharing or gifting of nonfood items may have transpired between slave families at Locust Grove. It is possible that food accompanied the ceramics in gift-giving activities. It is probably significant that the matched objects are considered luxury items by archaeologists. Often these kinds of artifacts are used to illustrate socioeconomic status of slave households (see especially Adams and Boling 1989). Sharing of these items, however, suggest that such "luxury" objects may have had different meanings for African American women (Singleton 1995:128). It might not have been important to have a matching tea set; rather, a saucer from a friend or family member symbolizing the reciprocal obligations may have been significant. Other studies of gifting, especially hxaro beads among the !Kung San (Wiessner 1982), illustrate that gifts are symbolic and useful in a social context. For the African American slaves at Locust Grove, the gifts of plates or teacups, rather than being viewed as high economic status items, could have been seen as objects used and appreciated in friendly social contexts in the quarters and symbolic of the reciprocal bonds between slave households and families.

The extension of bonds of kinship outside the immediate conjugal family would have been particularly important to slaves in Kentucky because of the apparent high risk of being sold down the river. In the event that a parent (either mother or father) was sold away, and the child or children kept behind, strong bonds of kinship outside the immediate household would help ensure the future of dependent offspring robbed of biological parents. Thus part of the importance of clothing exchange for children was to symbolically state an obligation to another person's child. Further, when faced with being overworked, driven too hard, or beaten, a reaction from the entire community would have been difficult for the slave owner to withstand. Finally, emotional support from within the community during life crises like birth, illness, and death would have been particularly important to a group of people often denied access to comforts of a formal church and professional medical care.

Conclusion

At Oxmoor Plantation, the documentary record in the form of private family letters written primarily by the plantation mistress, provides data concerning the lives of domestic slaves in the big house. Mammy Louisa, her daughter Beck, Caroline, Lucinda, and Charity worked in the mansion in the service of their white owners. Their owners, the Bullitts, perceived and treated these women in ways that reflected their ideas and ideals about the roles of black women. Occasionally, the Bullitts referred to these women with kinship terms such as *Mammy* and *Aunt*. These kinship terms helped define the behavior by the slaves and between the enslaved women and their owners. Within the roles created in part by the slave owners, these women found ways to operate for their own purposes and perhaps protect and provide for their families.

At Locust Grove, the documentary record is nearly silent about the forty slaves who lived and labored there. However, extensive archaeological excavations of three slave houses provided information about slave households. Analysis of decorated ceramics suggests that some amount of sharing or gifting took place between the households and may have operated within the slave community to create and promote solidarity within the quarters. This sharing or gifting was likely the domain of women. Solidarity in the slave quarters would have helped to protect individuals during times of stress such as illness, beatings, or threats of being sold down the river.

Enslaved women had gendered roles in the big house and gendered roles within the slave community. As they moved from the big house to the quarters, their roles switched, much as individuals code-switch in their conversations throughout the day. The relative importance (or visibility) of the role in the big house may not have correlated with the relative status of the woman within the slave community. Both types of gender roles, however, structured the lives of slave women. More important, through these gendered personae, women sought ways to protect their families from the brutality of slavery and create solidarity within the slave community. If it is true that slave women provided necessary structure and cohesiveness to the slave community through their actions and interactions with each other, then, indeed, "the jobs and services performed by slave women for the community were not peripheral but central to slave survival" (White 1985:22).

ACKNOWLEDGMENTS

I am grateful to the Filson Club and Jim Holmberg for providing me with an opportunity to examine the Bullitt family records. I am indebted to Dr. Blaine Hudson for his assistance in this project. Mrs. Bullitt kindly provided access to the documents and to her property. The project was funded by the Kentucky Heritage Council and the University of Southern Mississippi. Dave Pollack, Charles Faulkner, Gail Brockman, Zaynab Reilly, Jay Stottman, Berle Clay, Nick Young, and Philip Carr all provided wonderful help. Thanks to our writers' group of Amy Chasteen, Misty Jaffe, David Hunt, Ann Marie Kinnell, Carolyn Ware, and Shana Walton for their terrific and numerous comments on many versions of this chapter.

REFERENCES

Adams, William H., and Sarah J. Boling
    1989   Status and Ceramics for Planters and Slaves on Three Georgia
            Coastal Plantations. *Historical Archaeology* 24(4):69–96.
Aschenbrenner, Joyce
    1973   Extended Families among Black Americans. *Journal of Comparative
            Family Studies* 4:257–268.
Blassingame, John
    1979   *The Slave Community: Plantation Life in the Antebellum South.*
            Rev. ed. Oxford Univ. Press, New York.
Bullitt, Thomas Walker
    1995   *My Life at Oxmoor: Life on a Kentucky Farm before the War.* Privately
            printed, Louisville, Ky.

Cashdan, Elizabeth
 1985 Coping with Risk: Reciprocity among the Basarwa of Northern
   Botswana. *Man*, n.s., 20:454–474.

Duranti, Alessandro
 1992 Language in Context and Language as Context: The Samoan
   Respect Vocabulary. In *Rethinking Context: Language as an Inter-*
   active Phenomenon, edited by Alessandro Duranti and Charles
   Goodwin, pp. 77–97. Cambridge Univ. Press, Cambridge.

Foster, H. J.
 1983 African Patterns in the Afro-American Family. *Journal of Black*
   Studies 14(2):201–232.

Fox-Genovese, Elizabeth
 1988 *Within the Plantation Household: Black and White Women of the*
   Old South. Univ. of North Carolina Press, Chapel Hill.

Genovese, Eugene
 1976 *Roll, Jordan, Roll: The World the Slaves Made*. Random House,
   New York.

Hurston, Zora Neale
 1990 *Mules and Men*. Harper and Row, New York. Originally published
   1935 by J. B. Lippincott, Inc., Philadelphia.

McDaniel, Antonio
 1990 The Power of Culture: A Review of the Idea of Africa's Influence on
   Family Structure in Antebellum America. *Journal of Family History*
   15(2):225–238.

Ochs, Elinor
 1992 Indexing Gender. In *Rethinking Context: Language as an Interactive*
   Phenomenon, edited by Alessandro Duranti and Charles Goodwin,
   pp. 335–355. Cambridge Univ. Press, Cambridge.

Singleton, Theresa A.
 1995 The Archaeology of Slavery in North America. *Annual Review of*
   Anthropology 24:119–140.

Stack, Carol
 1974 *All Our Kin: Strategies for Survival in a Black Community*. Harper
   and Row, New York.

Sudarkasa, Niara
 1980 African and Afro-American Family Structure: A Comparison.
   Black Scholar 11(8):37–60.
 1981 Interpreting the African Heritage in Afro-American Family Organization. In *Black Families*, edited by Harriet McAdoo, pp. 37–53.
   Sage, Beverly Hills.

Webber, Thomas L.
  1978   *Deep Like the Rivers: Education in the Slave Quarter Community,
          1831–1865.* W. W. Norton, New York.
Wiessner, Polly
  1982   Risk, Reciprocity, and Social Influence on Kung San Economics.
          In *Politics and History in Band Societies,* edited by E. Leacock and
          R. Lee, pp. 61–84. Cambridge Univ. Press, Cambridge.
White, Deborah G.
  1985   *Ar'n't I a Woman? Female Slaves in the Plantation South.* W. W.
          Norton, New York.
Young, Amy L.
  1995   *Risk and Material Conditions of African American Slaves at Locust
          Grove: An Archaeological Perspective.* Ph.D. diss., Dept. of Anthro-
          pology, Univ. of Tennessee, Knoxville.
  1997a   Risk Management Strategies among African American Slaves at
          Locust Grove Plantation. *International Journal of Historical Archae-
          ology* 1:5–37.
  1997b   *Historical and Archaeological Investigations of Slaves and Slavery at
          Oxmoor Plantation.* Report submitted to the Kentucky Heritage
          Council, Frankfort, Ky.
Young, Amy L., and J. Blaine Hudson
  2000   Slave Life at Oxmoor. *The Filson Club History Quarterly*
          74(3):189–219.
Young, Amy L., Philip J. Carr, and Joseph E. Granger
  1998   How Historical Archaeology Works: A Case Study of Slave Houses
          at Locust Grove. *Kentucky Register* 96(2):167–194.

CHAPTER 6

Engendering Enslaved Communities on Virginia's and North Carolina's Eighteenth- and Nineteenth-Century Plantations

PATRICIA SAMFORD

A West African heritage was only one of a multitude of factors that affected an enslaved individual's sense of self and place within his or her world. Age, gender, marital status, occupation, and other components affected individuals' roles both within their immediate communities and the larger societies of which they were a part. The factors that create an individual's identity are complex. For example, a person can act as a parent in one instant and as a son or daughter in the next. Identities are not static but change innumerable times for any given person as they pass through life. Just as an individual assumes many roles and identities through the span of a lifetime of experiences, so too will there have been transformations between gendered roles on the different sides of the Atlantic. My intent is not to suggest that gender roles in West Africa and Virginia were identical; on the contrary, gender systems are variable and non-static (Wylie 1991). Instead, I propose that people drew upon their past experiences in forging new roles and communities for themselves, preserving cultural values "even in the midst of change" (Yentsch 1994:197).

Although the character of documentation complicates any study of enslaved peoples, investigating enslaved women is particularly difficult due to the double invisibility of race and gender (Kehoe 1992; White 1985). White colonial American views of women's subordinate status, for example, ensured that females were much less likely to be represented in the written documents than their male counterparts. Women's activities, generally hidden and often filtered through a male perspective, must be teased out of the documentary and archaeological evidence.

Cultures in Context

While there were many different West and Central African cultures whose members were enslaved in Virginia and North Carolina, I focus here on one West African society, the Igbo, who lived in the eighteenth century in what is present-day Nigeria. Nearly 50 percent of all African slaves arriving at Port York (located on the York River near Williamsburg) during two heavy importation periods in the early eighteenth century were from the Nigerian tribes of the Igbo, Ibibio, Efkins, and Mokos (Anstey 1975; Chambers 1996; Curtin 1969). I chose to focus on the Igbo for several reasons. First, the quality of the documentary and archaeological information on the Igbo is more detailed than for any of the other three groups. Additionally, colonial Virginia documents mention slave individuals of Igbo origin more than for any other group. Since much of the initial settlement of northeastern North Carolina was by Virginians, who brought their slaves with them (Kay and Cary 1995), grouping these two states is appropriate.

What was the nature of gender differences in Igbo culture just prior to and at the time of the European slave trade? Ethnohistoric and ethnographic sources reveal that, while there was certainly overlap between the spheres of men's and women's activities, there were substantial differences based on gender, both past and present (Afigbo 1981; Amadiume 1987; Gates 1987; Oramasionwu 1994).

At the time of the European slave trade,[1] the Igbo formed a stateless society characterized by small-scale social units with limited and localized concentrations of authority (Horton 1972). Their economy was based in agriculture, supplemented by hunting and fishing (Oguagha and Okpoko 1984). The development of their small-scale social and political organization was due, in large part, to a combination of their agricultural subsistence and the forest environment in which they lived. Since the scale at which land could be administered in the forest was limited, village settlements with descent-based political structures became the most effective unit of Igbo sociopolitical organization. These political systems were based on family and extended family units, linked by the spirits of deceased ancestors (Davidson 1977). A family unit, comprised of a man, his wives, children, and married sons and their families, resided in compounds of two to seven houses (Oramasionwu 1994:28). Ancestors, the spirits of deceased family members, were significant members of the extended family. Both men and women constructed ancestor shrines and regularly consulted ancestors for guidance and support (Gates 1987:15; Henderson 1972:169; McCall 1995:260).

Political authority was dispersed among a variety of organizational units, and since the precolonial Igbo operated under a dual-sex political system, there were organizations for both men and women (Okonjo 1976). Women formed powerful organized groups that settled marriage disputes and were in charge of death rituals (Achebe 1959:110; Isichei 1978; Oramasionwu 1994:37). They imposed fines on defaulting lineage members and were in charge of keeping the market and springs clean (Oramasionwu 1994:36). As in many other West African cultures, women in precolonial Igbo society were not marginalized as women have been in some Western cultures (Amadiume 1987, 1997; Paulme 1963). While a clear sexual division of labor existed, men and women's roles were seen as complementary.

When Igbos were forcibly removed from their native land and brought into Virginia and North Carolina, what were the economic, political, and social conditions of the culture they entered as enslaved individuals? Because the English and other European who settled in the American South were from literate societies, the eighteenth-century contexts for Virginia and North Carolina are much better understood than that of West Africa. The breadth and depth of the documentary records, examined exhaustively by historians and other scholars over the past hundred years, have made Virginia and North Carolina among the most studied of the American colonies.

During the eighteenth century, the tobacco economy that fueled the development of the Virginia colony began to give way to a new agricultural base of wheat and corn (Breen 1985; Kulikoff 1986; Menard 1980). Eighteenth-century Virginia Tidewater was characterized primarily by landowners farming small tracts with the assistance of a few enslaved individuals (Walsh 1997:14). Despite the numbers of small landholders, however, Virginia society, politics, and economics were under the control of a minority, the gentry landholders. Virginia society had gone from a relatively egalitarian society in the early seventeenth century to an increasingly hierarchical one beginning later in the century (Kulikoff 1986:4; McCartney 1997:88). The dominance of the egalitarian system had been supported by the steady supply of indentured labor, and with its disappearance and the growing reliance on African labor, the stage was set for the development of a new gentry class (Kulikoff 1986:37). These wealthy planters, descendants of some of the region's early settlers who prospered and gained political power, inherited land and labor wealth. At the turn of the eighteenth century, two-thirds of the land was owned by the wealthiest 5 percent of the population (Blackburn 1997:359). The elevated positions of the gentry allowed them to purchase additional labor and make improvements to their properties, as well as garner political power of their own (Kulikoff 1986).

Unlike Virginia, the North Carolina colony did not experience large-scale settlement during the seventeenth century, and the colony's economy varied more by region during the eighteenth century. While some planters experimented with rice in the southeastern part of the state, the primary export for the first-settled eastern regions was naval stores (Kay and Cary 1995). Lumber, tobacco, corn, wheat, and livestock were also important products for export to other colonies. The North Carolina piedmont began to be settled in the 1730s by individuals relocating from the eastern part of the state and by settlers from northern colonies like Maryland and Pennsylvania (Kay and Cary 1995). The North Carolina evidence presented in this chapter comes primarily from the northeastern region of the state, where it was more likely that slaves brought overland from Virginia would have been settled.

Enslaved people of African descent performed much of the labor for the production of these crops on gentry-owned plantations in Virginia and North Carolina. Although some individuals were housed in outbuildings constructed for other purposes, the enslaved predominantly lived in settlements or compounds adjacent to agricultural fields called quarters. During the eighteenth century, more than half of the enslaved on Virginia's middle and lower peninsulas lived on quarters with fewer than twenty slaves (Morgan 1998:41). It was on large plantations, like those properties whose quarter sites are used in this study, that local slave communities and community-based identities formed in the eighteenth century (Kulikoff 1986; Lee 1986; Sidbury 1997). I argue that multigenerational groups of extended families residing in quarter compounds bore basic similarities to Igbo kin-based societies and villages in West Africa.

While much of the American evidence presented here is derived from documentary sources, archaeological data from a number of gentry-owned plantations were also incorporated. The sites include seven Tidewater Virginia quarters located on the peninsula that lies between the James and York Rivers. They consisted of three quarters at Kingsmill Plantation's Utopia (Fesler 1998): the quarter at Carter's Grove Plantation (Kelso and Frank 1972), the Rich Neck Quarter (Franklin 1997), and Kingsmill Quarter (Kelso 1984). The occupation ranges of the seven sites ranged from the early eighteenth century to the first quarter of the following century. Late eighteenth- and early nineteenth-century quarters at Monticello (Sanford 1991) and Poplar Forest (Heath 1994) represent the Virginia Piedmont region. The North Carolina sites discussed here include Somerset Place, a nineteenth-century plantation in the northeastern part of the state (Steen 1995) and an eighteenth-century quarter located on the Eden House site, outside of Edenton (Lautzenheiser et al. 1998).

Men's and Women's Roles in Work

The primary economic activity for the Igbo was farming, and both men and women played critical, although differing, roles in agriculture. Yam and coco-yam were the two most important crops produced by the Igbo. Yams were viewed as male, and men controlled all aspects of the production and distribu-tion of this ritually important crop (Afigbo 1981:124; Amadiume 1987:29, 35). Women, on the other hand, were in charge of producing the "female" crops that formed the primary dietary staples, such as cocoyam, cassava, and plan-tain, as well as all other vegetables (Anyanwu 1976). Women had access to two types of land: garden land near the back of the compound and farmland either near compounds or on village outskirts (Amadiume 1987:34). Men and women both worked the farmlands where the major crops were grown. Men were in charge of the initial planting and later harvesting, while the daily job of tend-ing all crops fell to women. In the eighteenth century, women also helped men till the land and plant the crops (Gates 1987:14).

While men and women shared the products of the farmland, the gardens, where subsidiary crops such as melons and maize were grown, were exclusively a female domain, from the initial planting to the distribution of the crops. These garden plots were named for the ancestral women who originally farmed them, and these ancestral ties determined who had access to the land and controlled the distribution of agricultural products (McCall 1995:259–260). Women's work was critical for the maintenance of the family, and they derived power and distinction from successfully controlling and managing these crops (Amadiume 1987:30).

Raising and selling livestock, dogs, and fowl, as well as craft production, were additional sources of wealth for women (Achebe 1959:14; Amadiume 1987:31; Uchendu 1980). According to the memoirs of an eighteenth-century Igbo, Olaudah Equiano, Igbo women produced cloth, pottery, and tobacco pipes (Gates 1987). Since pottery was used both for household and ritual purposes, it formed an important female-controlled industry (Afigbo 1981:172; Anyanwu 1976:51). Although women were in charge of the subsistence economy, men traditionally owned and allocated the property upon which these crops were grown. Men's work included clearing bush and constructing house compounds, which were named after the men who cleared the land and established the space as a homestead (McCall 1995:259).[2] Men held a monopoly over ritual knowledge, craft specialization (such as blacksmithing) and external relations (Amadiume 1987:30). Men made baskets, trapped animals, crafted items of iron and wood, and tapped palm trees for wine production (Anyanwu 1976:139).

In the American South, both men and women worked as domestics and in the agricultural fields of the larger plantation, but here I am only considering work done during off times by the enslaved for the benefit of themselves and their families. For the enslaved, the short span of hours when they could work for themselves was surely the most important part of their day. Some of the avenues by which the enslaved could economically and physically benefit their families and communities included raising vegetables and poultry, hunting, fishing, or trapping, and crafting household items or tools. These activities would produce products that could be consumed, traded for other goods, or sold for cash.

Plantation account books and travelers' journals tell us that people enslaved in Virginia had personal gardens. In 1774 Philip Fithian noted the enslaved "digging up their small Lots of ground . . . for Potatoes, peas &c.," and Jefferson wrote of the enslaved at Monticello growing sweet potatoes (Fithian 1943:128). Because such documentation is relatively rare, archaeology assumes a special significance in the search for these gardens. Excavations around quarters where the enslaved lived have provided several types of evidence of those gardens. Although no planting beds or other distinctive garden features have been found, archaeological evidence consists of fenced or ditched enclosures where gardens could be kept safely out of the reach of free-ranging livestock and other animals. The early-eighteenth-century component at Utopia had a fenced enclosure between two of the quarter's three dwellings (Fesler 1998). At the late-eighteenth- and early-nineteenth-century quarters at Poplar Forest, Kingsmill, and Carter's Grove Plantation, there were traces of small fenced enclosures adjacent to the houses, where chickens were kept or gardens planted (Heath and Moncure 1998; Kelso 1984; Samford 1996). The mid-eighteenth-century component of the Utopia Quarter (44JC32) included a ditch feature adjacent to one dwelling that suggested the presence of a similar enclosure (Fesler 1998).

Even on sites with no traces of garden enclosures, plant remains were other tangible forms of gardening evidence at the quarters. At Utopia, the charred seeds from plants that may have been grown there included beans and corn, as well as peach pits and walnut shells (Fesler, personal communication, 1997). At Williamsburg's Rich Neck Quarter, ethnobotanical analysis showed sixteen different types of charred seeds in the household refuse, including cowpeas, squash, and lima beans (Franklin 1997; Mrozowski and Driscoll 1997).[3] Monticello's Mulberry Row assemblages included seeds from melons, beans, peaches, and chestnuts, and at Poplar Forest Quarter there was evidence of raspberries, cherries, peaches, huckleberries, persimmons, grapes, sunflowers, beans, corn, and wheat (Heath and Moncure 1998; Monticello Dept. of Archaeology 1997). While some of these foods were probably eaten fresh to supplement planter-supplied rations and add variety to the diet, some vegetables were also stored in subfloor pits for use during the winter months. Documentary evidence from early-nineteenth-century Virginia and North Carolina indicates that sweet potatoes were stored in subfloor pits (Douglass 1855; Singleton 1999; Washington 1965). Pollen and phytolith evidence from a hearth front subfloor pit at Utopia Quarter suggests that sweet potatoes or corn were stored in the pit, with grasses used as a lining or packing material for the food (Samford 2000).

Does documentary evidence suggest which members of the enslaved community were involved in gardening? Unfortunately, eighteenth-century observers of slave gardens neglected to reveal whether men or women were predominantly involved in cultivating the gardens, but interviews with former Virginia slaves born in the 1830s and 1840s mention only women in reference to gardening activities (Perdue et al. 1980:245, 311).

It may be possible to draw some parallels between food production in Igboland, Virginia, and North Carolina. Yams (*Dioscorea rotundata*), the main staple crop for the Igbo, are very similar to the American sweet potato (*Ipomoea batatas*). Chambers (1996), in his study on Virginia, argues that the use of subfloor pits as a storage area for this crop is an adaptation that can be tied to the prevalence of people of Igbo descent there. The sweet potato, a good source of vitamins, was adopted in Virginia and other parts of the upper South as a dietary staple by the enslaved.

It is interesting to postulate that enslaved males may have been responsible for the production of sweet potatoes, a crop closely paralleling the male-associated yam for the Igbo culture, while women worked the small subsistence gardens that contained a wider variety of crops crucial to family maintenance. While no documentary evidence has been found linking the production of sweet potatoes with males, there is a possible parallel in a Christmas tradition found only in southeastern Virginia and northeastern North Carolina. Jonkonnu appears to be a creolized tradition formed from a combination of Christian beliefs and the Igbo celebration of the New Yam harvest (Chambers 1996). In this celebration, elaborately costumed male dancers and singers would form a procession, traveling from house to house, performing for money. The celebration ended at the quarter, where dancing and singing would continue for long hours. This tradition is well documented in the mid-nineteenth century at Somerset Place, a plantation located in northeastern North Carolina (Fenn 1988). In Igbo culture, the New Yam harvest festival brings the community together in celebration of the bounty of the harvest, with feasting, drinking, and merrymaking.

In addition to supplementing diet with gardening, slaves also kept poultry at the quarters. In 1798 a visitor to Mount Vernon wrote about the quarters there, noting not only that "a very small garden planted with vegetables was close by" but also "5 or 6 hens, each one leading ten to fifteen chickens" (Niemcewicz 1965). Evidence from other excavations and plantation accounts show that tending poultry was a common slave activity. Eggshell has been found in small quantities with other food remains on quarter sites and plantation and merchant accounts record many instances of the enslaved trading eggs and poultry for other goods.[4]

Extrapolating from documents that record the economic activities of the enslaved community seems to suggest that primarily women were involved in the keeping of poultry, or at least the distribution of their products. These findings are consistent with Igbo women's activities. The poultry and their eggs were used both as provisions for feeding families and as items to barter or sell for other services or products. For example, entries in the Jane Frances Page Commonplace Book, dating between 1803 and 1806, list provisions given to enslaved Virginians on several Albemarle County plantations, as well as documenting instances of bartering between the plantation mistress and the enslaved labor force. Most of the transactions involved bartering various types of poultry for cuts of meat. Of the thirty-eight instances where gender could be determined, almost two-thirds of the transactions were by women, represented by fourteen or fifteen different individuals. This gender difference in bartering activity does not appear to be related to plantation demograph-ics, since the thirty-nine enslaved individuals listed as receiving clothing in 1804 were equally divided between males and females. Of the ten or eleven men who were recorded as bartering poultry, almost half of them were described as "old," while only three (20 percent) of the women were described in this fashion. It is interesting to posit that older men, retired from full-time work on the plantation, were spending their time in what was generally con-sidered a female enterprise.

Other than the larger number of transactions recorded in the Page Com-monplace Book, there appeared to be no significant differences in men and women's business dealings, although in several instances women traded poul-try for shawls rather than food. Meats obtained through bartering were the same cuts (bacon and middle cuts) being provisioned by the planter. These transactions suggest that the enslaved traded in order to increase meat allot-ments rather than to acquire higher quality cuts of meat. The data suggest that women, in addition to their daily work in the planter's agricultural fields, were instrumental in providing supplemental food and supplies for their fam-ilies. While the Page Commonplace Book provides a good example of a plan-tation's internal economy, it is a glimpse into just one early-nineteenth-century Virginia farm. More work with this and similar account books has been done by Ann Smart Martin (1997) and Barbara Heath (1997), and their analyses demonstrate numerous instances of the enslaved bartering and sell-ing foodstuffs and handcrafted items to planters.

Marketing and Economic Activities

Just as enslaved individuals were selling or bartering within the Virginia plan-tation economy, they were also a common presence in the local Virginia mar-kets (Heath 1997; Martin 1997). African American women were selling the products of their off-time labors—primarily eggs, chickens, and vegetables, although prepared foods and beer were also sold (Martin 1997). While the markets, with their hubbubs of noise, odors, and barnyard animals, were apparently places where women felt comfortable, perhaps venturing into the more formalized world of stores was not. Ann Martin's (1997) work with the

John Hook store slave account has shown that most accounts were held with men. Some of the men's purchases, such as sewing accessories, fabric, and ribbons, may have been purchases for women. It is unknown, however, whether these were gifts or if enslaved women requested that their male relatives or friends purchase them in their stead.

Another source that appears to corroborate the Virginia evidence for male dominance in stores is an early-nineteenth-century account book from the Mount Tizrah Plantation store in Person County, North Carolina. Between 1808 and 1810, Phillip Moore recorded numerous transactions with enslaved African Americans working on nearby plantations (Moore 1808–1810). Preliminary analysis of this account book shows that approximately 15 percent of Moore's business was with African Americans.[5] Most of the transactions noted men purchasing whiskey and brandy. Other purchases included bushels of potatoes, wheat, and corn, as well as flour by the pound. In some instances, men brought in crafted items, such as baskets, wooden tubs, and bed mats to exchange for cash. The names of twenty-five different men are listed, while only five enslaved women appeared in the account book. One of these women, Old Bess is recorded as picking up whiskey for Joe of Josiah Brown's farm, and others, such as Florence and Alise, purchased spirits for themselves.

The data in the Moore account book supplement and support the evidence from Virginia that men made up the majority of the customers in stores. Interestingly, a possible parallel can be drawn with Igbo economic activities, where much of the daily commerce occurs at local markets. The Igbo market is where a family's surplus foodstuffs, poultry, and livestock are sold. These markets play a central role in Igbo life; in addition to their economic functions, they serve as political, social, and ceremonial centers, points of communication between communities, and as arenas where the dramas of daily life are played out (Anyanwu 1976:228).

In accordance with a gender ideology that demarcates men's and women's spaces (Aniakor 1996), men are in charge of the external trade, while Igbo women maintain a monopoly on all aspects of the market (Amadiume 1987:39; Oramasionwu 1994:36; Uchendu 1980). Women do most buying and selling, both of men's and women's goods, and, in fact, the names of female ancestors constitute points of reference for distributing agricultural products (McCall 1995:260). That this degree of female power existed in the eighteenth century as well is suggested by the memories of Olaudah Equiano,[6] who remembered attending market days with his mother (Gates 1987:16). Since the market was one of the fastest ways to accumulate cash, most of a household's currency passed through female hands (Amadiume 1987:39) and gave women substantial economic power within the household and the larger family. Economic independence was a sign of status for a woman and skill in trading enhanced her desirability as a wife (Uchendu 1980:53).

Perhaps in Virginia and North Carolina, enslaved men and women viewed plantation and country stores as akin to external trade. Thus, women were less likely to transact business in stores than in the markets, an arena where women dominated in Igboland.

Family Organization

In Igboland, the household was a matricentric unit consisting of a woman and her children (Achebe 1959; Amadiume 1987, 1997), living with one or more other household units in a male-headed compound. Since the survival of each household unit was dependent upon the mother's resourcefulness and business acumen, training in farming and trading skills began early in life for girls (Uchendu 1980). A successful garden season or a surplus of poultry often made the difference in assuring the survival of the family through the lean months just prior to the yam harvesting.

In West Africa, Igbo women derived power and prestige from their wealth and ability to provide for their families. Such distinction was also most likely the case for enslaved women in the American South. Although studies over the past thirty years have demonstrated a high percentage of long-standing marriages within enslaved communities (Gutman 1976, White 1985), there were certainly many cases where spouses lived on separate quarters or plantations. In these instances, women headed households composed of themselves, their children, and often other family members. By cultivating gardens, gathering wild food plants, and raising poultry, African Americans were hedging their bets in favor of their families, supplementing the rations and supplies provided by plantation owners.

Archaeological evidence also indicates that the enslaved were hunting and trapping to add meat to the stewpot; archaeologists find gunflints and lead shot on virtually all African American sites, as well as bone from a variety of game. At the Utopia site component dated 1725–1750, the quarter inhabitants relied heavily on wild food, with the forests, rivers, and marshes around the quarter providing varied resources. Subfloor pit assemblages there contained several species of turtle, passenger pigeon, and wild mammals such as squirrel and woodchuck (Fesler 1998). Sites with ready access to major water sources also generally contain evidence (fish bone, net weights, fish hooks) that fishing was also a food-getting strategy. At Utopia Quarter, there were oyster, crab, and clamshells, and bones and scales from gar, carp, and catfish. While the documentary record is again largely silent on who was engaged in these activities, oral histories from the depression era suggest that hunting and fishing, as well as another form of dietary supplementation—that of liberating livestock from the planter's coffers—was done primarily by men (Perdue et al. 1980).

In addition to concern with their immediate kin of children, spouses, parents, and siblings, there is evidence from the nineteenth century that women formed supportive female networks that underpinned their strong group identity (Morton 1996; White 1985; see also Young, this volume). Through cooperative effort, for example, women divided childcare responsibilities and passed on knowledge and training in healing plants, cooking, and midwifery. Sometimes female knowledge and assistance took other forms. In the 1830s, Bethany Veney was separated from her baby and taken to Richmond to be sold. Using knowledge passed on to her from another enslaved woman, she was able to appear feverish and sickly on the auction block, thus attracting very little interest from potential buyers (Veney 1889). Her strategy paid off; unwilling to settle for the small price offered for Veney, the planter returned with her to Luray, Virginia, where she was able to be near her child. Doubtless there were innumerable other instances of enslaved women working together to preserve families. These support networks may have been similar to West African women's organizations that settled many community social matters (Achebe 1959; Oramasionwu 1994).

Spirituality

Evidence from historical and archaeological research shows that Africans and their descendants enslaved in the American South were slow to abandon many of their traditional African spiritual beliefs and practices. These familiar practices and beliefs, brought over aboard slave ships in the minds of the captives, provided guidance for the newly enslaved in restructuring their individual, family, and community identities under the bonds of enslavement. The archaeological evidence of West African–based spirituality in Virginia and North Carolina takes two forms: pit features cut through the clay soil under the floors of houses and spoon handles that appear to have been fashioned into objects that served religious functions.

The regular appearance of subfloor pits on slave quarters in Virginia and North Carolina suggests that their creation and use were tied to the presence of people of African descent (Fesler 1997b). Over 150 pits have been found on sixteen African American sites in Virginia alone, and they appear on sites in other states as well (Lautzenheiser at al. 1998; Samford 1996). Some slave houses contain only one or two subfloor pits, while others contain multiple pits—in some instances as many as eighteen (Kelso 1984). Archaeologists have long debated how subfloor pits were used, whether as root cellars for the preservation of fruits and vegetables, as "hidey holes" for stolen or valuable goods, or as personal storage spaces (Franklin 1997; Kelso 1984; Neiman 1997). Recent analysis suggests that they served in these capacities, as well as in a spiritual fashion (Samford 2000). Some pits contain assemblages of artifacts that bear resemblance to objects found on Igbo shrines.

The Utopia site (44JC32 and 44JC787), partially excavated during the 1970s by the Virginia Research Center for Archaeology and completed in the early 1990s by the James River Institute for Archaeology, was the location of a rural quarter outside of Williamsburg (Fesler 1997a; Kelso 1984). The site contained four temporal components, stretching from the beginning of the fourth quarter of the seventeenth century to about 1780. Archaeological and documentary evidence suggest that the second (circa 1700–1720), third (circa 1720–1750), and fourth (circa 1750–1780) components of the site were quarters for enslaved Africans and Afro-Virginians (Fesler 1997a; 1998). Each component contained two or three timber-framed houses, trash pits, and outbuildings.

Two subfloor pits from Utopia contained shrine assemblages. One pit (Feature 8) from the 1750–1780 occupation, contained a complete French wine bottle dating to the early 1760s, one of only two cowrie shells found at the site, and fragments of animal bone, wood, and white clay tobacco pipes. The configuration of a group of objects inside a shallow pan is similar to Igbo ancestral and divination shrines. Olaudah Equiano, an Igbo enslaved in eighteenth-century Virginia, noted in his autobiography that pipes and tobacco were placed in the graves of departed Igbo spiritual leaders (Gates 1987). The animal bones may also be significant since they include species that past and present Igbo hold sacred: namely, cows, sheep, and goats (Barbot 1732; Ifesieh 1986:68).

Another feature could be linked with women's spiritual activities. Feature 44, a four-by-three-foot rectangular pit with straight sidewalls and a flat bottom, was located in the southeastern corner of an earthfast structure whose occupation dated between 1720 and 1750. Excavation revealed that a .4-foot thick rounded platform of soil had been built up in the center of the feature's clay floor. Seven complete fossil scallop shells, three large cow bones, and two kaolin tobacco pipes had been arranged on the platform's surface.

The composition of the assemblage bears striking resemblance to objects associated with Igbo spiritual traditions (Jones 1931). Water, symbolized by the feature's fossil shells, is where the souls of the dead find temporary abodes while awaiting reincarnation and is considered sacred to the Igbo (Oramasionwu 1994:123–124). Additionally, all of the artifacts on the platform surface were white. Among the Igbo, as well as many other West African cultures, white is a sacred color associated with the spirit world and symbolizes purity, moral ideals, and the Supreme Being (Awolalu 1979:4; Cole and Aniakor 1984:216). Deities associated with water, such as Idemili, were particularly vital in Igbo culture and each had their own priest and cult objects (Cole and Aniakor 1984). The combination of white and water-related objects arranged on the earthen mound suggests that this pit may have contained a shrine that venerated Idemili, one of the Igbo water spirits. Idemili, the daughter of the Almighty God, came to earth in a pillar of water that rose from the sacred lake (Achebe 1987:93). The mound of soil upon which the shells rested perhaps represented the pillar of water "fusing earth to heaven at the navel of the black lake" (94), with the seven shells mirroring the seven chalk sticks in Achebe's novel *Anthills of the Savannah*.

As Igbo peoples spread throughout modern-day Nigeria and into the Diaspora, well away from the sacred waters, they continued to create shrines to Idemili. According to Igbo novelist Chinua Achebe (1987:94–95), these shrines were often simple and relatively plain, consisting of a stream, or a mound of earth, a stone, or an earthen bowl with seven pieces of chalk. Only women can make requests of Idemili (Achebe 1987).

Perhaps the most compelling evidence that this feature served as a shrine came from pollen analysis of soil samples. The sample was comprised overwhelmingly of pollen from native or cultivated grapes (Cummings and Moutoux 1999). Although pollen analysis cannot distinguish between the mere presence of grapes or a processed grape product like wine, the large quantity of grape pollen from Feature 44 suggests that the Igbo practice of pouring offerings of wine onto shrines continued in Virginia.

Igbo women also construct personal shrines that consist of pottery vessels buried in small holes in the floors of the women's houses (McCall 1995). Archaeological evidence consisting of buried complete ceramic vessels in several slave work areas in Virginia and Maryland appear to have been derivations of female personal shrines (Frank 1967; Samford 1996).

Other objects found on slave sites, both in the fill of subfloor pits and in other contexts, are suggestive of spiritual objects that further relate to ancestor veneration. Particularly interesting are a group of thirty cast pewter spoon handles from the mid- to late-eighteenth-century context at the Kingsmill Quarter. Most of these objects were found in the fill of subfloor pits in the quarter. The handles had been deliberately broken away from the spoon bowls, and in some instances the broken end had been smoothed or shaped into a point.[7] Sixty percent of the handles had been decorated with engraving that postdated the original manufacturing process. Most of the decorated spoons had been incised with linear zigzag patterns produced by a leatherworking pinking tool.[8] Other examples of the spoon handles were etched with straight lines that could have been produced with any sharp implement, including knives, awls, or heavy needles.

These engraved designs bear strong resemblance to several types of Igbo decorative motifs. The use of running lines of V-shaped decorative elements has precedent among cast bronze bells and other Igbo ritual objects (Neaher 1976; Shaw 1970),[9] some dating back as far as the tenth century. Other handles have designs that closely resemble Igbo body cicatrization motifs. These patterns are also found carved onto other wooden personal ritual objects called *ikenga* and other display figures. Body scarification serves multiple functions for the Igbo—they can be symbols of rank, clan, tribe, social, or marital status and sometimes are even done for medicinal or protective reasons (Adepegba 1976; Cole and Aniakor 1984). These spoon handles may have been used as divination tools. In Igbo culture, diviners were generally men.

Additionally, other items from some of the subfloor pits appeared to have been components of divination kits. Igbo divination kits included statue representations of deities, earthenware pottery, divination seeds, bones, pebbles, tortoise shells, and animal skulls (Arinze 1970:65). Possible divination items included the pierced pig metatarsals from the Eden House site and Rich Neck Quarter, fossilized sharks' teeth, and turtle shells.

Conclusion

Documents and archaeology provide brief flashes of illumination on the lives of individuals enslaved in Virginia. The shell-covered shrine hidden beneath the floor of the Utopia Quarter, with its parallels to the Igbo female deity Idemili, may have been one woman's attempt to bring about good fortune for her family. Engraved spoon handles may have been powerful divination tools in the hands of a Kingsmill Quarter man. The two shoulders of bacon that Nancy of Page Plantation obtained in the fall of 1803 in trade for her twelve chickens was meat that could be used to fill empty stomachs and flavor bland vegetables throughout the winter. At the same plantation, several months later, Old Aggy traded her chickens for a warm shawl to help ward off the evening chill. Taken alone, these journal entries show us individuals acting in the interest of themselves and their families. But by weaving together these slender threads of the past, it becomes possible to show that their West African heritage was an integral element in the lives enslaved men and women fashioned for themselves.

Certainly, the similarities that we can see between one particular West African culture and the late colonial period in Virginia cannot be attributed solely to the persistence of Igbo cultural traditions on this side of the Atlantic Ocean. A wide range of factors intersected to mold the shapes and textures of enslaved communities, not the least of which was the institution of slavery itself. Nevertheless, the enslaved worked to counter the negative effects of slavery by creating culturally rich communities on plantation quarters. Drawing upon memories of social and gender roles common in West Africa may have facilitated the development of such communities on Virginia plantations. While different in obvious ways, the seasonal rhythms and forms of agricultural work and the small group and extended family style of residing in quarters encountered by slaves in Virginia were in many respects similar to the rhythms of life in Igboland. Documentary and archaeological evidence suggests that the enslaved defined new roles for themselves based upon those they had known traditionally. The preservation of the family was central, and evidence in Virginia suggests that both men and women were interested in family stability and health. While there was certainly overlapping and intertwining of men's and women's roles in assuming responsibility for the family, women in particular appeared to be concerned with strategies that would assist in its economic well-being.

ACKNOWLEDGMENTS

Completion of this chapter would not have been possible without the assistance of many individuals. I would like to particularly thank my dissertation committee: Vin Steponaitis, Carole Crumley, Robert Ann Dunbar, Glenn Hinson, and James Peacock. Since much of my analysis focused on previously excavated archaeological sites, various institutions in Virginia made their collections available to me. Thanks are in order to Garrett Fesler and the staff at James River Institute for Archaeology in Jamestown, Virginia, and the staffs at the Virginia Division of Historic Landmarks, the Department of Archaeological Research at the Colonial Williamsburg Foundation, and the Department of Archaeology at Monticello. Many colleagues had a role in seeing this project through to its completion. Thank you to Leslie Bartlett; Nancy Bennett; Sara and Nick Bon-Harper; Bolaji Campbell; Henry Drewal; Jane Eastman; Joe Herbert; Diane Levy; Tom Maher; Ann, Carl, and Kate Martin; Trish McGuire; Chris Rodning; Jennie Smith; Martha Temkin; Amber Vanderwarker; and Greg Wilson. This project also benefited greatly from discussions with Tom Hargrove and Tim Mooney, two friends who did not live to see its completion.

NOTES

1. Many of the traditional patterns of social and political organization that were present in the eighteenth and nineteenth centuries still characterize Igbo society today.

2. For the importance of names in Igbo culture, see Aniakor (1996).

3. In Igboland, yams are boiled and then pounded into a stiff, doughy consistency (*foofoo*). Small balls of foofoo were eaten with vegetables and meat (Chambers 1996:118–119). Olaudah Equiano (1987:15) wrote of eighteenth-century Igbo foodways: "Bullocks, goats, and poultry, supply the greatest part of their food . . . The flesh is usually stewed in a pan; to make it savory we sometime use also pepper, and other spices . . . Our vegetables are mostly plaintains, eadas, yams, beans, and Indian corn."

4. Eggshell has been recovered from Utopia I (44JC32), Utopia II (44JC787), Kingsmill Quarter (44JC30), Monticello's Mulberry Row, and Rich Neck Quarter. The absence of eggshell from other sites may be more related to archaeological recovery methods than an accurate indicator of egg consumption at the sites.

5. There are numerous other recorded instances of planters sending slaves to purchase items on their behalf.

6. Equiano's memoirs are perhaps the most detailed portrayal available of eighteenth-century Igbo culture, a society that had no written language at the time. Since Equiano was taken from Africa as a preteen, the depth of his understanding of the workings of his village (particularly of the political and economic structures) has been called into question. A critical analysis of the narrative has evaluated the utility of Equiano's memoirs (Afigbo 1981). Afigbo (1981:148) suggests that the passages detailing women's roles and work appear to be the most accurate in the discussion of Igbo life, since Equiano's role as a youngest son meant that he spent most of his time in the company of his mother and other women.

7. Although it would be reasonable to argue that these spoons were used for eating and were simply discarded when they broke, several factors argue against this conclusion. The proportion of handles to bowls was very pronounced (four to one), suggesting that the handles were the portion of interest. Additionally, some of the handles showed signs of purposeful breaking; i.e., the handles had been twisted repeatedly to weaken the metal at its thinnest point where it joined the bowl. The broken ends of some of the other handles had been rounded or sharpened, perhaps to smooth away the jagged metal edges.

8. My thanks to Jay Gaynor, curator of metals at the Colonial Williamsburg Foundation for his assistance in describing various ways these marks could have been made.

9. The bronze objects Neaher studied were ethnographic and archaeological items, largely of indeterminate date.

REFERENCES

Achebe, Chinua
    1959   *Things Fall Apart.* Anchor Books, New York.
    1987   *Anthills of the Savannah.* Anchor Press, New York.
Adepegba, Cornelius O.
    1976   A Survey of Nigerian Body Markings and Their Relationship to
            Other Nigerian Arts. Ph.D. diss., Fine Arts Dept., Indiana Univ.,
            Bloomington.
Afigbo, Adiele E.
    1981   *Ropes of Sand: Studies in Igbo History and Culture.* Univ. Press Limited,
            in association with Oxford Univ. Press, Univ. of Nigeria Press, Nsukka.
Amadiume, Ifi
    1987   *Male Daughters, Female Husbands: Gender and Sex in an African
            Society.* Zed Books, London.

1997   *Reinventing Africa: Matriarchy, Religion, and Culture.* Zed Books, London.

Aniakor, Chike

1996   Household Objects and the Philosophy of Igbo Social Space. In *African Material Culture.* Edited by Mary Jo Arnoldi, Christraud M. Geary, and Kris L. Hardin. Indiana Univ. Press, Bloomington, pp. 214–242.

Anstey, Roger

1975   *The Atlantic Slave Trade and British Abolition, 1760–1810.* Humanities Press, Atlantic Highlands, New Jersey.

Anyanwu, Starling E. N.

1976   *The Igbo Family Life and Cultural Change.* Ph.D. diss., Univ. of Marburg, Marburg, Germany.

Arinze, Francis A.

1970   *Sacrifice in Ibo Religion.* Ibadan Univ. Press, Ibadan, Nigeria.

Awolalu, J. Omosade

1979   *West African Traditional Religion.* Onibonoje Press & Book Industries, Ibadan, Nigeria.

Barbot, James

1732   An Abstract of a Voyage to New Calabar River, or Rio Real, in the Year 1699. In *A Collection of Voyages and Travels,* compiled by Awnshawn and John Churchill. John Walthoe, London.

Blackburn, Robin

1997   *The Making of New World Slavery: From the Baroque to the Modern, 1492–1800.* Verso, New York.

Bloch, Maurice

1953   *The Historian's Craft.* Vintage Books, New York.

Breen, Timothy H.

1985   *Tobacco Culture: The Mentality of the Great Tidewater Planters on the Eve of Revolution.* Princeton Univ. Press, Princeton, N.J.

Chambers, Douglas Brent

1996   "He Gwine Sing He Country": Africans, Afro-Virginians, and the Development of Slave Culture in Virginia, 1690–1810. Ph.D. diss., Dept. of History, Univ. of Virginia, Charlottesville.

Cole, Herbert M., and Chike C. Aniakor

1984   *Igbo Arts: Community and Cosmos.* Museum of Cultural History, Univ. of California, Los Angeles.

Cummings, Linda Scott, and Thomas E. Moutoux

1999   Pollen and Phytolith Analysis at the Utopia I Site, 44JC32, Virginia. Paleo Research Labs Technical Report 98–20. Ms. on file,

Research Laboratories of Archaeology, Univ. of North Carolina, Chapel Hill.

Curtin, Philip
    1969   *The Atlantic Slave Trade: A Census*. Univ. of Wisconsin Press, Madison.

Davidson, Basil
    1977   A History of West Africa, 1000–1800. Longman, London.

Douglass, Frederick
    1855   *My Bondage and My Freedom*. Miller, Orton and Mulligan, New York.

Fenn, Elizabeth
    1988   "A Perfect Equality Seemed to Reign": Slave Society and Jonkonnu. *North Carolina Historical Review* 65 (Apr.):127–153.

Fesler, Garrett
    1997a Landscapes of Control and Autonomy: The Spatial Contestation of the Utopia Slave Quarter. Ms. on file, Dept. of Anthropology, Univ. of Virginia, Charlottesville.
    1997b A Quantitative Study of Architectural Changes in Slave Housing in the Piedmont and Chesapeake Regions of Virginia. Ms. on file, Dept. of Anthropology, Univ. of Virginia, Charlottesville.
    1998   Back to Utopia: An Interim Report on Renewed Archaeological Excavations at the Utopia Quarter, Field Seasons 1993–1996. Ms. on file, James River Institute for Archaeology, Williamsburg, Va.

Fithian, Philip Vickers
    1943   *Journal and Letters of Philip Vickers Fithian, 1773–1774: A Plantation Tutor of the Old Dominion*. Edited by Hunter Dickinson Farish. Colonial Williamsburg, Inc., Williamsburg, Va.

Frank, Neil
    1967   Brush-Everard House Kitchen and Surrounding Area, Block 29, Area E, Colonial Lots 164 and 165: Report on 1967 Archaeological Excavations. Ms. on file, Foundation Library, Colonial Williamsburg Foundation, Williamsburg, Va.

Franklin, Maria
    1997   Out of Site, Out of Mind: The Archaeology of an Enslaved Virginia Household, ca. 1740–1778. Ph.D. diss., Dept. of Anthropology, Univ. of California, Berkeley.

Gates, Henry Louis
    1987   *The Classic Slave Narratives*. New American Library, New York.

Gutman, Herbert
    1976   *The Black Family in Slavery and Freedom, 1750–1925*. Vintage Books, New York.

Heath, Barbara
  1994   An Interim Report on the 1993 Excavations: The Quarter Site
         at Poplar Forest, Forest, Virginia. Ms. on file, Corporation for
         Jefferson's Poplar Forest, Forest, Va.
  1997   Slavery and Consumerism: A Case Study from Central Virginia.
         *African American Archaeology: Newsletter of the African American
         Archaeology Network*, no. 19 (winter 1997):1, 58.
Heath, Barbara, and Amber Moncure
  1998   "The Little Spots Allow'd Them": The Archaeological Study
         of African American Yards. Ms. on file, Poplar Forest,
         Lynchburg, Va.
Henderson, Richard N.
  1972   *The King in Every Man: Evolutionary Trends in Onitsha Ibo Society
         and Culture.* Yale Univ. Press, New Haven.
Horton, Robin
  1972   Stateless Societies in the History of West Africa. In *History of
         West Africa*, edited by J.F.A. Ajayi and Michael Crowder.
         Columbia Univ. Press, New York.
Ifesieh, Emmanuel I.
  1986   Ritual Symbolism in Igbo Traditional Religion. *Africana
         Marburgensia* 9(1):50–82.
Isichei, Elizabeth
  1978   *Igbo Worlds: An Anthology of Oral Histories and Historical
         Descriptions.* Institute for the Study of Human Issues, Philadelphia.
Jones, G. I.
  1931   Photograph entitled "Portable Household Shrine." In the
         G. I. Jones Photographic Archive of Southeastern Nigerian
         Art and Culture. Available at http://www.siu.edu/anthro/
         mccall/jones/igbo/ika16.jpg.
Kay, Marvin L. Michael, and Lorin Lee Cary
  1995   *Slavery in North Carolina, 1748–1775.* Univ. of North Carolina,
         Chapel Hill.
Kehoe, Alice B.
  1992   The Muted Class: Unshackling Tradition. In *Exploring Gender
         through Archaeology: Selected Papers from the 1991 Boone Conference*,
         edited by Cheryl Claassen, pp. 23–32. Prehistory Press, Madison,
         Wis.
Kelso, William
  1984   *Kingsmill Plantations, 1619–1800: Archaeology of Country Life in
         Colonial Virginia.* Academic Press, New York.

Kelso, William M., and R. Neil Frank
     1972   A Report on Exploratory Excavations at Carter's Grove Plantation,
             James City County, Virginia (June 1970–Sept. 1971). Ms. on file,
             Colonial Williamsburg Foundation, Williamsburg, Va.
Kulikoff, Allan
     1986   *Tobacco and Slaves: The Development of Southern Cultures in the
             Chesapeake, 1680–1800.* Univ. of North Carolina Press, Chapel Hill.
Lautzenheiser, Loretta, Patricia M. Samford, Jaquelin Drane Nash,
Mary Ann Holm, and Thomas Hargrove
     1998   "I Was Moved of the Lord to Go to Carolina . . . " Data Recovery
             at Eden House Site 31BR52 Bertie County, North Carolina. Report
             prepared by Coastal Carolina Research for the North Carolina
             Dept. of Transportation.
Lee, Jean B.
     1986   The Problem of Slave Community in the Eighteenth-Century
             Chesapeake. William and Mary Quarterly, 3d ser., 43:333–361.
Martin, Ann Smart
     1997   Complex Commodities: The Enslaved as Producers and Consumers
             in Eighteenth-Century Virginia. Paper presented at the Omohundro
             Institute of Early American History and Culture Annual Confer-
             ence, Winston-Salem, N.C.
McCall, John C.
     1995   Rethinking Ancestors in Africa. *Africa* 65(2):256–270.
McCartney, Martha
     1997   *James City County: Keystone of the Commonwealth.* Donning
             Company Publishers, Virginia Beach.
Menard, Russell
     1980   The Tobacco Industry in the Chesapeake Colonies, 1617–1730:
             An Interpretation. *Research in Economic History* 5:109–177.
Monticello Dept. of Archaeology
     1997   Monticello Finds List for Buildings O, S, T and the Negro Quarter.
             On file with Monticello Archaeology Department, Thomas Jefferson
             Foundation, Charlottesville, Va.
Moore, Stephen
     1808–1810 Papers. 2205 Ser. 4.1. Vol. 16. Southern Historical Collection,
             Univ. of North Carolina, Chapel Hill.
Morgan, Phillip
     1998   *Slave Counterpoint: Black Culture in the Eighteenth-Century
             Chesapeake and Lowcountry.* Univ. of North Carolina Press,
             Chapel Hill.

Morton, Patricia
  1996   Introduction. *Discovering Women in Slavery: Emancipating Perspectives on the American Past.* Univ. of Georgia Press, Athens.
Mrozowski, Steve A., and L. H. Driscoll
  1997   Seeds of Learning: An Archaeological Analysis of the Rich Neck Plantation Slave Quarter. Ms. on file at the Dept. of Archaeological Research, Colonial Williamsburg Foundation.
Neaher, Nancy C.
  1976   Bronzes of Southern Nigeria and Igbo Metalsmithing Traditions. Ph.D. diss., Dept. of Art, Stanford Univ., Stanford, Calif.
Neiman, Fraser
  1997   Sub-Floor Pits and Slavery in Eighteenth- and Early-Nineteenth-Century Virginia. Paper presented at the Thirtieth Annual Meeting of the Society for Historical Archaeology, Corpus Christi.
Niemcewicz, Julian U.
  1965   *Under Their Vine and Fig Tree: Travels through America in 1797–1799, 1805 with some Further Account of Life in New Jersey.* Translated and edited by Metchie Budka. Grassmann Publishing Co., Elizabeth, N.J.
Oguagha, P. A., and Okpoko, A. I.
  1984   History and Ethnoarchaeology in Eastern Nigeria: A Study of Igbo-Igala Relations with Special Reference to the Anambra Valley. Cambridge Monographs in African Archaeology 7. B.A.R. International, Oxford.
Okonjo, Kamene
  1976   The Dual-Sex Political System in Operation: Igbo Women and Community Politics in Midwestern Nigeria. In *Women in Africa: Studies in Social and Economic Change*, edited by Nancy Hafkin and Edna G. Bay. Stanford Univ. Press, Stanford.
Oramasionwu, Ernest U.
  1994   The Enduring Power of Igbo Traditional Religion. Ph.D. diss. Univ. of Manitoba, Winnipeg, Manitoba.
Page, Jane Frances
  n.d.   Commonplace Book. Ms. on file, Virginia Historical Society, Richmond, Va.
Paulme, Denise (editor)
  1963   *Women of Tropical Africa.* Univ. of California Press, Berkeley.
Perdue, Charles L., Jr., Thomas E. Barden, and Robert K. Phillips
  1980   *Weevils in the Wheat: Interviews with Virginia Ex-Slaves.* Indiana Univ. Press, Bloomington.

Samford, Patricia M.

1996 The Archaeology of African American Slavery and Material Culture. In *William and Mary Quarterly*, 3d ser., 53(1):87–114.

2000 "Strong Is the Bond of Kinship": West African-Style Ancestor Shrines and Subfloor Pits on African American Quarters. Ph.D. diss., Dept. of Anthropology, Univ. of North Carolina, Chapel Hill.

Sanford, Douglas

1991 Middle Range Theory and Plantation Archaeology: An Analysis of Domestic Slavery at Monticello, Albemarle County, Virginia, ca. 1770–1830. *Quarterly Bulletin of the Archeological Society of Virginia* 46:20–30.

Shaw, Thurstan

1970 *Igbo-Ukwu: An Account of Archaeological Discoveries in Eastern Nigeria.* Faber and Faber, London.

Sidbury, James

1997 *Ploughshares into Swords: Race, Rebellion, and Identity in Gabriel's Virginia, 1730–1810.* Cambridge Univ. Press, New York.

Singleton, William Henry

1999 *Recollections of My Slavery Days.* Introduction and Annotations by Katherine Mellen Charron and David S. Cecelski. Division of Archives and History, North Carolina Dept. of Cultural Resources, Raleigh.

Steen, Carl

1995 *The Somerset Place Restoration Excavations 1994.* Diachronic Research Inc., Columbia, S.C. Submitted to the North Carolina Dept. of Cultural Resources Division of Archives and History, Historic Sites Section, Raleigh. Copies available from Historic Sites Section, Raleigh, N.C.

Uchendu, Patrick Kenechukwu

1980 The Changing Cultural Role of Igbo Women in Nigeria, 1914–1975. Ph.D. diss., School of Education, New York Univ., New York.

Veney, Bethany

1889 *Aunt Betty's Story: The Narrative of Bethany Veney, A Slave Woman.* Geo. H. Ellis, Boston. Available at http://sunsite.unc.edu/docsouth/veney/veney.html.

Walsh, Lorena

1997 *From Calabar to Carter's Grove: The History of a Virginia Slave Community.* Univ. Press of Virginia, Charlottesville.

Washington, Booker T.

    1965   *Up from Slavery.* Americanist Library, Boston. Originally published
            1901, Doubleday, New York.

White, Deborah G.

    1985   *Ar'n't I a Woman? Female Slaves in the Plantation South.*
            W. W. Norton, New York.

Wylie, Alison

    1991   Gender Theory and the Archaeological Record: Why Is There
            No Archaeology of Gender? In *Engendering Archaeology: Women
            and Prehistory.* Edited by Joan M. Gero and Margaret W. Conkey,
            pp. 31–54. Basil Blackwell, Cambridge.

Yentsch, Anne E.

    1994   *A Chesapeake Family and Their Slaves: A Study in Historical
            Archaeology.* Cambridge Univ. Press, Cambridge.

CHAPTER 7

Living Arrangements among Enslaved Women and Men at an Early-Eighteenth-Century Virginia Quartering Site

GARRETT R. FESLER

The practice of historical archaeology, like any of the social sciences, is full of assumptions. This study addresses one fundamental assumption: gender differences played a significant role in shaping the daily interaction of enslaved Africans living in early-eighteenth-century Virginia.[1] Gender relations will be examined among a group of enslaved Africans living on an early-eighteenth-century quartering site known as the Utopia Quarter,[2] located several miles outside of Williamsburg, Virginia (Map 7.1). Archaeological excavations were recently completed at the site, one of the earliest eighteenth-century slave field quarters to be studied extensively in the Chesapeake (see Samford 1996).[3] The findings from Utopia provide a rich source of archaeological data to address issues concerning social interaction between enslaved women and men at the site. Although the Utopia Quarter was occupied for nearly a century between 1670 and 1775, this analysis focuses on one period of that occupation, between the years 1700 and about 1730 (Fesler 2000), during a time of rapid expansion in the institution of slavery.

Intuitively, one can assume that almost universally, in virtually all cultures, gender differences between women and men play a decisive role in determining social relations.[4] And yet, due to a scarcity of information concerning African American slave culture in the New World, particularly for the Chesapeake region of North America, little is known about the day-to-day lives of African American slaves, especially prior to the American Revolution. While historians have reconstructed accounts of pre-Revolutionary slave life and culture in the Chesapeake with considerable success (see, for example, Berlin 1998; Kulikoff 1986; Morgan 1998; Sobel 1987; Stevenson 1996; Walsh 1997), and historical archaeologists have produced a wide array of site reports and case studies of slave habitation sites (see, for example, Ferguson 1992;

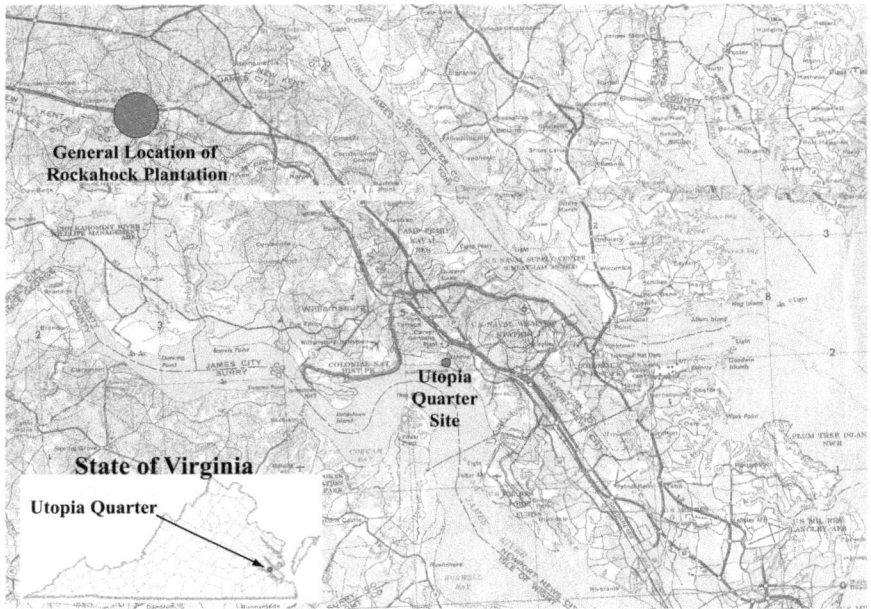

MAP 7.1.   Location of the Utopia Quarter on the U.S. Geological Survey, 1:100,000 scale quadrangle map (Williamsburg 1984).

Franklin 1997; Heath 1999; Higgens et al. 2000; Kelso 1984; Parker and Hernigle 1990; Pogue and White 1991; Samford 1996, 2000; Sanford 1995), gender relations among African American slaves at places like the Utopia Quarter continue to remain largely ambiguous and unknown, and many questions remain. Did enslaved Africans reassert forms of gender relations they knew from various West and Central African cultures of origin? Was this possible, given the circumstances of slavery? Did Anglo-American slave owners impose their own social standards upon their slaves, including gender mores? Or did slaves creolize several forms of gender relations, melding together old ways of living known from a variety of African pasts with new ways of living from their Anglo-American captors?

Whether or not answers to these questions can be gleaned from the archaeological record at places like the Utopia Quarter is open to debate. However, the approach here is to define how men and women organized themselves on the ground by isolating those spaces and places at the site that each gender principally inhabited. Based on the premise that Utopia's enslaved men and

women negotiated space in part due to the recognition of culturally constructed gender differences, the task at hand is to "map" their locations across
the site in an effort to pinpoint where women and men congregated, separately
and together. Three forms of archaeological evidence are used to investigate the
gendered spaces at Utopia: an examination of the architecture (interior spaces),
the overall layout of the site (exterior spaces), and the distribution of various
classes of artifacts associated with each household.

Whatever gendered patterns emerge from the data are then assessed in
terms of three primary living arrangements, each of which regarded gender as
a main organizing principal. First, it is possible that due to many planters'
initial preference for male laborers and the resulting demographic imbal-
ances, single-sex barracks may have been the preferred living arrangement
at Utopia. Second, perhaps because of the preponderance of African-born
adults living at Utopia at the time, the residents may have been able to replicate a living arrangement based on the indigenous village compound, a pan-
African phenomenon, which, if true to form, was highly segregated by gender. Third, although single-family or kin-based domestic units became the
norm in the middle and later eighteenth century, it is possible that kin and
family groups formed in these early years at Utopia and became the conven-
tional domestic unit. The archaeological patterns of each of these three
hypothesized gendered domestic units manifested themselves differently on
the landscape.

Eerie Silences

Although presently the shelves of most libraries are bending under the weight
of anthropological and archaeological books, articles, and journals devoted to
the study of gender (see Joyce and Claassen 1997:1), a comparatively small
amount of work on the topic has come from historical archaeologists (see, for
example, Little 1994; Scott 1994a; Seifert 1991; Wall 1994; Yentsch 1991a; 1991b).
And the number of historical archaeological case studies of gender at African
American sites is very sparse (see, for example, Muller 1994; Yentsch 1994).
Why the "eerie silence" on gender—as Margaret Conkey (1991:29) has termed
it—from practitioners of African American archaeology? Some point out that
persistent androcentric notions of the past may subvert certain studies (Roberts
1993; Spencer-Wood 1991). The failure to fully capture the past experiences of

African American men and women also may be due to chronic Anglocentric perspectives within current anthropological thinking (Dill 1990; Lott 1997:21; Moore 1988:190; Scott 1994b: 11; Singleton and Bograd 1995:29). Others concede that there is a general lack of theoretical tools from which to frame significant questions about race, gender, and slavery simultaneously (Collins 1997; hooks 1981; Lewis 1990:45; West and Fenstermaker 1997).

There are other obstructions impeding archaeological interpretations of gender. For one, falling into the trap of gender attribution is always a possibility. Too often research has been geared toward uncritically "identifying one set of objects with males and another with females" without assessing the gendered categories (Conkey and Spector 1984:25; see also Dobres 1995). It is wise to remember that gender does not structure the division of labor; rather, the source of gender difference is derived from the division of labor (Moore 1991:408; see also Watson 1997). With this in mind, a task-differentiation framework has been developed and applied successfully in archaeological contexts and will be employed at Utopia (see Conkey and Spector 1984:24–27; Gibb and King 1991; Spector 1983; 1991; 1993).[5] However, without credible ethnohistorical or ethnographic sources, there is a risk of perpetuating androcentric models of men's and women's roles.

The majority of researchers who grapple with issues of gender will readily concede that the essence of gender difference resides with differential access to power (Aries 1997:92). For example, Henrietta Moore suggests that difference "is always experienced relationally in terms of political discrimination, inequalities of power, and forms of domination" (1994:26).[6] In terms of archaeological studies of enslaved African Americans, the structure of gender is embedded within a cultural system of power and inequality that had an almost incalculable influence on the shape of male and female roles. Therefore, at sites of slavery such as the Utopia Quarter, gender differences were nested within a racist culture that already imposed differential access to power on its enslaved subjects; essentially, modes of gender relations among slaves could be considered a secondary level of difference compared to the inequities of the slave system (see Chafetz 1990).[7] Until recently, the imposition of power, violence, racism, exploitation of the slave system, and resistance to it have taken center stage in studies of plantation slavery, eclipsing subjects such as gender that were considered subsidiary slave social structures. Volumes such as this one are beginning to break free and fill the eerie silences.

Sources of Gender Relations at Utopia

In all settings, including the Utopia Quarter, gender norms were learned and adopted through interaction and experience. Slaves at Utopia fashioned their gender relations from two primary cultural sources, from Anglo-American gender norms imposed on them by their owners and overseers and from their own remembered understanding of how men and women were supposed to interact from the assorted West and Central African cultures that converged at the site.

Anglo-American conceptions of gender in early-eighteenth-century Virginia were recast by the colonial experience but essentially remained similar to those found in England at the time. For instance, Anglo-Virginian women and men continued to labor in separate spheres—women primarily in the domestic realm and men outside of it (Brown 1996:24–25). Sometimes this prototypical division of labor could not be maintained, such as in the latter decades of the seventeenth century when some female indentured servants and women living on impoverished farmsteads were forced by necessity to work "in the ground" (Main 1982:108–109), and, conversely, some men took on jobs usually reserved for women (Brown 1996:84–85). In time, sex ratios evened, mortality rates declined, and other demographic changes ameliorated the blending of gender roles among English colonists (Main 1982). By the early eighteenth century, with the influx of slave labor, most Anglo-American women of all ranks were saved the hardship of fieldwork except those in the most destitute straits (181).

Colonial housewifery generally centered on cooking, cleaning, washing, raising children, and gathering and preserving food (Brown 1996:25–27; Carr et al. 1991:72). Yet, depending on circumstances, variations in these tasks did occur, such as the amount of time spent grinding corn into meal (Carr et al. 1991:71). Some researchers suggest that the ideal division of labor advanced home production for white colonial women, while men concentrated outside the home on commodity production (see Kulikoff 1986:229–231). However, the ideal was rarely met; instead, the "division and segregation of domestic space along lines of gender and status was not easily established," as James Gibb and Julie King discovered in their archaeological analysis of activity areas on three seventeenth-century Maryland home lots (1991:112).

For each African slave who ended up making a home at the Utopia Quarter, the process of enslavement was physically and emotionally devastating.

Although unimaginably harrowing, study after study has proved that slavery altered but did not obliterate the cultural canon retained by enslaved Africans in the New World (for example, Berlin 1998; Kulikoff 1986; Morgan 1998; M. Mullin 1992; Walsh 1997). Forced to rebuild cultural conventions from scratch, often among potentially hostile strangers, many slaves struggled to reconstitute a coherent code of mores that they had known before their capture into slavery. Dozens of diverse culture areas throughout West and Central Africa, and even from as far away as Madagascar, fed the transatlantic slave trade (see Thomas 1997). Not only gender roles but also ways of living, family organization, rites of passage, and religious beliefs differed from place to place, and it would be a grave mistake to consider African culture as monolithic (see Posnansky 1999). And yet, while urging caution, most researchers will grant that the vast majority of African peoples caught up in the transatlantic slave trade shared some common cultural continuities, what Sidney Mintz and Richard Price (1992:9–10) call a system of collective "values . . . which may underlie and shape behavioral response." Historians sketch a distinctive world-view shared by Africans, including an emphasis on family and community; an acceptance of polygamy; communal land ownership; a similar understanding of nonrational causality; an emphasis on taboo, magic, and ritual; an attachment of place with spiritual significance; and a cyclical perception of time (Kolchin 1993:42; Sobel 1987:18–20; see also Boles 1983:40; Farnham 1987:70; Gomez 1998; Sudarkasa 1980:52). This suggests that enslaved Africans from different culture areas who lived at places like Utopia may have spoken different languages and had widely differing concepts of how to go about daily tasks, but their core values, including gender norms, often were quite compatible.

Utopia was occupied in the first several decades of the eighteenth century, at a time when the slave trade to the region was dominated by shipments from the Bight of Biafra (primarily Igbo) and, to a lesser extent, by imports from the Gold Coast (Koromanti), Angola, and Senegambia (Mandinga) (Curtin 1969:157; Kulikoff 1986:321; Morgan 1998:63). By all accounts, once landed in the Chesapeake, early-eighteenth-century slave masters imposed virtually no division of labor based on gender (Brown 1996:119; Carr and Walsh 1988; Davis 1981:8; hooks 1981:45; White 1985:114). Enslaved men and women worked in the fields side by side doing the same jobs and were counted equally as full hands (Shammas 1985:10; Walsh 1993:177; Yentsch 1994:173, 176, 367). This arrangement directly contradicted many African social norms in which men and women spent a majority of their time apart from each other, at work and at leisure (Casey 1991:142; M. Mullin 1992:172).

While early-eighteenth-century masters enforced a similar daily work routine on both men and women, most had little desire to disrupt life in the slave quarters as long as fieldwork kept apace, productivity remained high, and Old World ways of living did not threaten a master's authority. Most Chesapeake slave populations were able to construct their own gender norms in the quarters, but what kind of division of labor they instituted remains a contested topic among some historians. One side suggests that the debilitating nature of enslavement prompted women and men to set aside a strict division of labor so as to share equally the burden of domestic work (Davis 1981:18). Others propose the opposite, that in an effort to counteract the planter's perception that enslaved men and women were homogenous and interchangeable, slaves created a conspicuous division of labor within the quarters (J. Jones 1989:197). As egalitarian as the relationships between enslaved men and women may or may not have been, the quarters generally functioned as a woman's domain, in large part because women bore the children and took on the lion's share of child rearing, and these activities took place in the quarters. By virtue of this, women had a more significant physical presence at most slave quarters.

Motherhood and childcare traditionally were female provinces in most West and Central African cultures (Callaway 1993; White 1985:66). As such, women unable to bear children often became social outcasts (Mbiti 1991:64). In most African cultures women raised children with little or no help from their husbands but usually with the assistance of other women. In this manner, in many societies strong female kin networks formed. These extended kin connections were expressed spatially in segregated living arrangements in domestic compounds. Husbands and wives often slept separately, and the built landscape marked out a ranked residential hierarchy (see Bourdier and Minh-ha 1985; White 1985:65). African Olaudah Equiano indicated the significance of the physical order of his 1730s Igbo compound by noting that the head male's home sat in the center, with wives' huts on each side and the habitations of slaves and their families distributed on the fringes of the enclosure (Potkay and Burr 1995:170). Elsewhere, the spatial order of many compounds expressed various degrees of architectural, functional, hierarchical, social, and spiritual significance (Aniakor 1996; Bourdier and Minh-ha 1985:28).

In most African societies women had the primary responsibility for crop cultivation outside the compound (Nash 1982:182; Sobel 1987:28). One observer of the late-sixteenth-century Congolese noted, "The men do not work. Throughout the day they sit on the ground with their legs crossed. The women cultivate the land with hoe" (Fage 1989:155). Another recorded in 1594, "The women build the houses and work in the fields . . . and do all that men do elsewhere" (154). One traveler reported from Sierra Leone in 1507, "The women cultivate, sow, harvest and do everything" (154). More than three hundred years later, a nineteenth-century missionary commented on the strict gender division of labor by remarking, "You will often see a great, big man walking ahead with nothing in his hand but a cutlass, and a woman, his wife, coming on behind with a great big child on her back, and a load on her head" (hooks 1981:17). A priest visiting Sierra Leone in 1607 phrased it more bluntly, "[Men] make use of their wives in the fields as though they were slaves" (Fage 1989:155). Thus, African women typically did much of the work inside and outside the domestic sphere, although in most cultures their status remained subordinate to men (Fage 1989:155; hooks 1981:17).[8]

What becomes apparent from looking at the historical evidence for the early-eighteenth-century Chesapeake is that enslaved men and women experienced slavery differently (White 1985:62). For instance, even though they labored in fields together, English and African ideals of division of labor tended to confer greater mobility on enslaved males (75). Pregnancy, child rearing, and domestic work tended to restrict women to the plantation, while men were more likely to obtain skilled positions, allowing them to be hired out temporarily to other planters. Marriages between slaves on different plantations occurred frequently, and it was more common for husbands to travel "abroad" to visit wives and children, in large part because property rights over children were determined matrilineally (Mann 1990:149; Walsh 1997). Thus, enslaved men co-opted the wider landscapes, those paths that crisscrossed between plantations, as an "alternative territorial system" (Isaac 1982:53), leaving enslaved women to shape the domestic spaces in and around the quarters, further demonstrating that those women left a considerable imprint on sites such as Utopia.

Historical Background of Utopia

In October 1700 Virginia planter James Bray II (circa 1668–1725)[9] acquired a 1,280-acre plantation located not far outside the newly established town of Williamsburg (see Maps 7.1 and 7.2). Fronting the James River, the valuable property previously had belonged to Thomas Pettus Jr. (circa 1650–1690).

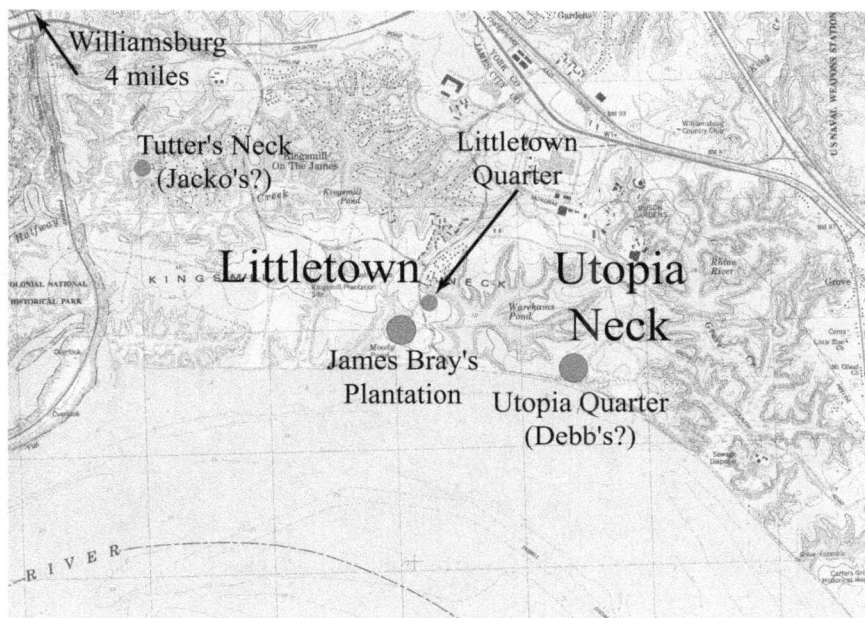

MAP 7.2.   Place-names in the vicinity of the Utopia Quarter on the U.S. Geological Survey, 1:24,000 scale quadrangle map (Hog Island 1984).

When Pettus died suddenly in 1690, his wife remarried within a matter of weeks to neighboring planter James Bray. The marriage set into motion a series of recurring court cases pitting Bray against several Pettus heirs for control of the Pettus estate. Eventually, Bray attained most of Pettus's former landholdings, including the deed to the 1,280-acre property known as Littletown and Utopia (Fesler 2000:32–33). In Pettus's day the western half of the property was known as Littletown, while the eastern half had long been called Utopia or Utopia Neck (see Map 7.2).[10]

Almost immediately upon acquiring Littletown/Utopia, Bray hired carpenters and masons to begin construction of an imposing brick house on the west end of the property that was to serve as his plantation seat. At or near the same time, Bray also ordered a series of timber-framed structures to be built on the Utopia section of the property to function as an outlying quarter for his growing labor force of enslaved Africans. Bray's workers erected three post-in-ground dwellings and a fourth smaller service building at Utopia, and these buildings stood for upwards of twenty-five years until shortly after his

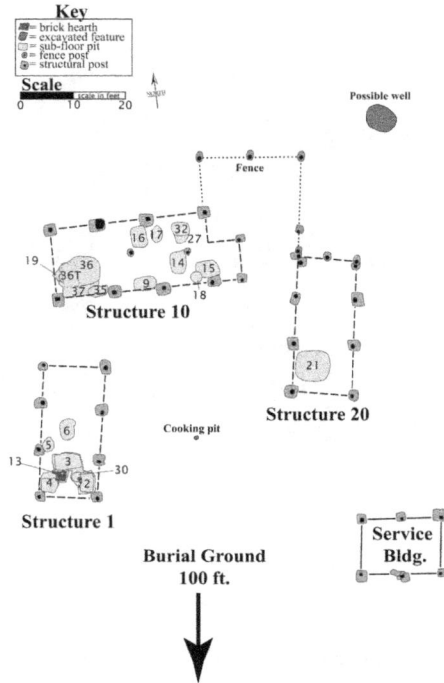

MAP 7.3.   Plan map of the Utopia Quarter, circa 1700–1730.

death in 1725 (Fesler 2000). As the site evolved under James Bray's ownership, the main components of Utopia consisted of a small outbuilding; three post-in-ground dwellings, each with between one and a dozen subfloor storage pits; a post-and-rail fence connecting two of the dwellings; a possible well; a cooking pit; and a small burial ground located several hundred feet to the south (see Map 7.3).

In 1726 a probate inventory was made of James Bray's estate, providing a comprehensive snapshot of the estate as it stood at the end of his life. According to the inventory, Bray had amassed a considerable fortune in land and personal property (Bray 1726). He owned many luxury items, such as a clock, silver tableware, a silver cane and sword, and two coats of arms, and the fields of his plantations were filled with nearly five hundred head of livestock, including fourteen horses (Bray 1726; Kelso 1984:38). In addition to the 1,280-acre Littletown/Utopia plantation, Bray owned several thousand additional acres in James City County and a number of prominent lots in the town of

Williamsburg. As for human property, Bray owned seventy adult slaves, more than seven enslaved children,[11] and the contracts on an unknown number of indentured servants (Bray 1726).

By probing the probate inventory, it is possible to reconstruct how James Bray managed his labor and resources at the end of his life and, from this, to develop a profile of how his male and female slaves were distributed across his plantations (Bray 1726) (Table 7.1). In addition to his home base at the Littletown manor house, Bray placed two outlying quarters on the 1,280-acre Littletown/Utopia property that he dubbed Debb's and Jacko's (Table 7.2).[12] He also operated six additional quarters on more than 2,000 acres known as Rockahock, located approximately twenty miles away in the northern extremes of James City County along the Chickahominy River (Table 7.3) (see Map 7.1). Each of the eight quarter parcels and the home plantation functioned as a small farm, and each probably encompassed between 350 to 450 acres, depending upon conditions, soil fertility, and staffing (see Table 7.1).

The locations of Littletown, Debb's, and Jacko's have been identified and excavated. Based on archaeological research, the Littletown slaves likely were headquartered at the plantation itself, either in buildings sited next to the main house, in a small nearby outbuilding, or at a quartering site several hundred yards to the north (Kelso 1973:17–20; 1977:85–86; 1984:104–106) (see Map 7.2). The Utopia site functioned as either Debb's or Jacko's quarter. Given the preponderance of livestock at Jacko's, including the only sheep on the plantation (see Table 7.1), the layout of the Utopia site does not seem to reflect large-scale animal penning, nor does the faunal assemblage indicate an increase in sheep elements.[13] Therefore, if for the moment it is presumed that Utopia was the site of Debb's Quarter, evidence strongly suggests that Jacko's was located at a place called Tutter's Neck located one and a half miles to the northwest from the Bray plantation (Kelso 1974:7–8; 1984:106–110; Noel Hume 1968) (see Map 7.2).[14]

The probate inventory for Littletown, Debb's, and Jacko's lumps the twenty-four adult slaves and four children into one list, perhaps a sign that there was some amount of fluidity between the three venues and people moved about frequently depending upon changing staffing needs (see Tables 7.1 and 7.2). The sex ratio almost reached parity among the twenty-four adults, but how the eleven men and thirteen women were apportioned between the three quarters remains unknown. The inventory is more explicit concerning the distribution of slaves on the six outlying quarters at Rockahock, listing the names

TABLE 7.1

Nine Quarter Farms Owned by James Bray in 1725

	Adult Female Slaves	Adult Male Slaves	Overseer or Foreman	Cattle	Swine	Sheep	Horses	Mean Acres	Acres in Use*
Littletown/Utopia									
Littletown	13	11		45			7	427	
Debb's			Forewoman	20	28			427	480
Jacko's			Foreman	33	66	45		427	
Rockahock									
Roger's	3	3	Overseer	32	21		4	370	120
Bridges	10	3	Overseer	18	39			370	260
Dubblerum's	3	3	Foreman	24	12		2	370	120
Nero's	3	2	Foreman		16			370	100
New Kent	8	3		19	18		1	370	220
Rockahock	3	2		25	30			370	100
Totals	43	27		216	230	45	14	3,500	1,400

*Based on an average allocation of twenty acres per adult fieldhand under a crop rotation system.

TABLE 7.2
Enslaved staff working at Littletown,
Debb's, and Jacko's in 1725

Women	Men	Girls	Boys	Total
Moll	Sam	Lucy	Spring	
Dye	Jack		Martin	
Janny	Caesar		Daniel	
Batty	Tom			
Flora	Jupiter			
Doll	Jacko			
Nanny	May			
Hope	Orson			
Debb	Mark			
Augor	Brinee			
Juno	Sandy			
Judy				
Pegg				
13	11	1	3	28

and gender of the slaves at each (see Table 7.3). Because of this, the Rockahock inventory can serve as a proxy of sorts for Littletown, Debb's, and Jacko's, allowing some inferences to be made concerning gender demographics there.

At the Rockahock property, Bray divided forty-six enslaved adults into six separate quarters, ranging between a low of five adults at Nero's and Rockahock Quarter to thirteen adult slaves at Bridges. The ratio of men to women at four of the six outlying plantations was almost at parity, while at Bridges and New Kent women outnumbered men roughly three to one. Overall, Bray placed thirty women (65 percent) and sixteen men (35 percent) on the Rockahock property, a ratio of close to two women for every man (see Table 7.3).

The predominance of women at Bridges and New Kent quarters is unusual for the time period. Most planters of the day preferred male laborers over female at a rate of two or three to one, quite opposite the pattern observed at the Rockahock property (see Kolchin 1987:208; Kulikoff 1986:66–68; Stevenson 1996:167; Treckel 1996:70; Walsh 1997:82–84). Most of Bray's con-

TABLE 7.3

Enslaved Staff Working at Six of James Bray's Rockahock Property in 1725

	Women		Men	Children	Equipment
Rogers's					
Quarter	Sarah		Frank	Nanny	Frying pan
(8)	Judy		George	Simon	Large iron pot
	Dye		Ben		Old gun
					Warming pan
Bridges					
Quarter	Parthenia	Phillis	Luke	Children	Iron pot
(13+)	Hannah	Maria	Thunder		
	Dinah	Janny	Peter		
	Patience	Parthenia			
	Betty	Lucy			
Dubblerum's					
Quarter	Sarah		Dubblerum	Child	Pot
(7)	Queen		Dick		
	Margaret		Sharper		
Nero's					
Quarter	Beauty		Nero	Children	
(5+)	Jammy		Cuffee		
	Amy				
New Kent					
Quarter	Venus	Abigall	Jupiter		Iron pots (2)
(11)	Nanny	Fanny	Cain		
	Bess	Patty	Tom		
	Esthar	Rachael			
Rockahock					
Quarter	Juno		Ned		
(5)	Elizabeth		Abell		
	Sugar				
Total = 49+	30		16	3+	

temporaries believed that African men were more capable of withstanding the severity of fieldwork. Ironically, few planters, probably including Bray, were aware that in the majority of West African cultures women did most of the agricultural fieldwork, while many of the men in those same cultures were relatively unfamiliar with its rigors (Brown 1996:115; Fage 1989:154–156; Keim 1983:148; Meillassoux 1991:111, 356 n. 22; Stevenson 1996:171; Treckel 1996:67).

Bray may have valued the reproductive capabilities of female slaves, whereas most of his contemporaries opted to buy new Africans off the boat when in need of more field hands.[15] Or, given the inflated value that European slave traders placed on men, Bray may have chosen to purchase more African women as a cost-saving measure (White 1985:64). Bray probably also realized that women in general tended to be more docile and less inclined to run away (Morgan 1998:526).

In the end, market forces likely determined most of Bray's choices. For instance, slave ships embarking from the Bight of Biafra dominated the Chesapeake trade in the early eighteenth century, and these ships often carried more enslaved women than men, making Bray's choices little more than an issue of supply and demand (Eltis 1998; Nwokeji 2001; Walsh 1997:79). For these reasons, and perhaps others, Bray apportioned his six Rockahock slave quarters with two adult women for every one adult man.

Yet the disproportionate number of women is deceiving. If the quarters at Bridges and New Kent are removed from the equation, there is virtual parity between men and women (see Table 7.1). In all probability, the divergence in numbers between enslaved men and women at Bridges and New Kent was a result of a specific management directive from Bray. The majority of women living at Bridges and New Kent may have been new arrivals, with Bray choosing to group them together with fewer new African men as a means to acclimate them to their situation. Bridges and New Kent may have functioned as training and seasoning quarters, places where newly arrived slaves adjusted to the environment, to their enslavement, to the demands of fieldwork, and to the daily regimen that would characterize the remainder of their lives.[16] Planters usually intermingled seasoned slaves with new arrivals to speed the process of assimilation (Walsh 1997:83). Moreover, Bray may have realized that gang labor was the most efficient manner for controlling and extracting work from new workers unqualified to take on individual tasks or to work without supervision. Chesapeake planters tended to favor assigning women to gang labor, especially as the eighteenth century progressed (Carr and Walsh 1988:179; Morgan 1988). However it occurred, having groups of enslaved African women cohabit and work together at Bridges and New Kent replicated typical domestic social organization in many West and Central African cultures where women and men were often strictly segregated, and this could have made the transition to slavery less demoralizing for some of these women (Casey 1991:142; Mullin 1992:172).

The presence of children at four of the six Rockahock quarters strongly suggests that conjugal pairings had occurred between adults at these locations (see Table 7.3). In fact, it is tempting to suggest that at Rogers's, Dubblerum's, and Nero's most of the women and men formed consensual unions. At Bridges two women named Parthenia strongly implies a mother and her Virginia-born teenage daughter were in residence, whereas the lack of children at New Kent and Rockahock indicate that both quarters may have been stocked primarily with recently purchased "new Negroes" (see Table 7.3). Bray may have actively encouraged his slaves to form monogamous bonds as a mechanism of control, something that became standard practice by midcentury (Berlin 1998:129–131; Walsh 1997:83–84). However, there appears to have been a shortage of marriage partners for some of the forty-three adult women under Bray's control. Some may have had to look outside the immediate confines of the quarters for mates.

Although the ratio of the eleven men to thirteen women at Littletown, Debb's, and Jacko's was close to equal, it cannot be ascertained who or how many lived at each of the three quartering areas. At the six Rockahock quarters, Bray placed an average of eight adults at each, and typically most field quarters in this era housed eight to ten adults (Kolchin 1993:33; Kulikoff 1986:330–331; Morgan 1998:36; G. Mullin 1972:48). Planters considered more than ten to fifteen slaves at any one quarter the maximum that an overseer could manage efficiently (Walsh 1997:87, 289 n. 26). If the twenty-four adults were distributed evenly between Littletown, Debb's, and Jacko's, then it is possible that between six and ten slaves lived at each of the three quarters.

Given the demographic snapshot of Bray's slaves in 1725, apparently he employed slave women at the same tasks as enslaved men, and in the case of Debb, a woman assumed the role of authority figure. Having senior male slaves such as Jacko, Dubblerum, and Nero serving as foremen was not unusual.[17] However, an eighteenth-century slave forewoman like Debb is almost unheard of in the history books, although later in the nineteenth century a few make reference to slave women serving as drivers, primarily leading gangs of other women and children (see Carr and Walsh 1988; Fogel 1989:45–49; Mann 1990:139). In the Chesapeake, an enslaved woman's stage of life or marital status usually determined her social position (Shammas 1985:25–26). In some West and Central African cultures, postmenopausal or celibate women sometimes achieved positions of leadership because of their desexualized status (see Ardener 1981:16; Barley 1994:63; Callaway 1981:172,

174; Sudarkasa 1987:38; Terborg-Penn 1987:51). Often these female elders attained powerful positions through special spiritual skills, healing, midwifery, or divination (Amadiume 1987; Goheen 1996; Steady 1987:17). Whether or not these types of skills were carried over on Virginia plantations, or if planters like Bray were aware of them, is difficult to know. Most likely, the residents of the quarter recognized and respected certain abilities Debb possessed, possibly based on indigenous values such as age or spiritual power. Bray may have appreciated the authority bestowed on Debb by her fellow slaves and followed the will of the community by openly recognizing its most eminent member.

In terms of gender, it is likely that women, whether conferred with authority like Debb or not, played the key role in structuring the living environment within the domestic settings of most Chesapeake quarters, whereas men focused their attention outside the site (Carr and Walsh 1988:182). In fact, given the traditional African segregation of male and female spheres of interaction, men may have spent the bulk of their leisure time fishing, hunting, visiting wives or relatives, or otherwise congregating away from the immediate confines of the site when circumstances allowed it. At Chesapeake domestic slave sites, apparently many men were absent or at the very least peripheral characters, while the women largely shaped the day-to-day interaction at the living quarters (Fesler 1997; Heath and Bennett 2000).

Architectural Analysis: Interior Space

Architecture, in terms of interior space, is one of the fundamental elements that had an effect on gender relations at places like Utopia. The buildings at the site created locales where space helped to shape gender roles and, simultaneously, where gender roles helped to shape that space (see Conkey and Spector 1984:24; Joyce and Claassen 1997:5–7; Little 1994:198; Singleton and Bograd 1995:29–30).[18] The size of each dwelling, its interior layout, the number of rooms, the number of subfloor pits, and other features all played a role in structuring the interior spaces and guiding interaction (Table 7.4).

A cursory examination of the posthole patterns for all four structures indicates that the builders followed the vernacular architectural norms of the time and presumably divided each of the three dwellings into two rooms, a

TABLE 7·4

Traits of the Four Post-in-Ground Structures at the Utopia Quarter

	Size (feet)	Square Feet	Rooms	Hall Subfloor Pits	Parlor Subfloor Pits	Total Subfloor Pits	Shed Addition	Floor Type	Chimney Type
Structure 1	12 x 28	336	2?	4	2	6	No	Dirt	End
Structure 10	15.5 x 32 6 x 8.5	547	3	4	8	12	6 x 8.5	Dirt	End
Structure 20	12 x 28	336	2?	1	0	1	No	Dirt	End
Service Building	12 x 16	192	1?	0	0	0	No	Dirt	End

"hall" and a "parlor" (see Carson et al. 1981). When occupied by Virginians of European heritage, the hall normally functioned as the larger, more public of the two rooms, and usually centered on a fireplace for cooking, eating, and warmth, whereas the parlor served as a more private chamber, usually for sleeping. The enslaved Africans transplanted to Utopia may have chosen to inhabit the structures following the European hall and parlor model, or they may have devised their own more culturally comfortable use of interior space. Utopia's architectural evidence provides some tentative insights on this issue.

Structure 1 was twelve by twenty-eight feet and contained six subfloor pits cutting into its dirt floor, four of them positioned at the south end of the building fronting a small hearth (see Map 7.3 and Table 7.4). None of the postholes showed evidence of repair, indicating that the structure probably stood for no more than twenty to thirty years (Carson et al. 1981:158). The carpenters may have partitioned the house into two rooms, a smaller hall in the south half and a larger parlor on the north end, although there is no direct evidence of this aside from the pattern of subfloor pit placement, which suggests that Pit 5 and Pit 6 were separated from the complex around the hearth (see Map 7.3). At least one door on the long east wall probably opened out into the courtyard, providing access to the outdoor cooking pit located not more than fifteen feet away (see Map 7.3). Whether another door on the west side provided cross-passage access remains unverified. Archaeologists turned up no evidence of window glass, nor any pieces of casement window leads in association with Structure 1, strongly suggesting that wooden shutters served as the only window coverings, if any. A small dry-laid hearth at the south end of the building fronted a wattle-and-daub fireplace and chimney, the structure's only source of heat.

The largest dwelling on the site, Structure 10, was sixteen by thirty-two feet with a six-by-eight-foot shed addition on the east end (see Map 7.3 and Table 7.4). Given the fact that only one post on the north wall of Structure 10 demonstrated any signs of repair, the dwelling probably stood for no longer than twenty to thirty years (Carson et al. 1981:158). On the west gable end a heavy concentration of ash, charcoal, and scorched sand betrayed the location of a fireplace with an exterior wattle-and-daub chimney. As evidenced by a small weight-bearing post stud located in the center of the building, the builders partitioned Structure 10 into two sixteen-by-sixteen-foot rooms, what would be considered a hall and parlor in vernacular architectural terms (see

Carson et al. 1981). The west end hall contained one large six-by-six-foot sub-floor pit (Subfloor Pit 36) that cut through the dirt floor fronting the fireplace; it had been modified and expanded several times. Archaeologists discovered traces of wooden sidewalls still in place, as well as a large hinge, proving that this particular subfloor pit had a lid. Compared to all the other subfloor pits at Utopia, this one was the most securable. Not only could the box be locked to prevent theft, but the walls and lid probably kept out most vermin.

The parlor in the east half of Structure 10 contained eight subfloor pits, all of which were smaller in size and shallower than the large subfloor pit in the hall. Except for Subfloor Pit 14, most of the parlor subfloor pits were arrayed along the edges of the interior walls presumably in an effort to keep the main area of foot traffic open and clear of obstacles (see Map 7.3). Based on the placement of subfloor pits, and the center partition, the main door to the building faced the courtyard and probably was located on the south wall adjacent to Subfloor Pit 9. Another door likely opened from the shed into a small fenced enclosure connecting the corner of Structure 10 to the corner of Structure 20. A possible single scrap of casement lead produced the only hint that the building possessed glazed windows. Given the lack of any additional evidence, it appears likely that most if not all the window coverings in Struc-ture 10 consisted of wooden shutters.

The dimensions of Structure 20 matched those of Structure 1, some twelve feet in width and twenty-eight feet in length (see Map 7.3 and Table 7.4). Dur-ing the life of the structure the north gable end needed extensive repair. To fix rotted posts, it was necessary to tear out the entire north wall. Both corner posts on that end were replaced, and a center gable post was added for addi-tional support. The new wall extended the length of the structure approxi-mately one additional foot.

Archaeologists uncovered no evidence to indicate how the builders inter-nally divided Structure 20. Presumably, like Structure 1, a partition separated the dwelling into two rooms, a hall and parlor. Like its twin structure across the way, a door probably opened onto the courtyard. Due to the extensive repair work on the north gable, and the positioning of the one and only sub-floor pit in the extreme southwest corner of the building presumably near a fireplace, it seems likely that the main heat source was located on the south end of the structure. Other than the single subfloor pit dug through the dirt floor, archaeologists encountered no other features inside Structure 20 (see

Map 7.3). A lack of window glass fragments and an errant casement lead in one of the postholes indicated that Structure 20 probably was not outfitted with glazed windows.

The twelve-by-sixteen-foot service building was located roughly twenty feet to the south of Structure 20. With no apparent source of heat, no subfloor pits, and no other signs of intensive domestic activity, this structure apparently was used for storage or some other utilitarian task.

Several strands of evidence indicate that the three dwellings all stood simultaneously at the site. The fence joining Structures 10 and 20 clearly illustrates their contemporaneity (see Map 7.3). Moreover, the cross-postholes for Structure 1 and 10 were placed off center in exactly the same manner, a unique architectural irregularity that suggests the buildings were erected at the same time by the same builder (see Carson et al. 1981:151–153). Furthermore, Structures 1 and 20 were identical in size, a strong indication that they were built together.

Although all three dwellings were spartan, Structure 10 contained several features that likely made it a slightly more attractive and habitable dwelling compared to the other two. Structure 10 had 61 percent more floor space and definitely had three discrete interior rooms (hall, parlor, and shed), whereas Structures 1 and 20 had no direct evidence of internal partitioning. If Structures 1 and 20 consisted of only one great room, this would have had a direct bearing on issues such as privacy and personal space and, in turn, on gender relations. Thus, assuming that privacy and the division of space was preferred by the inhabitants, in general it appears that the potential living conditions within Structure 10 were marginally better than those in Structures 1 and 20 due to the fact that it had additional usable space and rooms. At the very least, Structure 10 was experienced differently than the other two dwellings.

Spatial Analysis: Exterior Areas

While interior spaces within the dwellings had a significant impact on social interaction and gender relations, recent research suggests that enslaved African Americans spent the bulk of their time out of doors at work and at play in the yard (see, for example, Gundaker 1993; Hall 1990:170; Westmacott 1992). By chance or design, the layout of the Utopia Quarter appears to have facilitated social relations among the residents because the buildings faced inward toward each other to form an open-ended courtyard space in the center (see Map 7.3). This dynamic exterior yard space formed by the placement of the buildings seems to have produced a communal locale for the residents of the site to gather and interact. The courtyard at Utopia resembled the layout of "compounds" regularly observed in many Central and West African cultures at the time and up to the present.[19] A typical African compound was enclosed on all sides, forming an open space or courtyard in the center that provided shared space.

Although the design of the site is reminiscent of Central and West African living arrangements, the buildings themselves conform to standard English measurements and reflect an English vernacular architectural post-in-ground tradition (Carson et al. 1981; Glassie 1975; see also Anthony 1976a, b; S. Jones 1985; Vlach 1991). Bray must have employed a skilled carpenter familiar with English and Virginia architecture to oversee the construction project.[20] No doubt Bray's slaves provided most of the labor, cutting the trees, hewing the logs, fitting the frames together, and digging the postholes, but decisions concerning the sizes, locations, and details of the structures were supervised by a trained carpenter in consultation with Bray himself. Exactly why the builders laid out the four structures in a rather unorthodox configuration remains unknown. It is possible that one or more slaves may have convinced the carpenter to arrange the buildings into a compound. Or, perhaps Bray approved of the compound arrangement, believing the organization of the structures into a quasi-Panoptic open-ended square improved surveillance of them (see Fesler 1997). Whatever the case, upon arriving at their new quarters at Utopia, most of the enslaved Africans must have immediately sensed a remarkable coincidence; the four structures arrayed into a compound at Utopia replicated living spaces in a majority of West and Central African cultures, the very cultures from which most or all the newly arrived Africans had originated.

The seemingly familiar environment that the compound at Utopia created for its enslaved African inhabitants must have had a significant influence on the social relations among men and women operating in its spaces. It is possible that the compound setting stimulated the restoration of some traditional domestic patterns among its African residents, including living arrangements that were based on segregating men and women. If so, the distribution of artifacts associated with each of the dwellings may be able to illustrate this phenomenon.

Artifact Distribution Analysis: The Three Households

The analysis of the Utopia Quarter artifacts is based loosely on the artifact classification system Stanley South developed from his work several decades ago in the Carolinas (1977).[21] South's most general classification levels, what he termed the *group* and the *class* categories, are used for comparison of the Utopia household contexts, with several modifications. South concocted nine broad artifact groups: Kitchen, Bone, Architectural, Furniture, Arms, Clothing, Personal, Tobacco Pipe, and Activities. Within those nine groups, South proposed forty-two artifact classes, ranging from ceramics to military objects (South 1977:95–96). For analysis of Utopia all ethnobotanical materials have been moved from Activities and placed into a tenth group, Food. Colonoware pottery has been moved from Activities and grouped with the Kitchen data. Items such as mirror glass, fossilized shark's teeth, smoker's companions, decorative wire, decorative chain, and combs have been placed in the Personal group. Aiglets have been added to the Clothing group. Flint flakes have been added to the Arms group, under the assumption that they may have accumulated during the process of making and retouching gunflints.

Archaeologists recovered more than 31,000 artifacts from the Utopia Quarter, in addition to almost 180 pounds of charcoal, oyster shell, eggshell, mortar, daub, and brick. By eliminating from further study most of the noncultural items, the Native American ceramics and lithics, and all the materials tabulated by weight, 15,009 artifacts remain for analysis (Table 7.5). The primary objective of artifact analysis is to identify artifact patterns that reveal gendered spaces at Utopia. It is expected that all three of the hypothesized living arrangements—single-sex barracks, a village compound, or kin-based domestic units—created distinctive and identifiable artifact patterns within each of the dwelling units.[22] By comparing the artifact assemblages from each household, at both the group and class level, it may be possible to isolate locations of gendered activity, places where women and men assembled, and thereby draw some conclusions about how gender shaped social relations at Utopia.

Ascribing a particular set of data exclusively to women or to men is problematic. Each of the ten artifact groups provides a loose analytical framework for comparing the intensity of various domestic activities associated with each of the three households. Nonetheless, based on a task differentiation framework devised by Janet Spector (1983), modified by James Gibb and Julie King (1991) on several Chesapeake sites, and with the guidance of a detailed farm

TABLE 7.5
Groups and Classes of Utopia Quarter Artifacts

Kitchen Artifact Group	777	5.18%
1. Ceramics	181	
2. Wine bottles	464	
3. Case bottles	39	
4. Tumbler	1	
5. Pharmaceutical bottles	37	
6. Glassware	7	
7. Tableware	31	
8. Kitchenware	17	
Faunal (Bone) Group	5,913	39.40%
9. Bone fragments	5,913	
Architectural Group	5,757	38.36%
10. Window glass	1	
11. Hand wrought nails	5,723	
12. Spikes	14	
13. Construction hardware	16	
14. Door lock parts	3	
Furniture Group	13	0.09%
15. Furniture hardware	13	
Arms Group	184	1.23%
16. Shot and sprue	32	
17. Gunflints/flint flakes	152	
Clothing Group	275	1.83%
19. Buckles	4	
20. Thimble	1	
21. Buttons	14	
22. Scissors	1	
23. Straight pins	117	
24. Hook/eye fasteners	2	
24a. Aiglet	1	
25. Beads	135	
Personal Group	18	0.12%
28. Key	1	
29. Personal items	17	

(continued on next page)

TABLE 7.5 *(continued)*

Tobacco Pipe Group	1,247	8.31%
30a. English CTP	1,157	
30b. Local CTP	90	
Activities Group	449	2.99%
31. Construction tools	11	
32. Farm tools	2	
33. Toys	4	
34. Fishing gear	1	
37. Storage items	18	
39. Stable and barn	10	
40. Misc. hardware	40	
41. Other (scrap metal)	363	
Food Group	376	2.51%
38. Ethnobotanical Material	376	
Totals	15,009	100%

diary kept by George Washington in the 1780s (Carr and Walsh 1988), some artifact types can be correlated with activities principally performed by women or men (Table 7.6). For the purposes of analysis, the Kitchen, Bone, Food, and Clothing groups at Utopia are considered to be associated primarily with women, whereas the Arms, Tobacco Pipe, and Activities groups are regarded as men's endeavors. Three of the groups, Architecture, Furniture, and Personal, cannot reasonably be linked to either men or women and will be eliminated from any further study here.

None of the seven potentially gendered artifact groups can be considered the exclusive domain of one gender or the other. Some of the tasks enslaved men and women performed necessarily overlapped. For example, following the customary division of labor in most African cultures, enslaved women performed most of the duties in the kitchen, processing, preparing, and storing food (activities that encompass the Kitchen, Bone, and Food groups). However, both men and women used Kitchen group artifacts to consume and store foodstuffs, and Bone group artifacts accumulated in places where animals were butchered, prepared, consumed, and stored, activities shared by both women and men. Moreover, given the imbalanced sex ratio in the region in the early eighteenth century, some men may have been forced to take on

TABLE 7.6
Genders Associated with the Artifact Groups

Artifact Group	Gender
Kitchen	Women
Faunal (bone)	Women
Architectural	
Furniture	
Arms	Men
Clothing	Women
Personal	
Tobacco pipe	Men
Activities	Men
Food	Women

women's roles and prepare meals and perform other domestic tasks. In general, however, women are more strongly linked with all facets of food processing, preparation, consumption, and storage, whereas men were more likely to be involved to a lesser degree in the domestic setting, primarily with the processing and consumption of food. Therefore, the presence of Kitchen, Bone, and Food group artifacts represents a stronger association with women's activity (see Tables 7.5 and 7.6).

The Clothing group consists of both items worn on clothing and objects used in the production and maintenance of clothing, such as brass straight pins, thimbles, and scissors (see Table 7.5). Sewing normally was a woman's domain (see Galle, this volume). In addition, women were more likely to adorn themselves with decorative beads (or more decorative beads) than men, and given the fact that women commonly wore more layers of clothing than men, clothing fasteners and possibly even buttons were more likely to come from women's garments (see Baumgarten 1988). Given this, Clothing group artifacts appear to be more representative of women than men at places like Utopia.

Three of the artifact groups can be reasonably associated primarily with Utopia's male residents (see Table 7.6). The Arms group contains shot, sprue, and gun parts, gunflints, and flint flakes. All these items were involved with the use and maintenance of firearms for hunting, an arena that men were more likely to control. The Tobacco Pipe group contains both locally manufactured Chesapeake pipes and English pipes. Although both sexes enjoyed smoking tobacco, men may have dedicated themselves to the practice more often than women, meaning concentrations of tobacco pipe fragments may pinpoint places where men assembled. The Activities group consists of a wide range of artifacts generally used by men outside the domestic sphere, such as construction tools, farm tools, fishing gear, storage items, livestock equipment, and miscellaneous hardware. Again, at times there was overlap, and women may have found themselves carrying out tasks usually reserved for men. For example, the shortage of men at some of Bray's outlying quarters may have necessitated that women handle some men's work, such as hunting, fishing, repairing equipment, or caring for livestock. Circumstances for bridging the gap between men's and women's domains was always a possibility at the Utopia Quarter, largely dependent on outside forces imposed upon them by James Bray or other authority figures.

Of the seven artifact groups possibly related to gender, the faunal Bone group (39.4 percent) makes up more than one-third of the entire artifact collection. Tobacco Pipe group fragments comprise 8.3 percent of the assemblage, followed by Kitchen group artifacts at 5.2 percent, the Activities group (3 percent), the Food group (2.5 percent), the Clothing group (1.8 percent), and the Arms group (1.2 percent). These numbers provide a baseline mean for comparison with assemblages from each of the three households associated with Structures 1, 10, and 20.

Structure 1

The artifact assemblage recovered from the six subfloor pits in Structure 1 consisted of nearly 2,800 artifacts. The artifact profile generated by the seven artifact groups for Structure 1 tends to suggest an association with activities conducted by men (Table 7.7). The Arms and Tobacco Pipe groups, both presumably men's groups, produced a percentage of artifacts more than one standard deviation above the site's mean. However, the Activities group, again seemingly affiliated with men, came in at more than one standard deviation below the mean. Among the four women's artifact groups, only the Clothing group yielded a reading more than one standard deviation above the norm. The three domestic groups, Kitchen, Bone, and Food, all measured below the

TABLE 7.7
Profile of Artifact Groups Associated with Structure 1

	Structure 1 (%)	Mean (%)	Standard Deviation	Deviation from the Mean	Gender
Kitchen	4.65	4.87	1.91	-0.12	- Women
Bone	36.83	39.09	4.91	-0.46	- Women
Arms	2.97	1.52	1.31	1.11	+ Men*
Clothing	5.15	2.45	2.35	1.15	+ Women*
Tobacco pipe	15.73	9.18	6.28	1.04	+ Men*
Activities	1.57	2.80	1.07	-1.15	- Men*
Food	1.14	2.29	1.08	-1.06	- Women*

*More than one standard deviation above or below the mean.

mean, with Food more than one standard deviation below it (see Table 7.7). Although the evidence is not conclusive, men's artifact groups outweigh women's by a small margin. At the very least, the absence of women's artifact groups, particularly those directly associated with food processing, preparation, consumption, and storage suggest that Structure 1 was not the focal point of this type of activity.

Structure 10

Archaeologists recovered more than 6,700 artifacts associated with Structure 10. Subfloor Pit 36, the large storage cellar located in the hall, produced the vast majority of those artifacts (n=4,389), while the eight subfloor pits in the parlor yielded 1,901 artifacts. Structure 10's artifact group profile was almost exactly opposite the profile encountered in Structure 1, with women's artifact groups dominating in the majority of the seven groups (Table 7.8). In the three domestic categories, the Kitchen, Bone, and Food groups all were at or near one standard deviation above the mean. The only women's group to come in under the mean was the Clothing group. For the men's groups, only the Activities group deviated above the mean, whereas the Arms and Tobacco Pipe groups were slightly below it. Because of the apparent high degree of

TABLE 7.8

Profile of Artifact Groups Associated with Structure 10

	Structure 10 (%)	Mean (%)	Standard Deviation	Deviation from the Mean	Gender
Kitchen	6.88	4.87	1.91	1.05	+ Women*
Bone	44.73	39.09	4.91	1.15	+ Women*
Arms	1.16	1.52	1.31	-0.27	- Men
Clothing	1.23	2.45	2.35	-0.52	- Women
Tobacco Pipe	8.61	9.18	6.28	-0.09	- Men
Activities	3.37	2.80	1.07	0.53	+ Men
Food	3.28	2.29	1.08	0.92	+ Women

*More than one standard deviation above or below the mean.

food-related activities in Structure 10—especially those associated with Sub-floor Pit 36 in front of the hearth in the hall—of the three households, Structure 10 has the strongest association with women's activity.

Structure 20

Structure 20 produced almost five thousand artifacts, all but a handful extracted from Subfloor Pit 21. The overall artifact profile for Structure 20 did not indicate a clear connection with either sex. None of the seven artifact groups produced readings more than one standard deviation above the site's mean. In fact, only the Activities and Food groups generated a high enough relative number of artifacts to deviate above the norm. The other five categories deviated on the negative side of the mean, but not by a noticeably large percentage. All this indicates that neither women nor men dominated the activities in Structure 20, suggesting that both sexes contributed to the artifact assemblage in relatively equal proportions (see Table 7.9).

By comparing and contrasting the artifact group profiles for the three households, it becomes apparent that certain types of activities are more strongly associated with particular dwelling units. For example, Structure 10 yielded a significantly higher amount of Kitchen, Bone, and Food group arti-

TABLE 7.9
Profile of Artifact Groups Associated with Structure 20

	Structure 20 (%)	Mean (%)	Standard Deviation	Deviation from the Mean	Gender
Kitchen	3.07	4.87	1.91	-0.94	- Women
Bone	35.72	39.09	4.91	-0.69	- Women
Arms	0.42	1.52	1.31	-0.84	- Men
Clothing	0.96	2.45	2.35	-0.63	- Women
Tobacco pipe	3.21	9.18	6.28	-0.95	- Men
Activities	3.47	2.80	1.07	0.63	+ Men
Food	2.45	2.29	1.08	0.15	+ Women

facts than either Structures 1 or 20, indicating that it functioned as the most active indoor food processing, preparation, consumption, and storage zone at the site. Activity related to sustenance occurred in both Structure 1 and 20 but at a much reduced rate (compare with Tables 7.7, 7.8, and 7.9). Archaeologists recovered enough Kitchen group material from Structures 1 and 20 to indicate these activities were not confined exclusively to Structure 10. However, Structure 10 contained three to four times more ceramics, glass bottles and containers, and eating utensils than the other two dwellings, two to three times more faunal remains, and at least twice as many Food group items, strongly suggesting that it was a focal point for kitchen-related activity.

Structures 1 and 10 produced the vast majority of the Arms group artifacts, but only in Structure 1 did the percentage of these artifacts deviate significantly above the mean. All of Structure 1's Arms group artifacts were recovered from the subfloor pits arrayed around the hearth, suggesting that the fireplace in Structure 1 served as a regular setting for casting lead shot and making gunflints. The occupants of the hall in Structure 10 conducted these same two tasks as well, but on a reduced scale.

Based on raw numbers, archaeologists excavated more Clothing group artifacts from in front of the Structure 1 hearth (n=142) than from all the other contexts combined (n=130), primarily due to the 107 glass seed beads from the subfloor pits around the hearth (compare with Tables 7.7, 7.8, and 7.9). Archaeologists retrieved most of the artifacts associated with sewing, such as brass straight pins and iron scissors, from the halls of all three structures, seemingly in direct relation to the fireplaces in each dwelling. Mending clothing, sewing, darning, and perhaps quilting may have been activities conducted primarily in one's off-hours at night, whereupon firelight was essential. Because of the location of firelight, it seems reasonable to assume that over the years dropped and lost pins accumulated in the halls, and the high number of seed beads in the Structure 1 hall may be attributable to this phenomenon as well (see Kelso 1984:201–202).

Structures 1 and 10 produced most of the tobacco pipe fragments from the site, in comparison to the low number of pipe materials in Structure 20 (compare with Tables 7.7, 7.8, and 7.9). Tobacco smoking may have been one of the few leisure-time activities available to the residents of Utopia, and the presence or absence of broken tobacco pipes may delineate areas used for socializing and limited relaxation. Most of the pipes accumulated in the halls in both Structure 1 and 10, presumably a sign that much of the tobacco smoking took place in front of the hearth, whereas the inhabitants of Structure 20 were less inclined to gather and smoke tobacco there.

Most of the Activities group artifacts consisted of scrap metal (see Table 7.5). The remaining Activities group artifacts were distributed almost evenly throughout the three households, although higher percentages of them were found in Structures 10 and 20. All three structures contained evidence of construction and farm tools, storage containers, livestock equipment, and miscellaneous hardware, implying that men were regularly present.

The overall comparison of the three structures demonstrates that the hall in Structure 10 produced more domestic artifacts than the other contexts at the site. The principal locus of indoor food processing, preparation, consumption, and storage was the hearth in Structure 10. Furthermore, tobacco smoking, firearms maintenance, and sewing activity took place at elevated levels around the hearth in Structure 1. In general, the artifact group profiles of the three dwelling units suggest that Structure 1 was oriented toward men's activity and Structure 10 toward women's activity. Structure 20 provides a neutral reading, with neither women nor men dominating the profile.

As mentioned previously, none of the artifacts in any of the seven artifact groups can be associated exclusively with one sex or the other; within most of the groups there is the potential for gender overlap. In an effort to isolate artifact types with a direct correlation with one sex or the other, several specific

TABLE 7.10
Comparison of Women's and Men's Artifacts within the Utopia Dwellings

	Structure 1	%	Structure 10	%	Structure 20	%	Totals
Thimbles	0	0	0	0	1	100	1
Scissors	1	100	0	0	0	0	1
Straight pins	31	26	56	48	30	26	117
Beads	107	80	16	12	10	8	133
Toy marbles	0	0	2	50	2	50	4
Women's Artifacts	140	54	74	29	44	17	258
Shot and sprue	11	37	16	53	3	10	30
Gunflints and flint flakes	67	47	59	42	17	12	143
Construction tools	0	0	5	55	4	44	9
Fishing tackle	0	0	1	100	0	0	1
Livestock equipage	3	33	5	55	1	11	9
Men's Artifacts	81	42	86	45	25	13	192
Tobacco Pipe fragments	395	36	535	49	154	14	1,084

classes of artifacts were chosen for additional analysis (Table 7.10). Items such as sewing equipment (thimbles, scissors, and straight pins), glass beads, and toy marbles are considered strongly related to women, almost to the exclusion of men. At times men may have handled these artifacts, but for the most part, women did the lion's share of sewing and mending, were more likely to adorn themselves with glass beads, and were more involved with caring for children who might have played with marbles (although adults used marbles for games, gambling, and other leisure activities). Artifacts attributed to men include lead shot and sprue, gunflints and flint flakes, construction tools, fishing tackle, and livestock equipage. Again, women had access to these things, but men normally claimed the responsibility for performing these types of jobs.

Based on the types of artifacts ascribed to women in Table 7.10, more than half of all the women's artifacts turned up in the hall in Structure 1, largely due to the 107 beads recovered there. Structure 10 produced 29 percent of the women's artifacts, and Structure 20 yielded only 17 percent of them.

Artifacts related specifically to men's activity were arrayed throughout the buildings in a slightly different fashion than the women's artifacts. Structure 10 yielded 45 percent of the men's artifacts (32 percent in the hall and 13 percent in the parlor), while nearly the same amount, 42 percent of the men's artifacts, came from Structure 1. Structure 20 was on the low end of the scale and produced only 13 percent of the artifacts ascribed to men. According to these numbers, women and men tended to occupy the same interior spaces, although women may have had a stronger presence in Structures 1 and 20, whereas men may have asserted a more prominent role in Structure 10. These findings tend to contradict the earlier artifact group profiles which suggested that women predominated in Structure 10 and men in Structure 1, leading to the frustrating possibility that the archaeological evidence may not allow for any credible conclusions regarding men and women of Utopia.

Discussion

Many factors influence the mundane daily decisions people make about what roles and jobs women and men are expected to assume. The residents of Utopia seem to have established gender roles based on notions both old and new. Enslaved Africans toted cultural conceptions of the proper ways to interact to places such as Utopia like cultural suitcases. As they unpacked their baggage, the institution of Chesapeake slavery necessitated that these new arrivals jettison some of their cultural articles to comply with the system of violence and exploitation forced upon each one of them. Other old ways of living and interrelating were cobbled into the social fabric of Utopia to form a cultural bricolage recognizable and acceptable to both slave and master.

It is surmised that Utopia's cultural bricolage could have produced three possible living arrangements, all of which considered gender as a main organizing principle: (1) single-sex barracks; (2) a prototypical West or Central African "compound"; or (3) kin-based households. Although these systems of social organization did not remain static and may have changed over the life of the site, and additional cultural factors such as status, ethnicity, age, origin of birth, and so on, influenced how people stratified themselves into households, each of the three proposed living arrangements likely produced a distinctive archaeological imprint if put into use for any length of time at Utopia.

Evidence of Single-Sex Barracks at Utopia

In the early eighteenth century a few of the more prosperous planters began to accumulate populations of slaves that sometimes ranged in the dozens. Where formerly slaves and servants in the seventeenth century often lived in the same house with the master, planters like James Bray began housing groups of these alien "new Negroes" in separate quarters at places like Utopia (see Neiman 1980). Contrary to the makeup of Bray's slave population, on most plantations enslaved men tended to outnumber women five or ten to one (Kulikoff 1977:309). Whether planters intended to segregate the sexes, or their buying patterns simply facilitated housing men and women separately, some of the Chesapeake's earliest eighteenth-century enslaved Africans lived in what variously has been termed sex-segregated "dormitories" or "barracks" (Berlin 1998:113; Kolchin 1993:50; Kulikoff 1986:334; Morgan 1998:105–106). If single-sex barracks were in use at Utopia, they are expected to produce identifiable artifact assemblages that betray the dominant presence of either men or women.

According to the evidence, a principal amount of food-related activity took place in front of the hearth in Structure 10 and to a lesser extent at the hearths in Structures 1 and 20 (see Table 7.7, 7.8, and 7.9). If women performed the majority of the cooking, they must have taken on a conspicuous role in each of these structures. Presumably, a woman inhabited the same structure in which she cooked and asserted her authority over her hearth. The outside cooking pit was positioned closest to Structure 1 and across from Structure 20 (see Map 7.3), suggesting that the inhabitants of these two dwellings cooked a portion of their meals outdoors, perhaps moving inside during inclement weather. Outdoor cooking may explain why Structure 10 produced almost 400 percent more Kitchen group artifacts than both Structure 1 and 20.

Archaeologists retrieved 80 percent of the beads from Structure 1, and 27 percent of the sewing equipment. An almost identical amount of sewing equipment was recovered from Structure 20, while Structure 10 produced close to half the site's sewing articles. The distribution of sewing items and beads reinforces the notion that the hearths acted as loci for women's activity. The hearths in Structure 1 and 10 also attracted men's activity. Men apparently preferred knapping gunflints and casting lead shot in Structures 1 and 10, while Structure 20 seemingly was less inviting to both sexes. Based on tobacco pipe fragments, the residents enjoyed what little leisure time they had smoking in front of the hearths in Structure 1 and 10. Again, for some unknown reason the hearth in Structure 20 saw less activity than the other two, as measured by women's and men's artifacts and tobacco pipe fragments (see Table 7.10). Thus, the hearths in Structure 1 and 10 appeared to be the focal point of most indoor activity for both women and men. None of the three halls seemed to have been exclusively associated with one gender or the other.

While both men and women were present at the hearths of the three dwellings, the parlor in Structure 10 may have served primarily as a men's space. The challenge of living in cramped quarters, especially with unrelated individuals, prompted many slaves to dig subfloor pits as a means to store, curate, and protect personal belongings (Neiman 1997). Instead of placing one's worldly goods on a shelf or in a corner, open and vulnerable to theft, subfloor pits served as closets or lockers that could be covered and secured from others. Who would have been more inclined to carve out private storage spaces, men or women? With women spending the bulk of their time outside of fieldwork at the quarter, the need to store their belongings out of sight in a defined space may have been less crucial than men who were supposedly spending their off-hours away from the quarter. In some West and Central African cultures, women often participated in communal support networks when raising children and caring for their families, which may have neutralized their need for private space. The lack of small subfloor pits in Structure 20, therefore, may suggest a distinctly feminine space. Men, on the other hand, less inclined to pool their resources or form close alliances with other men in the homelands, could have manufactured privacy for themselves, even if it was a small hole in the parlor floor in Structure 10 to store a few meager belongings.

The archaeological evidence at Utopia raises the possibility that the occupants resided in sex-segregated dwellings. If this was the case, the parlor in Structure 10 probably accommodated men, and Structure 20 housed most of the women. However, the distribution of so-called male and female artifacts fails to establish a clear separation of men's and women's spheres. Instead, the artifact distributions suggest that women and men had equal access to all three Utopia dwellings and that both sexes left evidence of their presence.

Evidence of a Village Compound at Utopia

The idea that Africans enslaved in the Chesapeake engineered enough control in their lives to replicate a village compound that many of them knew from the homelands seems farfetched at best. Yet, almost inexplicably, the alignment of the buildings into a compound formation at Utopia paralleled the domestic landscape encountered throughout West and Central Africa. Except for different building materials, few would have noticed if the built landscape at Utopia had been transplanted into most areas of eighteenth-century Africa. The main feature of most African compounds was the presence of an open courtyard in the center surrounded by an assortment of buildings (see Bourdier and Minh-ha 1985). The head of the compound usually placed his dwelling in a central position, sometimes in the center of the courtyard, sometimes at the head of the other structures. Often women and men remained segregated in separate dwellings in a ranked social hierarchy. A headman's wives and children might live in a line of small huts, with the senior wives closest to the husband (Sobel 1987:124–126).[23] Other subordinates, sometimes the headman's sons, might live in another line of buildings in order of seniority. In most cases, the sexes were largely separated in the compounds and ate meals apart (see Potkay and Burr 1995:169), and if this way of living carried over to Utopia, household assemblages similar to single-sex barracks should be in evidence. However, in African compounds a central leadership figure was readily evident. Almost always male, the compound head organized the built landscape to support his dominant position (Fesler 1997). If a leader emerged at Utopia, the presence of higher status goods should be visible in one of the households.

As noted previously, archaeologists recovered the bulk of the artifacts from Structure 10. Structure 10 produced more Kitchen, Bone, Furniture, Personal, Activities, and Food group artifacts than Structures 1 and 20 combined. Architecturally, Structure 10 was larger, had a shed addition attached to it, and contained more architectural hardware than its two counterparts, including the only key and door lock parts, hinting at a level of security and privacy not attainable in the other dwellings. Even its largest subfloor pit acted as a lockbox, suggesting the unit's goods were worthy of protection from theft. The builders may have been instructed to make Structure 10 bigger, better built, and placed in a dominant position in relation to the other two dwellings because originally Bray intended it to house an overseer. In fact, it is quite likely that an overseer initially inhabited it. If so, this could account for the unusual layout of the compound: the structuring of the site conveyed both real and symbolic power to the occupant of Structure 10. At a later date Bray probably felt comfortable enough to withdraw the overseer and place Debb, Jacko, or one of his other more trusted slaves in charge.

Even if the original intent of the layout of the compound was to create an environment of control for an overseer occupying Structure 10, the architectural layout of the Utopia compound happened to correspond to the cardinal directions. Many West and Central African cultures perceived the universe as four-sided or cyclical, and they went to great lengths to align their living environment with the cardinal points (Aniakor 1996; Callaway 1981:173; Ferguson 1992; Thompson 1983, 1993). As such, Structure 10 was located to the north, Structure 1 to the west, Structure 20 to the east, and a burial ground to the south (Map 7.4). This arrangement likely placed the inhabitants of each building into spatial relationships with each other and the cosmos, and, by virtue of the location of the burial ground one hundred feet to the south, it also incorporated departed ancestors into the daily flow of space.

In Central African Congolese cultures, the position of landscape elements is a key feature of daily life. For example, north—the location of Structure 10—represents the height of the day, maleness, and authority, whereas south—the burial ground—equates to midnight and femaleness (Thompson 1983:109). Overall, the circle formed by the four compass points in the compound may have represented to its inhabitants the progress of the soul from birth, to full strength, to fading, and to renaissance (Thompson 1993:48–49) (see Map 7.4). In some cases compounds are aligned so that men's houses face the rising sun and women's face the setting sun, a spatial arrangement that reflected an underlying perception of male and female time, one in which men's time is oriented in the morning for work and women's in the evening for preparing meals (Lyons 1991). If sleeping quarters were segregated by gender at Utopia, the sun would have shone in the door of Structure 1, in the position of a men's house, and later the sun would have set on the entry of Structure 20, positioned as a women's house, as each faced into the compound.[24] In this manner, space could have reinforced gender hierarchies, and gender differences could be signaled by the layout and uses of architectural elements (see Bourdieu 1971; Yentsch 1991c).

The partitioning of room interiors also may have reflected meaningful separations of space. The vernacular European architectural practice of dividing a house into a public hall and a private parlor paralleled much African thinking of splitting the world into two halves, one private and one public (see Aniakor 1996). This is most evident in Structure 10, the dwelling spatially located in a position usually reserved for the head of the compound and the only dwelling with verifiable evidence of partitioning. The abundance of artifacts in the hall

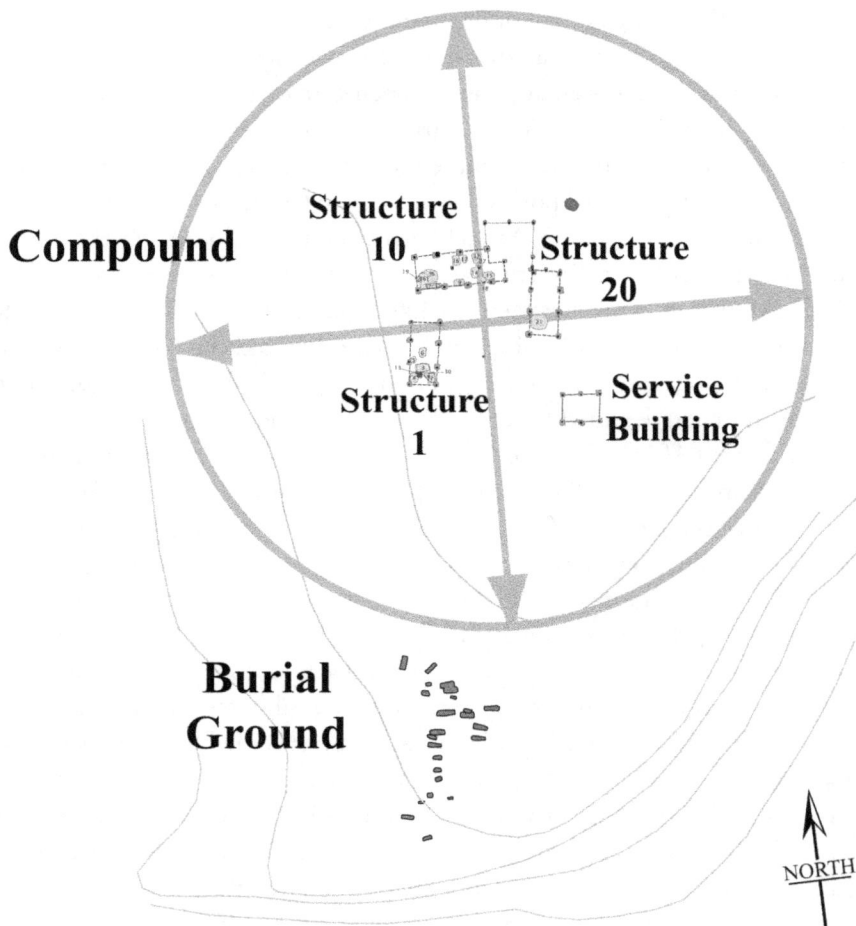

MAP 7.4.   Orientation of the Utopia Quarter compound in relation to cardinal directions.

(n=4,389) indicates it served as the most active indoor public space in the compound. In comparison, activity as measured by numbers of artifacts in the Structure 10 parlor (n=1,901) was reduced substantially in these more private spaces. Formal Igbo compounds still today are organized into female private spheres and male public ones (218).

Is it possible after toiling side by side all day in tobacco fields that enslaved African men and women retired to the Utopia Quarter and assembled into hierarchical social groupings that resembled an African village rather than a forced labor camp? The evidence strongly suggests that a headman (or head-woman) of some sort, a person of authority, inhabited Structure 10. Moreover, social subordinates may have occupied the Structure 10 parlor and the other two structures. How might this sort of ranking system have been imposed and was it based on gender? It is possible that "new Negroes" fresh off the boat were relegated to subordinate status and lumped together into one or more of the dwellings, while senior residents or Creoles assumed leadership roles (see Kulikoff 1986:333–334; Morgan 1998:467–477). The artifactual, architectural, and spatial differences present at the site strongly suggest that below the surface of enslavement Utopia's residents put into action a complex patchwork of ancestral ways of living. The Utopia Quarter seems to have functioned in many respects as an archetypal village compound.

Evidence of Kin-Based Households at Utopia

Historians surmise that the growth of the African American family in eighteenth-century Chesapeake failed to begin until several factors fell into place. Once the sex ratio reached parity and American-born Creole slaves became a majority, these demographic factors set into motion the necessary social components for family growth (see Berlin 1998; Kulikoff 1986; Morgan 1998). Slave owners also reaped the benefits of a more docile and controllable slave population by encouraging the formation of family units (see Walsh 1997:83). Thus, in most areas of the Chesapeake by midcentury the majority of enslaved Africans lived among kin.

In the early decades of the eighteenth century some of the first enslaved residents of Utopia must have found the conditions for family formation less than ideal. The population at Utopia consisted of unrelated, culturally het-erogeneous individuals, some speaking diverse languages and toiling long hours with little time to devote to breaking down the barriers of difference that separated them. If, however, Utopia's residents overcame these impedi-ments and began forging new family and kin groupings, the archaeological record may reflect this in several ways. First, household artifact assemblages may appear alike, indicating similar access to goods for each family. Moreover, each household should contain the components for self-sufficiency. Instead of sharing goods and contributing to the welfare of the community, or cooking communal meals of which all members partook, each household may have loosely competed with the others for survival.

Archaeologically, the question of kin-based households may best be considered by exploring issues of communal interaction and cooperation. Did each household prepare separate meals or contribute to a larger community whole? Although each dwelling had a hearth for cooking with a large subfloor pit fronting it, the preponderance of food-related activity seems to have taken place in Structure 10. Moreover, the scarcity of almost all types of domestic goods in Structure 20 demonstrates a much reduced level of subsistence and places the self-sufficiency of its inhabitants into question (see Table 7.9).

The layout of the site also bespeaks of a communal atmosphere. The orientation of all three buildings toward the open courtyard space in the middle facilitated social interaction, and no barriers prevented access from one dwelling to the other. There is no evidence that each household attempted to cordon off their own yard or garden in exclusion of others. Indeed, the one fence at the site connecting Structures 10 and 20 functioned as an animal pen in an area that was shared by both dwellings (see Map 7.3). Individuals seemed to have spent the majority of their time both indoors and outdoors in the company of others. This daily social intimacy may have frayed some nerves, but in general it likely prompted increased cooperation among the residents of Utopia and the structure of the site hastened the process. The abundance of subfloor pits inside the Structure 10 parlor suggests that privacy was at a premium and individuals coped by creating small niches of space for themselves, something that interrelated kin would be less inclined to do.

The circumstances of enslavement also may have facilitated community cooperation. With each member of the compound contributing their food allotment to the community pot, the burden of cooking and food acquisition was shared. After a long day of gang labor, the prospect of having the sole responsibility of pounding corn, butchering meat, gathering vegetables, and tending a fire to feed only oneself and perhaps immediate family members must have been daunting. By distributing the cooking chores, each individual saved some amount of time and effort, and by pooling resources the community as a whole provided better nourishment than any one individual could. Evidence of at least one cooking pit in the compound (and surely others that failed to leave an archaeological footprint) signals a cooking facility accessible to all residents. Perhaps in the winter or during bad weather the bulk of the cooking moved inside Structure 10, which served as a community "kitchen" of sorts when outdoor cooking became unfeasible.

Overall, most signs of a kin-based living arrangement at Utopia appear unsupported by the evidence. The artifacts and the spatial arrangement of the site hint at a more communal social orb. If so, some sort of sex-segregated living arrangement that recognized differences between men and women appears to have been the norm. No doubt some women and men paired off and produced children, as indicated by several children living on the plantation. However, the data at Utopia indicate that these nascent families failed to leave a recognizable material imprint in the archaeological record.

Conclusion

The initial question posed at the beginning of this study was whether gender differences played a significant role in shaping the daily interaction at Utopia. The interpretation of the architecture, spatial layout, and artifact patterns at the site indicate that gender indeed was on the minds of both master and slave. Intentional or not, James Bray's acquisition of almost twice as many enslaved women to men contrasted with the buying policies of his fellow planters and strongly suggests that he considered the gender makeup of his workforce important. The enslaved residents of Utopia (most native to Africa) arrived at the site with deeply rooted perceptions of proper gender roles and relations. Together, both master and slave negotiated an uneasy system of social interaction at Utopia largely based on concepts of gender.

Of the three hypothesized living arrangements, Utopia most closely resembles the appearance and bearing of an indigenous African compound based in part on segregated living arrangements for women and men. The two living arrangements were not mutually exclusive. The separation of men and women into demarcated spheres commonly occurred in West and Central African cultures. Thus, if Bray purposely housed women and men in separate dwellings, or the residents themselves decided upon this system, it was a satisfactory and familiar form of social organization for most of them.

The archaeological evidence collected from the Utopia Quarter demonstrates that the residents recalled cultural understandings of daily life from African pasts and expressed them in the arrangement of space, the use of architecture, and the distribution of artifacts. In particular, the layout of the compound, the pattern of subfloor pits and division of space inside some of the dwellings, and the distribution of particular artifact types further supports the likelihood that the sexes, perhaps of their own volition, segregated themselves at the site. At Utopia people shaped their living environment, while at the same time the living environment shaped their responses to it. This recursive relationship between person and place at Utopia mutually reinforced itself to create a domestic space that many of the residents must have come to think of as a home, however grudgingly (see Giddens 1979, 1984, 1991). Of course, this was not the objective of the original design of the compound. The builder, no doubt under the watchful eye of James Bray, seems to have believed that the compound arrangement of buildings would facilitate an overseer's authority, especially with that overseer ensconced in Structure 10 at the head of the compound. Yet Bray and his carpenter probably had no inkling that they had created a landscape that closely matched countless domestic compounds across the African continent.

At Utopia both women and men left an imprint in the archaeological record. The primary focus has been to evaluate three possible living arrangements based in large part upon gender: single-sex barracks, a compound similar to those in West and Central Africa, and kin-based households. The archaeological evidence is more evocative than conclusive. The architectural, spatial, and artifact assemblage data evoke a collective, communal living system in effect at Utopia, one that deemed the separation of the sexes a vital component of social life. Both the compound setting and the segregation of the sexes into rigid spheres were cultural systems directly derived from West and Central Africa, systems that virtually all of Utopia's inhabitants recognized and presumably preferred. It would be comforting to believe that the residents of Utopia were empowered by their circumstances, that the familiar cultural structure they encountered and nurtured at the site helped to make the harsh realities of enslavement a little less onerous. It is also possible that the daily reminder of a way of life with freedom that no longer existed was a burden, an *aide memoire* that made living at Utopia that much more unbearable.

ACKNOWLEDGMENTS

The archaeological work at Utopia would not have been possible without the financial support of Busch Properties, Inc., the owners of the property. Over the years scores of volunteers, field school students, and more than two dozen field archaeologists working for the James River Institute for Archaeology moved dirt at Utopia. I have also benefited from a legion of friends and scholars who have given advice, pointed toward resources, or thoughtfully pondered the evidence at Utopia. My thanks to all, and to Jillian Galle for having the wherewithal to take on the mammoth task of pulling this volume together.

NOTES

1. The term *enslaved Africans* refers to individuals whose ancestry originated on the African continent and who were enslaved in the Western world primarily because of the darker pigmentation of their skin. When the term *slave* is used, this is not intended to suggest that a person's primary identity was as such. Indeed, all individuals, slave or free, inhabited multiple identities depending upon the circumstances. During the course of a day, a female slave, for example, could also be a mother, wife, friend, sister, nurse, gardener, cook, provider, worker, artisan, and so on, or a combination of these roles.

2. For purposes of management efficiency, most Virginia planters divided their landholdings into subunits called quarters, usually managed by an overseer. The term *quarter* also refers to the actual dwelling units on these outlying farms (see H. Jones 1956:75).

3. The Chesapeake region encompasses Delaware, the District of Columbia, Maryland, Pennsylvania, Virginia, and West Virginia, generally those states that surround the Chesapeake Bay, the largest estuary in the Western Hemisphere, and its tidal tributaries east of the fall line (see Kulikoff 1986:18).

4. From an archaeological perspective, Rosemary Joyce and Cheryl Claassen (1997:7) point out, "Difference is . . . at the heart of the creation of distinctive settings for action, and distinctive kinds of action, that we can perceive archaeologically."

5. See Carr and Walsh (1988) for a slave task differentiation framework derived from George Washington's journals.

6. While gender relations are the current focus, this is not to imply that race, class, status, and other salient identities were not also present as structuring elements of social relations at places like Utopia. Moore uses the term *mutually imbricated* to suggest the interconnectedness of a range of identities at play at any given time (1994:50).

7. Susan Mann rather ingeniously suggests that "analyzing oppression within oppressed groups is like 'dancing on a minefield'" (1990:135; see also Ardener 1981:14–15; Morton 1996; Steady 1987:18–19).

8. For an alternative view, see Sudarkasa (1987), who suggests that deferential behavior to men occurred only within the conjugal relationship. See also Brown (1996:115) on European colonial writings on Africa.

9. There were several generations of James Brays in Virginia, beginning with James Bray I (circa 1631–1691), his son James Bray II (circa 1668–1725), and his grandson James Bray III (circa 1715–1744) (Fesler 2000). Since Bray I and Bray III are not referenced any further, roman numeral designations will not be used.

10. The name Utopia is derived from one of the original early-seventeenth-century owners named John Uty (Utie), who cleverly applied his surname to his plantation (Fesler 2000; Kelso 1984:35).

11. Six of the children are listed by name (four boys and two girls); however, in several instances the inventory lists "children" but provides no tally.

12. Bray placed slaves in charge at both quarters. On the inventory Debb is listed as one of the most senior of the thirteen women and Jacko among the eleven men (Bray 1726).

13. Caprines (sheep and goats) comprise 1.17 percent of the Period 2 faunal assemblage. In comparison with four other similar sites in Virginia dating to the same period, the percentage of caprines from those collections averages 1.78 percent. Although hardly scientific, it does not appear that Utopia contains an unusually high percentage of sheep elements (see Walsh et al. 1997:238–241).

14. James Bray's sister-in-law Judith purchased three hundred acres at Tutter's Neck in 1717. Judith subsequently died in 1720, and Bray may have acquired control of it as acting guardian for her son (Fesler 2000).

15. See Walsh (1997:117) for a discussion of the economic benefits and drawbacks to relying on natural increase versus regularly buying new slaves (see also Jordan 1968:70).

16. In the seventeenth century early English settlers in Virginia, weakened by their voyage and prone to disease and sickness in the New World, experienced a high death rate. The process of adjusting to the new environment was known as "seasoning," and in some cases "guest houses" were built to help people make the transition, something akin to crude sanatoriums. Incoming new Africans underwent similar adjustments, and in an effort to reduce the high mortality rate, some planters attempted to gradually acclimate their new slaves, sometimes choosing one quarter as a seasoning station (for slave mortality rate, see Kulikoff 1986:69).

17. In the Chesapeake region slaves with supervisory duties tended to be referred to as foremen rather than drivers, as was the usual term in the Lower South (Morgan 1998:218–219). The wealthiest Virginia planter in Bray's day, Robert "King" Carter, appointed slave foremen at forty-three of his forty-eight

field quarters, apparently using the position as a reward and a mechanism for keeping his slaves in line (Morgan 1998:208; Walsh 1997:86).

18. This approach relies heavily on theories of interaction originally developed by Erving Goffman (1959, 1961, 1986) and later amplified by Shirley Ardener (1981), Henrietta Moore (1996), and other practice theorists (Bourdieu 1977; Giddens 1979, 1984; Ortner 1996; Sahlins 1981).

19. For descriptions of past and present West African compounds, see Agorsah (1985:114); Aniakor (1996:216); Anthony (1976b:9); Bohannan and Bohannan (1968:14–22); Bourdier and Minh-ha (1985:14–17); Bradbury and Lloyd (1957); Clapperton (1829:73); Curtin (1967:74, 267); Dalzel (1967:xiii, 29, 125); Dantzig and Jones (1987:76); David (1971); Denyer (1978); Dike (1985:10); Freeman (1968:55, 138, 159); Gamble (1967:41); Guidoni (1987:197–198); Hair et al. (1992:88, 511–512); Jones (1985:196–197); Krapf-Askari (1969); Mollien (1967:248); Rutter (1971:154, 163); Schon and Crowther (1970:302); Schwerdtfeger (1971); Winterbottom (1969:81, 87).

20. In 1758 Virginia plantation owner Joseph Ball sent instructions to his plantation manager concerning the construction of new slave quarters. Ball described in detail the size, location, and components of the buildings he wanted built and firmly ordered, "Get a good Carpenter." (Joseph Ball to Joseph Chinn, October 7, 1758, Ball Letter Book).

21. The use of South's taxonomy to analyze the Utopia artifact collection should not be interpreted as an attempt to develop a slave pattern; it was chosen as an effective method to compare and contrast the assemblages within the site.

22. To simplify matters, each of the three dwelling units will be considered a household, although by definition the groups inhabiting each unit may not have functioned as households (see Bender 1967; Netting, Wilk, and Arnould 1984; Wilk and Rathje 1982).

23. One researcher suggests that the three main archaeological traits of polygyny are separate houses and hearths for wives and an open courtyard in the center (Chase 1991).

24. If men did smoke more tobacco than women, it is interesting to note that Structure 1 produced significantly high percentages of tobacco pipe fragments compared to the sitewide mean (see Table 7.7).

REFERENCES

Agorsah, E. Kofi
    1985   Archeological Implications of Traditional House Construction among the Nchumuru of Northern Ghana. *Anthropology* 26(1):103–115.

Amadiume, Ifi
    1987   *Male Daughters, Female Husbands: Gender and Sex in an African Society.* Zed Books, Atlantic Highlands, N.J.

Aniakor, Chike
    1996   Household Objects and the Philosophy of Igbo Space. In *African Material Culture*, edited by Mary Jo Arnoldi, Christraud M. Geary, and Kris L. Hardin, pp. 214–242. Indiana Univ. Press, Bloomington.

Anthony, Carl
    1976a   The Big House and the Slave Quarters, Part I: Prelude to New World Architecture. *Landscape* 20(3):8–19.
    1976b   The Big House and the Slave Quarters, Part II: African Contributions to the New World. *Landscape* 21(1):9–15.

Ardener, Shirley
    1981   Ground Rules and Social Maps for Women: An Introduction. *Women and Space: Ground Rules and Social Maps*, edited by Shirley Ardener, pp. 11–34. Croom Helm, London.

Aries, Elizabeth
    1997   Women and Men Talking: Are They Worlds Apart? In *Women, Men, and Gender: Ongoing Debates*, edited by Mary Roth Walsh, pp. 91–100. Yale Univ. Press, New Haven.

Ball, Joseph
    1744–1759   Joseph Ball Letter Book, 1744–1759. Ms. on file, microfilm M-21. John D. Rockefeller Jr. Library, Colonial Williamsburg Foundation, Williamsburg.

Barley, Nigel
    1994   *Smashing Pots: Works of Clay from Africa.* Smithsonian Institution Press, Washington, D.C.

Baumgarten, Linda
    1988   "Clothes for the People": Slave Clothing in Early Virginia. *Journal of Early Southern Decorative Arts* 14(2):26–70.

Bender, Donald R.
    1967   Refinement of the Concept of Household: Families, Co-residence, and Domestic Functions. *American Anthropologist* 69:493–504.

Berlin, Ira
    1998   *Many Thousands Gone: The First Two Centuries of Slavery in North America.* Belknap Press of Harvard Univ. Press, Cambridge, Mass.

Bohannan, Paul, and Laura Bohannan
    1968   *Tiv Economy.* Northwestern Univ. Press, Evanston, Ill.

Boles, John B.
  1983   *Black Southerners, 1619–1869.* Univ. Press of Kentucky, Lexington.
Bourdier, Jean-Paul, and Trinh T. Minh-ha
  1985   *African Spaces: Designs for Living in Upper Volta.* Africana Publishing
         Co., New York.
Bourdieu, Pierre
  1971   The Berber House. *Rules and Meanings: The Anthropology of Every-
         day Knowledge,* edited by Mary Douglas, pp. 98–110. Penguin
         Education, Suffolk, Great Britain.
  1977   *Outline of a Theory of Practice.* Cambridge Univ. Press, Cambridge.
Bradbury, R. E., and P. C. Lloyd
  1957   *The Benin Kingdom and the Edo-Speaking Peoples of South West
         Nigeria.* International African Institute, London.
Bray, James, II
  1726   James Bray II Will. Colonial Williamsburg Foundation Library,
         Williamsburg, Va.
Brown, Kathleen M.
  1996   *Good Wives, Nasty Wenches, and Anxious Patriarchs: Gender, Race,
         and Power in Colonial Virginia.* Univ. of North Carolina Press,
         Chapel Hill.
Callaway, Helen
  1981   Spatial Domains and Women's Mobility in Yorubaland, Nigeria.
         Women and Space: Ground Rules and Social Maps, edited by Shirley
         Ardener, pp. 168–186. Croom Helm, London.
  1993   "The Most Essentially Female Function of All": Giving Birth.
         Defining Females: The Nature of Women in Society, edited by
         Shirley Ardener, pp. 146–167. Berg Publishers, Providence, R.I.
Carr, Lois Green, and Lorena Walsh
  1988   Economic Diversification and Labor Organization in the Chesapeake,
         1650–1820. *Work and Labor in Early America,* edited by Stephen
         Innes, pp. 144–188. Univ. of North Carolina Press, Chapel Hill.
Carr, Lois Green, Russell R. Menard, and Lorena S. Walsh
  1991   *Robert Cole's World: Agriculture and Society in Early Maryland.*
         Univ. of North Carolina Press, Chapel Hill.
Carson, Cary, Norman F. Barka, William M. Kelso, Gary Wheeler Stone,
and Dell Upton
  1981   Impermanent Architecture in the Southern American Colonies.
         Winterthur Portfolio 16:135–196.

Casey, Joanna

    1991   One Man No Chop: Gender Roles in the Domestic Economy in Northern Ghana, West Africa. *The Archaeology of Gender: Proceedings of the Twenty-second Annual Chacmool Conference*, edited by Dale Walde and Noreen D. Willows, pp. 137–143. Univ. of Calgary Archaeological Association, Calgary.

Chafetz, Janet

    1990   *Gender Equity*. Sage Publishers, Newbury Park, Calif.

Chase, Sabrina M.

    1991   Polygyny, Architecture, and Meaning. *The Archaeology of Gender: Proceedings of the Twenty-second Annual Chacmool Conference*, edited by Dale Walde and Noreen D. Willows, pp. 150–158. Univ. of Calgary Archaeological Association, Calgary.

Clapperton, Hugh

    1829   *Journal of a Second Expedition into the Interior of Africa, from the Bight of Benin to Soccatoo*. J. Murray, London.

Collins, Patricia Hill

    1997   On West and Fenstermaker's "Doing Difference." In *Women, Men, and Gender: Ongoing Debates*, edited by Mary Roth Walsh, pp. 73–75. Yale Univ. Press, New Haven.

Conkey, Margaret W.

    1991   Does It Make a Difference? Feminist Thinking and Archaeologies of Gender. *The Archaeology of Gender: Proceedings of the Twenty-second Annual Chacmool Conference*, edited by Dale Walde and Noreen D. Willows, pp. 24–33. Univ. of Calgary Archaeological Association, Calgary.

Conkey, Margaret, and Janet Spector

    1984   Archaeology and the Study of Gender. In *Advances in Archaeological Method and Theory*, vol. 7, edited by Michael Schiffer, pp. 1–38. Academic Press, New York.

Curtin, Phillip

    1967   *Africa Remembered: Narratives by West Africans from the Era of the Slave Trade*. Univ. of Wisconsin Press, Madison.

    1969   *The Atlantic Slave Trade: A Census*. Univ. of Wisconsin Press, Madison.

Dalzel, Archibald

    1967   *The History of the Dahomey, an Inland Kingdom of Africa*. Frank Cass, London.

Dantzig, Albert, and Adam Jones (editors)

    1987   *Description and Historical Account of the Gold Kingdom of Guinea (1602)*. Oxford Univ. Press, New York.

David, Nicholas

1971   The Fulani Compound and the Archaeologist. *World Archaeology*
        3(2):111–131.

Davis, Angela Y.

1981   *Women, Race, and Class*. Vintage Books, New York.

Denyer, Susan

1978   *African Traditional Architecture: An Historical and Geographical
        Perspective*. Africana Publishing Co., New York.

Dike, Azuka A.

1985   *The Resilience of Igbo Culture: A Case Study of Awka Town*. Fourth
        Dimension Publishers, Enugu, Nigeria.

Dill, Bonnie Thornton

1990   The Dialectics of Black Womanhood. In *Black Women in America:
        Social Science Perspectives*, edited by Micheline R. Malson, Elizabeth
        Mudimbe-Boyi, Jean F. O'Barr, and Mary Wyer, pp. 65–77. Univ. of
        Chicago Press, Chicago.

Dobres, Marcia-Anne

1995   Beyond Gender Attribution: Some Methodological Issues for
        Engendering the Past. In *Gendered Archaeology*, Research Papers
        in Archaeology and Natural History No. 26, pp. 51–66. ANH
        Publications, Research School of Pacific Studies, Australian
        National Univ., Canberra, Australia.

Eltis, David

1998   Age and Sex: The Slave Trade in Comparative Perspective. Paper
        delivered at the Transatlantic Slaving and African Diaspora:
        Using the W. E. B. DuBois Institute Dataset of Slaving Voyages
        Conference, Williamsburg, Va.

Fage, J. D.

1989   Slaves and Society in Western Africa, 1445–c. 1700. In *The African
        Diaspora: Africans and Their Descendants in the Wider World to
        1800*, edited by the Black Diaspora Committee of Howard Univ.,
        pp. 145–163. Ginn Press, Needham Heights, Mass.

Farnham, Christie

1987   Sapphire? The Issue of Dominance in the Slave Family, 1830–1865.
        "To Toil the Livelong Day": America's Women at Work, 1780–1980,
        edited by Carol Groneman and Mary Beth Norton, pp. 68–83.
        Cornell Univ. Press, Ithaca.

Ferguson, Leland

1992   *Uncommon Ground: Archaeology and Early African America,
        1650–1800*. Smithsonian Institution Press, Washington, D.C.

Fesler, Garrett R.

1997   Landscapes of Control and Autonomy: The Spatial Contestation of the Utopia Slave Quarter. A paper presented to the Univ. of Virginia, Dept. of Anthropology, Charlottesville.

2000   Back to Utopia: An Interim Report on Renewed Archaeological Excavations at the Utopia Quarter, Field Seasons 1993–1996. Period 2 Occupation, ca. 1700–1730. Vol. II. James River Institute for Archaeology, Williamsburg, Va.

Fogel, Robert William

1989   *Without Consent or Contract: The Rise and Fall of American Slavery.* W. W. Norton & Co., New York.

Franklin, Maria

1997   Out of Site, Out of Mind: The Archaeology of an Enslaved Virginian Household, ca. 1740–1778. Ph.D. diss., Dept. of Anthropology, Univ. of California, Berkeley.

Freeman, Thomas Birch

1968   *Journals of Various Visits to the Kingdoms of Ashanti, Aku, and Dahomi in Western Africa.* Frank Cass, London.

Gamble, David P.

1967   *The Wolof of Senegambia, Together with Notes on the Lebu and the Serer.* International African Institute, London.

Gibb, James G., and Julia A. King

1991   Gender, Activity Areas, and Homelots in the Seventeenth-Century Chesapeake Region. *Historical Archaeology* 25(4):109–131.

Giddens, Anthony

1979   *Central Problems in Social Theory.* Univ. of California Press, Berkeley.

1984   *The Constitution of Society: Outline of the Theory of Structuration.* Univ. of California Press, Berkeley.

1991   *Modernity and Self-Identity: Self and Society in the Late Modern Age.* Polity Press, Cambridge, Mass.

Glassie, Henry

1975   *Folk Housing in Middle Virginia: A Structural Analysis of Historic Artifacts.* Univ. of Tennessee Press, Knoxville.

Goffman, Erving

1959   *The Presentation of Self in Everyday Life.* Anchor Books, New York.

1961   *Asylums: Essays on the Social Situation of Mental Patients and Other Inmates.* Anchor Books, New York.

1986   *Frame Analysis: An Essay on the Organization of Experience.* Northeastern Univ. Press, Boston.

Goheen, Miriam
1996   *Men Own the Fields, Women Own the Crops: Gender and Power in the Cameroon Grassfields.* Univ. of Wisconsin Press, Madison.
Gomez, Michael A.
1998   *Exchanging Our Country Marks: The Transformation of African Identities in the Colonial and Antebellum South.* Univ. of North Carolina Press, Chapel Hill.
Guidoni, Enrico
1987   *Primitive Architecture.* Rizzoli, New York.
Gundaker, Grey
1993   Tradition and Innovation in African American Yards. *African Arts* 26:58–71.
Hair, P. E. H., Adam Jones, and Robin Law (editors)
1992   *Barbot on Guinea: The Writings of Jean Barbot on West Africa, 1678–1712.* The Hakluyt Society, London. Univ. Press, Cambridge, Great Britain.
Hall, Edward T.
1990   *The Hidden Dimension.* Anchor Books Doubleday, New York.
Heath, Barbara J.
1999   *Hidden Lives: The Archaeology of Slave Life at Thomas Jefferson's Poplar Forest.* Univ. of Virginia Press, Charlottesville.
Heath, Barbara, and Amber Bennett
2000   "The Little Spots Allow'd Them": The Archaeological Study of African American Yards. *Historical Archaeology* 34(2):38–55.
Higgens, Thomas F., Benjamin Ford, Charles M. Downing, Veronica L. Deitrick, Stevan C. Pullins, and Dennis B. Blanton
2000   Wilton Speaks: Archaeology at an Eighteenth- and Nineteenth-Century Plantation. Data Recovery at Site 44HE493, Associated with the Proposed Route 895 Project, Henrico County, Virginia. William and Mary Center for Archaeological Research, College of William and Mary, Williamsburg, Va.
Books, Bell
1981   *Ain't I a Woman: Black Women and Feminism.* South End Press, Boston.
Isaac, Rhys
1982   *The Transformation of Virginia, 1740–1790.* Univ. of North Carolina Press, Chapel Hill.
Jones, Hugh
1956   *The Present State of Virginia* [1724]. Edited by Richard L. Morton. Univ. of North Carolina Press, Chapel Hill.

Jones, Jacqueline
    1989   "My Mother Was Much of a Woman": Black Women, Work, and
            the Family under Slavery. In *Women and the Family in a Slave
            Society*, edited by Paul Finkelman, pp. 195–229. Garland Publishing,
            New York.

Jones, Steven L.
    1985   The African American Tradition in Vernacular Architecture. In
            The Archaeology of Slavery and Plantation Life, edited by Theresa A.
            Singleton, pp. 195–213. Academic Press, Orlando.

Jordan, Winthrop D.
    1968   *White over Black: American Attitudes toward the Negro, 1550–1812.*
            Univ. of North Carolina Press, Chapel Hill.

Joyce, Rosemary A., and Cheryl Claassen
    1997   Women in the Ancient Americas: Archaeologists, Gender, and the
            Making of Prehistory. In *Women in Prehistory: North America and
            Mesoamerica*, edited by Cheryl Claassen and Rosemary A. Joyce,
            pp. 1–14. Univ. of Pennsylvania Press, Philadelphia.

Keim, Curtis A.
    1983   Women in Slavery among the Mangbetu. In *Women and Slavery
            in Africa*, edited by Claire C. Robertson and Martin A. Klein,
            pp. 144–159. Univ. of Wisconsin Press, Madison.

Kelso, William M.
    1973   An Interim Report: Historical Archaeology at Kingsmill, the
            1975 Season. Virginia Research Center for Archaeology,
            Yorktown, Va. Ms. on file, Virginia Dept. of Historic Resources,
            Richmond, Va.

    1974   An Interim Report on the Historical Archaeology at Kingsmill
            Plantation, the 1973 Season. Virginia Research Center for
            Archaeology, Yorktown, Va. Ms. on file, Virginia Dept. of
            Historic Resources, Richmond, Va.

    1977   An Interim Report: Historical Archaeology at Kingsmill, the
            1972 Season. Virginia Research Center for Archaeology,
            Yorktown, Va. Ms. on file, Virginia Dept. of Historic Resources,
            Richmond, Va.

    1984   *Kingsmill Plantations, 1619–1800: Archaeology of Country Life in
            Colonial Virginia.* Academic Press, Orlando.

Kolchin, Peter
    1987   *Unfree Labor: American Slavery and Russian Serfdom.* Belknap Press
            of Harvard Univ. Press, Cambridge, Mass.

1993   *American Slavery, 1619–1877.* Hill and Wang, New York.

Krapf-Askari, Eva
1969   *Yoruba Towns and Cities: An Enquiry into the Nature of Urban Social Phenomena.* Clarendon Press, Oxford, Great Britain.

Kulikoff, Allan
1977   The Beginnings of the Afro-American Family in Maryland. In *Law, Society, and Politics in Early Maryland,* edited by Aubrey C. Land, Lois Green Carr, and Edward C. Papenfuse, pp. 171–196. John Hopkins Univ. Press, Baltimore.
1986   *Tobacco and Slaves: The Development of Southern Cultures in the Chesapeake, 1680–1800.* Univ. of North Carolina Press, Chapel Hill.

Lewis, Diane K.
1990   A Response to Inequality: Black Women, Racism, and Sexism. In *Black Women in America: Social Science Perspectives,* edited by Micheline R. Malson, Elizabeth Mudimbe-Boyi, Jean F. O'Barr, and Mary Wyer, pp. 41–63. Univ. of Chicago Press, Chicago.

Little, Barbara J.
1994   "She Was . . . an Example to Her Sex": Possibilities for a Feminist Historical Archaeology. In *Historical Archaeology of the Chesapeake,* edited by Paul A. Shackel and Barbara J. Little, pp. 189–229. Smithsonian Institution Press, Washington, D.C.

Lott, Bernice
1997   Cataloging Gender Differences: Science or Politics? In *Women, Men, and Gender: Ongoing Debates,* edited by Mary Roth Walsh, pp. 19–23. Yale Univ. Press, New Haven.

Lyons, Diane
1991   The Construction of Gender, Time, and Space. *The Archaeology of Gender: Proceedings of the Twenty-second Annual Chacmool Conference,* edited by Dale Walde and Noreen D. Willows, pp. 108–113. Univ. of Calgary Archaeological Association, Calgary.

Main, Gloria L.
1982   *Tobacco Colony: Life in Early Maryland, 1650–1720.* Princeton Univ. Press, Princeton.

Mann, Susan A.
1990   Slavery, Sharecropping, and Sexual Identity. *Black Women in America: Social Science Perspectives,* edited by Micheline R. Malson, Elisabeth Mudimbe-Boyi, Jean F. O'Barr, and Mary Wyer, pp. 133–157. Univ. of Chicago Press, Chicago.

Mbiti, John S.

    1991   Flowers in the Garden: The Role of Women in African Religion.
          In *African Traditional Religions: In Contemporary Society*, edited by
          Jacob K. Olupona, pp. 59–72. Paragon House, New York.

Meillassoux, Claude

    1991   *The Anthropology of Slavery: The Womb of Iron and Gold*. Translated
          by Alide Dasnois. Univ. of Chicago Press, Chicago.

Mintz, Sidney W., and Richard Price

    1992   *The Birth of African American Culture: An Anthropological Perspective*.
          Beacon Press, Boston.

Mollien, Gaspard T.

    1967   *Travels in the Interior of Africa to the Sources of the Senegal and
          Gambia, Performed by Command of the French Government in the
          Year 1818*. Edited by T. E. Bowditch. Frank Cass, London.

Moore, Henrietta

    1988   *Feminism and Anthropology*. Univ. of Minnesota Press, Minneapolis.

    1991   Epilogue. In *Engendering Archaeology: Women and Prehistory*, edited
          by Joan M. Gero and Margaret W. Conkey, pp. 407–411. Blackwell,
          Cambridge, Mass.

    1994   *A Passion for Difference: Essays in Anthropology and Gender*. Indiana
          Univ. Press, Bloomington.

    1996   *Space, Text, and Gender: An Anthropological Study of the Marakwet
          of Kenya*. Guilford Press, New York.

Morgan, Phillip D.

    1988   Task and Gang Systems: The Organization of Labor on New World
          Plantations. In *Work and Labor in Early America*, edited by Stephen
          Innes, pp. 189–220. Univ. of North Carolina Press, Chapel Hill.

    1998   *Slave Counterpoint: Black Culture in the Eighteenth-Century
          Chesapeake and Lowcountry*. Univ. of North Carolina Press,
          Chapel Hill.

Morton, Patricia

    1996   Introduction. In *Discovering the Women in Slavery: Emancipating
          Perspectives on the American Past*, edited by Patricia Morton,
          pp. 1–26. Univ. of Georgia Press, Athens.

Muller, Nancy Ladd

    1994   The House of the Black Burghardts: An Investigation of Race,
          Gender, and Class at the W. E. B. Du Bois Boyhood Homesite.
          In *Those of Little Note: Gender, Race, and Class in Historical
          Archaeology*, edited by Elizabeth M. Scott, pp. 81–94. Univ. of
          Arizona Press, Tucson.

Mullin, Gerald W.
   1972   *Flight and Rebellion: Slave Resistance in Eighteenth-Century Virginia.*
          Oxford Univ. Press, New York.
Mullin, Michael
   1992   *Africa in America: Slave Acculturation and Resistance in the American
          South and the British Caribbean, 1736–1831.* Univ. of Illinois Press,
          Urbana and Chicago.
Nash, Gary B.
   1982   *Red, White, and Black: The Peoples of Early America.* Prentice-Hall,
          Englewood Cliffs, N.J.
Neiman, Fraser
   1980   *The "Manner House" before Stratford: Discovering the Clifts
          Plantation.* A Stratford Handbook, Stratford, Va.
   1997   Sub-Floor Pits and Slavery in Eighteenth- and Early-Nineteenth-
          Century Virginia. A paper presented at the Society for Historical
          Archaeology annual meeting, Corpus Christi, Tex.
Netting, Robert McC., Richard R. Wilk, and Eric J. Arnould
   1984   Introduction. *Households: Comparative and Historical Studies of the
          Domestic Group,* edited by Robert McC. Netting, Richard R. Wilk,
          and Eric J. Arnould, pp. xiii–xxxviii. Univ. of California Press,
          Berkeley.
Noel Hume, Ivor
   1968   *Excavations at Tutter's Neck in James City County, Virginia, 1960–1961.*
          Contributions from the Museum of History and Technology,
          Paper 53. Smithsonian Institution, Washington, D.C.
Nwokeji, G. Ugo
   2001   African Conceptions of Gender and the Slave Traffic. *William and
          Mary Quarterly,* 3d ser., 58(1):47–68.
Ortner, Sherry B.
   1996   Making Gender: Toward a Feminist, Minority, Postcolonial,
          Subaltern, etc. Theory of Practice. In *Making Gender: The Politics
          and Erotics of Culture,* pp. 1–20. Beacon Press, Boston.
Parker, Kathleen A., and Jacqueline L. Hernigle
   1990   *Portici: Portrait of a Middling Plantation in Piedmont, Virginia.*
          Occasional Report #3, Regional Archeology Program, National
          Capital Region, National Park Service, Washington, D.C.
Pogue, Dennis, and Esther White
   1991   Summary Report on the "House for Families" Slave Quarter Site
          (44FX762/40–47), Mount Vernon Plantation, Mount Vernon, Va.
          Mount Vernon Ladies' Association, Mount Vernon, Va.

Posnansky, Merrick

1999   West Africanist Reflections on African American Archaeology.
        I, Too, Am America: Archaeological Studies of African American Life,
        edited by Theresa A. Singleton, pp. 21–38. Univ. Press of Virginia,
        Charlottesville.

Potkay, Adam, and Sandra Burr (editors)

1995   *Black Atlantic Writers of the Eighteenth Century: Living the New
        Exodus in England and the Americas*. St. Martin's Press, New York.

Roberts, Catherine

1993   A Critical Approach to Gender as a Category of Analysis in Archae-
        ology. In *Women in Archaeology: A Feminist Critique*, edited by
        H. du Cros and L. Smith, pp. 16–21. Dept. of Prehistory, Research
        School of Pacific Studies, Australian National Univ., Canberra,
        Australia.

Rutter, Andrew

1971   Ashanti Vernacular Architecture. *Shelter in Africa*, edited by Paul
        Oliver, pp. 153–171. Praeger Publishers, New York.

Sahlins, Marshall

1981   *Historical Metaphors and Mythical Realities: Structure in the Early
        History of the Sandwich Islands Kingdom*. Univ. of Michigan Press,
        Ann Arbor.

Samford, Patricia

1996   The Archaeology of African American Slavery and Material Culture.
        William and Mary Quarterly, 3d ser., 53(1):87–114.

2000   Power Runs in Many Channels: Subfloor Pits and West African-
        Based Spiritual Traditions in Colonial Virginia. Ph.D. diss.,
        Dept. of Anthropology, Univ. of North Carolina, Chapel Hill.

Sanford, Douglas Walker

1995   The Archaeology of Plantation Slavery at Thomas Jefferson's
        Monticello: Context and Process in an American Slave Society.
        Ph.D. diss., Dept. of Anthropology, Univ. of Virginia,
        Charlottesville.

Schon, James F., and Samuel Crowther

1970   *Journals of the Rev. James Frederick Schon, and Mr. Samuel Crowther:
        Who, with the Sanction of Her Majesty's Government, Accompanied the
        Expedition Up the Niger in 1841 on Behalf of the Church Missionary
        Society*. Frank Cass, London.

Schwerdtfeger, Friedrich

1971   Housing in Zaria. *Shelter in Africa*, edited by Paul Oliver, pp. 58–79.
        Praeger Publishers, New York.

Scott, Elizabeth M. (editor)

1994a *Those of Little Note: Gender, Race, and Class in Historical Archaeology.*
Univ. of Arizona Press, Tucson.

1994b Through the Lens of Gender: Archaeology, Inequality, and Those
"of Little Note." In *Those of Little Note: Gender, Race, and Class in
Historical Archaeology*, edited by Elizabeth M. Scott, pp. 3–24.
Univ. of Arizona Press, Tucson.

Seifert, Donna J. (editor)

1991 Gender in Historical Archaeology. Special Issue of *Historical
Archaeology* 25(4).

Shammas, Carole

1985 Black Women's Work and the Evolution of Plantation Society in
Virginia. *Labor History* 26(1):5–28.

Singleton, Theresa A., and Mark D. Bograd

1995 *The Archaeology of the African Diaspora in the Americas.* Society for
Historical Archaeology, Guides to the Archaeological Literature of
the Immigrant Experience in America, No. 2. Braun-Brumfield,
Ann Arbor, Mich.

Sobel, Mechal

1987 *The World They Made Together: Black and White Values in Eighteenth-
Century Virginia.* Princeton Univ. Press, Princeton.

South, Stanley

1977 *Method and Theory in Historical Archaeology.* Academic Press,
San Diego, Calif.

Spector, Janet D.

1983 Male/Female Task Differentiation among the Hidatsa: Toward
the Development of an Archaeological Approach to the Study of
Gender. In *The Hidden Half: Studies of Plains Indian Women*, edited
by Patricia Albers and Beatrice Medicine, pp. 77–99. Univ. Press of
America, Lanham, Md.

1991 What This Awl Means: Towards a Feminist Archaeology. In
Engendering Archaeology: Women and Prehistory, edited by Joan M.
Gero and Margaret W. Conkey, pp. 388–406. Blackwell,
Cambridge, Mass.

1993 *What This Awl Means: Feminist Archaeology at a Wahpeton Dakota
Village.* Minnesota Historical Society Press, St. Paul.

Spencer-Wood, Suzanne M.

1991 Toward a Feminist Historical Archaeology of the Construction
of Gender. *The Archaeology of Gender: Proceedings of the Twenty-
second Annual Chacmool Conference*, edited by Dale Walde and

Noreen D. Willows, pp. 234–244. Univ. of Calgary Archaeological Association, Calgary.

Steady, Filomina Chioma

1987   African Feminism: A Worldwide Perspective. *Women in Africa and the African Diaspora*, edited by Rosalyn Terborg-Penn, Sharon Harley, and Andrea Benton Rushing, pp. 3–24. Howard Univ. Press, Washington, D.C.

Stevenson, Brenda E.

1996   *Life in Black and White: Family and Community in the Slave South.* Oxford Univ. Press, New York.

Sudarkasa, Niara

1980   African and Afro-American Family Structure: A Comparison. *Black Scholar* 11:37–60.

1987   "The Status of Women" in Indigenous African Societies. *Women in Africa and the African Diaspora*, edited by Rosalyn Terborg-Penn, Sharon Harley, and Andrea Benton Rushing, pp. 25–41. Howard Univ. Press, Washington, D.C.

Terborg-Penn, Rosalyn

1987   African Feminism: A Theoretical Approach to the History of Women in the African Diaspora. *Women in Africa and the African Diaspora*, edited by Rosalyn Terborg-Penn, Sharon Harley, and Andrea Benton Rushing, pp. 43–63. Howard Univ. Press, Washington, D.C.

Thomas, Hugh

1997   *The Slave Trade: The Story of the Atlantic Slave Trade, 1440–1870.* Simon & Schuster, New York.

Thompson, Robert Farris

1983   *Flash of the Spirit: African and Afro-American Art and Philosophy.* Vintage Books, New York.

1993   *Face of the Gods: Art and Altars of Africa and the African Americans.* Museum for African Art, New York.

Treckel, Paula A.

1996   *To Comfort the Heart: Women in Seventeenth-Century America.* Twayne Publishers, New York.

Vlach, John Michael

1991   Afro-American Domestic Artifacts in Eighteenth-Century Virginia. In *By the Work of Their Hands: Studies in Afro-American Folklife*, edited by John M. Vlach, pp. 53–72. Univ. Press of Virginia, Charlottesville.

Wall, Diana DiZerega
> 1994   *The Archaeology of Gender: Separating the Spheres in Urban America.* Plenum Press, New York.

Walsh, Lorena
> 1993   Slave Life, Slave Society, and Tobacco Production in the Tidewater Chesapeake, 1620–1820. In *Cultivation and Culture: Labor and the Shaping of Slave Life in the Americas,* edited by Ira Berlin and Phillip D. Morgan, pp. 170–199. Univ. Press of Virginia, Charlottesville.
>
> 1997   *From Calabar to Carter's Grove: The History of a Virginia Slave Community.* Univ. Press of Virginia, Charlottesville.

Walsh, Lorena S., Ann Smart Martin, and Joanne Bowen
> 1997   Provisioning Early American Towns. The Chesapeake: A Multi-disciplinary Case Study. Final Performance Report. Colonial Williamsburg Foundation, Williamsburg, Va.

Watson, Carol
> 1997   Gender versus Power as a Predictor of Negotiation Behavior and Outcomes. In *Women, Men, and Gender: Ongoing Debates,* edited by Mary Roth Walsh, pp. 145–152. Yale Univ. Press, New Haven.

West, Candace, and Sarah Fenstermaker
> 1997   Doing Difference. In *Women, Men, and Gender: Ongoing Debates,* edited by Mary Roth Walsh, pp. 58–72. Yale Univ. Press, New Haven.

Westmacott, Richard
> 1992   *African American Gardens and Yards in the Rural South.* Univ. of Tennessee Press, Knoxville.

White, Deborah G.
> 1985   *Ar'n't I a Woman? Female Slaves in the Plantation South.* W. W. Norton & Co., New York.

Wilk, Richard R., and William Rathje
> 1982   Household Archaeology. *American Behavioral Scientist* 23(6):617–639.

Winterbottom, Thomas M.
> 1969   *An Account of the Native Africans in the Neighbourhood of Sierra Leone, to Which Is Added an Account of the Present State of Medicine among Them.* Frank Cass, London.

Yentsch, Anne
> 1991a   The Symbolic Divisions of Pottery: Sex-Related Attributes of English and Anglo-American Household Pots. In *The Archaeology of Inequality,* edited by Randall H. McGuire and Robert Paynter, pp. 192–230. Blackwell, Cambridge, Mass.

1991b Engendering Visible and Invisible Ceramic Artifacts, Especially Dairy Vessels. *Historical Archaeology* 25(4):132–155.

1991c Access and Space, Symbolic and Material, in Historical Archaeology. *The Archaeology of Gender: Proceedings of the Twenty-second Annual Chacmool Conference*, edited by Dale Walde and Noreen D. Willows, pp. 252–262. Univ. of Calgary Archaeological Association, Calgary.

1994   *A Chesapeake Family and Their Slaves: A Study in Historical Archaeology*. Cambridge Univ. Press, New York.

CHAPTER 8

African American Men, Women, and Children in Nineteenth-Century Natchez, Mississippi: An Analysis of the City Cemetery Sexton's Records

MARIE ELAINE DANFORTH

The reconstruction of health patterns among nineteenth-century African Americans has proved challenging. The amount of scholarly attention the issue has received is sporadic at best, leading researchers to generally draw upon all sources of information available. One of the most successful approaches has been to use both historical and anthropological data to examine nutritional and disease experiences. Although historical documents are often biased, biological indicators are less easily manipulated. In turn, the human skeleton tends to record only chronic conditions, and few of the lesions that do occur are attributable to a single etiology (Ortner and Putschar 1985). Thus, the amplification provided by historical documents is critical. Archaeological excavation offers yet a third independent source of data from which health patterns of African American men and women living during the 1800s may be investigated. Such a research design has yielded highly successful results at a number of historical sites (for example, LaRoche and Blakey 1997; Rose 1985).

Interestingly, most of these historical sites have represented the extremes in terms of community size for African Americans during this time period. The studies focused on either very large cities, such as Philadelphia and New York, or rural settlements, such as Cedar Grove, Arkansas, and Elko Switch, Alabama (LaRoche and Blakey 1997; Rankin-Hill 1997; Rose 1985; Turner 1989). Overlooked are towns and small cities even though these communities theoretically represent a transitional ground in terms of health experiences and correlated factors. Their residents would have experienced fewer diseases related to contact with soil and animals and experienced more diseases associated with population density and sanitation. Economic opportunities would have also varied somewhere between farming and manufacture and industry. Social support networks may have been less kin based than in rural regions since many residents were immigrants (Wharton 1947) but lacked the highly organized social institutions seen in cities (Rankin-Hill 1997).

In the present study, the health patterns of African American men and women are considered in the small city of Natchez, Mississippi. Using data gained from the sexton's records of the city cemetery, mortality patterns at various points in the life cycle for males and females are reconstructed. These data are then compared to similar data gained from historical and bioarchaeological studies of other African American populations of the time. Through such analysis, we can help better understand how the residents of Natchez coped with the unique environmental and economic challenges presented to them.

Nineteenth-Century Natchez

Before 1865 Natchez was comprised primarily of townhouses of wealthy planters who had large land tracts in outlying areas of Mississippi and Louisiana. Even though the number of inhabitants ranged from only six to nine thousand in the mid to late 1800s, it either was the most or the second most populous (after Vicksburg) city in the state (Eighth, Ninth, and Tenth U.S. Censuses). Natchez also had one of the largest black segments as well, with African Americans constituting from one-third to over one-half of the population. Jobs performed by the slaves residing in the city included some fieldwork, since the homes often had large grounds with gardens, but also would have consisted of activities related to maintenance of the house, such as cooks and maids. Some slaves may also have assisted in the running of businesses (Davis 1994).

The black population of Natchez became even larger after the Civil War. Much of the growth was related to the city being a federal haven for slaves during the war, but Natchez also experienced in-migration of African Americans from rural regions, as occurred in a number of Mississippi towns after 1865 (Wharton 1947:100). Although immediately after the war there was a concerted effort to replace black labor with that of others, especially European immigrants, "unsatisfactory as Negro labor might have been, Mississippi had discovered that it was definitely superior to any she might obtain in its place at similar cost" (Wharton 1947:103; also Rabinowitz 1992:16). There was some competition for black laborers, and those in Natchez supported themselves in a variety of positions, both skilled and unskilled. Local census information of the late 1800s lists their occupations as including seamstresses, painters, blacksmiths, laundresses, and schoolteachers (Trammell 1998). Thus, the study of nineteenth-century African American health at Natchez offers many interesting contrasts for examining sex roles.

The Natchez Cemetery Database

The Natchez City Cemetery was established in 1822, replacing two cemeteries located closer to the center of the city. Eventually, it came to have a number of separate sections, such as Catholic Hill and Public Grounds, based on religious, economic, and racial criteria (Map 8.1). The African American areas are generally on the fringes of the cemetery near the bayou, where today there is a problem of graves washing out. Using the sexton's records, Robert Shumway of Vidalia, Louisiana, collected information on a total of 21,438 interments dating from 1822 until 1909 (personal communication). The data include the individual's name, age at death, cause of death, attending physician, area of burial in cemetery, and occasional additional comments.

Among the entries are records of some nine thousand African Americans, of which the earliest dates to 1834. Very little information is available for the 1,592 entries before 1865 (Table 8.1). Most are described as simply "A Negro Man/Woman/Child/Boy/Girl/Infant" with a few having a first name listed. Less than 20 percent of the interments had any additional data. When an age at death was given, it was often rounded since nearly all end in "5" or "0." Most of these individuals appear to have been slaves, as evidenced by phrases such as "Property of . . . " in the comments section, although a handful of entries note "Free Person of Color." In comparison, the number of African American interments in the sexton's records dating after 1865 was very large; thus, I have chosen to use those interments dating only until 1890. This date represents the twenty-five-year span after the end of the war and predates the effects of many late nineteenth-century medical advances, such as bacteriological identification of specific diseases and landmark improvements in public health (Peterson 1979). The entries for the final sample of some 2,478 interments were much more complete than those predating 1865. Nearly all had first and/or last names and date of death, and about 85 percent had additional information as well.

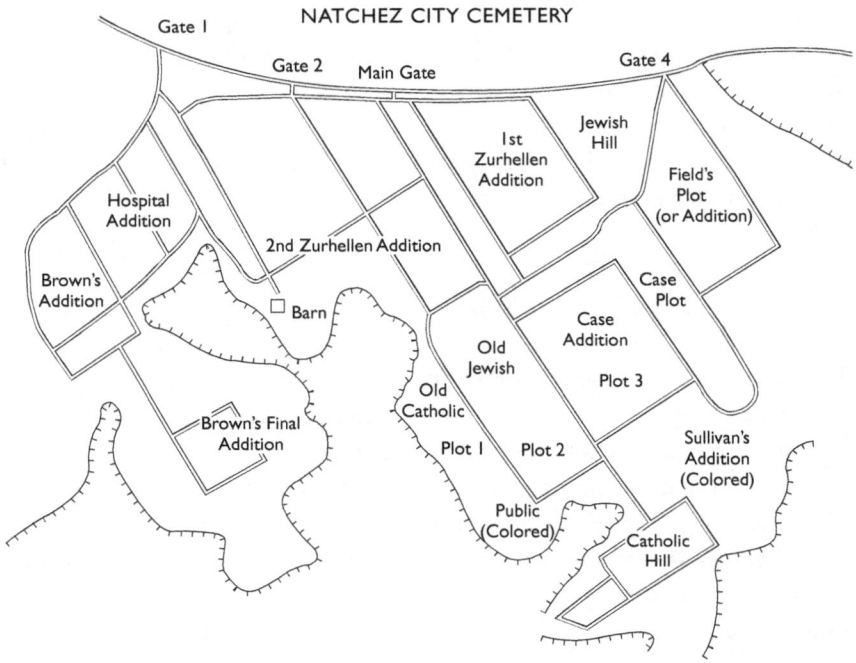

MAP 8.1.   Layout of Natchez City Cemetery.

For this analysis, the database was somewhat modified. The first task was assignment of sex. The first name was most commonly used for this. Several of the less traditional names, such as Beverly and Creasy, were given sex designations if they could be found in census records or in nineteenth-century genealogies posted on the Internet. The only entries for whom gender was largely indeterminable were those juveniles described only as "Child of. . . ." Age assignment, in comparison, was much more straightforward. If an age-at-death were given, it was kept as is, even though many were obviously estimations. Meeker (1976:19) has argued that owners at times misrepresented the ages of slaves, making juveniles older and the elderly younger.

Assessment of cause of death was problematic because most diagnoses of the time were based entirely on the presentation of symptoms. To help alleviate some of the confusion caused by the general lack of understanding of disease etiology and terminology of the day, the causes of death were reclassified into broad categories following Savitt (1978:145), as may be seen in Table 8.2.

TABLE 8.1

Age and Sex Distribution of African American Burials
in Natchez Cemetery, 1834–1890

| | 1834–1865 | | | |
	Males	Females	Undetermined	Total
Neonates	0	0	31	31
Infant child			228	228
2 wks–1 yr	0	0	77	77
1–5 yrs	3	3	52	58
5–15 yrs	25	19	18	62
Boy/girl/child of unspecified age	42	26	230	298
15–30 yrs	34	15	1	50
30–45 yrs	19	19	0	38
45–60 yrs	17	22	0	39
60–75 yrs	15	8	0	23
75 + yrs	10	12	2	24
Man/woman/adult of unspecified age	364	286	14	664
Total	529	410	653	1,592

| | 1865–1890 | | | |
	Males	Females	Undetermined	Total
Neonates	19	24	1	44
2 wks–1 yr	136	95	8	239
1–5 yrs	313	272	15	600
5–15 yrs	100	110	5	215
15–30 yrs	181	188	7	376
30–45 yrs	128	135	2	265
45–60 yrs	140	140	2	282
60–75 yrs	129	123	4	256
75 + yrs	84	105	2	191
Total	1,230	1,192	46	2,468

TABLE 8.2
Classification of Causes of Deaths in Natchez Cemetery, 1834–1890

Accidents—Includes burns,* drowning,* spider bite, exposure,* swallowing lye,* killed, shot, fractures, suicide, wounds

Cholera—Includes Asiatic cholera, epidemic cholera, cholera morbus,* cholera asphixia, cholera sporadic

Diarrheal disease—Includes diarrhea,* flux, dysentery,* cholera infantum*

Digestive disease—Includes hepatitis, inflammation of the liver,* stomach cramps, bilious colic,* duodenitis, gastric fever,* gastritis,* indigestion, bowel inflammation,* colic cramp,* hemorrhage of bowels,* abdominal congestion,* peritonitis,* thrush,* obstruction of gall duct, obstruction of bowels, gastroenteritis, perityphlitis, enteritis, abscess of liver, liver complaint, oedema of glottis, intestinal catarrh

Diphtheria—Includes croup*

Dropsy—Includes ascites,* hydrothorax,* anasarca

Female diseases—Includes metritis, inflammation of uterus, disease of uterus, ovarian dropsy, uterine myomata

Fevers, unclassifiable—Includes bilious fever,* congestive fever,* congestive chill,* typhus fever,* malignant fever, pernicious fever, prevailing fever, intermittent fever, continued fever, erysipelas

Gangrene—Includes mortification of foot

Heart disease—Includes heart hypertrophy, valvular disease, carditis, aortal aneurism, endocarditis, mitral insufficiency, fatty heart, angina maligna, varioloid, mitral regurgitation, tricuspid regurgitation

Intemperance—Includes alcoholism, delirium tremens, mania portu [*sic*]

Joint Disease—Includes rheumatism, suppuration of joints, morbus coxarius

Malaria—Includes remittent fever,* swamp fever, typhomalarial fever, remittent bilious fever

Marasmus—Includes inanition

Maternity-related diseases—Includes puerperal fever,* child bed, child birth, postpartum hemorrhage, other "puerperal" conditions

Measles—Includes morbilli

Mental illness—Includes chronic mania, senility

Mumps

Neoplasms—Includes face cancer, womb cancer, epithelioma uterus, ovarian tumor, cerebral tumor, hemorrhage from bursting of tumor

Nervous system disease—Includes apoplexy,* epilepsy,* cerebral malformation, paralysis,* spinal meningitis, neuralgia,* acute meningitis, brain congestion,* hydrocephalus,* brain fever,* brain inflammation,* loco ataxis, fits,* disease of the spine,* spasms, cerebral typhus, myelitis, meningeal effusion, hemiplegia, cerebritis

(continued on next page)

TABLE 8.2 *(continued)*

Old age

Respiratory diseases—Includes lung abscess,* asthma,* bronchitis,* lung
congestion,* lung hemorrhage,* influenza,* pneumonia,* catarrh,* bilious
pleurisy,* empyema, oedema of lungs, cold, typhoid pneumonia

Scarlet fever—Includes inflammation of throat,* laryngitis,* inflammation of
larynx, sequela scarletina

Smallpox

Syphilis

Teething—Includes dentition

Tetanus—Includes lockjaw, trismus, trismus infantum

Tuberculosis—Includes scrofulary consumption,* phthisis,* tabes mesenterica,*
consumption,* scrofula

Typhus

Typhoid fever

Urinary disease—Includes nephritis, cystitis, extravasation of urine, suppression
of urine, Bright's disease, bladder inflammation, uremic poisoning,
albiminuria, chronic nephritis, inflammation of kidneys

Whooping cough—Includes pertussis

Worms—Includes vermis, helminthiasis

Yellow fever

---

*Diseases also classified into category by Savitt (1978:145).

This scheme worked for more than 80 percent of the entries, but a few dying from conditions such as "hives" and "epixtasis" (nosebleed) remained unclassified. Similarly, a few of the classification categories, most importantly "teething" and "old age," were so common that they were kept as is despite their imprecise meanings.

All demographic analysis followed procedures outlined in Weiss (1973). This sample is unusual compared to that used in most demographic studies since calculations are made using a death cohort rather than a birth cohort for two reasons. First, the limited time frame involved in the present study would not allow many birth cohorts, especially those dating to after the Civil War, to include all members through their deaths. Second, most interpretations of mortality patterns seen in the Natchez City Cemetery database will involve comparison with bioarchaeological analysis of other nineteenth-century African American populations, which also represent death cohorts.

Such an approach has been used with other cemetery studies as well (for example, Maples and Anderson 1989–90).

General Mortality Patterns

Life expectancy, which is the mean number of years lived by all members of a population, is often used as a general measure of a group's adaptational success. Although some 371 African Americans dying before 1865 were given ages in the sexton's records (Table 8.1), it was impossible to calculate a reliable estimate of life expectancy since the age at death was given for so few infants. In contrast, the post-1865 sample appears to be a highly representative sample of the population. Life expectancy for this group is 29.32 years (N=2,243) (Table 8.3), which is roughly comparable to values seen in most other populations from the time (Table 8.4). When life expectancies for the individual sexes are considered, women at Natchez live as long, if not slightly longer, than males, a pattern seen at most other sites as determined from both bioarchaeological and census data. Unfortunately, the data at Natchez do not lend themselves for analysis of changes in life expectancy before and after emancipation, which is unfortunate since a controversy exists among historians concerning the issue. Eblen (1974) argues there was little change from 1850 until 1900, whereas Meeker (1976) suggests postwar conditions caused life expectancy to decrease by seven years in black males and four years in black females. The experience of African Americans at the Cedar Grove site in Arkansas, where the mean age at death was about fourteen, would lend support to Meeker's position, at least for rural populations (Rose 1985).

Mortality Profiles and Causes of Death in Subadults

Infants. Infant mortality among humans is always high relative to the rest of childhood, and the figures seen in the Natchez sample closely adhere to this pattern (Weiss 1973). In the slave population, some 2.5 percent of neonates (those under age two weeks) died, as did some 40 percent of infants (those under age one) (Figure 8.1). This is somewhat higher than the 30 percent rate of infant mortality estimated for slaves by Farley (1965:395) but much lower than the 54 percent estimated by Steckel (1986b:452). In terms of causes of death among the slave sample, all neonates were simply listed as being stillborn,

TABLE 8.3

Life Table for African Americans in Natchez City Cemetery, 1865–1890

Age (x)	D_x	d_x	l_x	q_x	L_x	T_x	e^0_x
0–.99	523	2,083	10,000	.2083	8,959	293,268	29.32
1–4	331	1,319	7,917	.1666	29,030	284,359	35.92
5–9	112	446	6,598	.0676	31,875	255,329	38.70
10–14	86	343	6,152	.0558	29,903	223,454	36.32
15–19	123	490	5,809	.0844	27,820	193,551	33.12
20–24	145	578	5,319	.1087	25,150	165,731	31.16
25–29	123	490	4,741	.1034	22,480	140,581	29.65
30–34	90	359	4,251	.0845	20,358	118,101	27.78
35–39	101	402	3,892	.1033	18,455	97,743	25.11
40–44	98	390	3,490	.1117	16,475	79,288	22.72
45–49	99	394	3,100	.1271	14,515	62,813	20.26
50–54	119	474	2,706	.1752	12,345	48,298	17.85
55–59	86	343	2,232	.1537	10,303	35,953	16.11
60–64	100	398	1,889	.2107	8,450	25,650	13.58
65–69	92	367	1491	.2461	6,538	17,200	11.54
70–74	78	311	1124	.2767	4,843	10,662	9.49
75–79	76	303	813	.3773	3,308	5,819	7.15
80–85	66	263	510	.5157	1,893	2,511	4.92
85 +	62	247	247	1.0000	618	618	2.50

D_x= Absolute number of individuals dying within age interval.
d_x= (Percentage of total sample dying within age interval) x 100.
l_x= Number of initial population cohort of 10,000 still alive at start of age interval.
q_x= Probability of dying prior to reaching next age interval.
L_x= Life-years lived by initial cohort of 10,000 during interval x.
T_x= Life-years remaining for initial cohort of 10,000.
e^0_x= Age-specific life expectancy.

and no single cause emerged as primary among the nine given for those dying as infants. In comparison, infant mortality rates in the post-1865 sample dropped by half to 21 percent (Figure 8.1 and Table 8.3). These findings are comparable to the 26 percent death rate seen in the free black Philadelphia population in the mid-1800s (Rankin-Hill 1997). These data are also similar to

TABLE 8.4

Estimations of Life Expectancies in Eighteenth- and Nineteenth-Century
African Americans by Gender

	Males	Females	Total Population[a]
Skeletal Samples			
Clifts Plantation, Va.[b] (early 1700s?)	30.5	34	
Belleview Plantation, S.C. (n=2)[c] (1738–1756)	40+	45+	
College Landing, Va. (n=17)[d] (1790–1820)	36.3	36.3	
Catoctin Furnace, Md. (n=24)[e] (1790–1840)	35.7	35.4	
First African Baptist Church, Phila (n=75)[f] (1823–1841)	44.8	38.9	
Charleston-area Plantation, S.C. (n=36)[g] (1840–1870)	34.7	39.7	
Natchez, Miss. (n=2468) (1865–1890)	31.1	31.9	29.3
Elko Switch, AL (n=22)[h]			31.7
Cedar Grove, AR (n=80)[i]			14
Demographic data			
Blacks (late 1800s)[j]	33.0	34.4	33.7
Mississippi blacks (1900)[k]	32.5	35.0	

NOTES: [a]Total Population includes those individuals for whom sex could not be determined, including all juveniles. [b]Kelley and Angel (1987); [c]Rathbun (1991); [d]Kelley and Angel (1987); [e]Kelley and Angel (1987); [f]Angel et al (1987); [g]Rathbun (1987); [h]Turner (1989); [i]Rose (1985); [j]Eblen (1974); [k]Lewis (1942).

the 21.8 percent death rate in males and 18.6 percent death rate in females reported in the 1880 Census (Tenth U.S. Census). However, the findings are lower than the 34 percent infant mortality rate seen at Cedar Grove (Rose 1985).

The primary cause of death among infants in the postwar sample was tetanus (also lockjaw, or trismus nacentum), which claimed some 57 percent

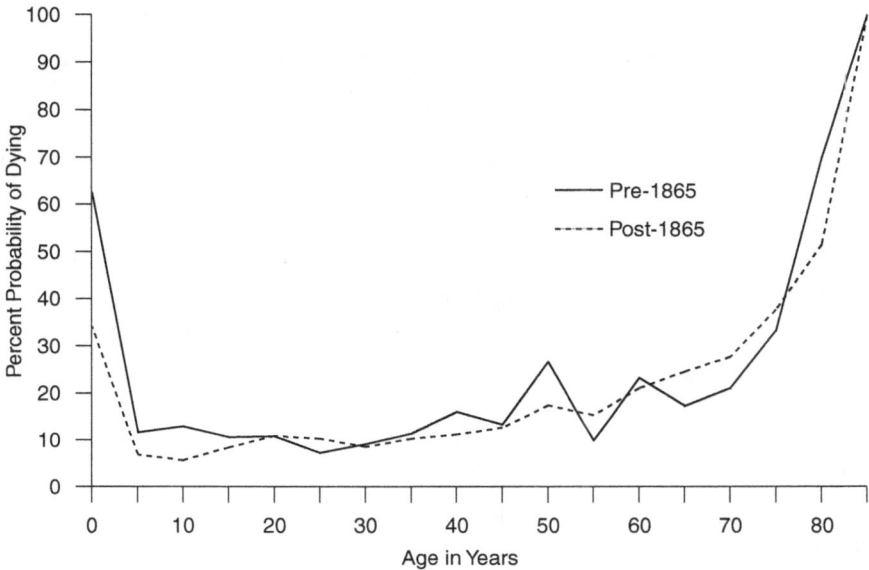

FIG. 8.1. Comparison of probability of dying (q_x) for African Americans in Natchez before and after 1865.

of those dying before age one (Table 8.5). Savitt (1978:122) attributes the high rate of bacterial infection to the mishandling of the umbilical stump, such as by covering it with mud. Kiple and King (1982:101–104), however, argue that the disease manifested may actually have been tetany, which is related to deficiencies of Vitamin D and other nutrients in the mother. According to practices of the time, enslaved women, who were already often malnourished, were often kept indoors for the late part of their pregnancies. This was especially problematic considering the darker skin typical of African Americans, because their higher concentration of melanin already was filtering out much of the ultraviolet light necessary for Vitamin D production. A further contribution to the possibility of Vitamin D deficiency is the inability of most individuals of African ancestry to digest milk (Cardell and Hopkins 1978). Convulsions were also a common cause of death among slave children (Savitt 1978:145), and the continued presence of convulsions during the postbellum period suggests that the cultural practices involved were being maintained despite the changing times.

Although there was no gender bias evident among those infants dying of tetanus or convulsions, the mortality rate seen among male infants was nearly

TABLE 8.5
Leading Causes of Death by Age in African Americans
in Natchez Cemetery, 1865–1890

0–1 Years (N)	1–5 Years (N)	5–15 Years (N)
Total (281)*	Total (187)*	Total (149)*
Nervous system diseases (78)	Nervous system diseases (40)	Tuberculosis (23)
Tetanus (52)	Diarrheal diseases (26)	Nervous system diseases (22)
Respiratory diseases (46)	Teething (21)	Respiratory diseases (18)
Diarrheal diseases (27)	Digestive diseases (19)	Typhoid fever (17)
Digestive diseases (25)	Respiratory diseases (19)	Unclassified fevers (15)

15–45 Years (N)	45+ Years (N)
Total (604)*	Total (679)*
Tuberculosis (177)	Heart disease (114)
Respiratory diseases (91)	Debility (83)
Nervous system diseases (35)	Nervous system diseases (71)
Accidents (32)	Old age (56)
Typhoid fever (31)	Respiratory diseases (54)
Dropsy (54)	

*Number of individuals in category with cause of death listed.

50 percent higher than that of females (Figure 8.2). This gendered difference in infant mortality rates, which is seen in most human populations, has been offered as evidence of a biological advantage in survival for females, possibly as a result of the need of their greater numbers to ensure species continuation (Stini 1969; Stinson 1985). One potential manifestation of this biological edge is that girls are generally four to six weeks more mature at birth (Tanner 1978:58). In the Natchez sample, male infants were three times as likely to die of respiratory illness, presumably from less developed lungs, and twice as likely to die of digestive/diarrheal causes, which may reflect a less developed immune system. In certain societies, such differences in survival may be one cause of male preferencing for access to food and health care, such as through longer nursing, in certain societies (for example, Callan and Kee 1981). The great differential in female survival in Natchez, which was more than twice as large as the 20 percent level that was still found in the United States during

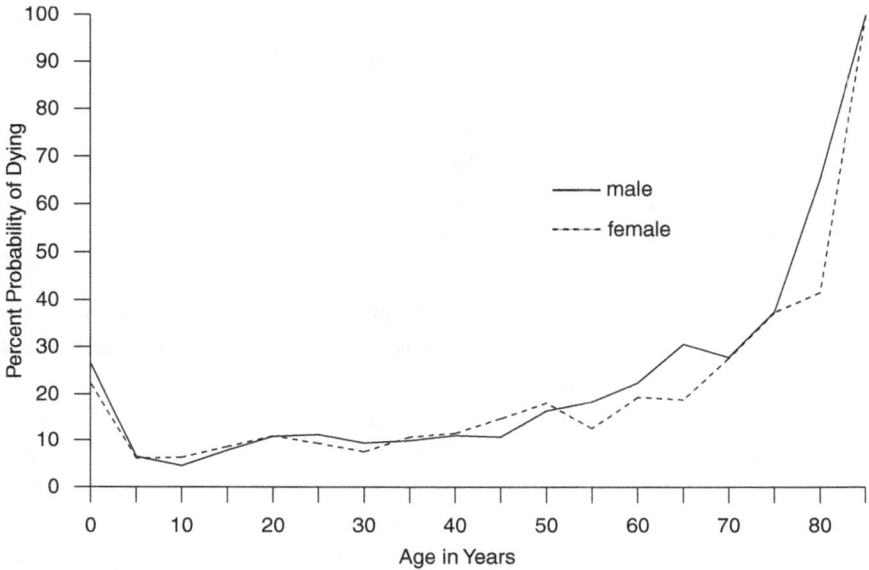

FIG. 8.2.   Comparison of probability of dying (q_x) for male and female African Americans in Natchez from 1865 to 1890.

the 1990s (MacDorman and Atkinson 1995), may suggest that any preferencing among infants by sex for access to resources that occurred in nineteenth-century Natchez was not effective.

Children. In most human populations, rates of death fall after infancy, and in later childhood they are the lowest during the human lifetime. This may reflect a winnowing of the weak during infancy. Such a pattern was indeed seen at Natchez as well (Figure 8.1), where the likelihood of death between ages five and ten was only one-third that of the first year of life. Despite this marked drop, however, the juvenile mortality rates at Natchez were still somewhat high. One possible explanation for the excessive mortality may be found in stature. Steckel (1986a) found that enslaved children were extremely short but underwent a tremendous growth spurt during adolescence, becoming much taller adults than anticipated. He speculates that younger children were exceedingly undernourished. It was only when they approached adulthood and became economically valuable that they received a more adequate diet. This practice may have continued even after emancipation. An even more probable, although not mutually exclusive, explanation involves attitudes concerning which foods were deemed appropriate for children (Kiple and King 1982:97). Slave children were routinely given hominy, cornbread, and fat since such a trio was thought to provide the most necessary nutrients. It was only when they became adolescents that they were considered to be able to handle meat, which of course provided the missing protein that was so critical to growth. Evidence for continuation of these food practices after the Civil War may be tangentially found in the high rates of malnutrition among children in the late-nineteenth-century skeletal series from Cedar Grove, Arkansas (Rose 1985).

Nervous system diseases remained the leading cause of death among children in Natchez (Table 8.5), with most instances involving convulsions. In this age group, a gender difference in nervous system diseases is seen with females affected twice as often, although the reason is unknown. Digestive and diarrheal problems became the next leading cause of deaths, which undoubtedly were related to the changing diet of children as they were weaned at about age one and then introduced to many new bacteria found in replacement foods. The timing of deaths supports such an interpretation since infants and children at Natchez died most commonly during the warmer months, as was also seen among free blacks in Philadelphia and slaves in New Orleans (Rankin-Hill 1997:83; Steckel 1986b:442). In fact, Steckel (1986b:444) argues that such a pattern of seasonality was an urban phenomenon. The children also undoubtedly ingested many germs as they increasingly explored their environments and enlarged their range of social contact, especially through playmates.

Accidents also became a more common cause of death during this stage of life. A large number of boys, especially during the prewar period, died of drowning or falls, whereas girls more often died of burns and poisoning. These causes of death may reflect the greater independence of the children away from their caretakers' watchful eyes, but they also suggest that juveniles as young as age five were already beginning to assume some of their adult roles. Girls may have been assisting with cooking or laundering chores, and boys may have been fishing or working with boats. It has been speculated that the large number of drownings among blacks was related in part to their "denser bones." Although some have indeed claimed that individuals of African ancestry have heavily mineralized bone, the difference it makes in the body weight of an adult is only about one pound (Merz et al. 1956). It would seem that the low body fat levels that undoubtedly characterized most young boys of the time would have had more effect in quickly drowning a child with little buoyancy.

When these patterns for childhood mortality are compared with those from other contemporary black populations, some interesting patterns emerge.

Tetanus, teething, and convulsions were top causes of death among Virginia slave children and free black children in Philadelphia in the mid-1800s (Rankin-Hill 1997; Savitt 1978:143) as well as in the post-1865 period at Natchez. Only three juveniles at Natchez, however, were listed as dying of worms, which, at the time, was generally considered to be a disease of African Americans and was a leading cause of death among slaves (Kiple and King 1982:113; Savitt 1978:143). The lack of infestation in children may somewhat reflect the more urban setting in which they lived since they probably came into contact with soil and farm animals less frequently. Also supporting a contrast in mortality patterns with rural settings are the findings from the free black population at Cedar Grove (Rose 1985). Some 55 percent of children at that site were dead by age fifteen, as compared to only about 40 percent at Natchez (Table 8.3). Causes of death at Cedar Grove cannot be easily determined because so few leave skeletal lesions, but those present suggest that infants may have been dying from malaria and congenital syphilis, whereas juveniles suffered from extensive nutritional deficiencies.

In yet another difference from the disease experience of Virginia slaves, only four infants in Natchez are listed as dying of smothering. Also perceived to be a black disease, slave owners attributed it to weary or careless mothers overlaying their infants as they shared a bed. Johnson provides evidence for such a cause by noting that the incidence of smothering was highest in those areas, such as the cotton belt, where slaves were forced to work the hardest and thus the mothers were the most tired at night (Johnson 1981:515–516). Such an interpretation could explain the low incidence of smothering at Natchez, since black women, throughout the time period under consideration, had more domestic rather than field duties. It is noteworthy, however, that the four smothered infants in Natchez all died in the 1880s, at which time Johnson notes rates for this cause of death had plummeted to one-fourth those seen during slavery (Johnson 1981:518).

In contrast, Kiple and King (1982:107–109) and Savitt (1978:123–127) have argued that the high rate of smothering was manifestation of the disease modernly identified as sudden infant death syndrome. In SIDS, a baby stops breathing for unknown reasons, although current research suggests it may be related to a number of factors, including respiratory conditions, sleeping position, poor prenatal care, and low birth weight (SIDS Network 1998). The typical SIDS death usually occurs in the winter months and is most common in children older than two months. The four "smothered" children at Natchez conform to seasonality expectations in that two deaths occurred in December and one in March, but all of the infants affected were less than six weeks old at death, which is a bit younger than what is typically seen in SIDS cases.

Older Children and Adolescents. Children during later childhood and adolescence had relatively low death rates, but the causes of death resembled those seen in adults. Tuberculosis and unclassified fevers join the previously seen nervous and respiratory system diseases (Table 8.5). One female, age 17, died in childbirth. Since the reported age of first births among slaves was about age 20.7, it is surprising that more young women did not die of maternal causes, especially since adolescents are somewhat more vulnerable to delivery problems due to still-growing pelvises (Steckel 1985:103). Accidents also continued to be a common cause of death for young males, but the causes involved a greater variety of more dangerous tasks, as indicated by the comments "hit by railrode carr" and "tunnel falling in."

Mortality Patterns and Causes of Death in Adults

Young Adults. The leading cause of mortality by far among the twenty- to forty-five-year-olds at death, both before and after the Civil War, was tuberculosis. These findings contradict the belief expressed in certain medical writings of the late nineteenth century that the disease was almost entirely a postbellum occurrence among blacks (Kiple and King 1982:139; Ornstein 1937; Walton 1897), but it does support the interpretation that African Americans compared to whites were particularly susceptible to tuberculosis, especially the military variety that is the most fatal form (Kiple and King 1982:139–146; Walton 1897). Others have argued that this disease was just part of a vulnerability of those of African descent to respiratory diseases in general, caused by a number of factors, including no previous exposure to bacterial pneumonias in Africa (Savitt 1988:126–127). Rates of the disease at Natchez may actually have been higher than those seen in Tables 8.5 and 8.6, since tuberculosis was often also identified as typhoid and dropsy. It also reinforces the notion that tuberculosis was a disease of the young adult (Condran and Cheney 1982).

There were some gender differences in causes of death among young adults (Table 8.6). In many populations today, young adult females typically exhibit higher death rates than do males due to the risks of childbirth. At Natchez, however, females showed slightly lower mortality levels in the young adult age group, with only 6 percent dying of maternal complications. The low

TABLE 8.6

Leading Causes of Death by Gender (Adults over Age 15)
in African Americans in Natchez Cemetery

1834–1865	
Males (N)	Females (N)
Total (283)*	Total (225)*
Tuberculosis (58)	Tuberculosis (52)
Cholera (31)	Old age (33)
Unclassified fever (28)	Cholera (17)
Respiratory diseases (22)	Dropsy (15)
Old age (22)	Heart disease (14)

1865–1890	
Males (N)	Females (N)
Total (580)*	Total (635)*
Tuberculosis (91)	Tuberculosis (134)
Respiratory diseases (85)	Heart diseases (79)
Heart diseases (60)	Nervous system diseases (52)
Nervous system diseases (54)	Respiratory diseases (47)
Debility (49)	Dropsy (46)
Accidents (48)	Debility (41)
Urinary system diseases (34)	Old age (40)
Dropsy (32)	Neoplasms (25)
Diarrheal diseases (27)	Digestive diseases (24)
Unclassified fevers (20)	Diarrheal diseases (17)

*Number of individuals in category with cause of death listed.

rate may be attributed to the fact that many of these women were urban dwellers who worked in domestic settings, which may have provided them access, either officially or unofficially, to more food. Cities, especially those located on a river, also potentially had a greater variety of foods available than did more isolated communities. Thus, these women were not vulnerable to death during childbirth from constitutions already compromised by poor nutrition, as has been argued by Rose (1985) to explain, based on skeletal evidence, the peak in female deaths between ages thirty and forty in the Cedar Grove series. This argument falls short because McKeown and Record (1962) note that poor nutrition was the leading variable in tuberculosis deaths, and women were much more likely to fall victim to that disease than were young males. Rather, the sex differences in mortality levels and causes of death probably reflect males dying six times more often of accidents and murder. Many of the accidents involved being shot, and a number of the injuries are suggestive of dangerous occupations (for example, "from falling timber," "boiler explosion"). Evidence of violence was also common among males at the Cedar Grove site, where some 20 percent exhibited healed cranial fractures (Rose 1985:143).

The only difference in the causes of death at Natchez between the pre- and post-1865 samples was the presence of cholera in the earlier period, during which it was the second leading cause of death among young adults. No one in the Natchez City Cemetery died of cholera after 1871; this suggests that public health measures had taken effect in the city as in most of the rest of the United States, with the last reported cholera case anywhere in the nation being in 1873 (Rosenberg 1962:226). The disappearance of cholera as a primary cause of death is easily seen in the seasonality of deaths in the Natchez post-1865 sample in which the number of deaths level out. In contrast, blacks in Philadelphia and New Orleans during the mid-1800s showed much higher mortality in spring and summer, largely due to cholera (Rankin-Hill 1997; Steckel 1986b:442).

Older Adults. Within the samples from both periods, several individuals are listed as surviving to at least one hundred, although it is hard to say how many may have had their longevity embellished. Although many in the pre-1865 sample died of dropsy, cholera, and tuberculosis, the leading cause of death by far among those over age forty-five was old age (Table 8.5). The "old age" generalization may indicate a lack of concern for the cause of death in this age group or an attitude of the inevitability of the human body reaching its natural end, although it was applied only to those who were at least sixty-five years old. In the post-1865 group, the leading cause of death was heart disease, followed by debility and nervous system diseases. The situation of fewer individuals succumbing to old age probably indicates increased recognition of the degenerative processes that contribute to death of an older adult.

When patterns of mortality by gender are considered, some interesting findings emerge for this group. Most unexpected was that female mortality rates at age forty-five increased dramatically and were nearly 50 percent greater than that of males. One clue might be that the cause of death most evident in this group is heart disease, which may reflect the loss of the protective benefits of estrogen due to menopause. Although age forty-five is rather young for menopause by contemporary standards, it is very typical among populations under stress (Leidy 1994). Also providing indirect support for menopause commonly occurring during the mid-forties is the fact that the oldest age at which a woman died in childbirth was forty-five.

The expected pattern of mortality rates rising much faster for males than for females among the very old is seen at Natchez. Women are twice as likely to reach eighty-five years compared to males (Figure 8.2), just as women were twice as likely to die of the listed cause of "old age." Another consequence of their longer lives was a much higher incidence of cancer. The most common organs affected by neoplasms are those exclusive to females, such as the breast and uterus. In a parallel situation, males in this age group also die in greater numbers from urinary problems, presumably related to enlarged prostate glands.

The causes of death for older adults at Natchez are comparable with those of other nineteenth-century black populations. Savitt (1978:145) reports the top five causes among Virginia slaves were tuberculosis, old age, respiratory diseases, nervous system diseases, and diarrheal diseases. Among the pre-1865 Natchez sample, diarrheal diseases were less common, but yellow fever and cholera were more common, which is easily attributable to Natchez's location as a river city. The drop in yellow fever rates in the post-1865 Natchez sample is surprising, however, since the disease continued to ravage cities on the Mississippi River for the entire time period under analysis. The only yellow fever deaths among African Americans at Natchez were associated with an 1871 epidemic. Surprisingly, no African Americans in the city appear to have died during the famous 1878 epidemic that affected much of the state, including more than one thousand deaths in nearby Vicksburg (Patterson 1992:858). Partial explanation may be found in the fact that even though blacks contracted yellow fever, their mortality rates were generally about one-tenth that seen in whites (Kiple and King 1982:46). The protection from severe cases of the disease also possibly resulted in it being correctly diagnosed. Interestingly, children were thought to be totally immune from the disease (Patterson 1992:862), which is also reflected in the Natchez sample.

Conclusion

The health experiences seen among the black residents of nineteenth-century Natchez provide one of the first glimpses into life in a river city in the Deep South. In many ways, the residents exhibit patterns characteristic of nearly all human populations. Firstly, infant mortality is relatively high, with baby boys taking the brunt of the mortality because of their delayed physical development, especially in the lungs. Secondly, mortality is comparatively low during childhood but rises once again as the effects of male deaths from violence and accidents and female deaths from childbirth begin to occur in young adulthood. Finally, at the end of the life span, African American women in Natchez were twice as likely to live to age eighty.

Many of the health experiences also reflect those commonly seen in African Americans of the time. More than one-fourth of infants died within the first year of life. Most often the cause was tetanus or convulsions, which reflect either tetany (Kiple and King 1982) or cultural practices concerning the umbilicus. Children at times died of accidental causes, such as burning or drowning, that suggest they had already begun many of their adult activities. Young adults fell victim most frequently to tuberculosis. Although tuberculosis was the most common killer of whites as well, blacks seemed to contract a particularly serious and deadly form. This was probably part of a susceptibility to respiratory diseases in general among those of African descent.

Changes and continuities in health patterns in blacks throughout the past century are also reflected in the Natchez data. Infant mortality rates dropped by more than one-third between antebellum to postbellum times, although the causes remained the same. Unfortunately, few other statistics could be gleaned from the pre-1865 sample because of lack of information, but compared to the experiences seen in other slave populations, postbellum African Americans in Natchez saw their babies succumb much less often to smothering. If the cause of smothering is actually SIDS, as many researchers believe (Kiple and King 1982; Savitt 1978), then this may suggest that infants grew larger at birth and/or were better nourished, two of the most important factors in the appearance of SIDS. If the cause of death is related to weary mothers overlaying infants, then it may reflect the less demanding work of black women living in urban Natchez. Causes of death also became more specific in the later nineteenth century, most likely reflecting better medical identification of individual disease processes. Public sanitation was also beginning to have an effect, as seen in the entire disappearance of cholera after 1870. Unfortunately, other indicators suggest that times did not change entirely, such as the continuing presence of tuberculosis. Also seen were higher than anticipated rates of childhood mortality, which may have resulted from the continuing practice of denying youngsters meat in their diets based on the belief that it was inappropriate for their systems. It also may suggest that they were involved in many relatively dangerous activities that increased their likelihood of dying from accidental causes.

A few patterns in the cemetery data do suggest beneficial health effects of Natchez being a small city. This, of course, is contrary to most expectations of increased disease in urban settings because of easier transmission of infectious disease as well as poorer sanitation. Such findings, however, were not seen in analysis of two skeletal series from rural communities in the late 1800s. Instead, Elko Switch (Turner 1989) and Cedar Grove (Rose 1985) showed higher childhood mortality and lower life expectancies. Compared to slave populations (Savitt 1978), postbellum Natchez children died far less often from worms and diarrheal/digestive diseases, which may be related to less exposure to soil and animals. The better than anticipated health among the city-dwelling Natchez residents could have resulted from a wider variety of food resources because of river trade, better medical care because of the presence of a local charity hospital, and increased economic opportunities because of a broader job market. Improved health status in urban settings has also been seen in other populations, including those recovered from the cemetery at the First African Baptist Church in Philadelphia (Rankin-Hill 1997), the eighteenth-century slave cemetery from New Orleans (Owsley et al. 1987), and the Freedman Cemetery in Dallas (Rathbun et al. 1998).

These findings also reveal interesting gender patterns of nineteenth-century African American residents of Natchez, as they relate both to culture and biology. One of the most pervasive manifestations of this is that women appear to have enjoyed life expectancies several years longer than those of men, a demographic pattern that has not always been true. In premodern societies, females succumbed earlier from a variety of causes, most especially the stresses of childbirth and hard work, but better nutrition and modern medical care have reversed the situation (Ascádi and Nemeskéri 1970). Of course, the greater biological vulnerability of male infants is more difficult to overcome since much is related to developmental timing. Also contributing to the greater longevity of women was the much lower mortality rate of young girls compared to that of their brothers, which indicates that males were not enjoying much, if any, preferential treatment. This in turn may suggest that females were considered to be valuable both socially and/or economically. The deaths among children caused by accidents show that the juveniles adopted traditional roles and that they adopted these roles early. By age five, girls were working in domestic chores, whereas boys were more likely to labor outside, such as in fishing.

By adulthood, however, it appears that women were able to greatly reduce the danger associated with their tasks, whereas accidents continued to claim the lives of many men. This probably reflects the fact that experience alone could not make their jobs entirely safe, but perhaps they were also more prone to take chances. Males were also apparently more involved with violence than women, as evidenced by the number of causes of death listed as murder and gunshots. One surprising find in the Natchez data was that if nineteenth-century African American women were bearing children in late adolescence, they were not dying from it. A final aspect of the longer life expectancy of African American women in Natchez during the late 1800s is that a relatively large percentage were widows in old age. Since they were often succumbing to degenerative diseases such as heart conditions or cancer, this may be an indication that there was a strong support network to provide them care.

In summary, Natchez confirmed many health patterns seen in other black populations from the nineteenth century. Their unique combination, however, provides the first glimpse into experiences of those in a small city since previous studies have focused on either large urban centers or rural settings. Analysis of the Natchez Cemetery records also offers the advantage of large sample size, a problem plaguing many of the skeletal studies. It is hoped that this study will encourage the further examination of other cemetery records. The information they contain may seem limited, but it nevertheless can provide mortality patterns that complement the osteological record. In turn, these patterns can be tested and then reevaluated using data from the archaeological record and other historical documents as researchers attempt to reconstruct the life experiences of those buried in the nineteenth century.

ACKNOWLEDGMENTS

I would like to thank Robert Shumway of Vidalia, Louisiana, who collected the data from the sexton's records at the Natchez City Cemetery. Without his time and efforts, this chapter would not have been possible. I am also grateful to Amy Young for introducing me to the cemetery project and for all of her help and encouragement in my attempts to understand life for the African American residents of Natchez in the 1800s. Finally, I would like to thank the editors, Jillian Galle and Amy Young, for all their valuable suggestions in revising this chapter. All errors remain mine.

REFERENCES

Angel, J. Lawrence, Jennifer Olsen Kelley, Michael Parrington, and Stephanie Pinter
  1987   Life Stresses of the Free Black Community as Represented by the First African Baptist Church, Philadelphia, 1823–1841. *American Journal of Physical Anthropology* 74:213–220.
Ascádi, G., and J. Nemeskéri
  1970   *History of Human Life Span and Mortality.* Akadémiai Kaidó, Budapest.
Callan, V. J, and P. K. Kee
  1981   Sons or Daughters? Cross-Cultural Comparisons of the Sex Preferences of Australian, Greek, Italian, Malay, Chinese, and Indian Parents in Australia and Malaysia. *Population and Environment* 4:97–108.
Cardell, N. S., and M. M. Hopkins
  1978   The Effect of Milk Intolerance on the Consumption of Milk by Slaves in 1860. *Journal of Interdisciplinary History* 8:507–513.
Condran, G. A., and R. Cheney
  1982   Mortality Trends in Philadelphia: Age and Cause Specific Rates, 1870–1930. *Demography* 19:97–123.
Davis, Ronald L. F.
  1994   *The Black Experience in Natchez, 1720–1880.* Eastern National Park and Monument Association.
Eblen, J. E.
  1974   New Estimates of the Vital Rates of the United States Black Population during the Nineteenth Century. *Demography* 11:301–319.
Farley, Reynolds
  1965   The Demographic Rates and Social Institutions of the Nineteenth Century Negro Population: A Stable Population Analysis. *Demography* 2:389.
Johnson, Michael T.
  1981   Smothered Slave Infants: Were Slave Mothers at Fault? *Journal of Southern History* 47:493–520.

Kelly, Jennifer Olsen, and J. Lawrence Angel
    1987   Life Stresses of Slavery. *American Journal of Physical Anthropology*
        74(2):199–212.

Kiple, Kenneth F., and Virginia Himmelsteib King
    1982   *Another Dimension to the Black Diaspora: Diet, Disease, and Racism.*
        Cambridge Univ. Press, London.

La Roche, Cheryl J., and Michael L. Blakey
    1997   Seizing Intellectual Power: The Dialogue at the New York African
        Burial Ground. *Historical Archaeology* 31:84–106.

Leidy, Lynnette E.
    1994   Biological Aspects of Menopause: Across the Lifespan. *Annual*
        Reviews of Anthropology 23:231–254.

Lewis, Julian H.
    1942   *The Biology of the Negro.* Univ. of Chicago Press, Chicago.

MacDorman, Marian F., and Jonnae O. Atkinson
    1995   *Infant Mortality Statistics from Linked Birth/Infant Death Data Set—*
        1995 Period Data. Monthly Vital Statistics Summaries and Supple-
        ments, vol. 46, no. 6, Suppl. 2. National Center for Health Statistics,
        Hyattsville, Md.

Maples, Trina C., and John L Anderson
    1989–90 Gone but Not Forgotten: A Study of Mid-Nineteenth Demogra-
        phy at Fairview Cemetery, Albany, Indiana. *Ohio Valley Historical*
        Archaeology 7, no. 8:33–41.

McKeown, T., and R. G. Record
    1962   Reasons for Decline in Mortality in England and Wales during the
        Nineteenth Century. *Population Studies* 16:94–122.

Meeker, Edward
    1976   Mortality Trends of Southern Blacks, 1850–1910. *Explorations in*
        Economic History 13:13–42.

Merz, A. L., Mildred Trotter, and R. R. Peterson
    1956   Estimation of Skeletal Weight in the Living. *American Journal of*
        Physical Anthropology 14:589–609.

Ornstein, George
    1937   The Leading Cause of Death among Negroes: Tuberculosis. *Journal*
        of Negro Education 6:303–313.

Ortner, Donald J, and Walter G. J. Putschar
    1985   *Identification of Pathological Conditions in Human Skeletal Remains.*
        Smithsonian Press, Washington.

Owsley, Douglas W., Charles E. Orser Jr., Robert W. Mann,
Peer H. Moore-Jansen, and Robert L. Montgomery
    1987   Demography and Pathology of an Urban Slave Population
            from New Orleans. *American Journal of Physical Anthropology*
            74:185–197.
Patterson, K. David
    1992   Yellow Fever Epidemics and Mortality in the United States,
            1693–1905. *Social Science and Medicine* 34:855–865.
Peterson, J. A.
    1979   The Impact of Sanitary Reform upon American Urban Planning,
            1840–1890. *Journal of Social History* 13:83–103.
Rabinowitz, Howard N.
    1992   *The First New South, 1865–1920*. Harlan Davidson, Arlington
            Heights, Ill.
Rankin-Hill, Lesley M.
    1997   *A Biohistory of Nineteenth-Century Afro-Americans: The Burial
            Remains of a Philadelphia Cemetery*. Bergin and Garvey,
            Westport.
Rathbun, R. Ted
    1987   Health and Disease at a South Carolina Plantation, 1840–1860.
            American Journal of Physical Anthropology 74:239–253.
    1991   Status and Health in Colonial South Carolina: Belleview
            Plantation, 1738–1756. In *What Mean These Bones?* edited by
            M. L. Powell, P. S. Bridges, and A. M. Mires, pp. 148–164.
            Univ. of Alabama Press, Tuscaloosa.
Rathbun, R. Ted, Richard Steckel, Keith Condon, and Thomas A. Crist
    1998   African American Biohistory: Relative Rankings in the Health
            and Human History Project (abstract). *American Journal of
            Physical Anthropology* Suppl. 26:184.
Rose, Jerome C.
    1985   *Gone to a Better Land: A Biohistory of a Black Cemetery in the
            Post-Reconstruction South*. Arkansas Archaeological Survey
            Research Series 25, Fayetteville.
Rosenberg, Charles E.
    1962   *The Cholera Years*. Univ. of Chicago Press, Chicago.
Savitt, Todd L.
    1978   *Medicine and Slavery: The Diseases and Health Care of Blacks in
            Antebellum Virginia*. Univ. of Illinois Press, Urbana.

1988   Slave Health and Southern Distinctiveness. In *Disease and Distinctiveness in the American South*, edited by Todd L. Savitt and James H. Young, pp. 120–153. Univ. of Tennessee, Knoxville.

SIDS Network
1998   Sudden Infant Death Syndrome at http://www.sids-network.org, October 25, 1998.

Steckel, Richard
1985   *The Economics of U.S. Slave and Southern White Fertility*. Garland, New York.
1986a   Birth Weights and Infant Mortality among American Slaves. *Explorations in Economic History* 23:173–198.
1986b   A Dreadful Childhood: Excess Mortality of American Slaves. *Social Science History* 10:427–465.

Stini, William A.
1969   Nutritional Stress and Growth: Sex Differences in Adaptive Response. *American Journal of Physical Anthropology* 31:417–426.

Stinson, Sara
1985   Sex Differences in Environmental Sensitivity during Growth and Development. *Yearbook of Physical Anthropology* 28:123–148.

Tanner, James M.
1978   *Foetus into Man: Physical Growth from Conception into Maturity*. Harvard Univ. Press, Cambridge.

Trammell, Tanya
1998   The More Things Change: Economic Status and Disease among Mulattoes in Natchez, 1870–1890. Paper presented at the meetings of the Southern Anthropological Association, Wilmington.

Turner, Kenneth R.
1989   Biological Analysis. In *Elko Switch Cemetery: An Archaeological Perspective*, edited by M. G. Shogren, K. R. Turner, and J. C. Perroni, pp. 191–228. Alabama State Museum of Natural History, Division of Archaeology, Report of Investigations 58, Tuscaloosa.

Walton, J. T.
1897   The Comparative Mortality of the White and Colored Races in the South. *Charlotte Medical Journal* 10:291–294.

Weiss, Kenneth M.
1973   *Demographic Models for Anthropology*. Memoirs of the Society for American Archaeology No. 27, Washington.

Wharton, Vernon Lane
1947   *The Negro in Mississippi, 1865–1890*. Univ. of North Carolina Press, Chapel Hill.

CHAPTER 9

Feminine Voices from beyond the Grave: What Burials Can Tell Us about Gender Differences among Historic African Americans

KRISTIN J. WILSON AND MELANIE A. CABAK

Most archaeologists now agree that culture and society, not biology, define gender roles (Conkey and Gero 1991:8; Rogers 1980:12). During the antebellum period, slaveholders shaped many aspects of African American gender roles in part by assigning enslaved men and women their daily tasks. It was typical for households to be matriarchal and for extended families, particularly female relatives, to help raise children. The strongest interpersonal bonds among slave families were usually between mother and child as opposed to the European-American pattern that privileged the husband and wife as the basis for the family unit (White 1991:118). Primary sources (for example, Hurmence 1990; Kemble 1984) reveal these differences, as well as many others, in the relationships and roles of enslaved African American men and women.

Gender is fluid (Conkey and Gero 1991:8, 10), and although some aspects of gender roles shaped by slavery certainly continued after emancipation, others changed. Just as archaeology contributes to a better understanding of other aspects of historic African American lifeways (for example, Ferguson 1992; Schuyler 1980; Singleton 1985) archaeology also provides insight into past African American gender roles. This chapter focuses on how gender influenced African American folk beliefs and physical well-being in the late nineteenth and early twentieth centuries. We examined burial data from six cemeteries in the southeastern United States to explore what gender differences might find expression in the material culture of folk cures and whether poor physical health might contribute to an adherence to a belief in, or use of, folk remedies. Artifacts and skeletal remains provide insight into gender-based material differences and trends associated with physical health. We argue that interment with cultural materials believed to possess spiritual or medicinal qualities and relative physical health may indicate treatment or condition in life that relates to gender roles.

Previous Studies

Archaeologists understand quite a bit about historic African American burial practices, but this knowledge rarely extends to gender comparisons. In particular, few cultural resource management reports, necessarily written under tight budgetary and time constraints, go beyond sex identification of the skeletal remains to provide an analysis of gender. However, some bioarchaeological studies of African American burials attempt to connect questions of health and gender, though in small burial populations that make extrapolation and generalization difficult.

Several studies document African American burial customs, which often show strong continuity with traditional West African practices (Cabak 1994; Handler and Lange 1978; Jordan 1982; LaRoche 1994; Thompson 1984; Vlach 1991). For example, the surface of graves in West Africa typically included items such as ceramic vessels, bottles, and cooking pots (Chatelain 1896:17; Glave 1891:825; Nassau 1904:232). African American graves throughout the rural Southeast likewise often contained similar mortuary goods (Blassingame 1972:37; Combes 1972:56; Courlander 1976:288; Puckett 1972:104–107; Vlach 1991:42). Oral histories and historic narratives tell us that items on these graves were usually placed there for spiritual reasons (Courlander 1976:288; Glave 1891:825; Puckett 1972:105–110; Thompson 1984:134; Vlach 1991:42). Despite this extensive knowledge about how African Americans treated the surface of graves, few researchers consider how these practices may reveal gender influences.

In this chapter, we consider the types of grave goods found not on the surface of the graves but within interments, and we attempt to link these artifacts to gender roles. Handler and Lange's (1978:200) research indicates that West Africans "commonly placed goods inside the grave with the corpse." From the data examined for this study, it appears that despite the large number of burials examined, it was rare to include grave goods, perhaps indicating a departure from West African burial customs. Since our data come from burials dating to the late nineteenth to early twentieth century, this pattern may reflect both spatial and temporal distance from West African origins. In addition, most of the interments in our sample date after emancipation, when many changes in southern life were under way. These changes probably affected all aspects of African American life, including burial customs, though perhaps differently according to gender, age, and other factors.

Archaeological reports do not often contend with gender differences in detail. One reason for this apparent neglect may be in part due to the limited number of graves containing artifacts, which renders it difficult to discuss the material basis of gender. Poor bone preservation, precluding sex identification, is another obstacle in exploring disparities in treatment by gender. Handler and Lange (1978:201) found no "correlation between the presence or absence of grave goods and particular age or sex groups" in their research of West African burial customs. Researchers emphasize that some burials containing unusually high numbers of grave goods reveal closer relationships to West African customs. For example, Handler et al. (1979) thought that one elderly male, who was buried in Newton Cemetery in Barbados with many artifacts, may represent a medicine man or "witch doctor" (Handler et al. 1979). In the African Burial Ground in New York City, the burial of one adult female, who exhibited dental modification, contained blue waist beads. This woman, who died in the eighteenth century, may have been born in Africa (LaRoche 1994). Researchers do not yet have a clear understanding of gender differences among African American burial practices. Nevertheless, the data available suggest that burials of both African American women and men may exhibit West African cultural traits.

There are several studies that focus on the human remains of African Americans (for example, Braley 1992; Braley and Moffat 1995; Dockall et al. 1996; Rathbun and Scurry 1991; Reitz et al. 1985; Rose 1985; Shogren et al. 1989). These researchers discuss some African American gender differences in health and nutrition using skeletal data. Rose (1985) and Shogren et al. (1989) note a skewed demographic profile toward females in several historic African American communities, possibly resulting from cultural factors such as male out-migration. Other researchers recognize gendered patterns such as higher incidence of violent trauma in males from a Georgia tenant farmers' cemetery (Braley and Moffat 1995) and higher levels of lead in female remains at a coastal plantation (Reitz et al. 1985). As a point of departure in their study involving colonial African American skeletal populations, Rathbun and Scurry (1991:164) point out that archaeologists should consider gender and age differences when

examining the relationship between status and health. African American gender health differences rarely receive attention as part of a single study because
most burial populations are small and sample sizes limit meaningful discussion. Mainly due to the paucity of reliably sexed skeletal populations, and
partly due to a lack of interest in gender research, broad studies linking health
and gender in historic African American populations, such as intersite comparisons, regional or temporal summaries, and intercultural comparisons are
infrequent or nonexistent. In addition, much of the archaeological work in
historic African American cemeteries takes place under contract archaeology
and the results of the work are only available in gray literature with limited cir-
culation. This chapter addresses this problem to a certain extent, as we glean
the majority of our data from contract archaeology reports.

Data and Methodology

We collected data for this study from six southern cemeteries across the South
that were in use mainly during the postbellum period. A few earlier graves may
be present in the data set, as most burials did not have inscribed headstones
with dates. The Redfield Cemetery, in central Georgia, dates to the late-
nineteenth and early-twentieth centuries and contained eighty burials, fifty-
two of which are included in this study (Braley and Moffat 1995). The human
remains recovered in this cemetery were in a state of extremely poor preservation, which severely limited the number of burials we could include in our
analysis. The Cedar Grove Cemetery in southwest Arkansas probably dates
between 1890 and 1927 (Rose 1985). The cemetery contained seventy-nine
burials; our study includes seventy-eight. We also examined the data from
fifty-four of the fifty-six burials disinterred from the Elko Switch Cemetery in
northern Alabama (Shogren et al. 1989). Based on artifacts associated with the
graves and historic documents, the graves at this cemetery date between 1850
and 1920. The Phillips Cemetery, located in La Marque, Texas, contained fifty-
three burials dating from the late-nineteenth- to the early-twentieth-centuries
(Dockall et al. 1996). We included twenty-six of these burials in our study, as
well as data from sixty-six of the seventy-nine burials found at the Deepstep
A.M.E. Church Cemetery in middle Georgia. This cemetery dates from circa
1860 to 1920 and contained burials from slaves, tenant farmers, and members
of the A.M.E. Church. Finally, we analyzed data from sixty graves found at the

late-nineteenth- to early-twentieth-century Hopewell Baptist Church Cemetery excavated in Gwinnett County, Georgia. We excluded burials postdating 1920. In sum, our data set consists of 336 burials dating from 1850 to 1920.

For our analysis, we assume all people buried in historically designated African American cemeteries were of African American descent. We only use the burial data from individuals whose biological sex could be reliably determined, and we admittedly conflate biological sex and social gender. We clearly note any burials listed as "probably" female or male. We included data from infants, children, and young teenagers in one general subadult category, as sex determinations from immature remains are unreliable. We placed adults in three age categories consisting of young adult (ages twenty-one to thirty-four), middle adult (ages thirty-five to forty-nine), and old adult (fifty and older). We also retained a category of unidentified adults when we had a determination of gender but not the age group.

We tabulated the data related to artifacts and physical characteristics of the skeletal remains. We totaled all the personal artifacts, such as jewelry, or artifacts classified as grave goods, by burial. To limit our scope, we excluded coffin hardware and clothing artifacts (like buttons, rivets, and eyelets), although it would be interesting to examine gender differences in these materials as well. When the information was available, we recorded the placement of an artifact, such as beads found near the neck or around the head.

We investigated the health of the representative populations by reviewing skeletal data in published reports or from the excavators' original field notes. The bones often record information about the health and nutrition of a person. Several researchers use data about diet and disease to interpret the social dynamics of past groups (for example, Powell et al. 1991; Verano and Ubelaker 1992). Meaningful social roles divide along gender lines, which in historic American society are typically, but not always, derived from biological sex. We examined gender patterns in age at death and in the relative prevalence of such pathologies as systemic infection, trauma, and activity-related bone remodeling and degeneration. Knowledge of health differences between genders may impact interpretation of artifact findings, especially in the case of artifacts thought to have been imbued with medicinal characteristics.

Analysis of age at death within a population can give some indication of relative health between males and females and among age groups. Systemic infection, which is identifiable as multiple lesions of the periosteum, or cortex of bone, was a common contributor to mortality before the mid-twentieth

TABLE 9.1

Burial Data Examined

Cemetery	No. of Burials	Females	Probable Females	Males	Probable Males	Subadults
Cedar Grove	78	18	3	13	2	42
Deepstep	66	11	1	9	0	45
Elko Switch	52	13	4	9	0	26
Hopewell	60	11	1	7	2	39
Phillips	26	10	10	11	0	4
Redfield	54	3	0	9	5	37
Total	336	66	10	58	9	193

century advent of antibiotics. Systemic infection in archaeological skeletal remains can sometimes be attributed to specific diseases such as tuberculosis, rickets, or syphilis, but most are categorized as nonspecific. Researchers may recognize localized infections, usually the result of external injury, as small areas of remodeled bone. Many past populations exhibit signs of anemia, an illness stemming from iron deficiency or sickle-shaped red blood cells. Sickle-cell anemia is particularly common among African Americans, most likely due to a combination of historical factors (for example, West African origin, surviving the Middle Passage) and perhaps even biological adaptation to malarial conditions (Stuart-Macadam 1992; compare with Goodman 1994).

A gendered comparison of trauma and activity-related bony changes can aid our understanding of relative health risk, lifestyle differences, and division of labor. Trauma refers to fractures, dislocations, cuts, and gunshot wounds, all of which can alter social dynamics, affect one's ability to work, and, of course, cause death. Activity-related remodeling and degeneration of bone includes premature development of arthritis and osteophytosis, Schmorl's nodes (or lesions of the vertebrae), enthesiopathies (areas of excavated bone from overuse of muscles), and hyperdevelopment of muscle attachments. The presence of activity-related conditions not only suggest type of work performed but also may provide insight into quality of life.

We noted the sex and age of each individual and recorded all pathological characteristics along with which skeletal elements were affected. Infection and trauma were listed as active or healed. Bone preservation was highly variable

TABLE 9.2

Burials by Age Groups and Gender

Group	Number
Women	
Young adults (21–34)	20
Middle adults (35–49)	12
Old adults (50+)	19
Adults of unknown age	25
Men	
Young Adults (21–34)	10
Middle Adults (35–49)	16
Old Adults (50+)	15
Adults of Unknown Age	26
Subadults	193
Total	336

among cemeteries, which makes comparisons between cemeteries difficult. In addition, possible inconsistencies in the skeletal data may relate to inter-observer bias and a historic lack of standards for data collection from human skeletal remains (addressed in Buikstra and Ubelaker 1994). We included all burials in analysis because in many cases we could not determine from the CRM report whether no pathology existed or whether the preservation precluded identification of pathologies. Nevertheless, the sample size and information available was sufficient to recognize some apparent relationships between gender and health.

As previously noted, the data set for this study consists of 336 burials (Table 9.1). The sample sizes of males and females are similar, whereas the number of subadults exceeds the number in either adult category. This trend is due to the fact that we could incorporate all subadults into our sample, whereas we excluded adult burials if we could not determine gender with reasonable accuracy. Furthermore, historic populations tended to experience much higher mortality of infants and children than we see today. Table 9.2 presents the adults by categories of age group and gender. This table also illustrates that the sample size of women and men by specific age group is not very large. It is important to include age group in this analysis of gender differences for several

TABLE 9.3

Burial Artifacts in the Study Sample

Artifact	Number
Beads	11
Bottles	12
Brooches	2
Bullets/Shot	5
Ceramics	5
Coins	16
Combs	14
Crucifix	1
Decorative Pins	5
Dental jewelry	2
Earrings	6
Eggshell	4
Finger Rings	13
Flower Pot	1
Foil	1
Glass, other	7
Key	1
Medallions	3
Newspaper	1
Other	6
Styrofoam	1
Toys	3

reasons. The interpretation of health indicators varies by age, gender roles tend to change throughout a person's lifetime, and older generations often conserve cultural traditions, whereas younger ones tend to modify traditions.

Artifacts

The burials in this study contained a wide range of artifacts. A total of 90, or 27 percent, of the 336 burials contained artifacts that we did not classify as

TABLE 9.4
Burials with Jewelry by Gender

Artifact Type	WOMEN		MEN		SUBADULTS	
	n	%	n	%	n	%
Beads	7	9	0	0	4	2
Brooches	2	3	0	0	0	0
Decorative pins	5	7	0	0	1	1
Earrings	6	8	0	0	0	0
Finger rings	11	15	1	2	1	1

clothing or coffin hardware. Table 9.3 shows that most items occurred in small frequencies. Common artifacts found in burials include coins, rings, and glass, particularly in the form of bottles. We selected two categories of artifacts to examine in detail: those that may have been used as jewelry and those that may be related more exclusively to folk beliefs.

Historic photos and other images illustrate that African Americans (particularly women) used jewelry such as beads and earrings in their daily lives. We identified five different types of jewelry in the burials. These categories consist of beads, brooches, earrings, decorative pins, and finger rings (Table 9.4). The most prevalent artifacts were finger rings, probably wedding rings. Women's burials yielded the highest percentages of jewelry, which is consistent with current-day trends in the United States but perhaps a departure from the historic West African custom of men wearing beads and other jewelry. We found only finger rings with men.

Examining these artifacts by gender and age group indicates some interesting trends. With the exception of beads, young and middle-age adult women were more often buried with jewelry items than elderly women (Table 9.5). This pattern suggests that older women did not adorn themselves as frequently with jewelry as younger women did. It is possible that families were less likely to bury older women with their jewelry for some reason. Archaeologists found beads most often with women older than thirty-five or with children. We suspect that perhaps these individuals seemed to be in more need of the protection and medicinal qualities afforded by the beads. We identified no discernible pattern among the adult men, probably due to the general lack of jewelry interred with them.

TABLE 9.5

Adults with Jewelry Artifacts by Age Group and Gender

Women

Artifact Type	YOUNG ADULTS		MIDDLE ADULTS		OLD ADULTS		UNKNOWN AGE ADULTS		TOTAL	
	n	%	*n*	%	*n*	%	*n*	%	*n*	%
Beads	0	0	4	33	3	16	0	0	7	9
Brooches	1	5	0	0	0	0	1	4	2	3
Decorative pins	2	10	1	8	2	11	0	0	5	7
Earrings	3	15	3	25	0	0	0	0	6	8
Finger rings	4	20	2	17	2	11	3	12	11	15

Men

Artifact Type	YOUNG ADULTS		MIDDLE ADULTS		OLD ADULTS		UNKNOWN AGE ADULTS		TOTAL	
	n	%	*n*	%	*n*	%	*n*	%	*n*	%
Beads	0	0	0	0	0	0	0	0	0	0
Brooches	0	0	0	0	0	0	0	0	0	0
Decorative pins	0	0	0	0	0	0	0	0	0	0
Earrings	0	0	0	0	0	0	0	0	0	0
Finger rings	0	0	1	6	0	0	0	0	1	2

TABLE 9.6

Burials with Artifacts Associated with Folk Beliefs

	WOMEN		MEN		SUBADULTS	
Artifact Type	*n*	*%*	*n*	*%*	*n*	*%*
Folk Beliefs						
Ceramic vessels	4	5	0	0	2	1
Coins	3	4	2	3	6	3
Coins, pierced	3	4	0	0	2	1
Eggshells	2	3	1	2	1	1
Medicine bottles	1	1	5	8	3	2
Foil	1	1	0	0	0	0
Possible Folk Beliefs						
Beads	7	9	0	0	0	0
Rings	11	15	1	2	1	1

The mortuary data presents several artifacts that may be indicative of folk practices (Table 9.6). Many researchers suggest that loved ones placed coins in graves to keep the deceased's eyes from opening (Crissman 1994; Puckett 1972:84), to ward off spirits (Rose 1985:61), or to pay passage on the boat to the afterlife (Handler and Lange 1978). Eleven burials contained coins, which were distributed evenly among our sample of men, women, and children. The placement of these coins includes one woman who had a dime in her left hand, which may be related to the belief of paying a fee for the passage to afterlife or back to Africa. Three individuals (a woman and two men) had coins in their eye sockets. In the remaining burials, coins were recovered in either the general coffin fill or the excavator did not record the location of the coins.

Many people in the early-twentieth century reported that African Americans sometimes wore pierced coins around their ankles and necks (Escott 1979:109; Puckett 1972:288, 314; Rawick 1972a:215, 1972b:205; WPA 1974:92, 125). Coins could ward off conjuring, bring good luck, and cure many ailments such as indigestion or rheumatism. For example, in South Carolina, people recalled that it was "good luck to tie a dime around a baby's neck" or "a silver coin tied around one's ankle will warn the person wearing it if they have been poisoned, by turning black" (Folklore Project [1930s]:1655:1–2).

Five burials, those of women and children only, contained pierced coins. In three burials, all middle age or elderly women, the drilled coin was recovered near the chest or throat, possibly indicating they had been worn around the neck (Table 9.6). It appears equally possible that these women wore the coins for protection throughout their lives or to cure the sicknesses that ultimately caused death. We do not know the location of the coins in the other two burials. Although the sample of burials containing pierced coins is small, they generally occur with women or children, although the historic records indicate that men also wore coins for a variety of purposes.

Archaeologists give a number of explanations for the African American practice of placing a saucer full of salt on the corpse. Its intent may relate to keeping away evil spirits or to slow bloating of the abdomen, or the saucer may have been one of the last items used by the deceased (Rose 1985:96). Archaeologists report ceramics placed with the corpse outside the South in places such as Philadelphia (Parrington 1987:60) and Barbados (Handler and Lange 1978:136). The practice of placing a dish containing salt on the deceased apparently was common among the English and has also been reported in Jamaica and among European Americans in Appalachia (Crissman 1994; Fremmer 1972).

Six burials, including those of four women and two children, contained ceramics including four saucers. Archaeologists recovered these saucers from near the chest or the pelvis. One of the other ceramic artifacts was a flowerpot found at the foot of the coffin. Another unidentified ceramic sherd was found in the general coffin fill of a child. As with the pierced coins, ceramics, particularly saucers, occurred only with women or children in our sample. These saucers are probably evidence of folk beliefs among the deceased or those who prepared the deceased for burial. Perhaps women and children were thought to be more vulnerable to evil spirits and in greater need of protection afforded by the plate of salt or from jewelry as mentioned above. Alternatively, women, as the ones who prepared the dead for burial, were able to maintain closer relationships with women relatives and children as those relationships took precedence over husband-wife associations in the family dynamics of the time.

Rose (1985:43) found eggshells in four burials in the Cedar Grove Cemetery in Arkansas. He offers several possible explanations as to why people buried their dead with eggshells. First, according to Puckett (1972), slaves associated eggs with conjuring, goiter, good luck, wealth, and sorrow. An informant claims that people were buried with an egg when the cause of death was mysterious, and by the time the egg broke (in the coffin) the cause of death would be known. In this cemetery, eggshells were found in the burials of women, men, and children, suggesting that age or gender were not factors in determining whom among the deceased was buried with eggshells.

Archaeologists have found medicine bottles on the surface and inside the graves at African American cemeteries (Rose 1985; Watters 1994). According to Puckett (1972:104), African Americans in Mississippi and South Carolina placed the medicine bottle last used by the deceased "turned upside down with the corks loosened so the medicine would soak in the grave." One of the authors of this essay (Wilson) excavated a grave in Barnwell, South Carolina, that contained a partially full, upside-down medicine bottle attached with mortar to the masonry of a brick-lined burial shaft. At least nine burials in our sample contained medicinal containers. Numerous burials contained unidentified glass bottles, some of which may have been medicinal. Interestingly, there appears to be clear gender differences with the placement of these containers with the deceased. Almost all glass containers were found with men or children. Only one burial of a woman contained medicine bottles, and her burial contained between six and eight medicine and whisky bottles. That woman may have died under remarkable circumstances or held an unusual role in society, as the quantity of medicine and alcohol bottles appears to carry some meaning. It may be that medicine bottles were usually included with men and boys. It is interesting to note that men in our sample were more likely to suffer from infectious disease, perhaps prompting more common use of medicines.

The burial of one woman contained metallic foil. The gleam of tinfoil, according to some folklorists, represents the "flash" of the departed spirit. The act of placing tinfoil in or on a grave may be a gesture to the dead (Thompson 1984:139).

In addition to the above-listed artifacts, several other items may also pertain to folk beliefs. The jewelry artifacts include items such as rings, necklaces, hair combs, and pins. We acknowledge that many of these artifacts may have served dual purposes of adornment and as elements of folk practice.

As stated previously, several of the burials, particularly those of women, contained rings. Many of these rings were probably wedding rings or adornment. Rings in this context carry additional meaning. For example Julia Henderson, a former slave, stated that for cramps she wore "a brass ring on my finger or wrist" (Rawick 1972b:325). This type of medicinal quality attributed to metal can be seen today in the popularity of copper wristbands said to prevent every ailment from arthritis to heart attacks.

The graves of seven women and four children contained beads. Certainly these beads functioned as jewelry, but African Americans may have valued beads for their medicinal qualities. One reference to this belief comes from a photograph of an elderly African American woman taken by a fieldworker with the Farm Services Administration who included a caption stating that the woman wore "black beads to prevent heart trouble" (Nixon 1938). An example of dual use may be the African American woman in the Elko Switch Cemetery who was buried with a necklace of thirty-three black wire-wound beads and one blue-faceted glass bead. Excavators found the blue bead placed in the center of the strand of beads (Shogren et al. 1989), which may reflect aesthetic or spiritual purposes. Scholars suggest that historic African Americans prized blue beads as good luck charms (Stine et al. 1996).

Only 8 percent of the burials (n=28) in our sample contain artifacts that we could associate with folk beliefs. Including artifacts that may have served dual functions, such as beads and rings, increases this count to only 13 percent (n=44) of the burials. We do not know if this pattern simply represents a departure from West African customs due to temporal or spatial distance or if other factors are at play.

Skeletal Evidence

Many of the individuals with preserved skeletal remains exhibited evidence of infection (Table 9.7). Localized periostitis, which is a relatively minor infection, was most common among males in the middle adult years. Women with localized periostitis tended to be young adults. Children had the fewest localized infections, at 8 percent of the sample populations. This pattern may be due in part to decreased survivorship by children from injuries and infections that would not be fatal to adults. Many children may have died before the bones could record the infection.

Nonspecific systemic infections are not usually attributable to a particular disease but represent fairly severe illnesses that may cause incapacitation for a lengthy period or death. Fifteen percent of the men and 11 percent of the women in this study exhibited nonspecific periostitis. Only 8 percent of children suffered from this ailment.

TABLE 9.7

Pathology by Gender

Pathology	WOMEN		MEN		SUBADULTS	
	n	%	n	%	n	%
Localized infection	8	11	10	15	15	8
Nonspecific Systematic infection	8	11	10	15	15	8
Tuberculosis	3	4	2	3	5	3
Rickets	1(?)	1	1	1	2	1
Anemia	6	8	9	13	17	9
Syphilis	1(?)	1	0	0	0	0
Trauma	5	7	11	16	0	0
Violent trauma	4	5	5	7	0	0
Activity-related changes	22	29	15	22	0	0

Anemia, which may have been due to dietary iron deficiency or sickle cell in these populations often appears postcranially as periostitis. Surprisingly, males appear to have been most affected by anemia, perhaps due to more limited access to iron-rich foods and greater labor demands. Women and children expressed this pathology at nearly equal rates and perhaps accessed better foods while cooking. A small number of men, women, and children suffered from tuberculosis or rickets. One woman showed signs of syphilis, but the skeletal indicators were not distinct from those of rickets, thus we draw no conclusion here. Overall, nearly half of the men in our study showed some form of infection, whereas only 36 percent of women had infections. It is possible that greater risk of injury or poorer overall health resulted in greater exposure to pathogens for men. About one-fifth of the children showed signs of healed or active infections. The osteological paradox emerges here as other children may have died before evidence of their illnesses could affect bone.

Men in this study exhibit more traumatic injuries than women. In fact, chi-square tests show that the difference in the prevalence of trauma between men and women is significant at the .10 level. Broken limbs, dislocated joints, and gunshot wounds were among the evidence of trauma seen in the 23 percent of the men in our sample populations. Five males of various ages suffered

TABLE 9.8
Relative Age at Death

Age Group	WOMEN		MEN	
	n	%	n	%
Old adult	19	25	15	22
Middle adult	12	16	16	24
Young adult	20	26	10	15
Unknown	25	33	26	39
Total	76	100	67	100

possible violent trauma, including three with probable gunshot wounds, one who may have been hanged, and one who suffered multiple rib fractures along with a blow to the head. A small percentage of women reveal possible violence-related trauma. One woman who died between 20 to 29 years of age had a fragment of knife stuck in her hip. A middle adult woman likely died from a gunshot wound, and an elderly woman suffered a blow to the head that probably caused her death. An additional five women endured fractures such as crushed toes, broken ribs, and a foot injury. No children exhibited any trauma. Clearly the adult population, at least, was at risk for violence and accidents, and men were particularly susceptible. Violence accelerated during the stressful times of Reconstruction, perhaps affecting those buried in the graves examined here. In addition, accidents would be expected in jobs requiring hard manual labor that most African American men regularly engaged in.

Men and women exhibited about the same rates of early arthritis, hyper-development of muscle attachments, and overused joints, all activity-related bony changes. There were no such conditions apparent in the remains of any of the children. Schmorl's nodes, osteophyte development, and vertebral ossification are all common ailments related to severe back stress. Three individuals (a man, an elderly woman, and a young woman) from Phillips Cemetery showed hyperdeveloped radii with enthesiopathies. This condition suggests hard labor, involving repetitive use of the lower arm muscles.

Table 9.8 shows that about one-fourth of both men and women lived to their old adult years. Gender differences in age at death emerge in the young and middle adult age categories. A chi-square test indicates that the pattern of women dying more often in the young adult years versus males who tended to die once they reached middle adulthood features a .10 level of statistical significance. The higher risk of death faced by women during their childbearing years may account for this trend. Otherwise, both genders show similar mortality in these populations.

Conclusion

This study compiles burial data from six cemeteries located in the Southeast, consisting of a sample of 336 individuals. Mortuary behavior and health and nutrition show gender differences. Although not surprising, the data indicate that women were buried with jewelry more often than men. Perhaps this trend indicated jewelry use similar to that of European Americans. In West Africa, both men and women adorned themselves with objects such as beads and bracelets.

Perhaps more important, a few burials contain artifacts that demonstrated continuity with West African and African American belief systems. The material culture reflecting folk health beliefs seems to revolve mainly around women as caregivers for children and the women themselves. The analysis indirectly suggests that it was mostly the women who maintained folk beliefs, particularly in the realm of health care. For example, pierced coins and beads, believed to ward off sickness and evil and actually worn by the deceased, were found only with women and children, as were the perhaps similarly magical ceramic dishes. Maybe women and children needed more protection due to perceived weakness or susceptibility to the supernatural, or perhaps women were better skilled manipulators of otherworldly matters. Certainly child mortality and death during childbirth were significant threats with which mothers contended. Folk remedies and magical fetishes would afford some degree of protection and peace of mind.

The presence of eggshells and unpierced coins found in all types of burials is less clear. The placement of these goods may reflect the beliefs of those who prepared the deceased for burial (most likely women) or beliefs held by the deceased. These items may relate to circumstances unassociated with gender or age, such as eggshells, which may indicate that survivors supposed mysterious death. It is worth considering the pattern of bead usage by older women and children. Perhaps the older women carried on past traditions and shared them with their charges (as many do today), whereas younger women had less use for earlier customs.

Like today, the postbellum era appears to have been especially hard on the health of African American men, although few gender differences were apparent in the amount of activity-related stress on the skeletal system. Men from the study population appear to have been more susceptible to infection and trauma, whereas women were more likely to die as young adults. Perhaps the higher rates of infection among men relate to the prevalence of medicine bottles in their graves. If women were more likely to die from childbirth, they would have had less need for medicines. Whereas men, who apparently suffered more accidents, violence, and infectious disease, could hope to receive successful treatment. Women, as the caretakers of the family and keepers of home remedies and folk treatments and the ones primarily responsible for taking care of the dead, probably placed the bottles in the graves of the men to ease the pain of the deceased and to symbolically relieve their own pain. The trend that shows men in our study group were less likely to wear items associated with folk beliefs and healing characteristics yet more likely to have medicine in their graves lends some support to this idea. Wearing a fetish item was probably the choice of the individual, whereas inclusion of grave goods would have been the choice of the loved ones left behind.

Our analysis of the data contained in the gray literature of CRM reports shows that a gendered perspective of burial data can yield some interesting patterns. Though artifacts relating to folk beliefs are rare and skeletal preservation remains an obstacle, small sample sizes can be combined to answer larger questions about the past. Historic African American men and women led lives that were distinct based on their assigned and assumed gender roles. Different life roles and duties probably meant distinctive worldviews and, of course, different health risks. Archaeologists can read some of these distinctions in the material record to help explain the past. In this examination, women as primary caregivers and as the likely ones to administer home remedies, maintain folk beliefs, and prepare the dead for burial, influence what view of the past archaeologists get to see. Clearly, gender should be an important element of any discussion on African American burial practices. Further research, which could come from new excavations or combining previously collected data, might examine gender differences in coffin hardware, clothing items, historic health data, physical stature, and gravestones to help explain differences and similarities in burial treatment between historic

African American men and women. It is hoped that synthesizing some of these data will result in a much better understanding of life and death of historic African Americans.

REFERENCES

Blassingame, John W.
   1972   *The Slave Community: Plantation Life in the Antebellum South.*
          Oxford Univ. Press, New York.
Braley, Chad O.
   1992   *Archaeological and Archival Investigations at the Deepstep A.M.E.*
          Church Cemetery, Washington County, Georgia. Prepared by South-
          eastern Archaeological Services, Athens. Submitted to Englehard
          Corporation, Gordon, Ga.
Braley, Chad O., and William G. Moffat
   1995   *Archaeological and Historical Investigations of Redfield Cemetery,*
          Jones County, Georgia. Volume I, Report. Prepared by Southeastern
          Archaeological Services, Athens. Submitted to Macon Water
          Authority, Macon, Ga.
Buikstra, Jane E., and Douglas H. Ubelaker
   1994   *Standards for Data Collection from Human Remains.* Arkansas
          Archaeological Survey Research Series 44, Fayetteville.
Cabak, Melanie A.
   1994   *Reconnaissance Survey of Site 1 of the Proposed Three Rivers Landfill,*
          Savannah River Site, Aiken County, South Carolina. Technical
          Report 20, Savannah River Archaeological Research Program,
          South Carolina Institute of Archaeology and Anthropology,
          Univ. of South Carolina, Columbia.
Chatelain, H.
   1896   Angolan Customs. *Journal of African Folk-lore.* Vol. 9.
Combes, John D.
   1972   Ethnography, Archaeology, and Burial Practices among Coastal
          South Carolina Blacks. *Conference on Historic Site Archaeology*
          Papers 7:52–61.
Conkey, Margaret W., and Joan M. Gero
   1991   Tensions, Pluralities, and Engendering Archaeology: An Introduc-
          tion to Women and Prehistory. In *Engendering Archaeology: Women*
          and Prehistory, edited by J. Gero and M. Conkey, pp. 3–30. Basil
          Blackwell, Cambridge.

Courlander, Harold
    1976   *A Treasury of Afro-American Folklore.* Crown Publishers, New York.
Crissman, James K.
    1994   *Death and Dying in Central Appalachia.* Univ. of Illinois Press,
            Urbana and Chicago.
Dockall, Helen D., J. F. Powell, and D. Gentry Steele
    1996   *Home Hereafter: An Archaeological and Bioarchaeological Analysis of an
            Historic African American Cemetery (41GV125).* Center for Environ-
            mental Archaeology, Texas A & M Univ. Reports of Investigations,
            No. 5.
Escott, Paul D.
    1979   *Slavery Remembered: A Record of Twentieth-Century Slave Narratives.*
            Univ. of North Carolina Press, Chapel Hill.
Ferguson, Leland
    1992   *Uncommon Ground: Archaeology and Early African America,
            1650–1800.* Smithsonian Institution Press, Washington D.C.
Folklore Project
    [1930s] Folklore Project, Work Projects Administration, No. 1655, D-27A(1),
            D-4-27B(1); No. 1885, D-4-27A, F-2-18A. Ms. on file, Manuscripts
            Division, South Caroliniana Library, Univ. of South Carolina,
            Columbia.
Fremmer, Ray
    1972   Dishes in Colonial Graves: Evidence from Jamaica. *Historical
            Archaeology* 7:58–62.
Glave, E. J.
    1891   Fetishism in Congo Land. *Century Magazine* 41:7825.
Goodman, Alan H.
    1994   Cartesian Reductionism and Vulgar Adaptationism: Issues in
            the Interpretation of Nutritional Status in Prehistory. In *Paleo-
            nutrition: The Diet and Health of Prehistoric Americans,* edited
            by Kristin D. Sobolik, pp. 163–177. Center for Archaeological
            Investigations, Southern Illinois Univ. at Carbondale, Occasional
            Paper No. 22.
Handler, Jerome S., and Frederick W. Lange
    1978   *Plantation Slavery in Barbados: An Archaeological and Historical
            Investigation.* Harvard Univ. Press, Cambridge, Mass.
Handler, Jerome S., Frederick W. Lange, and Charles E. Orser
    1979   Carnelian Beads in Necklaces from a Slave Cemetery in Barbados,
            West Indies. *Ornament* 4(2):15–18.

Hurmence, Belinda (editor)

    1990   *Before Freedom: Forty-eight Oral Histories of Former North and South Carolina Slaves.* Mentor for Penguin Books, New York.

Jamieson, Ross W.

    1992   Material Culture and Social Death: African American Burial Practices. *Historical Archaeology* 29(4):39–58.

Jordan, Terry G.

    1982   *Texas Graveyards: A Cultural Legacy.* Univ. of Texas Press, Austin.

Kemble, Frances Anne

    1984   *Journal of a Residence on a Georgia Plantation in 1838–1839,* edited by John A. Scott. Univ. of Georgia Press, Athens.

LaRoche, Cheryl J.

    1994   Beads from the African Burial Ground, New York City: A Preliminary Assessment. *Beads* 6:2–20.

Nassau, Robert Hamill

    1904   *Fetishism in West Africa.* Duckworth, London.

Nixon, Herman Clarence

    1938   *Forty Acres and Steel Mules.* Univ. of North Carolina Press, Chapel Hill.

Parrington, Michael

    1987   Cemetery Archaeology in the Urban Environment: A Case Study from Philadelphia. In *Living in Cities: Current Research in Urban Archaeology.* Special Publication Series, No. 5, edited by Edward Staski, pp. 48–55. Society for Historical Archaeology, California, Pennsylvania.

Powell, Mary Lucas, Patricia S. Bridges, and Ann Marie Wagner Mires (editors)

    1991   *What Mean These Bones? Studies in Southeastern Bioarchaeology.* Univ. of Alabama Press, Tuscaloosa.

Puckett, Newbell Niles

    1972   *Folk Beliefs of the Southern Negro.* Negro Universities Press, New York. Originally published 1926 by Univ. of North Carolina Press.

Rathbun, Ted A., and James D. Scurry

    1991   Status and Health in Colonial South Carolina: Belleview Plantation, 1738–1756. In *What Mean These Bones? Studies in Southeastern Bioarchaeology,* edited by M. L Powell, P. S. Bridges, and A. M. Wagner Mires, pp. 148–164. Univ. of Alabama Press, Tuscaloosa.

Rawick, George P.

    1972a   *Texas Narratives, Parts 1 and 2.* Vol. 4, *The American Slave: A Composite Autobiography.* Greenwood Publishing Co., Westport, Conn.

1972b *Georgia Narratives, Parts 1 and 2.* Vol. 12, *The American Slave: A Composite Autobiography.* Greenwood Publishing Co., Westport, Conn.

Reitz, Elizabeth J., Tyson Gibbs, and Ted A. Rathbun
1985 Archaeological Evidence for Subsistence on Coastal Plantations. In *The Archeology of Slavery and Plantation Life,* edited by Theresa A. Singleton, pp. 163–194. Academic Press, Orlando, Fla.

Rogers, Barbara
1976 *The Domestication of Women.* Tavistock, London.

Rose, Jerome C.
1985 Gone to a Better Land: A Biohistory of a Rural Black Cemetery in the Post-Reconstruction South. Arkansas Archaeological Survey Research Series 25, Fayetteville.

Schuyler, Robert L. (editor)
1980 *Archaeological Perspectives on Ethnicity in America: Afro-American and Asian American Culture History.* Baywood, Farmingdale, New York.

Shogren, Michael G., Kenneth R. Turner, and Jody C. Perroni
1989 Elko Switch Cemetery: An Archaeological Perspective. Report of Investigation 58. Division of Archaeology, Alabama State Museum of Natural History, Moundsville.

Singleton, Theresa (editor)
1985 *The Archaeology of Plantation Life and Slavery.* Academic Press, New York.

Stine, Linda Francis, Melanie A. Cabak, and Mark D. Groover
1996 Blue Beads as African American Cultural Symbols. *Historical Archaeology* 30(3):49–75.

Stuart-Macadam, Patricia
1992 Porotic Hyperostosis: A New Perspective. *American Journal of Physical Anthropology* 87:39–47.

Thompson, Robert Farris
1984 *Flash of the Spirit: African and Afro-American Art and Philosophy.* Vintage Books, New York.

Verano, John W., and Douglas H. Ubelaker (editors)
1992 *Disease and Demography in the Americas.* Smithsonian Institute Press, Washington, D.C.

Vlach, John M.
1991 *By the Work of Their Hands: Studies in Afro-American Folklife.* Univ. Press of Virginia, Charlottesville.

Watters, David R.

    1994   Mortuary Patterns at the Harnery Site Slave Cemetery, Montserrat in Caribbean Perspective. *Historical Archaeology* 28(3):56–73.

White, Deborah G.

    1991   Female Slaves in the Plantation South. In *Before Freedom Came: African American Life in the Antebellum South*, edited by Edward D. C. Campbell Jr., pp. 101–122. Museum of the Confederacy, Richmond and Univ. Press of Virginia, Charlottesville.

Work Projects Administration (WPA)

    1974   *Drums and Shadows: Survival Studies among the Georgia Coastal Negroes.* Univ. of Georgia Press, Athens, Reprint Co., Spartanburg, S.C. Originally published 1940, Savannah Unit, Georgia Writers' Project, Work Projects Administration.

An End to the Eerie Silence

LARRY MCKEE

In addressing the topic of gender within the archaeological study of African American life, the authors in this volume have taken on some of historical archaeology's most challenging questions and issues. What are the limits to the utility of excavated data and to the interpretive statements that can be made about this evidence? Should our studies be driven by what the ground can tell us, or should we start with research questions unconstrained by such boundaries? In the end these concerns are tied to how we view the articulation between different sources of evidence and insight on the past, be it from a bag of artifacts, a diary written in the nineteenth century, or a body of sociological theory. Historical archaeology in its most successful and productive form ignores the walls between these categories and moves toward uniting whatever is available and useful in coming to viable conclusions about what happened in the past. Most of the authors in this volume boldly subscribe to this approach, and the results they present go far beyond whatever limits some may apply to archaeological evidence. In doing so, they have provided a well-spoken end to the "eerie silence" (Conkey 1991:29, cited in Fesler, this volume) about gender within the archaeological study of African American life.

Although all the authors are concerned with gender in African American life, with a special emphasis on the period of enslavement, all start from a conceptual consideration of gender within human experience as a whole. All use what can be termed as the modern view of gender, which can be summarized in this way: Men and women had and have very different roles within society. The differences are culturally constructed and thus vary from setting to setting, and sometimes from hour to hour, and also become transformed as these settings change. These differences are also usually strongly linked to assignments and divisions of labor and to divisions of authority and power.

The strength of these differences is also such that to ignore gender's influence in any kind of social analysis is to risk missing essential evidence and essential paths to understanding.

Gender's role in structuring African American life has obvious interconnections with the oppression of slavery and its aftermath. "That gender was on the minds of both master and slave . . . seems indisputable," notes Garrett Fesler in his contribution to this volume. This "mindfulness" was heightened by the tensions tied to taboos about sexual relations between black and white and the white community's enhanced recognition of the divisions of the masculine and feminine within the Old South's "honor" culture. Looking at the enslaved as just "raced" but not "gendered" individuals eliminates key parts of our field of vision about the African American past, especially in terms of seeing how the particulars of gender could be used in strategies of resistance. A statement from Laurie Wilkie's contribution says it best. "Until [we] recognize the importance of gender within this community, our 'unengendered' interpretations of the African American past will fail to properly illuminate social dynamics and interactions within this community."

Archaeologists' forays into gender studies were originally driven by the impulse to use the material record as a way to counteract the large-scale invisibility of women in most documentary sources. This desire to reestablish the place of women in the way the past is seen and understood has obvious parallels to the rise of archaeological studies of African American life. As these pursuits have matured and become entwined, as seen in this volume, the point has moved away from the simplistic goal of digging up "female artifacts" and "Africanisms." The goal has become to use what we know about gender and race in furthering our interpretations, to see these as defining elements of the social environment in which people lived, and to keep the influence of each in mind as we try to make sense of particular times and places in the past.

Of course there is both the room and the necessity within our focus on the social dynamics of the past to bring the specifics of women's activities back to light. As Patricia Samford points out, black women have been subjected to the "double invisibility of race and gender," and many of the contributors here provide reconstructions of women's roles and activities at a level of detail best compared to ethnography. Samford provides examples of slave women as savvy market entrepreneurs and as the "structural engineers" of family life, and Fesler builds on this view in describing the key roles of women in defining the details and dynamics of entire quarter communities in early eighteenth-century Virginia. Laurie Wilkie delves into the way an early-twentieth-century Alabama midwife mixed old and new in dealing with the dangers of childbirth. Barbara Heath analyzes the surprisingly detailed records of slave purchases in central Virginia. Thomas and Thomas carefully unravel how both men and women put forth a complex presentation of self based on the "layering" of personal appearance, and Cabak and Wilson show how this presentation continued into the grave. Amy Young considers the importance and key features of role switching through the course of an enslaved woman's day. Jillian Galle's study of archaeological assemblages of sewing equipment goes beyond seeing slave seamstresses as "just" impressively skilled craft workers to show their role as central players and cultural mediators within plantation communities. All in all, this is an impressive array of scholarship, speaking loud and clear about the specifics and active role of gender in African American life. The authors are due congratulations for the courage they have shown in taking their interpretations beyond just the descriptive. The silence is truly broken.

Now that the silence is broken the conversation can begin. Some of the authors here have noted that in talking about gender there is a need to address the broader social category of individual identity and how identity is defined by factors such as gender, age, race, cultural tradition, etc. Certainly the archaeological record is quite blurred in terms of the visibility of individuals. Again, the point is not so much to search for the individual in the ground but to use knowledge of the role of individuals in human interaction in studying and interpreting the past. Individuals certainly take on much of their identity from being born male or female, some of this defined by biological "essentialism," some thrust on a person by society's standards and expectations. Patricia Samford notes in her contribution that African traditions provided "internalized ideas about what the proper roles and behavior for men and women were," which served as an important foundation for the evolution of gender roles within New World slavery. Thomas and Thomas argue that "there are no social situations in which gender is not a key aspect of an individual's identity." But in considering identity and individual action and influence in the African American past, the question arises about whether or not race and enslavement overshadows gender. What happens when age, intellect, religion, kinship, height, weight, etc. are put into the mix as well? Can we see and understand enough from our blurred sources to tease out the effects of the different influences on African American identity, or does a focus on these multiple variables compound the complexity too much and dilute our discussions to the point of ineffectiveness?

The well-reasoned consensus within this volume is that gender remains key, in spite of and perhaps even because of the harsh realities of race-based slavery in colonial- and antebellum-period America. Thomas and Thomas make the case for gender as having a "master status" in defining identity, and Elizabeth Scott's introductory essay amplifies this idea in presenting social identity as an inseparable compound of race, class, and gender. Scott, drawing on Nancy Hewitt's (1992) thinking, suggests that it is pointless to isolate these elements from one another. Truly understanding the interplay among such keystones of identity is clearly a challenge, given there is no readymade body of theory that considers race, gender, and slavery simultaneously. Scott responds by encouraging an emphasis on the dynamic element—the way relations play out between those in different roles, with different identities. We should not be trying to pin down and describe identity; we should be trying to see it at work in the course of social action. These are the kind of concepts that move the consideration of gender and identity away from something we need to remind ourselves about and toward something we absolutely have to use in making sense of the past.

Scott also comments that "by asking how gender helped shape lives in the past, we bring the focus onto people." It is always useful to be reminded of the ultimate point of our studies, especially on those days when the work seems to be more about lab backlogs, funding shortfalls, and report deadlines. What would Gracy, the Hermitage seamstress, think of our intense scrutiny of a handful of pins that slipped between the cracks in her small dwelling's floor? I hope she would be pleased to know of our interest in the details of her life and the life of her family and community.

The tough struggle over trying to see and use personal identity in archaeological research brings with it some necessary consideration about where to fit in these questions within the course of a typical research project. The contributors here are clearly in favor of having gender and identity right up front, as an organizing principle to be used in designing research just as it was an organizing principle in the original social and physical definition of the sites we are studying. For instance, in taking on the study of a slave quarter most of us conceptualize the occupants as not just members of a monolithic category labeled "slaves," but also as fathers, mothers, children, siblings, grandparents, aunts, uncles, cousins, neighbors, and work partners. We rarely if ever see hard evidence of such an array of individuals, but knowing of the presence of all these people in their different roles reminds us of the lively complexity of the communities we study. Garrett Fesler's study of the Utopia Quarter "operationalizes" this approach in a successful way, in considering how the site was organized and "negotiated . . . in part due to a recognition of culturally constructed gender differences."

Another useful way to put ideas about social identity to work is at the level of artifact analysis. In these pages Thomas and Thomas provide some useful discussion linking common artifacts to the actions individuals take in modifying their appearance and presenting themselves to the world. Barbara Heath takes on another topic, artifact acquisition patterns, in exploring the choices made by "enslaved shoppers" in nineteenth-century Virginia. In linking store ledgers and artifact assemblages she brings to light surprising evidence of the socially if not financially significant economic power achieved by some slaves through small-scale production and manufacturing and shows how this "consumerism" was influenced by gender, age, and marital status.

The chapters in this volume make it clear that putting gender and other elements of social identity to work in archaeological interpretations does not involve simple applications of linear formulas and monolithic definitions. Cases differ, and analysts have differing interests and research strategies. The success of these works suggests there is no need to establish some codified norms or procedures in taking on the topic.

It is overly optimistic to think that a single volume can put an end to the years of ignorance and silence about gender in archaeological research on the African American past. But the theoretical reach and data-rich detail presented here should make this volume a standard reference and a strong foundation for further explorations for years to come. This foundation is solidified by the true community represented by the list of contributors. Most of us have known each other for at least five and in some cases ten and fifteen years. The resulting cross-pollination of our projects and interpretations inevitably strengthens the results. This also makes for a style of scholarship that is both professionally and personally quite satisfying.

REFERENCES

Conkey, Margaret W.
    1991   Does It Make a Difference? Feminist Thinking and Archaeologies of Gender. *The Archaeology of Gender: Proceedings of the Twenty-second Annual Chacmool Conference*, edited by Dale Walde and Noreen D. Willows, pp. 24–33. Univ. of Calgary Archaeological Association, Calgary.
Hewitt, Nancy A.
    1992   Compounding Differences. *Feminist Studies* 18(2):313–326.

Selected Bibliography

Agorsah, E. Kofi
    1985   Archaeological Implications of Traditional House Construction among the Nchumuru of Northern Ghana. *Anthropology* 26(1): 103–115.

Angel, J. Lawrence, Jennifer Olsen Kelley, Michael Parrington, and Stephanie Pinter
    1987   Life Stresses of the Free Black Community as Represented by the First African Baptist Church, Philadelphia, 1823–1841. *American Journal of Physical Anthropology* 74:213–220.

Aniakor, Chike
    1996   Household Objects and the Philosophy of Igbo Social Space. In *African Material Culture*, edited by M. J. Arnoldi, C. M. Geary, and K. L. Hardin, pp. 214–242. Indiana Univ. Press, Bloomington.

Bassett, John Spencer (editor)
    1926–1935 *Correspondence of Andrew Jackson.* 7 vols. Carnegie Institute of Washington, Washington, D.C.

Baumgarten, Linda
    1988   "Clothes for the People": Slave Clothing in Early Virginia. *Journal of Early Southern Decorative Arts* 14(2):26–70.
    1991   Plains, Plaid, and Cotton: Woolens for Slave Clothing. *Ars Textrina* 15:203–221.

Bender, Donald R.
    1967   Refinement of the Concept of Household: Families, Co-residence, and Domestic Functions. *American Anthropologist* 69:493–504.

Berlin, Ira
    1998   *Many Thousands Gone: The First Two Centuries of Slavery in North America.* The Belknap Press of Harvard Univ. Press, Cambridge, Massachusetts.

Betts, Edwin Morris (editor)

    1987   *Thomas Jefferson's Farm Book*. Univ. Press of Virginia, Charlottesville.

Blassingame, James W.

    1976   Status and Social Structure in the Slave Community: Evidence from New Sources. In *Perspectives and Irony in American Slavery*, edited by Harry P. Owens, pp. 137–151. Univ. Press of Mississippi, Jackson.

Brown, Kathleen M.

    1994   *Good Wives, Nasty Wenches, and Anxious Patriarchs: Gender, Race, and Power in Colonial Virginia*. Univ. of North Carolina Press, Chapel Hill.

Breeden, James O.

    1980   *Advice among Masters: The Ideal in Slave Management in the Old South*. Greenwood Press, Westport, Conn.

Campbell, Edward D. C., and Kym S. Rice (editors)

    1991   *Before Freedom Came: African American Life in the Antebellum South*. Univ. Press of Virginia, Charlottesville.

Campbell, Marie

    1946   *Folks Do Get Born*. Rinehart and Co., New York.

Carr, Lois Green, and Lorena Walsh

    1987   Economic Diversification and Labor Organization in the Chesapeake, 1650–1820. *Work and Labor in Early America*, edited by Stephen Innes, pp. 144–188. Univ. of North Carolina Press, Chapel Hill.

Carson, Cary, Norman F. Barka, William M. Kelso, Gary Wheeler Stone, and Dell Upton

    1981   Impermanent Architecture in the Southern American Colonies. *Winterthur Portfolio* 16:135–196.

Coe, Emily

    1995   Granny Midwives: Grandmother to Nurse Midwives. Paper presented at the American Anthropological Association Meetings, Washington, D.C.

Collins, Patricia Hill

    1994   Shifting the Center: Race, Class, and Feminist Theorizing about Motherhood. In *Mothering: Ideology, Experience, and Agency*, edited by E. N. Glenn, G. Chang, R. Forcey. Routledge, New York.

    2000   *Black Feminist Thought: Knowledge, Consciousness, and the Politics of Empowerment*. 2d ed. Routledge, New York.

Conkey, Margaret W.

    1991   Does It Make a Difference? Feminist Thinking and Archaeologies of Gender. *The Archaeology of Gender: Proceedings of the Twenty-second*

Annual Chacmool Conference, edited by Dale Walde and Noreen D. Willows, pp. 24–33. Univ. of Calgary Archaeological Association, Calgary.

Conkey, Margaret W., and Joan Gero

1991   *Engendering Archaeology: Women in Prehistory*. Basil Blackwell, Oxford.

Conkey, Margaret, and Janet Spector

1984   Archaeology and the Study of Gender. In *Advances in Archaeological Method and Theory*, vol. 7, edited by Michael Schiffer, pp. 1–38. Academic Press, New York.

Crader, Diana

1990   Slave Diet at Monticello. *American Antiquity* 55:690–717.

Delle, James A., Stephen A. Mrozowksi, and Robert Paynter (editors)

2000   *Lines That Divide: Historical Archaeologies of Race, Class, and Gender*. Univ. of Tennessee Press, Knoxville.

Edwards-Ingram, Ywone D.

1998   An Inter-Disciplinary Approach to African American Medicinal and Health Practices in Colonial America. *Watermark* 20(3):67–73.

2001   African American Medicine and the Social Relations of Slavery. In *Race and the Archaeology of Identity*, edited by Charles Orser, pp. 34–53. Univ. of Utah Press, Salt Lake City.

Farley, Reynolds

1965   The Demographic Rates and Social Institutions of the Nineteenth Century Negro Population: A Stable Population Analysis. *Demography* 2:389.

Ferguson, Leland G.

2000   "The Cross Is a Magic Sign": Marks on Eighteenth-Century Bowls from South Carolina. In *I, Too, Am America: Archaeological Studies of African American Life*, edited by Theresa A. Singleton, pp. 116–131. Univ. Press of Virginia, Charlottesville.

Fogel, Robert William

1995   *Without Consent or Contract: The Rise and Fall of American Slavery*. W. W. Norton, New York.

Foster, Helen Bradley

1997   *"New Raiments of Self"': African American Clothing in the Antebellum South*. Berg, Oxford.

Fox-Genovese, Elizabeth

1988   *Within the Plantation Household: Black and White Women in the Old South*. Univ. of North Carolina Press, Chapel Hill.

Franklin, Maria
    1997   *Out of Site, Out of Mind: The Archaeology of an Enslaved Virginia Household, ca. 1740–1778.* Ph.D. diss., Dept. of Anthropology, Univ. of California, Berkeley.
    2001   A Black Feminist-Inspired Archaeology? In *Journal of Social Archaeology* 1(1):108–125.

Franklin, Maria, and Garrett Fesler (editors)
    2002   *Historical Archaeology, Identity Formation, and the Interpretation of Ethnicity.* Colonial Williamsburg Research Publications, Colonial Williamsburg Foundation, Williamsburg.

Fraser, Gertrude
    1998   *African American Midwifery in the South.* Harvard Univ. Press, Cambridge.

Genovese, Eugene D.
    1976   *Roll Jordan Roll: The World the Slaves Made.* Vintage Books, New York.

Gero, Joan M., and Margaret W. Conkey (editors)
    1991   *Engendering Archaeology: Women and Prehistory.* Cambridge, Basil Blackwell.

Goffman, Erving
    1959   *The Presentation of Self in Everyday Life.* Double Day, Garden City, New York.

Gomez, Michael A.
    1995   *Exchanging our Country Marks: The Transformation of African Identities in the Colonial and Antebellum South.* Univ. of North Carolina Press, Chapel Hill.

Gruber, Anna
    1991   The Archaeology of Mr. Jefferson's Slaves. Master's thesis, Winterthur Program in Early American Culture, Univ. of Delaware, Winterthur.

Gutman, Herbert
    1976   *The Black Family in Slavery and Freedom, 1750–1925.* Vintage Books, New York.

Handler, Jerome S. and Frederick W. Lange
    1978   *Plantation Slavery in Barbados: An Archaeological and Historical Investigation.* Harvard Univ. Press, Cambridge, Massachusetts.

Hatch, Peter J.
    2001   African American Gardens at Monticello. *Twin Leaf, Thomas Jefferson Center for Historic Plants Annual Journal and Catalogue,* no. 13:14–20.

Heath, Barbara J.
    1998   Slavery and Consumerism: A Case Study from Central Virginia. *African American Archaeology, Newsletter of the African American Archaeology Network* 19:1–8.
    1999   Buttons, Beads, and Buckles: Contextualizing Adornment within the Bounds of Slavery. In *Historical Archaeology, Identity Formation, and the Interpretation of Ethnicity*, edited by Maria Franklin and Garrett Fesler, pp. 47–69. Colonial Williamsburg Research Publications, Colonial Williamsburg Foundation, Williamsburg.

Heath, Barbara, and Amber Bennett
    2000   'The little Spots allow'd them': The Archaeological Study of African-American Yards. *Historical Archaeology* 34(2):38–55.

Herskovits, Melville
    1941   *Myth of the Negro Past*. Beacon Press, Boston.

Hewitt, Nancy A.
    1992   Compounding Differences. *Feminist Studies* 18(2):313–326.

Hodder, Ian
    2000   Agency and Individuals in Long-Term Process. In *Agency in Archaeology*, edited by Marcia-Anne Dobres and John Robb, pp. 21–33. Routledge, London.

Hunt, Patricia
    1996   The Struggle to Achieve Individual Expression through Clothing and Adornment: African American Women under and after Slavery. In *Discovering the Women in Slavery*, edited by Patricia Morton, pp. 227–240. Univ. of Georgia Press, Athens.

Hurston, Zora Neale
    1934   Characteristics of Negro Expression. In *Negro: An Anthology*, edited by Nancy Cunard. Wishart and Company, London. Reprinted in The Sanctified Church, Turtle Creek, Berkeley (1981).

Jamieson, Ross W.
    2000   Dona Luisa and Her Two Houses. In *Lines That Divide: Historical Archaeologies of Race, Class, and Gender*, edited by James A. Delle, Stephen A. Mrozowski, and Robert Paynter, pp. 142–167. Univ. of Tennessee Press, Knoxville.

Johnson, Michael T.
    1981   Smothered Slave Infants: Were Slave Mothers at Fault? *Journal of Southern History* 47:493–520.

Jones, Jacqueline
    1995   *Labor of Love, Labor of Sorrow: Black Women, Work, and the Family, from Slavery to the Present*. Vintage Books, New York.

Keckley, Elizabeth
    1868   *Behind the Scenes: Thirty Years a Slave and Four Years in the White House*. G. W. Carleton & Co., New York.

Kehoe, Alice B.
    1992   The Muted Class: Unshackling Tradition. In *Exploring Gender through Archaeology: Selected Papers from the 1991 Boone Conference*, edited by Cheryl Claassen, pp. 23–32. Prehistory Press, Madison.

Kelso, William
    1984   *Kingsmill Plantations, 1619–1800: Archaeology of Country Life in Colonial Virginia*. Academic Press, New York.

Kulikoff, Allan
    1986   *Tobacco and Slaves: The Development of Southern Cultures in the Chesapeake, 1680–1800*. Univ. of North Carolina Press, Chapel Hill.

Little, Barbara
    1994   "She Was . . . an Example to her Sex": Possibilities for a Feminist Historical Archaeology. In *Historical Archaeology of the Chesapeake*, edited by Paul A. Shackel and Barbara J. Little, pp. 189–204. Smithsonian Institution Press, Washington, D.C.

Mann, Susan A.
    1988   Slavery, Sharecropping, and Sexual Identity. *Black Women in America: Social Science Perspectives*, edited by Micheline R. Malson, Elisabeth Mudimbe-Boyi, Jean F. O'Barr, and Mary Wyer, pp. 133–157. Univ. of Chicago Press, Chicago.

Martin, Ann Smart
    1993   Buying into the World of Goods: Eighteenth-Century Consumerism and the Retail Trade from London to the Virginia Frontier. Ph.D. diss., Dept. of History, College of William and Mary, Williamsburg.

McKee, Larry
    1996   The Earth Is Their Witness. *Sciences* 35(2):36–41.
    1999   Food Supply and Plantation Social Order: An Archaeological Perspective. In *I, Too, Am America: Archaeological Studies of African American Life*, edited by Theresa A. Singleton, pp. 218–239. Univ. Press of Virginia, Charlottesville.

Meeker, Edward
    1976   Mortality Trends of Southern Blacks 1850–1910. *Explorations in Economic History* 13:13–42.

Mellon, James (editor)
    1988   *Bullwhip Days: The Slaves Remember*. Avon Books, New York.

Mintz, Sidney W., and Richard Price
1992   *The Birth of African-American Culture: an Anthropological Perspective.* Beacon Press, Boston.

Moore, Henrietta
1988   *Feminism and Anthropology.* Univ. of Minnesota Press, Minneapolis.

Morgan, Philip D.
1998   *Slave Counterpoint: Black Culture in the Eighteenth-Century Chesapeake and Lowcountry.* Univ. of North Carolina Press, Chapel Hill.

Morton, Patricia (editor)
1996   *Discovering the Women in Slavery: Emancipating Perspectives in the American Past.* Univ. of Georgia Press, Athens.

Neiman, Fraser
1997   Sub-Floor Pits and Slavery in Eighteenth- and Early-Nineteenth-Century Virginia. Paper presented at the Thirtieth Annual Meeting of the Society for Historical Archaeology, Corpus Christi, Texas.

Orser, Charles E.
1992   Beneath the Material Surface of Things: Commodities, Artifacts, and Slave Plantation. *Historical Archaeology* 26(3):95–104.

Perdue, Charles, Thomas Barden, and Robert Phillips
1976   *Weevils in the Wheat: Interviews with Virginia Ex-Slaves.* Indiana Univ. Press, Bloomington.

Proctor, Molly
1990   *Needlework Tools and Accessories.* B. T. Batsford, London.

Puckett, Niles Newbell
1968   *Folk Beliefs of the Southern Negro.* Greenwood Publishing, New York.

Purser, Margaret
1991   "Several Paradise Ladies Are Visiting in Town": Gender Strategies in the Early Industrial West. *Historical Archaeology* 25(4):6–16.

Rankin-Hill, Lesley M.
1995   *A Biohistory of Nineteenth-Century Afro-Americans: The Burial Remains of a Philadelphia Cemetery.* Bergin and Garvey, Westport.

Rathbun, R. Ted
1987   Health and Disease at a South Carolina Plantation: 1840–1860. *American Journal of Physical Anthropology* 74:239–253.

Rathbun, R. Ted
1991   Status and Health in Colonial South Carolina: Bellview Plantation 1738–1756. In *What Mean These Bones?*, edited by M. L. Powell, P. S. Bridges, and A. M. Mires, pp 148–164. Univ. of Alabama Press, Tuscaloosa.

Rathbun, R. Ted, Richard Steckel, Keith Condon, and Thomas A. Crist
    1998   African-American Biohistory: Relative Rankings in the Health and
            Human History Project (abstract). *American Journal of Physical
            Anthropology* Suppl 26, p 184.
Rawick, George P. (editor)
    1972   *The American Slave: A Composite Autobiography*. Vol. 16. Greenwood
            Publishing Co., Westport, Conn.
Reitz, Elizabeth J., Tyson Gibbs, and Ted R. Rathbun
    1985   Archaeological Evidence for Subsistence on Coastal Plantations. In
            The Archeology of Slavery and Plantation Life, edited by Theresa A.
            Singleton, pp. 163–194. Academic Press, Orlando, Florida.
Rogers, Gay Ann
    1983   *An Illustrated History of Needlework Tools*. John Murray Publishers,
            London.
Russell, Aaron E.
    1997   Material Culture and African American Spirituality at the
            Hermitage. *Historical Archaeology* 31(2):63–80.
Samford, Patricia
    1996   The Archaeology of African American Slavery and Material Culture.
            William and Mary Quarterly, 3d ser., 53(1):87–114.
    1998   "Strong Is the Bond of Kinship": West African–Style Ancestor
            Shrines and Subfloor Pits on African American Quarters. In
            *Historical Archaeology, Identity Formation, and the Interpretation
            of Ethnicity*, edited by Maria Franklin and Garrett Fesler,
            pp. 71–91. Colonial Williamsburg Research Publications,
            Colonial Williamsburg Foundation, Williamsburg.
    2000   "Strong Is the Bond of Kinship": West African–Style Ancestor
            Shrines and Subfloor Pits on African American Quarters.
            Ph.D. diss., Dept. of Anthropology, Univ. of North Carolina,
            Chapel Hill.
Savitt, Todd L.
    1988   Slave Health and Southern Distinctiveness. In *Disease and Distinc-
            tiveness in the American South*, edited by Todd L. Savitt and James
            Harvey Young, pp. 120–153. Univ. of Tennessee Press, Knoxville.
Schlotterbeck, John T.
    1995   The Internal Economy of Slavery in Rural Piedmont Virginia.
            In *The Slaves' Economy: Independent Production by Slaves in the
            Americas*, edited by Ira Berlin and Philip D. Morgan, pp. 170–181.
            Frank Cass, London.

Scott, Elizabeth M. (editor)

　　1994a *Those of Little Note: Gender, Race, and Class in Historical Archaeology.*
　　　　　Univ. of Arizona Press, Tucson.

　　1994b Through the Lens of Gender: Archaeology, Inequality, and Those
　　　　　"of Little Note." In *Those of Little Note: Gender, Race, and Class in
　　　　　Historical Archaeology,* edited by Elizabeth M. Scott, pp. 3–24.
　　　　　Univ. of Arizona Press, Tucson.

Seifert, Donna

　　1991　Within Sight of the White House: The Archaeology of Working
　　　　　Women. *Historical Archaeology* 25(4):82–108.

Seifert, Donna J. (editor)

　　1991　Gender in Historical Archaeology. Special Issue of *Historical
　　　　　Archaeology*:25(4).

Shackel, Paul A., and Barbara Little (editors)

　　1994　*Historical Archaeology of the Chesapeake.* Smithsonian Institution
　　　　　Press, Washington, D.C.

Singleton, Theresa (editor)

　　1985　*The Archaeology of Plantation Life and Slavery.* Academic Press,
　　　　　New York.

Singleton, Theresa

　　1995　The Archaeology of Slavery in North America. *Annual Review of
　　　　　Anthropology* 24:119–140.

　　1999　*I, Too, Am America: Archaeological Studies of African American Life.*
　　　　　Univ. Press of Virginia, Charlottesville.

Sobel, Mechal

　　1988　*The World They Made Together: Black and White Values in Eighteenth-
　　　　　Century Virginia.* Princeton Univ. Press, Princeton.

Spector, Janet D.

　　1993　*What This Awl Means: Feminist Archaeology at a Wahpeton Dakota
　　　　　Village.* Minnesota Historical Society Press, St. Paul.

Stanton, Lucia

　　2001　*Free Some Day: The African American Families of Monticello.*
　　　　　Monticello Monograph Series, Thomas Jefferson Foundation,
　　　　　Charlottesville.

Steckel, Richard

　　1986a Birthweights and Infant Mortality among American Slaves.
　　　　　Explorations in Economic History 23:173–198.

　　1986b A Dreadful Childhood: Excess Mortality of American Slaves.
　　　　　Social Science History 10:427–465.

Stevenson, Brenda E.
    1996   Gender Convention, Ideals, and Identity among Antebellum
            Virginia Slave Women. In *More Than Chattel: Black Women
            and Slavery in the Americas*, edited by David Barry Gaspar
            and Darlene Clark Hine, pp. 169–190. Indiana Univ. Press,
            Bloomington.
Stine, Linda France, Melanie A. Cabak, and Mark D. Groover
    1996   Blue Beads as African American Cultural Symbols. *Historical
            Archaeology* 30(3):49–75.
Tandberg, Gerilyn
    1980   Field Hand Clothing in Louisiana and Mississippi during the
            Antebellum Period. *Dress* 5:89–104.
Tandberg, Gerilyn, and Sally Graham Durand
    1981   Dress-Up Costumes for Field Slaves of Antebellum Louisiana and
            Mississippi. *Costume* 15:41–48.
Thomas, Brian
    1995   *Community among Enslaved African Americans on The Hermitage
            Plantation, 1820s–1850s*. Ph. D. Diss., Dept. of Anthropology,
            State Univ. of New York at Binghamton, New York. University
            Microfilms, Ann Arbor, Mich.
    1998   Power and Community: The Archaeology of Slavery at the
            Hermitage Plantation. *American Antiquity* 63(4):531–551.
Thompson, Robert Farris
    1983   *Flash of the Spirit*. Random House, New York.
Turner, Kenneth R.
    1989   Biological Analysis. In *Elko Switch Cemetery: An Archaeological Per-
            spective*, edited by M. G. Shogren, K. R. Turner, and J. C. Perroni,
            pp. 191–228. Alabama State Museum of Natural History, Division
            of Archaeology, Report of Investigations 58, Tuscaloosa.
Ulrich, Laurel T.
    1991   *A Midwife's Tale: The Life of Martha Ballard, Based on Her Diary,
            1785–1812*. Vintage, New York.
Vlach, John M.
    1978   *The Afro-American Tradition in Decorative Arts*. Cleveland Museum
            of Art, Cleveland.
    1980   Arrival and Survival: The Maintenance of an Afro-American
            Tradition in Folk Art and Craft. In *Perspectives on American Folk
            Art*, edited by M. G. Quimby and Scott T. Swank, pp. 177–217.
            W. W. Norton, New York.

Wall, Diana DiZerega

1995   *The Archaeology of Gender: Separating the Spheres in Urban America.*
Plenum Press, New York.

1999   Examining Gender, Class, and Ethnicity in Nineteenth-Century
New York. *Historical Archaeology* 33(1):102–117.

Walsh, Lorena

1997   *From Calabar to Carter's Grove: The History of a Virginia Slave
Community.* Univ. Press of Virginia, Charlottesville.

Weiner, Annette, and Jane Schneider (editors)

1989   *Cloth and the Human Experience.* Smithsonian Institution Press,
Washington, D.C.

Whelan, Mary K.

1991   Gender and Historical Archaeology: Eastern Dakota Patterns in the
Nineteenth Century. *Historical Archaeology* 25(4):17–32.

White, Deborah G.

1985   *Ar'n't I a Woman? Female Slaves in the Plantation South.* W. W.
Norton, New York.

1991   Female Slaves in the Plantation South. In *Before Freedom Came:
African American Life in the Antebellum South*, edited by Edward D.
C. Campbell Jr. and Kym S. Rice, pp. 101–122. Univ. Press of Vir-
ginia, Charlottesville.

Wiessner, Polly

1982   Risk, Reciprocity, and Social Influence on Kung San Economics.
In *Politics and History in Band Societies*, edited by E. Leacock and
R. Lee, pp. 61–84. Cambridge Univ. Press, Cambridge.

Wilkie, Laurie A.

1997   Secret and Sacred: Contextualizing the Artifacts of African American
Magic and Religion. *Historical Archaeology* 31(4):81–106.

2000   *Creating Freedom.* Louisiana State Univ. Press, Baton Rouge.

Wobst, H. Martin

1977   Stylistic Behavior and Information Exchange. In *For the Director:
Research Essays in Honor of James B. Griffin*, edited by Charles E.
Cleland, pp. 317–342. Anthropological Papers No. 61. Museum of
Anthropology, Univ. of Michigan, Ann Arbor.

Wylie, Alison

1992   Gender Theory and the Archaeological Record: Why Is There No
Archaeology of Gender? In *Engendering Archaeology: Women in
Prehistory*, edited by Margaret W. Conkey and Joan Gero, pp. 31–54.
Basil Blackwell, Oxford.

Yentsch, Anne E.
    1994   *A Chesapeake Family and Their Slaves; A Study in Historical Archae-ology*. Cambridge Univ. Press, Cambridge.
Young, Amy
    1995a Archaeological Evidence of African-Style Ritual and Healing Practices in the Upland South. *Tennessee Anthropologist* 21(2):139–155.
    1995b *Risk and Material Conditions of African American Slaves at Locust Grove: An Archaeological Perspective*. Ph.D. diss., Dept. of Anthropology, Univ. of Tennessee, Knoxville.
    1997   Risk Management Strategies among African American Slaves at Locust Grove Plantation. *International Journal of Historical Archaeology* 1:5–37.

Contributors

Melanie A. Cabak earned an M.A. from the University of South Carolina. She specializes in historical archaeology and has published numerous articles and reports on topics like gender in historic Inuit communities, the symbolism of blue beads on slave sites, and the archaeology of rural modernization. Her main interests are African American plantation and farmstead studies and caring for her three young children.

Marie Danforth is a professor of anthropology at University of South Mississippi, where she has taught since 1987. She received her Ph.D. from Indiana University in 1989. Her research interests focus on the interaction of health and culture change, and she has conducted bioarchaeological studies on skeletal collections from Mesoamerica and the southeastern United States. Her most recent work has involved looking at coastal adaptations in prehistoric populations in Mississippi and Alabama.

Garrett R. Fesler is a senior archaeologist with the James River Institute for Archaeology, Inc., in Williamsburg, Virginia. He earned an M.A. in history from the College of William and Mary and a Ph.D. in anthropology from the University of Virginia.

Jillian E. Galle is the project manager of the Digital Archaeological Archive of Chesapeake Slavery at Monticello. From 1998 to 2000 she served as a research archaeologist at the Hermitage, home of Andrew Jackson in Nashville, Tennessee. She is currently pursuing a doctorate in anthropology from the University of Virginia.

Barbara J. Heath directs the Department of Archaeology and Landscapes at Thomas Jefferson's Poplar Forest, where she has worked since 1992. Dr. Heath is also an adjunct faculty member in the anthropology department at the University of Virginia and has taught at Sweet Briar College. She has worked on sites throughout Virginia and in the Caribbean. Heath is the author of *Hidden Lives: The Archaeology of Slave Life at Thomas Jefferson's Poplar Forest*, and she has contributed articles on her work to several journals and edited volumes.

Larry McKee is a senior program manager with the cultural resource division of TRC, Inc. From 1988 through 1999 he served as director of archaeology at the Hermitage, home of Andrew Jackson in Nashville, Tennessee.

Patricia Samford is the director at Historic Bath, North Carolina's oldest town. She also serves as the regional manager for the northeast region of North Carolina State Historic Sites, which encompasses four sites, including Historic Bath, Historic Halifax, Somerset Plantation, and Historic Edenton. Her professional interests include African American archaeology, archaeological manifestations of spirituality, and cultural identity.

Elizabeth M. Scott is an assistant professor at Illinois State University in the Department of Sociology and Anthropology. She has published several articles and book chapters on topics related to the historical archaeology of gender and social inequality. Her primary interests are in French and British colonial societies in the Great Lakes and Mississippi Valley regions.

Brian W. Thomas is operations manager for TRC Garrow Associates, Inc., in Atlanta. He received a Ph.D. in anthropology from the State University of New York at Binghamton, with a specialization in historical archaeology. His primary interest is in African American archaeology.

Larissa Thomas directs the archaeology program for the Atlanta office of TRC Garrow Associates, Inc. She received her Ph.D. in anthropology from the State University of New York at Binghamton. Her research interests center on gender, political economy, and the Mississippian period in the prehistoric Southeast.

Laurie A. Wilkie is an associate professor in the Department of Anthropology at the University of California, Berkeley. Her research explores how people engage with material culture in their daily lives, with a particular focus on the archaeology of the recent past.

Kristin J. Wilson received an M.A. in anthropology with a dual emphasis on archaeology and physical anthropology from the University of South Carolina. She is currently working toward a doctorate in sociology at Georgia State University in Atlanta, writing supplemental textbook materials, and conducting ethnographic interviews of cocaine users and their families. Her interests pivot around issues of women's health and folk medicine from prehistoric to contemporary societies.

Amy L. Young is an assistant professor in the Department of Anthropology and Sociology at the University of Southern Mississippi. She is primarily interested in southern culture and has worked on many historic sites across the southern United States. She has published articles in *Southeastern Archaeology, International Journal of Historical Archaeology, North American Archaeologists, MidContinental Journal of Archaeology, and Mississippi Archaeology.*

Index

Note: Italicized page numbers represent tables